American Values in Transition

A READER

American Values in Transition

A READER

edited by
ROBERT C. BANNISTER
SWARTHMORE COLLEGE

HARCOURT BRACE JOVANOVICH, INC.
New York   Chicago   San Francisco   Atlanta

Preface

"Tune in, turn on, drop out," "Off the pigs," "Do your own thing," "Out of the closets, into the streets." These slogans, obscuring more than they explain, are but a few of the symptoms of the alleged "crisis" of the past decade. In Dallas and Detroit, at Berkeley and Kent State, this crisis has been painfully real. But the slogans, and the shift in values they portend, have been scarcely less explosive than bullets and firebombs. Indeed, in the view of the French observer Jean-François Revel, the present "American revolution" is "the first revolution in history in which disagreement on values and goals is more pronounced than disagreement on the means of existence."

The present collection highlights points of view about six values that have been heatedly debated no less frequently in the past than at present: personal freedom, marriage and the family, the melting pot, success, progress, and the "democratic system." Designed to place current issues in historical, philosophical, and literary perspective, the book may be used in one of several ways. As intellectual history, the ongoing debate will invite consideration of the economic, political, and social factors that underlie specific values, as well as of changes in fundamental attitudes informing specific arguments. Philosophically, seemingly irreconcilable differences will require careful analysis of epistemological and metaphysical assumptions, and close scrutiny of the reasoning by which conclusions are reached. Perhaps most importantly, the variety of literary forms, the often subtle use of language to achieve effect, will provide not only opportunities for literary analysis, but inspiration for readers to attempt their own formulations is essays, poetry, or even short stories.

The book would not have appeared, I should add, were it not for the shrewd counsel and perceptive advice I have received from others. I wish especially to thank Thomas Inge of Virginia Commonwealth University, Monroe Beardsley of Temple, John M. Blum of Yale, Richard Ludwig of Princeton, and Robert Ferm of Middlebury College, each of whom made useful suggestions. Howard Williams of the Swarthmore College Library was of great help in arranging interlibrary loans. Eleanor Bennett, secretary of the Swarthmore History Department, bore all deadlines with unfailing good cheer. William A. Pullin of Harcourt Brace Jovanovich first suggested the project to me and has patiently overseen it at every stage.

Robert C. Bannister

Contents

Introduction

"A glance at our country and its present moral condition fills the mind with alarming apprehensions." [1] So began a lament in an American magazine almost a century and a half ago. Similar concern has surfaced regularly during our history, from the jeremiads in which late seventeenth-century Puritans bewailed the decline of sanctity in their Bible Commonwealth to contemporary neo-Marxist predictions of a culture consumed by its own "contradictions." Despite perennial cautions against "washing the country's linen before the world," national soul-searching continues unabated. Wishing to be the most perfect nation in history, America *has* succeeded in becoming the most self-conscious.

While Americans bemoan the decay of "traditional values," they have seldom agreed on their substance. With the American Revolution still raging, the French-born Hector St. John de Crevecoeur in *Letters from an American Farmer* (1782) posed the issue in his now famous question, "What, then, is the American, this new man?" Although perceptive answers have appeared in a score of classic studies—from Tocqueville's *Democracy in America* (1831) to David Potter's *People of Plenty* (1954)—the question continues to provoke discussion. During the 1950s "national purpose" became almost a national obsession, prompting *Life* at the close of the decade to launch a full-scale symposium on the issue. The turmoil of the 1960s, and the much discussed "generation gap," left the question changed but no less urgent. As a commentator in *The New York Times* put it recently: "The country is longing for change—not only in things but in values." [2]

This collection, highlighting past and present discussion of six American values—personal freedom, marriage and the family, the melting pot, success, progress, and the "democratic system"—is designed to place the issues in historical, philosophical, and literary perspective. In studying values, certain general questions inevitably arise. (1) What are values? (2) Can one legitimately isolate six values from the many norms that shape social behavior? (3) Are different values related? Do

[1] Quoted in A. B. Hulbert, "Habit of Going to the Devil," *Atlantic Monthly*, 138 (1926), 804–06.
[2] Anthony Lewis, "Notes from Overground," *The New York Times*, April 12, 1971.

they harmonize or conflict? (4) Are values "relative"? Can one locate a single cause for differences in values within a society? (5) What causes change in a nation's values?

In defining values, sociologists warn that one must go beyond common notions of "good" and "bad." Values, writes Robin M. Williams, must have a "conceptual" element. Abstractions from an individual's immediate experience, values are the criteria by which specific goals are chosen; they are not the goals themselves. A house in the suburbs, two cars, and an impressive bank account, however much desired, are not values in this sense. Rather, they are objects chosen because the individual holds certain (socially determined) notions concerning success, marriage and the family, and perhaps individual freedom. Values, in the language of sociology, are "affectively charged: they represent actual or potential emotional motivation,"[3] a fact that has become painfully evident during the past decade.

The issues represented here satisfy these definitions and also meet further tests that distinguish dominant values from subordinate ones. Each has been extensively held among the population throughout much of our history. Intensely affirmed, each has inspired effort, activity, and propaganda from prestigious individuals and groups within the society. Other values, frequently mentioned in discussions of the American character, could undoubtedly be added: hard work, equality, humanitarianism, patriotism and loyalty, peace, and Manifest Destiny. Some of these will emerge in the readings. Humanitarianism and a belief in equality inform the struggle for women's rights, and equality and democracy are closely related. Attitudes toward peace and war, patriotism and loyalty, and America's role in the world, too complex to be treated directly in a reader of this size, appear implicitly in discussions of progress, democracy, and even individual freedom.

Values, thus, are interrelated. Success, the melting pot, and other single values are actually clusters, often overlapping, sometimes reinforcing one another. For example, success, in the nineteenth century, involved hard work, individual effort, and even humanitarian concern. Are such clusters internally consistent? Is the overall value system harmonious? On this point there is sharp disagreement. Tension, even contradiction within a value system, is not hard to find. Success threatens equality, while "equality of opportunity," a slogan devised to reconcile the two, runs counter to the ideal of the family, with its implicit guarantee of economic and educational advantage for children of the well-to-do. "A common aspect of modern life," writes the psy-

[3] Robin M. Williams, Jr. *American Society: A Sociological Interpretation,* 2nd ed. (New York: Alfred A. Knopf, 1960), Chapter 11.

chologist Carl Rogers, "is living with absolutely contradictory values." [4] Other observers, however, have sought to identify a consensus underlying obvious tensions, noting such basic values as egalitarianism, optimism, and the belief in a fundamental moral law. Although these two views, termed *pluralist* and *monist*, primarily involve matters of emphasis, the question whether conflict or consensus lies at the heart of American history remains an extremely important one.

Conflict over values, to the degree it is not resolvable, also raises the possibility that values are merely relative to time and place. Easy generalizations here are dangerous. Although many Americans speak knowingly of a "generation gap" at least one study suggests that other factors, especially amount of education, are more important than age. Disagreement should be assessed in the light of many factors, including an author's age and sex, social and economic status, and ethnic, racial, and geographical background. Alternately, apparent differences may simply reflect changes in the objective situation. The growth of business bureaucracy, changing patterns of immigration, technological advance—such factors, which may often be gleaned "between the lines," are crucial in judging different arguments.

Because of the complexity of social values, major changes, long in the making, may finally involve only a subtle shift in a delicate balance. Whether one adopts a pluralist or monist view, no value system will appear entirely consistent. Most individuals in most societies learn to live with a measure of potential contradiction: motherhood and career, family privilege and egalitarian norms, property and human rights. When, at crucial points in history, such tension becomes unbearable, logic intrudes. "If all men are equal then . . ." So have begun the arguments of Abolitionists, labor leaders, suffragettes, and countless others who have shaped our past. In recent years, "terrible simplifiers" —to use the term that Jacob Burckhardt, the nineteenth-century historian of the Renaissance, applied to such individuals—again challenge the compromises of the past. Yet societies, even less than individuals, rarely live by logic alone. In all statements of values, evasion, ambiguity, even contradiction, are certainly as prevalent as any pretended consistency.

Since generations, we are told, last only a few years nowadays, it seems none too soon to reflect on the debates of the past decade. Has a permissive, even debauched, America begun her "decline and fall"? Will a new postwar era, the Age of the Silent Majority, see a return to some imagined "normalcy"? Or has a "new American Revolution"

---

[4] Carl R. Rogers, "Toward a Modern Approach to Values," *Journal of Abnormal and Social Psychology*, 68 (1964), 160–68.

American Values in Transition

A READER

Manners
and
Morals

The First American "Bust":
Morton of Merrymount

The events that serve as the basis for the many later accounts of the settlement at Merry Mount began in 1625 when Thomas Morton, an English lawyer and trader, settled at Pasonagessit (the present Quincy, Massachusetts). His party, led by a Captain Wollaston, consisted of a small group of "gentlemen" and a number of indentured servants. When, after several months, Wollaston and some followers went to Virginia, Morton established a sort of Bohemian trading post and led the remainder of the settlers in a wild revel that was unappreciated by their more staid neighbors. Punning on the Latin, Morton named the site, which overlooked Boston Bay, "Ma-re Mount."

Morton's activities, vividly described in the accounts below, soon inspired the Puritan Separatists, who had lived in nearby Plymouth since 1620, to crush the enterprise. In 1628 they dispatched Captain Miles Standish, the "Captaine Shrimp" of Morton's account, to arrest the "Lord of Misrule." Following a Keystone Cops escapade in which Morton temporarily escaped, he was recaptured and sent to England. In September 1628, John Endecott and a band of settlers from Massachusetts Bay visited Merry Mount, cut down the maypole that Morton had erected, and renamed the spot Mount Dagon, after the sea idol on whose feast day Samson had pulled down the pillars of the Gaza temple.

This colorful episode of New England history has perennially captured the American imagination. In addition to the accounts below, John Lathrop Motley, a contemporary of Hawthorne's, treated it in his two-volume **Merrymount** (1849). In the twentieth century it has been the subject of Richard L. Stokes's **Merrymount—A Dramatic Poem for Music** (1932) and Robert Lowell's "Endecott and the Red Cross," **The Old Glory** (1965). See Richard C. Sterne, "Puritans at Merrymount," **American Quarterly**, 22 (Winter 1970), 847–58 for an instructive comparison of these treatments.

3

Of the Revells of New Canaan

THOMAS MORTON (1590?–1647), trader and adventurer, was born in England. Arriving in Massachusetts in 1622, he spent a lifetime in battle with the Puritan authorities. After the Merry Mount episode he was deported in 1628, returned the following year, and was again exiled in 1630. While preparing **The New English Canaan** (1637), a delightful bit of revenge in which he indulged his ribald wit and flair for puns, he worked actively with those forces in England who wished to invalidate the charter of the Massachusetts Bay Company. When once again he returned to America, he was imprisoned in Boston in 1644 and died in Maine three years later.

14

The inhabitants of Pasonagessit, (having translated the name of their habitation from that ancient Salvage name to Ma-re Mount, and being resolved to have the new name confirmed for a memorial to after ages,) did devise amongst themselves to have it performed in a solemne manner, with Revels and merriment after the old English custome; [they] prepared to sett up a Maypole upon the festivall day of Philip and Iacob, and therefore brewed a barrell of excellent beare and provided a cafe of bottles, to be spent, with other good cheare, for all commers of that day. And because they would have it in a compleat forme, they had prepared a song fitting to the time and present occasion. And upon Mayday they brought the Maypole to the place appointed, with drumes, gunnes, pistols and other fitting instruments, for that purpose; and there erected it with the help of Salvages, that came thether of purpose to see the manner of our Revels. A goodly pine tree of 80. foote longe was reared up, with a peare of buckshorns nayled one somewhat neare unto the top of it: where it stood, as a faire sea marke for directions how to finde out the way to mine Hoste of Ma-re Mount.

·   ·   ·

There was likewise a merry song made, which, (to make their Revells more fashionable,) was sung with a Corus, every man bearing his part;

OF THE REVELLS OF NEW CANAAN. From Thomas Morton, *New English Canaan* (1637), ed. by C. F. Adams, Jr. (Boston: 1883), 276–77, 279–80, 282–87.

which they performed in a daunce, hand in hand about the Maypole, whiles one of the Company sung and filled out the good liquor, like gammedes and Iupiter.

The Songe

Cor.

 Drinke and be merry, merry, merry boyes;
 Let all your delight be in the Hymens ioyes;
 Iô to Hymen, now the day is come,
 About the merry Maypole take a Roome.
  Make greene garlons, bring bottles out
  And fill sweet Nectar freely about.
  Uncover thy head and feare no harme,
  For hers good liquor to keepe it warme.
 Then drinke and be merry, &c.
 Iô to Hymen, &c.
  Nectar is a thing assign'd
  By the Deities owne minde
  To cure the hart opprest with greife,
  And of good liquors is the cheife.
 Then drinke, &c.
 Iô to Hymen, &c.
  Give to the Mellancolly man
  A cup or two of 't now and than;
  This physick will soone revive his bloud,
  And make him be of a merrier moode.
 Then drinke, &c.
 Iô to Hymen, &c.
  Give to the Nymphe thats free from scorne
  No Irish stuff nor Scotch over worne.
  Lasses in beaver coats come away,
  Yee shall be welcome to us night and day.
 To drinke and be merry &c.
 Iô to Hymen, &c.

This harmles mirth made by younge men, (that lived in hope to have wifes brought over to them, that would save them a laboure to make a voyage to fetch any over,) was much distasted of the precise Seperatists, that keepe much a doe about the tyth of Muit and Cummin, troubling their braines more then reason would require about things that are indifferent: and from that time sought occasion against my honest Host of Ma-re Mount, to overthrow his ondertakings and to destroy his plantation quite and cleane.

.   .   .

15

Of a great Monster supposed to be at Ma-re-Mount; and the prepara-tion made to destroy it.

The Seperatists, envying the prosperity and hope of the Plantation at Ma-re Mount, (which they perceaved beganne to come forward, and to be in a good way for gaine in the Beaver trade,) conspired together against mine Host especially, (who was the owner of that Plantation,) and made up a party against him; and mustred up what aide they could, accounting of him as of a great Monster.

Many threatening speeches were given out both against his person and his Habitation, which they divulged should be consumed with fire: And taking advantage of the time when his company, (which seemed little to regard theire threats,) were gone up into the Inlands to trade with the Salvages for Beaver, they set upon my honest host at a place called Wessaguscus, where, by accident, they found him. The inhabitants there were in good hope of the subvertion of the plantation at Mare Mount, (which they principally aymed at;) and the rather because mine host was a man that indeavoured to advaunce the dignity of the Church of England; which they, (on the contrary part,) would laboure to vilifie with uncivile termes: enveying against the sacred booke of common prayer, and mine host that used it in a laudable manner amongst his family, as a practise of piety.

.   .   .

Much rejoycing was made that they had gotten their cappitall enemy, (as they concluded him;) whome they purposed to hamper in such sort that hee should not be able to uphold his plantation at Ma-re Mount.

The Conspirators sported themselves at my honest host, that meant them no hurt, and were so joccund that they feasted their bodies, and fell to tippeling as if they had obtained a great prize; like the Trojans when they had the custody of Hippeus pinetree horse.

Mine host fained greefe, and could not be perswaded either to eate or drinke; because hee knew emptines would be a meanes to make him as watchfull as the Geese kept in the Roman Cappitall: whereon, the contrary part, the conspirators would be so drowsy that hee might have an opportunity to give them a slip, insteade of a tester. Six persons of the conspiracy were set to watch him at Wessaguscus: But hee kept waking; and in the dead of night, (one lying on the bed for further suerty,) up gets mine Host and got to the second dore that hee was to passe, which, notwithstanding the lock, hee got open, and shut it after him with such violence that it affrighted some of the conspirators.

The word, which was given with an alarme, was, ô he 's gon, he 's gon, what shall wee doe, he 's gon! The rest, (halfe a sleepe,) start up in a maze, and, like rames, ran theire heads one at another full butt in the darke.

Theire grande leader, Captaine Shrimp, tooke on most furiously and tore his clothes for anger, to see the empty nest, and their bird gone.

The rest were eager to have torne theire haire from theire heads; but it was so short that it would give them no hold. Now Captaine Shrimp thought in the losse of this prize, (which hee accoumpted his Master peece,) all his honor would be lost for ever.

In the meane time mine Host was got home to Ma-re Mount through the woods, eight miles round about the head of the river Monatoquit that parted the two Plantations, finding his way by the helpe of the lightening, (for it thundred as hee went terribly;) and there hee pre-pared powther, three pounds dried, for his present imployement, and foure good gunnes for him and the two assistants left at his howse, with bullets of severall sizes, three hounderd or thereabouts, to be used if the conspirators should pursue him thether: and these two persons promised theire aides in the quarrell, and confirmed that promise with health in good rosa solis.

Now Captaine Shrimp, the first Captaine in the Land, (as hee sup-posed,) must doe some new act to repaire this losse, and, to vindicate his reputation, who had sustained blemish by this oversight, begins now to study, how to repaire or survive his honor: in this manner, callinge of Councell, they conclude.

Hee takes eight persons more to him, and, (like the nine Worthies of New Canaan,) they imbarque with preparation against Ma-re-Mount, where this Monster of a man, as theire phrase was, had his denne; the whole number, had the rest not bin from home, being but seaven, would have given Captaine Shrimpe, (a quondam Drummer,) such a wellcome as would have made him wish for a Drume as bigg as Diogenes tubb, that hee might have crept into it out of sight.

Now the nine Worthies are approached, and mine Host prepared: having intelligence by a Salvage, that hastened in love from Wessa-guscus to give him notice of their intent.

One of mine Hosts men prooved a craven: the other had prooved his wits to purchase a little valoure, before mine Host had observed his posture.

The nine worthies comming before the Denne of this supposed Monster, (this seaven headed hydra, as they termed him,) and began, like Don Quixote against the Windmill, to beate a parly, and to offer quarter, if mine Host would yeald; for they resolved to send him for England; and bad him lay by his armes.

But hee, (who was the Sonne of a Souldier,) having taken up armes in his just defence, replyed that hee would not lay by those armes, because they were so needefull at Sea, if hee should be sent over. Yet, to save the effusion of so much worty bloud, as would haue issued out of the vaynes of these 9. worthies of New Canaan, if mine Host should have played upon them out at his port holes, (for they came within danger like a flocke of wild geese, as if they had bin tayled one to another, as coults to be sold at a faier,) mine Host was content to yeelde upon quarter; and did capitulate with them in what manner it should be for more certainety, because hee knew what Captaine Shrimpe was.

Hee expressed that no violence should be offered to his person, none to his goods, nor any of his Howsehold: but that hee should have his armes, and what els was requisit for the voyage: which theire Herald retornes, it was agreed upon, and should be performed.

But mine Host no sooner had set open the dore, and issued out, but instantly Captaine Shrimpe and the rest of the worthies stepped to him, layd hold of his armes, and had him downe: and so eagerly was every man bent against him, (not regarding any agreement made with such a carnall man,) that they fell upon him as if they would have eaten him: some of them were so violent that they would have a slice with scabbert, and all for haste; untill an old Souldier, (of the Queenes, as the Proverbe is,) that was there by accident, clapt his gunne under the weapons, and sharply rebuked these worthies for their unworthy practises. So the matter was taken into more deliberate consideration.

Captaine Shrimpe, and the rest of the nine worthies, made themselves, (by this outragious riot,) Masters of mine Hoste of Ma-re Mount, and disposed of what hee had at his plantation.

This they knew, (in the eye of the Salvages,) would add to their glory, and diminish the reputation of mine honest Host; whome they practised to be ridd of upon any termes, as willingly as if hee had bin the very Hidra of the time.

Thomas Morton of Merrymount

WILLIAM BRADFORD (1590–1657), governor of the Plymouth colony between 1621 and 1651, was born in Yorkshire, England. In his youth he himself defied authority, joining the Separatist Puritan church at Scrooby in 1606 against the wishes of his parents, and emigrating to Holland three years later. He remained there until setting sail for the New World in 1620. As governor he was noted for his common sense, and particularly for maintaining good relations with the Indians. He composed his **History,** a document distinguished by the discipline and stark simplicity of its prose, between 1631 and 1651, although it was not published in full until the mid-nineteenth century.

About some three or four years before this time, there came over one Captain Wollaston (a man of pretty parts) and with him three or four more of some eminency, who brought with them a great many servants, with provisions and other implements for to begin a plantation. And pitched themselves in a place within the Massachusetts which they called after their Captain's name, Mount Wollaston. Amongst whom was one Mr. Morton, who it should seem had some small adventure of his own or other men's amongst them, but had little respect amongst them, and was slighted by the meanest servants. Having continued there some time, and not finding things to answer their expectations nor profit to arise as they looked for, Captain Wollaston takes a great part of the servants and transports them to Virginia, where he puts them off at good rates, selling their time to other men; and writes back to one Mr. Rasdall (one of his chief partners and accounted their merchant) to bring another part of them to Virginia likewise, intending to put them off there as he had done the rest. And he, with the consent of the said Rasdall, appointed one Fitcher to be his Lieutenant and govern the remains of the Plantation till he or Rasdall returned to take further order thereabout. But this Morton abovesaid, having more craft than honesty (who had been a kind of pettifogger of Furnival's Inn) in the others' absence watches an opportunity (commons being but hard amongst them) and got some strong drink and other junkets and made them a feast; and after they were merry, he began to tell them he would give them good counsel. "You see," saith he, "that many of your fellows are carried to Virginia, and if you stay till this Rasdall return, you will also be carried away and sold for slaves with the rest. Therefore I would advise you to thrust out this Lieutenant Fitcher, and I, having a part in the Plantation, will receive you as my partners and consociates; so may you be free from service, and we will converse, plant, trade, and live together as equals and support and protect one

THOMAS MORTON OF MERRYMOUNT. From William Bradford, *Of Plymouth Plantation* (1631–51), modernized version edited by Samuel Eliot Morison. Copyright © 1952. Reprinted by permission of Alfred A. Knopf, Inc.

another," or to like effect. This counsel was easily received, so they took opportunity and thrust Lieutenant Fitcher out o' doors, and would suffer him to come no more amongst them, but forced him to seek bread to eat and other relief from his neighbours till he could get passage for England.

After this they fell to great licentiousness and led a dissolute life, pouring out themselves into all profaneness. And Morton became Lord of Misrule, and maintained (as it were) a School of Atheism. And after they had got some goods into their hands, and got much by trading with the Indians, they spent it as vainly in quaffing and drinking, both wine and strong waters in great excess (and, as some reported) £10 worth in a morning. They also set up a maypole, drinking and dancing about it many days together, inviting the Indian women for their consorts, dancing and frisking together like so many fairies, or furies, rather; and worse practices. As if they had anew revived and celebrated the feasts of the Roman goddess Flora, or the beastly practices of the mad Bacchanalians. Morton likewise, to show his poetry composed sundry rhymes and verses, some tending to lasciviousness, and others to the detraction and scandal of some persons, which he affixed to this idle or idol maypole. They changed also the name of their place, and instead of calling it Mount Wollaston they call it Merry-mount, as if this jollity would have lasted ever. But this continued not long, for after Morton was sent for England (as follows to be declared) shortly after came over that worthy gentleman Mr. John Endecott, who brought over a patent under the broad seal for the government of the Massachusetts. Who, visiting those parts, caused that maypole to be cut down and rebuked them for their profaneness and admonished them to look there should be better walking. So they or others now changed the name of their place again and called it Mount Dagon.

Now to maintain this riotous prodigality and profuse excess, Morton, thinking himself lawless, and hearing what gain the French and fishermen made by trading of pieces, powder and shot to the Indians, he as the head of this consortship began the practice of the same in these parts. And first he taught them how to use them, to charge and discharge, and what proportion of powder to give the piece, according to the size or bigness of the same; and what shot to use for fowl and what for deer. And having thus instructed them, he employed some of them to hunt and fowl for him, so as they became far more active in that employment than any of the English, by reason of their swiftness of foot and nimbleness of body, being also quick-sighted and by continual exercise well knowing the haunts of all sorts of game. So as when they saw the execution that a piece would do, and the benefit that might come by the same, they became mad (as it were) after them and would not stick to give any price they could attain to for them; accounting their bows and arrows but baubles in comparison of them.

And here I may take occasion to bewail the mischief that this wicked man began in these parts, and which since, base covetousness prevailing in men that should know better, has now at length got the upper hand and made this thing common, notwithstanding any laws to the contrary. So as the Indians are full of pieces all over, both fowling pieces, muskets, pistols, etc. . . .

O, the horribleness of this villainy! How many both Dutch and English have been lately slain by those Indians thus furnished, and no remedy provided; nay, the evil more increased, and the blood of their brethren sold for gain (as is to be feared) and in what danger all these colonies are in is too well known. O that princes and parliaments would take some timely order to prevent this mischief and at length to suppress it by some exemplary punishment upon some of these gain-thirsty murderers, for they deserve no better title, before their colonies in these parts be overthrown by these barbarous savages thus armed with their own weapons, by these evil instruments and traitors to their neighbours and country! But I have forgot myself and have been too long in this digression; but now to return.

This Morton having thus taught them the use of pieces, he sold them all he could spare, and he and his consorts determined to send for many out of England and had by some of the ships sent for above a score. The which being known, and his neighbours meeting the Indians in the woods armed with guns in this sort, it was a terror unto them who lived stragglingly and were of no strength in any place. And other places (though more remote) saw this mischief would quickly spread over all, if not prevented. Besides, they saw they should keep no servants, for Morton would entertain any, how vile soever, and all the scum of the country or any discontents would flock to him from all places, if this nest was not broken. And they should stand in more fear of their lives and goods in short time from this wicked and debased crew than from the savages themselves.

So sundry of the chief of the straggling plantations, meeting together, agreed by mutual consent to solicit those of Plymouth (who were then of more strength than them all) to join with them to prevent the further growth of this mischief, and suppress Morton and his consorts before they grew to further head and strength. . . .

[They] first resolved jointly to write to him, and in a friendly and neighbourly way to admonish him to forbear those courses, and sent a messenger with their letters to bring his answer.

But he was so high as he scorned all advice, and asked who had to do with him, he had and would trade pieces with the Indians, in despite of all, with many other scurrilous terms full of disdain. They sent to him a second time and bade him be better advised and more temperate in his terms, for the country could not bear the injury he did. It was against their common safety and against the King's proclamation. He answered in high terms as before; and that the King's proclamation was no law, demanding what penalty was upon it. It was answered, more than he could bear—His Majesty's displeasure. But insolently he persisted and said the King was dead and his displeasure with him, and many the like things. And threatened withal that if any came to molest him, let them look to themselves for he would prepare for them.

Upon which they saw there was no way but to take him by force; and having so far proceeded, now to give over would make him far more haughty and insolent. So they mutually resolved to proceed, and obtained of the Governor of Plymouth to send Captain Standish and some other aid with him, to take Morton by force. The which accordingly was done. But they found him to stand stiffly in his defense, having made fast his doors, armed his consorts, set divers dishes of powder and bullets ready on the table; and if they had not been over-armed with drink, more hurt might have been done. They summoned him to yield, but he kept his house and they could get nothing but scoffs and scorns from him. But at length, fearing they would do some violence to the house, he and some of his crew came out, but not to yield but to shoot; but they were so steeled with drink as their pieces were too heavy for them. Himself with a carbine, over-charged and almost half filled with powder and shot, as was after found, had thought to have shot Captain Standish; but he stepped to him and put by his piece and took him. Neither was there any hurt done to any of either side, save that one was so drunk that he ran his own nose upon the point of a sword that one held before him, as he entered the house; but he lost but a little of his hot blood.

Morton they brought away to Plymouth, where he was kept till a ship went from the Isle of Shoals for England, with which he was sent to the Council of New England, and letters written to give them information of his course and carriage. And also one was sent at their common charge to inform their Honours more particularly and to prosecute against him. But he fooled of the messenger, after he was gone from hence, and though he went for England yet nothing was done to him, not so much as rebuked, for aught was heard, but returned the next year. Some of the worst of the company were dispersed and some of the more modest kept the house till he should be heard from. But I have been too long about so unworthy a person, and bad a cause.

The Maypole of Merry Mount

NATHANIEL HAWTHORNE (1804–1864), born in Salem, Massachusetts, numbered among his ancestors a judge in the witchcraft trials that took place there more than a century before. A graduate of Bowdoin College (1825), he turned to the Puritan past in many of the **Twice Told Tales** (1837) that first gained him notice. Sharing little of the optimism of the Transcendentalists, near whom he lived for a time in Concord, he used Puritan history to explore the darker recesses of the human soul in **The Scarlet Letter** (1850) and **The House of Seven Gables** (1851), his best known works.

Bright were the days at Merry Mount, when the Maypole was the banner staff of that gay colony! They who reared it, should their banner be triumphant, were to pour sunshine over New England's rugged hills, and scatter flower seeds throughout the soil. Jollity and gloom were contending for an empire. Midsummer eve had come, bringing deep verdure to the forest, and roses in her lap, of a more vivid hue than the tender buds of Spring. But May, or her mirthful spirit, dwelt all the year round at Merry Mount, sporting with the Summer months, and revelling with Autumn, and basking in the glow of Winter's fireside. Through a world of toil and care she flitted with a dreamlike smile, and came hither to find a home among the lightsome hearts of Merry Mount.

.   .   .

But what was the wild throng that stood hand in hand about the Maypole? It could not be that the fauns and nymphs, when driven from their classic groves and homes of ancient fable, had sought refuge, as all the persecuted did, in the fresh woods of the West. There were Gothic monsters, though perhaps of Grecian ancestry. On the shoulders of a comely youth uprose the head and branching antlers of a stag; a second, human in all other points, had the grim visage of a wolf; a third, still with the trunk and limbs of a mortal man, showed the beard and horns of a venerable he-goat. There was the likeness of a bear erect, brute in all but his hind legs, which were adorned with pink silk stockings. And here again, almost as wondrous, stood a real bear of the dark forest, lending each of his fore-paws to the grasp of a human hand, and

THE MAYPOLE OF MERRY MOUNT. From Nathaniel Hawthorne, *Twice-Told Tales* (1837).

as ready for the dance as any in that circle. His inferior nature rose half-way to meet his companions as they stooped. Other faces wore the similitude of man or woman, but distorted or extravagant, with red noses pendulous before their mouths, which seemed of awful depth, and stretched from ear to ear in an eternal fit of laughter. Here might be seen the Salvage Man, well known in heraldry, hairy as a baboon, and girdled with green leaves. By his side, a noble figure, but still a counterfeit, appeared an Indian hunter, with feathery crest and wampum belt. . . .

Had a wanderer, bewildered in the melancholy forest, heard their mirth, and stolen a half-affrighted glance, he might have fancied them the crew of Comus, some already transformed to brutes, some midway between man and beast, and the others rioting in the flow of tipsy jollity that foreran the change. But a band of Puritans, who watched the scene, invisible themselves, compared the masques to those devils and ruined souls with whom their superstition peopled the black wilderness.

Within the ring of monsters appeared the two airiest forms that had ever trodden on any more solid footing than a purple and golden cloud. One was a youth in glistening apparel, with a scarf of the rainbow pattern crosswise on his breast. His right hand held a gilded staff, the ensign of high dignity among the revellers, and his left grasped the slender fingers of a fair maiden, not less gayly decorated than himself. Bright roses glowed in contrast with the dark round their feet, or had sprung up spontaneously there. Behind this lightsome couple, so close to the Maypole that its boughs shaded his jovial face, stood the figure of an English priest, canonically dressed, yet decked with flowers, in heathen fashion, and wearing a chaplet of the native vine leaves. By the riot of his rolling eye, and the pagan decorations of his holy garb, he seemed the wildest monster there, and the very Comus of the crew.

"Votaries of the Maypole," cried the flower-decked priest, "merrily, all day long, have the woods echoed to your mirth. But be this your merriest hour, my hearts! Lo, here stand the Lord and Lady of the May, whom I, a clerk of Oxford, and high priest of Merry Mount, am presently to join in holy matrimony. Up with your nimble spirits, ye morris-dancers, green men, and glee maidens, bears and wolves, and horned gentlemen! Come; a chorus now, rich with the old mirth of Merry England, and the wilder glee of this fresh forest; and then a dance, to show the youthful pair what life is made of, and how airily they should go through it! All ye that love the Maypole, lend your voices to the nuptial song of the Lord and Lady of the May!"

This wedlock was more serious than most affairs of Merry Mount, where jest and delusion, trick and fantasy, kept up a continual carnival. The Lord and Lady of the May, though their titles must be laid down at sunset, were really and truly to be partners for the dance of life, beginning the measure that same bright eve. The wreath of roses, that hung from the lowest green bough of the Maypole, had been twined for them, and would be thrown over both their heads, in symbol of their flowery union. When the priest had spoken, therefore, a riotous uproar burst from the rout of monstrous figures.

"Begin you the stave, reverend Sir," cried they all; "and never did the woods ring to such a merry peal as we of the Maypole shall send up!"

Immediately a prelude of pipe, cithern, and viol, touched with practised minstrelsy, began to play from a neighboring thicket, in such a mirthful cadence that the boughs of the Maypole quivered to the sound. But the May Lord, he of the gilded staff, chancing to look into his Lady's eyes, was wonder-struck at the almost pensive glance that met his own.

"Edith, sweet Lady of the May," whispered he reproachfully, "is yon wreath of roses a garland to hang above our graves, that you look so sad? O, Edith, this is our golden time! Tarnish it not by any pensive shadow of the mind; for it may be that nothing of futurity will be brighter than the mere remembrance of what is now passing."

"That was the very thought that saddened me! How came it in your mind too?" said Edith in a still lower tone than he, for it was high treason to be sad at Merry Mount. "Therefore do I sigh amid this festive music. And besides, dear Edgar, I struggle as with a dream, and fancy that these shapes of our jovial friends are visionary, and their mirth unreal, and that we are no true Lord and Lady of the May. What is the mystery in my heart?"

Just then, as if a spell had loosened them, down came a little shower of withering rose leaves from the Maypole. Alas, for the young lovers! No sooner had their hearts glowed with real passion than they were sensible of something vague and unsubstantial in their former pleasures, and felt a dreary presentiment of inevitable change. From the moment that they truly loved, they had subjected themselves to earth's doom of care and sorrow, and troubled joy, and had no more a home at Merry Mount. That was Edith's mystery. Now leave we the priest to marry them, and the masquers to sport round the Maypole, till the last sunbeam be withdrawn from its summit, and the shadows of the forest mingle gloomily in the dance. Meanwhile, we may discover who these gay people were.

Two hundred years ago, and more, the old world and its inhabitants became mutually weary of each other. Men voyaged by thousands to the West: some to barter glass beads, and such like jewels, for the furs of the Indian hunter; some to conquer virgin empires; and one stern band to pray. But none of these motives had much weight with the colonists of Merry Mount. Their leaders were men who had sported so long with life, that when Thought and Wisdom came, even these unwelcome guests were led astray by the crowd of vanities which they should have put to flight. Erring Thought and perverted Wisdom were made to put on masques, and play the fool. The men of whom we speak, after losing the heart's fresh gayety, imagined a wild philosophy of pleasure, and came hither to act out their latest day-dream. They gathered followers from all that giddy tribe whose whole life is like the festal days of soberer men. In their train were minstrels, not unknown in London streets: wandering players, whose theatres had been the halls of noblemen; mummers, rope-dancers, and mountebanks, who would long be missed at wakes, church ales, and fairs; in a word, mirthmakers of every sort, such as abounded in that age, but now began to be discountenanced by the rapid growth of Puritanism. Light had their footsteps been on land, and as lightly they came across the sea. Many had been maddened by their previous troubles into a gay despair; others were as madly gay in the flush of youth, like the May Lord and his Lady; but whatever might be the quality of their mirth, old and young were gay at Merry Mount. The young deemed themselves happy. The elder spirits, if they knew that mirth was but the counterfeit of happiness, yet followed the false shadow wilfully, because at least her garments glittered brightest. Sworn triflers of a lifetime, they would not venture among the sober truths of life even to be truly blest.

.   .   .

Unfortunately, there were men in the new world of a sterner faith than these Maypole worshippers. Not far from Merry Mount was a settlement of Puritans, most dismal wretches, who said their prayers before daylight, and then wrought in the forest or the cornfield till evening made it prayer time again. Their weapons were always at hand to shoot down the straggling savage. When they met in conclave, it was never to keep up the old English mirth, but to hear sermons three hours long, or to proclaim bounties on the heads of wolves and the scalps of Indians. Their festivals were fast days, and their chief pastime the singing of psalms. Woe to the youth or maiden who did but dream of a dance! The selectman nodded to the constable and there sat the light-heeled reprobate in the stocks; or if he danced, it was round the whipping-post, which might be termed the Puritan Maypole.

.   .   .

In due time, a feud arose, stern and bitter on one side, and as serious on the other as anything could be among such light spirits as had sworn allegiance to the Maypole. The future complexion of New England was involved in this important quarrel. Should the grizzly saints establish their jurisdiction over the gay sinners, then would their spirits darken all the clime, and make it a land of clouded visages, of hard toil, of sermon and psalm forever. But should the banner staff of Merry Mount be fortunate, sunshine would break upon the hills, and flowers would beautify the forest, and late posterity do homage to the Maypole.

After these authentic passages from history, we return to the nuptials of the Lord and Lady of the May. Alas! we have delayed too long, and must darken our tale too suddenly. As we glance again at the Maypole, a solitary sunbeam is fading from the summit, and leaves only a faint, golden tinge blended with the hues of the rainbow banner. Even that dim light is now withdrawn, relinquishing the whole domain of Merry Mount to the evening gloom, which has rushed so instantaneously from the black surrounding woods. But some of these black shadows have rushed forth in human shape.

Yes, with the setting sun, the last day of mirth had passed from Merry Mount. The ring of gay masquers was disordered and broken; the stag lowered his antlers in dismay; the wolf grew weaker than a lamb; the bells of the morris-dancers tinkled with tremulous affright. The Puritans had played a characteristic part in the Maypole mummeries. Their darksome figures were intermixed with the wild shapes of their foes, and made the scene a picture of the moment when waking thoughts start up amid the scattered fantasies of a dream. The leader of the hostile party stood in the centre of the circle, while the rout of monsters cowered around him, like evil spirits in the presence of a dread magician. No fantastic foolery could look him in the face. So stern was the energy of his aspect, that the whole man, visage, frame, and soul, seemed wrought of iron, gifted with life and thought, yet all of one substance with his headpiece and breastplate. It was the Puritan of Puritans; it was Endicott himself!

"Stand off, priest of Baal!" said he, with a grim frown, and laying no reverent hand upon the surplice. "I know thee, Blackstone![1] Thou art the man who couldst not abide the rule even of thine own corrupted church, and hast come hither to preach iniquity, and to give example of it in thy life. But now shall it be seen that the Lord hath sanctified this wilderness for his peculiar people. Woe unto them that would defile it! And first, for this flower-decked abomination, the altar of thy worship!"

And with his keen sword Endicott assaulted the hallowed Maypole. Nor long did it resist his arm. It groaned with a dismal sound; it showered leaves and rosebuds upon the remorseless enthusiast; and finally, with all its green boughs and ribbons and flowers, symbolic of departed pleasures, down fell the banner staff of Merry Mount. As it

---

[1] Did Governor Endicott speak less positively, we should suspect a mistake here. The Rev. Mr. Blackstone, though an eccentric, is not known to have been an immoral man. We rather doubt his identity with the priest of Merry Mount.

sank, tradition says, the evening sky grew darker, and the woods threw forth a more sombre shadow.

"There," cried Endicott, looking triumphantly on his work, "there lies the only Maypole in New England! The thought is strong within me that, by its fall, is shadowed forth the fate of light and idle mirth-makers amongst us and our posterity. Amen, saith John Endicott."

"Amen!" echoed his followers.

But the votaries of the Maypole gave one groan for their idol. At the sound, the Puritan leader glanced at the crew of Comus, each a figure of broad mirth, yet, at this moment, strangely expressive of sorrow and dismay.

"Valiant captain," quoth Peter Palfrey, the Ancient of the band, "what order shall be taken with the prisoners?"

"I thought not to repent me of cutting down a Maypole," replied Endicott, "yet now I could find in my heart to plant it again, and give each of these bestial pagans one other dance round their idol. It would have served rarely for a whipping-post!"

"But there are pine-trees enow," suggested the lieutenant.

"True, good Ancient," said the leader. "Wherefore, bind the heathen crew, and bestow on them a small matter of stripes apiece, as earnest of our future justice. Set some of the rogues in the stocks to rest them-selves, so soon as Providence shall bring us to one of our own well-ordered settlements, where such accommodations may be found. Further penalties, such as branding and cropping of ears, shall be thought of hereafter."

"How many stripes for the priest?" inquired Ancient Palfrey.

"None as yet," answered Endicott, bending his iron frown upon the culprit. "It must be for the Great and General Court to determine, whether stripes and long imprisonment, and other grievous penalty, may atone for his transgressions. Let him look to himself! For such as violate our civil order, it may be permitted us to show mercy. But woe to the wretch that troubleth our religion!"

"And this dancing bear," resumed the officer. "Must he share the stripes of his fellows?"

"Shoot him through the head!" said the energetic Puritan. "I suspect witchcraft in the beast."

"Here be a couple of shining ones," continued Peter Palfrey, point-ing his weapon at the Lord and Lady of the May. "They seem to be of high station among these misdoers. Methinks their dignity will not be fitted with less than a double share of stripes."

Endicott rested on his sword, and closely surveyed the dress and aspect of the hapless pair. There they stood, pale, downcast, and appre-hensive. Yet there was an air of mutual support, and of pure affection seeking aid and giving it, that showed them to be man and wife, with the sanction of a priest upon their love. The youth, in the peril of the moment, had dropped his gilded staff, and thrown his arm about the Lady of the May, who leaned against his breast, too lightly to burden him, but with weight enough to express that their destinies were linked together, for good or evil. They looked first at each other, and then into the grim captain's face. There they stood, in the first hour of wedlock, while the idle pleasures, of which their companions were the emblems, had given place to the sternest cares of life, personified by the dark Puritans. But never had their youthful beauty seemed so pure and high as when its glow was chastened by adversity.

"Youth," said Endicott, "ye stand in an evil case, thou and thy maiden wife. Make ready presently, for I am minded that ye shall both have a token to remember your wedding day!"

"Stern man," cried the May Lord, "how can I move thee? Were the means at hand, I would resist to the death. Being powerless, I entreat. Do with me as thou wilt, but let Edith go untouched!"

"Not so," replied the immitigable zealot. "We are not wont to show an idle courtesy to that sex which requireth the stricter discipline. What sayest thou, maid? Shall thy silken bridegroom suffer thy share of the penalty, besides his own?"

"Be it death," said Edith, "and lay it all on me!"

Truly, as Endicott had said, the poor lovers stood in a woeful case. Their foes were triumphant, their friends captive and abased, their home desolate, the benighted wilderness around them, and a rigorous destiny, in the shape of the Puritan leader, their only guide. Yet the deepening twilight could not altogether conceal that the iron man was softened; he smiled at the fair spectacle of early love; he almost sighed for the inevitable blight of early hopes.

"The troubles of life have come hastily on this young couple," observed Endicott. "We will see how they comport themselves under their present trials ere we burden them with greater. If, among the spoil, there be any garments of a more decent fashion, let them be put upon this May Lord and his Lady, instead of their glistening vanities. Look to it, some of you."

"And shall not the youth's hair be cut?" asked Peter Palfrey, looking with abhorrence at the love-lock and long glossy curls of the young man.

"Crop it forthwith, and that in the true pumpkin-shell fashion," answered the captain. "Then bring them along with us, but more gently than their fellows. There be qualities in the youth, which may make him valiant to fight, and sober to toil, and pious to pray; and in the maiden, that may fit her to become a mother in our Israel, bringing up babes in better nurture than her own hath been. Nor think ye, young ones, that they are the happiest, even in our lifetime of a moment, who misspend it in dancing round a Maypole!"

And Endicott, the severest Puritan of all who laid the rock foundation of New England, lifted the wreath of roses from the ruin of the Maypole, and threw it, with his own gauntleted hand, over the heads of the Lord and Lady of the May. It was a deed of prophecy. As the moral gloom of the world overpowers all systematic gayety, even so was their home of wild mirth made desolate amid the sad forest. They returned to it no more. But as their flowery garland was wreathed of the brightest roses that had grown there, so, in the tie that united them, were intertwined all the purest and best of their early joys. They went heavenward, supporting each other along the difficult path which it was their lot to tread, and never wasted one regretful thought on the vanities of Merry Mount.

Two Nineteenth-Century Views

I Sing the Body Electric

WALT WHITMAN (1819–1892), America's best known poet, was born on eastern Long Island and at age four moved to Brooklyn, where he later pursued a career as a school teacher and journalist. In 1855 he published the first edition of **Leaves of Grass,** a collection of poems hailed by Emerson as "the most extraordinary piece of wit and wisdom America has yet contributed." Poet of the people, Whitman was nonetheless long rejected by common folk and critics alike. **Leaves of Grass** was termed obscene by the Philadelphia Society for the Suppression of Vice, and was also attacked by Anthony Comstock. "I Sing the Body Electric," added in 1860 to the "Children of Adam" poems, may rightly be said to be his version of "The Maypole of Merry Mount." One critic has termed it "a kind of sermon addressed to the life-deniers" (Edwin H. Miller, **Walt Whitman's Poetry** [New York: Houghton Mifflin, 1968], 130).

I SING THE BODY ELECTRIC.   From Walt Whitman, *Leaves of Grass*, 3rd ed., (1860).

I sing the body electric,
The armies of those I love engirth me and I engirth them,
They will not let me off till I go with them, respond to them,
And discorrupt them, and charge them full with the charge of the soul.

Was it doubted that those who corrupt their own bodies conceal themselves?

And if those who defile the living are as bad as they who defile the
  dead?
And if the body does not do fully as much as the soul?
And if the body were not the soul, what is the soul?

2

The love of the body of man or woman balks account, the body itself
  balks account,
That of the male is perfect, and that of the female is perfect.

The expression of the face balks account,
But the expression of a well-made man appears not only in his face,
It is in his limbs and joints also, it is curiously in the joints of his hips
  and wrists,
It is in his walk, the carriage of his neck, the flex of his waist and knees,
  dress does not hide him,
The strong sweet quality he has strikes through the cotton and broad-
  cloth,
To see him pass conveys as much as the best poem, perhaps more,
You linger to see his back, and the back of his neck and shoulder-side.

The sprawl and fulness of babes, the bosoms and heads of women, the
  folds of their dress, their style as we pass in the street, the contour
  of their shape downwards,
The swimmer naked in the swimming-bath, seen as he swims, through
  the transparent green-shine, or lies with his face up and rolls silently
  to and fro in the heave of the water.
The bending forward and backward of rowers in row-boats, the horse-
  man in his saddle,

Girls, mothers, house-keepers, in all their performances,

The group of laborers seated at noon-time with their open dinner-kettles, and their wives waiting,

The female soothing a child, the farmer's daughter in the garden or cow-yard,

The young fellow hoeing corn, the sleigh-driver driving his six horses through the crowd,

The wrestle of wrestlers, two apprentice-boys, quite grown, lusty, good-natured, native-born, out on the vacant lot at sun-down after work,

The coats and caps thrown down, the embrace of love and resistance,

The upper-hold and under-hold, the hair rumpled over and blinding the eyes;

The march of firemen in their own costumes, the play of masculine muscle through clean-setting trowsers and waist-straps,

The slow return from the fire, the pause when the bell strikes suddenly again, and the listening on the alert,

The natural, perfect, varied attitudes, the bent head, the curv'd neck and the counting;

Such-like I love—I loosen myself, pass freely, am at the mother's breast with the little child,

Swim with the swimmers, wrestle with wrestlers, march in line with the firemen, and pause, listen, count.

3

I knew a man, a common farmer, the father of five sons,

And in them the fathers of sons, and in them the fathers of sons.

This man was of wonderful vigor, calmness, beauty of person,

The shape of his head, the pale yellow and white of his hair and beard, the immeasurable meaning of his black eyes, the richness and breadth of his manners,

These I used to go and visit him to see, he was wise also,

He was six feet tall, he was over eighty years old, his sons were massive, clean, bearded, tan-faced, handsome,

They and his daughters loved him, all who saw him loved him,

They did not love him by allowance, they loved him with personal love,

He drank water only, the blood show'd like scarlet through the clear-brown skin of his face,

He was a frequent gunner and fisher, he sail'd his boat himself, he

had a fine one presented to him by a ship-joiner, he had fowling-
pieces presented to him by men that loved him,
When he went with his five sons and many grand-sons to hunt or fish,
you would pick him out as the most beautiful and vigorous of the
gang,
You would wish long and long to be with him, you would wish to
sit by him in the boat that you and he might touch each other.

4

I have perceiv'd that to be with those I like is enough,
To stop in company with the rest at evening is enough,
To be surrounded by beautiful, curious, breathing, laughing flesh is
enough,
To pass among them or touch any one, or rest my arm ever so lightly
round his or her neck for a moment, what is this then?
I do not ask any more delight, I swim in it as in a sea.

There is something in staying close to men and women and looking
on them, and in the contact and odor of them, that pleases the soul
well,
All things please the soul, but these please the soul well.

5

This is the female form,
A divine nimbus exhales from it from head to foot,
It attracts with fierce undeniable attraction,
I am drawn by its breath as if I were no more than a helpless vapor,
all falls aside but myself and it,
Books, art, religion, time, the visible and solid earth, and what was
expected of heaven or fear'd of hell, are now consumed,
Mad filaments, ungovernable shoots play out of it, the response like-
wise ungovernable,
Hair, bosom, hips, bend of legs, negligent falling hands all diffused,
mine too diffused,
Ebb stung by the flow and flow stung by the ebb, love-flesh swelling and deliciously aching,

Limitless limpid jets of love hot and enormous, quivering jelly of love,
    white-blow and delirious juice,
Bridegroom night of love working surely and softly into the pros-
    trate dawn,
Undulating into the willing and yielding day,
Lost in the cleave of the clasping and sweet-flesh'd day.

This the nucleus—after the child is born of woman, man is born of
    woman,
This the bath of birth, this the merge of small and large, and the out-
    let again.

Be not ashamed women, your privilege encloses the rest, and is the
    exit of the rest,
You are the gates of the body, and you are the gates of the soul.

The female contains all qualities and tempers them,
She is in her place and moves with perfect balance,
She is all things duly veil'd, she is both passive and active,
She is to conceive daughters as well as sons, and sons as well as daugh-
    ters.

As I see my soul reflected in Nature,
As I see through a mist, One with inexpressible completeness, sanity,
    beauty,
See the bent head and arms folded over the breast, the Female I see.

6

The male is not less the soul nor more, he too is in his place,
He too is all qualities, he is action and power,
The flush of the known universe is in him,
Scorn becomes him well, and appetite and defiance become him well,
The wildest largest passions, bliss that is utmost, sorrow that is utmost
    become him well, pride is for him,
The full-spread pride of man is calming and excellent to the soul,
Knowledge becomes him, he likes it always, he brings every thing to
    the test of himself,

Whatever the survey, whatever the sea and the sail he strikes soundings
   at last only here,
(Where else does he strike soundings except here?)

The man's body is sacred and the woman's body is sacred,
No matter who it is, it is sacred—is it the meanest one in the laborers'
   gang?
Is it one of the dull-faced immigrants just landed on the wharf?
Each belongs here or anywhere just as much as the well-off, just as
   much as you,
Each has his or her place in the procession.

(All is a procession,
The universe is a procession with measured and perfect motion.)

Do you know so much yourself that you call the meanest ignorant?
Do you suppose you have a right to a good sight, and he or she has no
   right to a sight?
Do you think matter has cohered together from its diffuse float, and
   the soil is on the surface, and water runs and vegetation sprouts,
For you only, and not for him and her?

7

A man's body at auction,
(For before the war I often go to the slave-mart and watch the sale,)
I help the auctioneer, the sloven does not half know his business.

Gentlemen look on this wonder,
Whatever the bids of the bidders they cannot be high enough for it,
For it the globe lay preparing quintillions of years without one animal
   or plant,
For it the revolving cycles truly and steadily roll'd.

In this head the all-baffling brain,
In it and below it the makings of heroes.

Examine these limbs, red, black, or white, they are cunning in tendon
   and nerve,
They shall be stript that you may see them.

Exquisite senses, life-lit eyes, pluck, volition,
Flakes of breast-muscle, pliant backbone and neck, flesh not flabby,
   good-sized arms and legs,
And wonders within there yet.

Within there runs blood,
The same old blood! the same red-running blood!
There swells and jets a heart, there all passions, desires, reachings, aspira-
   tions,
(Do you think they are not there because they are not express'd in
   parlors and lecture-rooms?)

This is not only one man, this the father of those who shall be fathers
   in their turns,
In him the start of populous states and rich republics,
Of him countless immortal lives with countless embodiments and en-
   joyments.

How do you know who shall come from the offspring of his offspring
   through the centuries?
(Who might you find you have come from yourself, if you could trace
   back through the centuries?)

8

A woman's body at auction,
She too is not only herself, she is the teeming mother of mothers,
She is the bearer of them that shall grow and be mates to the mothers.

Have you ever loved the body of a woman?
Have you ever loved the body of a man?
Do you not see that these are exactly the same to all in all nations and
   times all over the earth?

If any thing is sacred the human body is sacred,
And the glory and sweet of a man is the token of manhood untainted,
And in man or woman a clean, strong, firm-fibred body, is more beauti-
   ful than the most beautiful face.

Have you seen the fool that corrupted his own live body? or the fool
that corrupted her own live body?
For they do not conceal themselves, and cannot conceal themselves.

9

O my body! I dare not desert the likes of you in other men and women,
nor the likes of the parts of you,
I believe the likes of you are to stand or fall with the likes of the soul,
(and that they are the soul,)
I believe the likes of you shall stand or fall with my poems, and that
they are my poems,
Man's, woman's, child's, youth's, wife's, husband's, mother's, father's,
young man's, young woman's poems,
Head, neck, hair, ears, drop and tympan of the ears,
Eyes, eye-fringes, iris of the eye, eyebrows, and the waking or sleeping
of the lids,
Mouth, tongue, lips, teeth, roof of the mouth, jaws, and the jaw-hinges,
Nose, nostrils of the nose, and the partition,
Cheeks, temples, forehead, chin, throat, back of the neck, neck-slue,
Strong shoulders, manly beard, scapula, hind-shoulders, and the ample
side-round of the chest,
Upper-arm, armpit, elbow-socket, lower-arm, arm-sinews, arm-bones,
Wrist and wrist-joints, hand, palm, knuckles, thumb, forefinger, finger-
joints, finger-nails,
Broad breast-front, curling hair of the breast, breast-bone, breast-side,
Ribs, belly, backbone, joints of the backbone,
Hips, hip-sockets, hip-strength, inward and outward round, man-balls,
man-root,
Strong set of thighs, well carrying the trunk above,
Leg-fibres, knee, knee-pan, upper-leg, under-leg,
Ankles, instep, foot-ball, toes, toe-joints, the heel;
All attitudes, all the shapeliness, all the belongings of my or your body
or of any one's body, male or female,
The lung-sponges, the stomach-sac, the bowels sweet and clean,
The brain in its folds inside the skull-frame,
Sympathies, heart-valves, palate-valves, sexuality, maternity,
Womanhood, and all that is a woman, and the man that comes from
woman,

The womb, the teats, nipples, breast-milk, tears, laughter, weeping,
   love-looks, love-perturbations and risings,
The voice, articulation, language, whispering, shouting aloud,
Food, drink, pulse, digestion, sweat, sleep, walking, swimming,
Poise on the hips, leaping, reclining, embracing, arm-curving and
   tightening,
The continual changes of the flex of the mouth, and around the eyes,
The skin, the sunburnt shade, freckles, hair,
The curious sympathy one feels when feeling with the hand the naked
   meat of the body,
The circling rivers the breath, and breathing it in and out,
The beauty of the waist, and thence of the hips, and thence downward
   toward the knees,
The thin red jellies within you or within me, the bones and the marrow
   in the bones,
The exquisite realization of health;
O I say these are not the parts and poems of the body only, but of the
   soul,
O I say now these are the soul!

Free-Love Traps

ANTHONY COMSTOCK (1844–1915) was born in rural Connecticut
of colonial ancestry. After serving in the Civil War, he began in
1869 a lifelong crusade against "the sewer mouth of society" in an
antiobscenity drive for the YMCA. Backed by influential New York-
ers, he was appointed a special agent for the post office in 1873.
In less than two years he seized 130,000 pounds of books, 194,000
pictures, and 60,300 "articles made of rubber for immoral purposes." Founder and secretary of the Society for the Suppression of
Vice in New York, he was eventually responsible for the arrest of
some 3,600 men, women, and children. **Traps for the Young** (1883)
was a sequel to **Frauds Exposed; or How the People are Deceived
and Robbed, and Youth Corrupted** (1880).

When a boy I used to construct in the woods what was called a
stone-trap. This was formed by taking a large flat stone and setting it

FREE-LOVE TRAPS. From Anthony Comstock, *Traps for the Young* (1883).

up on one edge at an angle of about forty-five degrees, and fastening it there by means of three notched sticks. The end of one directly under the centre of the stone was baited with a sweet apple. The rabbit or squirrel nibbling the apple would spring the trap and be crushed to death.

The thing I mention now crushes self-respect, moral purity, and holy living. Sure ruin and death are the end to the victims caught by this doctrine, which is now becoming so prevalent. It is a bid to the lowest and most debased forms of living, and is dangerous to youth and adults alike. It takes the word "love," that sweetens so much of earth, and shines so brightly in heaven, and making that its watchword, distorts and prostitutes its meaning, until it is the mantle for all kinds of license and uncleanness. It should be spelled l-u-s-t, to be rightly understood, as it is interpreted by so-called liberals.

I can liken it to nothing more striking than the rude stone trap, so far as its results go.

As advocated by a few indecent creatures calling themselves reformers—men and women foul of speech, shameless in their lives, and corrupting in their influences—we must go to a sewer that has been closed, where the accumulations of filth have for years collected, to find a striking resemblance to its true character. I know of nothing more offensive to decency, or more revolting to good morals, than the class of publications issuing from this source. Science is dragged down by these advocates, and made a pretended foundation for their argument, while their foul utterances are sought to be palmed off upon the public as scientific efforts to elevate mankind. With them, marriage is bondage; love is lust; celibacy is suicide; while fidelity to marriage vows is a relic of barbarism. All restraints which keep boys and girls, young men and maidens pure and chaste, which prevent our homes from being turned into voluntary brothels, are not to be tolerated by them.

Nothing short of turning the whole human family loose to run wild like the beasts of the forest, will satisfy the demands of the leaders and publishers of this literature.

.   .   .

These agencies are active. They publish their false doctrines and theories, hold public meetings where foul-mouthed women address audiences of males—principally youth and old men—and the result of this seed-sowing is an enervated, lazy, shiftless, corrupt breed of human beings, devoid of common decency, not fit companions, in many cases. to run with swine.

My first experience with this crew was in Boston. Their leader had printed a most obscene and loathsome book. This book is too foul for description.

This foul book was advertised at a low price, and a special effort was made for "boy, girl, and women agents" to sell the same. This leader and his wife made it their business to hold free-love conventions, for the purpose of educating the youth in this line. He appropriated the mails of the United States, and made them his efficient agents in disseminating the book. Every volume had an advertisement for "boy and girl agents."

I secured the evidence, and procured a warrant in the United States Court at Boston for his arrest. I was especially deputed to execute this warrant. I went to his residence, and there learned that he was in Boston, holding a free-love convention. I returned there, reaching the hall where this convention was being held about 8.30 P.M. I was alone. I went up to the convention, bought a ticket, and as I entered the hall heard the speaker railing at "that Comstock." I took a seat without being recognized. The address was made up of abuse of myself and disgusting arguments for their cause.

I looked over the audience of about 250 men and boys. I could see lust in every face. After a little the wife of the president (the person I was after) took the stand, and delivered the foulest address I ever heard. She seemed lost to all shame. The audience cheered and applauded. It was too vile; I had to go out. I wanted to arrest the leader and end the base performance. There my man sat on the platform, puffed up with egotism. I looked at him and at the 250 eager faces, anxious to catch every word that fell from his wife's lips.

Discretion said, It is not wise to make yourself known. Duty said, There's your man, take him. But I was alone. In not one face in all that throng of his sympathizers was there enough manliness to encourage a hope of help, in case I required it.

I left the room with this one sentiment uppermost in my mind: "It is infamous that such a thing as this is possible in any part of our land, much more in Boston. It must be stopped. But how?" I went down the two flights of stairs to the street. The fresh air never was more refreshing. I resolved to stop that exhibition of nastiness, if possible. I looked for a policeman. As usual, none was to be found when wanted. Then I sought light and help from above. I prayed for strength to do my duty, and that I might have success. I knew God was able to help me. Every manly instinct cried out against my cowardly turning my back on this horde of lusters. I determined to try. I resolved that one man in America at least should enter a protest.

I had been brought over from the depot in a carriage. I had the driver place his carriage at the door leading up to the hall. I returned to the hall. This chieftain's wife continued her offensive tirade against common decency. Occasionally she referred to "that Comstock." Her husband presided with great self-complacency. You would have thought he was the champion of some majestic cause instead of a mob of free-lusters. I sat down again in the audience. The stream of filth continued until it seemed to me I could not sit a moment longer. Just then the leader passed from the stage into the anteroom. The audience were carried away with the vile talk. The baser the expressions, the louder they applauded.

I followed him out, and said to him quietly, "Is your name——?" [1]

With much self-conceit, he responded in the affirmative.

I simply said, "I have a warrant for your arrest for sending obscene matter through the mail. You are my prisoner."

He gasped out, "Who are you?"

I replied, "I am a deputy United States marshal."

"Well," he said, "if you'll excuse me I'll just go in and address the convention a moment."

I had been expecting this, and said at once, "You are now in custody, and you cannot harangue that crowd any more tonight."

Then he tried other devices to get into the hall; he wanted his overcoat and hat.

I said, "No, you cannot go in there again tonight. I then turned to one of his doorkeepers, a man about six feet two inches high, who was selling these obscene books as the people passed in and out, and said, "Are you a friend of this man?"

"Waal, you bet I am," he replied.

"Then," said I, "you had better get his hat and coat, or he'll go without them."

Then the prisoner wanted to go in and see his wife. I said, "No; call her out." As the six-footer brought the hat and coat, his wife-orator came out, having excused herself for a moment, and, much to my surprise, the audience kept their seats.

It began to be a little warm. Any moment an alarm might be given and this mob break loose. I kept cool, but it required an effort.

She wanted to know what was going to be done with her husband. I quietly replied, "Taken to Charles Street Jail."

"Well," she said, "I'll just go in and adjourn the convention, and then will come out and go with you, if you will wait a few moments."

I felt obliged, out of respect to my wife, sisters, and lady friends, to decline the kind offer of her (select) company. It was about all I wanted to do to have one of that slimy crowd in charge.

I knew that as soon as she returned and announced the arrest there would be a scene. I was in no mood for a bigger show than I had already witnessed. I had my money's worth and more, and was fully satisfied.

The prisoner desired to tarry. He did not readily respond to my

[1] There is no occasion for advertising him, and so I omit the name.

gentle hint to come. Time was safety with me then. I said, "Come;" and then took him by the shoulder (or neck, or thereabouts), and he moved toward the foot of the stairs. We got part way down the top flight, and I heard a tremendous yell. Then came, in less time than it takes to write it, a rush of many feet, pell-mell over benches and seats, in their scramble to see who would get out and down first. I took my man by the nape of the neck and we went down the next flight rather lively, and into the carriage. Before the first one of the audience touched the sidewalk, we were half a block away; for before I could get the carriage door closed, my Jehu, thinking discretion the better part of valor, whipped his steeds into a gentle run, away ho! for Charles Street Jail, where we arrived in safety.

Thus, reader, the devil's trapper was trapped. . . . Lust, to the careful observer, as surely shows itself in the face, look, and the expression of the eye, as do the marks of intemperance.

It is seen on the cars in the face of the man who stares the lady out of countenance. It is marked in the manner and expression of young men who seem to go to church for the express purpose of standing on the curbstone in front of the church door, at the close of the service, to watch and stare at the maidens as they come out. The poke in the ribs and laugh to attract attention, so often seen and heard from these gutter-statuaries, all argue nothing for common breeding or decency.

There is in Brooklyn a well-dressed man, with chin whiskers almost white, who makes a business of travelling about on crowded ferry-boats and horse-cars, and standing on street corners, to insult women as they pass. This miserable creature was very much outraged because he was exposed while offering an insult to a poor but in every way modest working-girl, on a ferry-boat recently.

Many ladies complain of insults from this creature. Well for him that husbands or brothers are not by when he treads on ladies' toes, or nudges them with his knee or elbow. These cowards always take good care to see that the lady is alone before advertising by their acts that they are unclean. They are devoured with vileness, and act out to the full their base natures.

To the young man or woman let me say, shun evil thoughts. They breed evil practices, and these soon will sink you so low that none are mean enough to do you reverence. These traps are numerous. They crush out common decency. They sap the physical well-being in the man or woman, and reduce humanity below the level of the brute. What license has done for the Turks, this free-love doctrine is doing for America.

War in Bohemia

MALCOLM COWLEY (1898–   ), free-lance writer, literary critic, and long-time associate editor of the **New Republic,** was born in Belsano, Pennsylvania. After graduating from Harvard in 1920, he journeyed to France, where he observed at first hand the "lost generation" of American expatriates. In **Exile's Return,** a chronicle of this generation written in the depths of the Depression, he expressed his conviction that the times demanded a renewed sense of social responsibility.

. . . Greenwich Village was not only a place, a mood, a way of life: like all bohemias, it was also a doctrine. Since the days of Gautier and Murger, this doctrine had remained the same in spirit, but it had changed in several details. By 1920, it had become a system of ideas that could roughly be summarized as follows:

1. The idea of salvation by the child.—Each of us at birth has special potentialities which are slowly crushed and destroyed by a standardized society and mechanical methods of teaching. If a new educational system can be introduced, one by which children are encouraged to develop their own personalities, to blossom freely like flowers, then the world will be saved by this new, free generation.

2. The idea of self-expression.—Each man's, each woman's, purpose in life is to express himself, to realize his full individuality through creative work and beautiful living in beautiful surroundings.

3. The idea of paganism.—The body is a temple in which there is nothing unclean, a shrine to be adorned for the ritual of love.

4. The idea of living for the moment.—It is stupid to pile up treasures that we can enjoy only in old age, when we have lost the capacity for enjoyment. Better to seize the moment as it comes, to dwell in it intensely, even at the cost of future suffering. Better to live extravagantly, gather June rosebuds, "burn my candle at both ends. . . . It gives a lovely light."

5. The idea of liberty.—Every law, convention or rule of art that prevents self-expression or the full enjoyment of the moment should

be shattered and abolished. Puritanism is the great enemy. The crusade against puritanism is the only crusade with which free individuals are justified in allying themselves.

6. The idea of female equality.—Women should be the economic and moral equals of men. They should have the same pay, the same working conditions, the same opportunity for drinking, smoking, taking or dismissing lovers.

7. The idea of psychological adjustment.—We are unhappy because we are maladjusted, and maladjusted because we are repressed. If our individual repressions can be removed—by confessing them to a Freudian psychologist—then we can adjust ourselves to any situation, and be happy in it. (But Freudianism is only one method of adjustment. What is wrong with us may be our glands, and by a slight operation, or merely by taking a daily dose of thyroid, we may alter our whole personalities. Again, we may adjust ourselves by some such psycho-physical discipline as was taught by Gurdjieff. The implication of all these methods is the same—that the environment itself need not be altered. That explains why most radicals who became converted to psychoanalysis or glands or Gurdjieff [1] gradually abandoned their political radicalism.)

8. The idea of changing place.—"They do things better in Europe." England and Germany have the wisdom of old cultures; the Latin peoples have admirably preserved their pagan heritage. By expatriating himself, by living in Paris, Capri or the South of France, the artist can break the puritan shackles, drink, live freely and be wholly creative.

All these, from the standpoint of the business-Christian ethic then represented by the *Saturday Evening Post*, were corrupt ideas. This older ethic is familiar to most people, but one feature of it has not been sufficiently emphasized. Substantially, it was a *production* ethic. The great virtues it taught were industry, foresight, thrift and personal initiative. The workman should be industrious in order to produce more for his employer; he should look ahead to the future; he should save money in order to become a capitalist himself; then he should exercise personal initiative and found new factories where other workmen would toil industriously, and save, and become capitalists in their turn.

During the process many people would suffer privations: most workers would live meagerly and wrack their bodies with labor; even the employers would deny themselves luxuries that they could easily pur-

---

[1] George Ivanovich Gurdjieff, a Russian living in France, had worked out a system of practical mysticism based largely on Yoga. His chief disciple was A. E. Orage, the editor of the *New English Weekly*. In the spring of 1924, when Orage was in New York, he gained a great many converts, chiefly among older members of the Greenwich Village set.

chase, choosing instead to put back the money into their business; but after all, our bodies were not to be pampered; they were temporary dwelling places, and we should be rewarded in Heaven for our self-denial. On earth, our duty was to accumulate more wealth and produce more goods, the ultimate use of which was no subject for worry. They would somehow be absorbed, by new markets opened in the West, or overseas in new countries, or by the increased purchasing power of workmen who had saved and bettered their position.

That was the ethic of a young capitalism, and it worked admirably, so long as the territory and population of the country were expanding faster than its industrial plant. But after the war the situation changed. Our industries had grown enormously to satisfy a demand that suddenly ceased. To keep the factory wheels turning, a new domestic market had to be created. Industry and thrift were no longer adequate. There must be a new ethic that encouraged people to buy, a *consumption* ethic.

It happened that many of the Greenwich Village ideas proved useful in the altered situation. Thus, *self-expression* and *paganism* encouraged a demand for all sorts of products—modern furniture, beach pajamas, cosmetics, colored bathrooms with toilet paper to match. *Living for the moment* meant buying an automobile, radio or house, using it now and paying for it tomorrow. *Female equality* was capable of doubling the consumption of products—cigarettes, for example—that had formerly been used by men alone. Even *changing place* would help to stimulate business in the country from which the artist was being expatriated. The exiles of art were also trade missionaries: involuntarily they increased the foreign demand for fountain pens, silk stockings, grapefruit and portable typewriters. They drew after them an invading army of tourists, thus swelling the profits of steamship lines and travel agencies. Everything fitted into the business picture.

I don't mean to say that Greenwich Village was the source of the revolution in morals that affected all our lives in the decade after the war, and neither do I mean that big business deliberately plotted to render the nation extravagant, pleasure worshiping and reckless of tomorrow.

The new moral standards arose from conditions that had nothing to do with the Village. They were, as a matter of fact, not really new. Always, even in the great age of the Puritans, there had been currents of licentiousness that were favored by the immoderate American climate and held in check only by hellfire preaching and the hardships of settling a new country. Old Boston, Providence, rural Connecticut, all had their underworlds. The reason puritanism became so strong in America was perhaps that it had to be strong in order to checkmate its enemies. But it was already weakening as the country grew richer in the twenty years before the war; and the war itself was the puritan crisis and defeat.

All standards were relaxed in the stormy-sultry wartime atmosphere. It wasn't only the boys of my age, those serving in the army, who were transformed by events: their sisters and younger brothers were affected in a different fashion. With their fathers away, perhaps, and their mothers making bandages or tea-dancing with lonely officers, it was possible for boys and girls to do what they pleased. For the first time they could go to dances unchaperoned, drive the family car and park it by the roadside while they made love, and come home after midnight, a little tipsy, with nobody to reproach them in the hallway. They took advantage of these stolen liberties—indeed, one might say that the revolution in morals began as a middle-class children's revolt.

But everything conspired to further it. Prohibition came and surrounded the new customs with illicit glamour; prosperity made it possible to practice them; Freudian psychology provided a philosophical justification and made it unfashionable to be repressed; still later the sex magazines and the movies, even the pulpit, would advertise a revolution that had taken place silently and triumphed without a struggle. In all this Greenwich Village had no part. The revolution would have occurred if the Village had never existed, but—the point is important—it would not have followed the same course. The Village, older in revolt, gave form to the movement, created its fashions, and supplied the writers and illustrators who would render them popular. As for American business, though it laid no plots in advance, it was quick enough to use the situation, to exploit the new markets for cigarettes and cosmetics, and to realize that, in advertising pages and movie palaces, sex appeal was now the surest appeal.

The Greenwich Village standards, with the help of business, had spread through the country. Young women east and west had bobbed their hair, let it grow and bobbed it again; they had passed through the period when corsets were checked in the cloakroom at dances and the period when corsets were not worn. They were not very self-conscious when they talked about taking a lover; and the conversations ran from mother fixations to birth control while they smoked cigarettes between the courses of luncheons eaten in black-and-orange tea shops just like those in the Village. People of forty had been affected by the younger generation: they spent too much money, drank too much gin, made love to one another's wives and talked about their neuroses. Houses were furnished to look like studios. Stenographers went on parties, following the example of the boss and his girl friend and her husband. The "party," conceived as a gathering together of men and women to drink gin cocktails, flirt, dance to the phonograph or radio and gossip about their absent friends, had in fact become one of the most popular American institutions; nobody stopped to think how short its history had been in this country. It developed out of the "orgies" celebrated by the French 1830 Romantics, but it was introduced into this country by Greenwich Villagers—before being adopted by salesmen from Kokomo and the younger country-club set in Kansas City.

Wherever one turned the Greenwich Village ideas were making their way: even the *Saturday Evening Post* was feeling their influence. Long before Repeal, it began to wobble on Prohibition. It allowed drinking, petting and unfaithfulness to be mentioned in the stories it published; its illustrations showed women smoking. Its advertising columns admitted one after another of the strictly pagan products—cosmetics, toilet tissues, cigarettes—yet still it continued to thunder against Greenwich Village and bohemian immorality. It even nourished the illusion that its long campaign had been successful. On more than one occasion it announced that the Village was dead and buried: "The sad truth is," it said in the autumn of 1931, "that the Village was a flop." Perhaps it was true that the Village was moribund—of that we can't be sure, for creeds and ways of life among artists are hard to kill. If, however, the Village was really dying, it was dying of success. It was dying because it became so popular that too many people insisted on living there. It was dying because women smoked cigarettes on the streets of the Bronx, drank gin cocktails in Omaha and had perfectly swell parties in Seattle and Middletown—in other words, because American business and the whole of middle-class America had been going Greenwich Village.

Do It!

JERRY RUBIN (1944–   ), founder of the Youth International Party (Yippies), appeared in numerous demonstrations during the 1960s, including the one at the Democratic Convention in 1968. A defendant in the celebrated trial of the "Chicago Seven," he is presently appealing his conviction. **Do It** (1970), a Yippie manifesto, perhaps best proves one of his favorite dicta: "We are the people our parents warned us against."

DO IT! From Jerry Rubin, *Do It!* Copyright © 1970 by the Social Education Foundation. Reprinted by permission of Simon & Schuster, Inc.

1: Child of Amerika

I am a child of Amerika.

If I'm ever sent to Death Row for my revolutionary "crimes," I'll order as my last meal: a hamburger, french fries and a Coke.

I dig big cities.

I love to read the sports pages and gossip columns, listen to the radio and watch color TV.

I dig department stores, huge supermarkets and airports. I feel secure (though not necessarily hungry) when I see Howard Johnson's on the expressway.

I groove on Hollywood movies—even bad ones.

I speak only one language—English.

I love rock 'n' roll.

I collected baseball players' cards when I was a kid and wanted to play second base for the Cincinnati Reds, my home team.

I got a car when I was sixteen after flunking my first driver's test and crying for a week waiting to take it a second time.

I went to the kind of high school where you had to pass a test to get *in.*

I graduated in the bottom half of the class.

My classmates voted me the "busiest" senior in the school.

I had short, short, short hair.

I dug *Catcher in the Rye.*

I didn't have pimples.

I became an ace young reporter for the Cincinnati *Post and Times-Star.* "Son," the managing editor said to me, *"someday you're going to be a helluva reporter, maybe the greatest reporter this city's ever seen."*

I loved Adlai Stevenson.

My father drove a truck delivering bread and later became an organizer in the Bakery Drivers' Union. He dug Jimmy Hoffa (so do I). He died of heart failure at fifty-two.

My mother had a college degree and played the piano. She died of cancer at the age of fifty-one.

I took care of my brother, Gil, from the time he was thirteen.

I dodged the draft.

I went to Oberlin College for a year, graduated from the University of Cincinnati, spent 1½ years in Israel and started graduate school at Berkeley.

I dropped out.
I dropped out of the White Race and the Amerikan nation.
I dig being free.
I like getting high.
I don't own a suit or tie.
I live for the revolution.
I'm a yippie!
I am an orphan of Amerika.

10: We Are All Human Be-ins

One day some Berkeley radicals were invited over to the Buddhist temple of some San Francisco hippies. We got high and decided to get the tribes of Haight-Ashbury and Berkeley together.

A Gathering of the Tribes. Golden Gate Park. Free music by all of the rock bands in the city.

The hippies were calling it a Human "Be-in."

Nobody knew what the fuck a Be-in was.

We got stoned on some outasight grass. One Berkeley radical asked: "What are going to be the demands of this demonstration?"

The hippies patiently explained to him that it wasn't a "demonstration" and that we were just going to *be* there.

"People will turn each other on."

"Only good vibes."

"But no demands."

The Berkeley radical kept demanding that there be demands. So somebody gave him a pencil and paper and told him to write some.

It got to be so heavy that one S.F. hippie jumped up and said, "There's got to be more love in this room: *Roll some more joints.*"

People in the streets knew something was up. They seemed to catch on right away. If it had been a political demonstration they would have asked, "What are the issues? What are the demands? Why should we go?"

But this time everybody knew.

The purpose was just to *be.*

Golden Gate Park:

Rock music.

Grass.

Sun. Beautiful bodies.

Paint.

Ecstasy. Rainbows. No strangers!

Everybody smiling. *No picket signs or political banners.*

Our nakedness was our picket sign.

We played out our fantasies like children. We were kids playing "grown-up games." You can be whatever you want to be when you're a kid.

We were cowboys and Indians, pirates, kings, gypsies and Greeks. It was a panorama of history.

The rock bands created a tribal, animal energy.

We were a religion, a family, a culture, with our own music, our own dress, our own human relationships, our own stimulants, our own media.

And we believed that our energy would *turn on the world.*

All of that energy in one place at one time was the Atom Bomb explosion of the youth culture.

The Be-in: a new medium of human relations. A magnet drawing together all the freaky, hip, unhappy, young, happy, curious, criminal, gentle, alienated, weird, frustrated, far-out, artistic, lonely, lovely people to the same place at the same time. We could see one another, touch one another and realize that *we* were not *alone.*

All of our rebellion was reaffirmed.

It was a new consciousness.

Instead of *talking* about communism, people were beginning to *live* communism.

The fragmented life of capitalist Amerika—the separation between work and play, school and fun, property and freedom—was reconstituted by the joyous celebrants.

Neither the civil rights movement, the Free Speech Movement or the antiwar movement achieved its stated goals. They led to deeper discoveries—that revolution did not mean the end of the war or the end of racism. Revolution meant the creation of new men and women.

Revolution meant a new life.

On earth.

Today.

Life is the act of living.
Revolution is the act of revolution.

We are all human be-ins.

14: Our Leaders Are Seven-Year-Olds

Amerika says: **Don't!**
The yippies say: **Do It!**

Everything the yippies do is aimed at three-to-seven-year-olds.
We're child molesters.
Our message: Don't grow up. Growing up means *giving up your dreams.*

Our parents are waging a genocidal war against their own kids. The economy has no use or need for youth. Everything is already built. *Our existence is a crime.*
The logical next step is to kill us. So Amerika drafts her young niggers and sends us to die in Vietnam.

The function of school is to keep white middle-class youth off the streets. *High schools and colleges are fancy baby-sitting agencies.*
Vietnam and the school system are the two main fronts in Amerika's genocidal campaign against the youth. Jails and mental hospitals follow closely.

Amerika says: *History is over.* Fit in. The best system in the history of man has been discovered—it's yours. Nothing else is possible because man is selfish, greedy, tainted by Original Sin. If we don't fit in, they lock us up.
But for the masses of people throughout the world, history is just beginning. We kids want to start again too, rebuilding from scratch.
We want to be heroes, like those we read about in the history books. We missed the First Amerikan Revolution. We missed World War II. We missed the Chinese and Cuban Revolutions. Are we supposed to spend our futures grinning and watching TV all the time?

A society which suppresses adventure makes the only adventure the suppression of that society.
Republican fat-cat businessmen see their kids become SDS leaders. War profiteers' children become hippies. Senators' kids are arrested at pot parties.
Generational war cuts across class and race lines and brings the revolution into every living room.

The revolution toppled the high schools in 1968. Soon it will go to the junior highs and then the grade schools.

The leaders of the revolution are seven-year-olds.

20: Fuck God

A dying culture destroys everything it touches.

Language is one of the first things to go.

Nobody really communicates with words anymore. Words have lost their emotional impact, intimacy, ability to shock and make love.

Language *prevents* communication.

> CARS LOVE SHELL
> How can I say
> "I love you"
> after hearing:
> "CARS LOVE SHELL."

Does anyone understand what I *mean?*

Nigger control is called "law and order." Stealing is called "capitalism."

A *"REVOLUTION"* IN TOILET PAPER.
A *"REVOLUTION"* IN COMBATING MOUTH ODOR!
A *"REVOLUTIONARY"* HOLLYWOOD MOVIE!
Have the capitalists no respect?

But there's one word which Amerika hasn't destroyed.

One word which has maintained its emotional power and purity.

Amerika cannot destroy it because she dare not use it.

It's illegal!

It's the last word left in the English language:

FUCK!!!

One bright winter day in Berkeley, John Thomson crayoned on a piece of cardboard "FUCK WAR," sat down with it and was arrested within two minutes. Two more people sat down with signs saying "FUCK WAR." *They* were arrested.

The Filthy Speech Movement had been born.

Everyone at school plays with himself verbally. The Free Speech Movement ended our virginity—we challenged outside society and the cops came on campus to get us. But once they left, everybody went back to playing with himself.

Once you've had sex, jacking off is a drag. Campus sexual frustration led John to start the Filthy Speech Movement.

"Nobody would have gotten excited if I held a sign which said 'Kill Vietnamese,' " John said.

So he said "FUCK WAR" and four mighty letters brought the Great University to a Grinding Halt.

Old people everywhere freaked out. *"Fuck, man, is this what Free Speech is coming to?"* Fucking Clark Kerr the fucking president of the fucking university fucking resigned. He said the fucking future of the whole mother-fucking university was at stake. Fuck him, he's a fucking asshole. He said that if FUCK wasn't fucking banished from the minds and mouths of the fucking students, then things were gonna get pretty fucked up.

But most political radicals got uptight and wouldn't defend FUCK. Activists in the Free Speech Movement ostracized the FUCK-heads— they said FUCK wasn't "serious"! They got a sudden pure speech fetish.

Things *did* get fucked-up. In a unity move, Clark Kerr came back and fucked the fucking students. They were expelled from the university and given jail terms. Few politicos gave a fuck.

The Free Speech Movement was raped in the same bed with the Filthy Speech Movement. The movement was badly divided. It was an early sign of the split between political radicals and the hippie/yippies.

How can you separate politics from sex? It's all the same thing: Body politic.

POLITICO-SEXUAL REALITY: The naked human body is immoral under Christianity and illegal under Amerikan law. Nudity is called "indecent exposure." Fuck is a dirty word because you have to be naked to do it. Also it's fun.

When we start playing with our "private parts," our parents say "Don't do that." The mother commits a crime against her child when she says "Don't do that."

We're taught that our shit stinks. We're taught to be ashamed of how we came into the world—fucking. We're taught that if we dig balling, we should feel guilty.

We're taught: body pleasure is immoral!

We're really taught to hate ourselves!

Puritanism leads us to Vietnam. Sexual insecurity results in a super-masculinity trip called imperialism. Amerikan foreign policy especially in Vietnam, makes no sense except sexually. Amerika has a frustrated penis, trying to drive itself into Vietnam's tiny slit to prove it is The Man.

The revolution declares war on Original Sin, the dictatorship of parents over their kids, Christian morality, capitalism and supermasculinity trips.

The yippie political strategy is to ally with Billy Graham. Keep the word "fuck" dirty! At the same time we yippies fight for the right to say fuck whenever we want to. It's a contradiction—but in contradictions like this lie the genius of making a revolution.

Our tactic is to send niggers and longhair scum invading white middle-class homes, fucking on the living room floor, crashing on the chandeliers, spewing sperm on the Jesus pictures, breaking the furniture and smashing Sunday school napalm-blood Amerika forever.

We will do whatever is forbidden.

We will outrage Amerika until the bourgeoisie dies of apoplexy.

We will turn Amerika's colleges into nudist camps.

We will find new ways of living together and raising our kids.

FUCKFUCKFUCKFUCKFUCKFUCKFUCKFUCKFUCKFUCKFUCKFUCKFUCK
FUCKFUCKFUCKFUCKFUCKFUCKFUCKFUCKFUCKFUCKFUCKFUCKFUCK
FUCKFUCKFUCKFUCKFUCKFUCKFUCKFUCKFUCKFUCKFUCKFUCKFUCK
FUCKFUCKFUCKFUCKFUCKFUCKFUCKFUCKFUCKFUCKFUCKFUCKFUCK
FUCKFUCKFUCKFUCKFUCKFUCKFUCKFUCKFUCKFUCKFUCKFUCKFUCK
FUCKFUCKFUCKFUCKFUCKFUCKFUCKFUCKFUCKFUCKFUCKFUCKFUCK
FUCKFUCKFUCKFUCKFUCKFUCKFUCKFUCKFUCKFUCKFUCKFUCKFUCK
FUCKFUCKFUCKFUCKFUCKFUCKFUCKFUCKFUCKFUCKFUCKFUCKFUCK
FUCKFUCKFUCKFUCKFUCKFUCKFUCKFUCKFUCKFUCKFUCKFUCKFUCK
FUCKFUCKFUCKFUCKFUCKFUCKFUCKFUCKFUCKFUCKFUCKFUCKFUCK
FUCKFUCKFUCKFUCKFUCKFUCKFUCKFUCKFUCKFUCKFUCKFUCKFUCK
FUCKFUCKFUCKFUCKFUCKFUCKFUCKFUCKFUCKFUCKFUCKFUCKFUCK
FUCKFUCKFUCKFUCKFUCKFUCKFUCKFUCKFUCKFUCKFUCKFUCKFUCK
FUCKFUCKFUCKFUCKFUCKFUCKFUCKFUCKFUCKFUCKFUCKFUCKFUCK
FUCKFUCKFUCKFUCKFUCKFUCKFUCKFUCKFUCKFUCKFUCKFUCKFUCK
FUCKFUCKFUCKFUCKFUCKFUCKFUCKFUCKFUCKFUCKFUCKFUCKFUCK
FUCKFUCKFUCKFUCKFUCKFUCKFUCKFUCKFUCKFUCKFUCKFUCKFUCK
FUCKFUCKFUCKFUCKFUCKFUCKFUCKFUCKFUCKFUCKFUCKFUCKFUCK
FUCKFUCKFUCKFUCKFUCKFUCKFUCKFUCKFUCKFUCKFUCKFUCKFUCK
FUCKFUCKFUCKFUCKFUCKFUCKFUCKFUCKFUCKFUCKFUCKFUCKFUCK
FUCKFUCKFUCKFUCKFUCKFUCKFUCKFUCKFUCKFUCKFUCKFUCKFUCK
FUCKFUCKFUCKFUCKFUCKFUCKFUCKFUCKFUCKFUCKFUCKFUCKFUCK
FUCKFUCKFUCKFUCKFUCKFUCKFUCKFUCKFUCKFUCKFUCKFUCKFUCK
FUCKFUCKFUCKFUCKFUCKFUCKFUCKFUCKFUCKFUCKFUCKFUCKFUCK
FUCKFUCKFUCKFUCKFUCKFUCKFUCKFUCKFUCKFUCKFUCKFUCKFUCK
FUCKFUCKFUCKFUCKFUCKFUCKFUCKFUCKFUCKFUCKFUCKFUCKFUCK
FUCKFUCKFUCKFUCKFUCKFUCKFUCKFUCKFUCKFUCKFUCKFUCKFUCK
FUCKFUCKFUCKFUCKFUCKFUCKFUCKFUCKFUCKFUCKFUCKFUCKFUCK
FUCKFUCKFUCKFUCKFUCKFUCKFUCKFUCKFUCKFUCKFUCKFUCKFUCK
FUCKFUCKFUCKFUCKFUCKFUCKFUCKFUCKFUCKFUCKFUCKFUCKFUCK
FUCKFUCKFUCKFUCKFUCKFUCKFUCKFUCKFUCKFUCKFUCKFUCKFUCK
FUCKFUCKFUCKFUCKFUCKFUCKFUCKFUCKFUCKFUCKFUCKFUCKFUCK
FUCKFUCKFUCKFUCKFUCKFUCKFUCKFUCKFUCKFUCKFUCKFUCKFUCK
FUCKFUCKFUCKFUCKFUCKFUCKFUCKFUCKFUCKFUCKFUCKFUCKFUCK
FUCKFUCKFUCKFUCKFUCKFUCKFUCKFUCKFUCKFUCKFUCKFUCKFUCK
FUCKFUCKFUCKFUCKFUCKFUCKFUCKFUCKFUCKFUCKFUCKFUCKFUCK

A Gay Manifesto

CARL WITTMAN (1943–   ), a native of New Jersey, graduated from Swarthmore College in 1964. Politically active as an undergraduate, he formulated his views concerning student activism and the civil rights movement in two articles later published in **The New Student Left** (1966), edited by Mitchell Cohen and Dennis Hale. His subsequent experience with draft resistance provided the background for his "Waves of Resistance," **Liberation,** 13 (November 1967), 29–33. "A Gay Manifesto" was written in the fall of 1969, soon after gay liberation groups began to form in San Francisco.

San Francisco is a refugee camp for homosexuals. We have fled here from every part of the nation, and like refugees elsewhere, we came not because it is so great here, but because it was so bad there. By the tens of thousands, we fled small towns where to be ourselves would endanger our jobs and any hopes of a decent life; we have fled from blackmailing cops, from families who disowned or "tolerated" us; we have been drummed out of the armed services, thrown out of schools, fired from jobs, beaten by punks and policemen.

And we have formed a ghetto, out of self-protection. It is a ghetto rather than a free territory because it is still theirs. Straight cops patrol us, straight legislators govern us, straight employers keep us in line, straight money exploits us. We have pretended everything is OK, because we haven't been able to see how to change it—we've been afraid.

In the past year there has been an awakening of gay liberation ideas and energy. How it began we don't know; maybe we were inspired by black people and their freedom movement; we learned how to stop pretending from the hip revolution. Amerika in all its ugliness has surfaced with the war and our national leaders. And we are revulsed by the quality of our ghetto life.

Where once there was frustration, alienation, and cynicism, there are new characteristics among us. We are full of love for each other and are showing it; we are full of anger at what has been done to us. And as we recall all the self-censorship and repression for so many years, a reservoir

A GAY MANIFESTO. From the *Activist*, 10 (1970). Reprinted by permission of Carl Wittman and the Activist Publishing Company.

of tears pours out of our eyes. And we are euphoric, high, with the initial flourish of a movement.

We want to make ourselves clear: our first job is to free ourselves; that means clearing our heads of the garbage that's been poured into them. This article is an attempt at raising a number of issues, and presenting some ideas to replace the old ones. It is primarily for ourselves, a starting point of discussion. If straight people of good will find it useful in understanding what liberation is about, so much the better.

It should also be clear that these are the views of one person, and are determined not only by my homosexuality, but by my being white, male, middle class. It is my individual consciousness. Our group consciousness will evolve as we get ourselves together—we are only at the beginning.

On Orientation

What homosexuality is: Nature leaves undefined the object of sexual desire. The gender of that object is imposed socially. Humans originally made homosexuality taboo because they needed every bit of energy to produce and raise children: survival of species was a priority. With overpopulation and technological change, that taboo continued only to exploit us and enslave us.

As kids we refused to capitulate to demands that we ignore our feelings toward each other. Somewhere we found the strength to resist being indoctrinated, and we should count that among our assets. We have to realize that our loving each other is a good thing, not an unfortunate thing, and that we have a lot to teach straights about sex, love, strength, and resistance.

Homosexuality is *not* a lot of things. It is not a makeshift in the absence of the opposite sex; it is not hatred or rejection of the opposite sex; it is not genetic; it is not the result of broken homes except inasmuch as we could see the sham of American marriage. *Homosexuality is the capacity to love someone of the same sex.*

Bisexuality: Bisexuality is good; it is the capacity to love people of either sex. The reason so few of us are bisexual is because society made such a big stink about homosexuality that we got forced into seeing ourselves as either straight or non-straight. Also, many gays got turned off to the ways men are supposed to act with women and vice-versa, which is pretty fucked-up. Gays will begin to turn on to women when 1) it's something that we do because we want to, and not because we should, and 2) when women's liberation changes the nature of heterosexual relationships.

We continue to call ourselves homosexual, not bisexual, even if we do make it with the opposite sex also, because saying "Oh, I'm Bi" is a cop-out for a gay. We get told it's OK to sleep with guys as long as we sleep with women, too, and that's still putting homosexuality down. We'll be gay until everyone has forgotten that it's an issue. Then we'll begin to be complete.

Heterosexuality: Exclusive heterosexuality is fucked up. It reflects a fear of people of the same sex, it's anti-homosexual, and it is fraught with frustration. Heterosexual sex is fucked up, too; ask women's liberation about what straight guys are like in bed. Sex is aggression for the male chauvinist; sex is obligation for the traditional woman. And among the young, the modern, the hip, it's only a subtle version of the same. For us to become heterosexual in the sense that our straight brothers and sisters are is not a cure, it is a disease.

.   .   .

On Roles

Mimicry of straight society: We are children of straight society. We still think straight: that is part of our oppression. One of the worst of straight concepts is inequality. Straight (also white, English, male-capitalist) thinking views things in terms of order and comparison. A is before B, B is after A; one is below two is below three; there is no room for equality. This idea gets extended to male/female, on top/on bottom, spouse/not spouse, heterosexual/homosexual, boss/worker, white/black and rich/poor. Our social institutions cause and reflect this verbal hierarchy. This is Amerika.

We've lived in these institutions all our lives. Naturally we mimic the roles. For too long we mimicked these roles to protect ourselves—a survival mechanism. Now we are becoming free enough to shed the roles which we've picked up from the institutions which have imprisoned us.

"Stop mimicking straights, stop censoring ourselves."

Marriage: Marriage is a prime example of a straight institution fraught with role playing. Traditional marriage is a rotten, oppressive institution. Those of us who have been in heterosexual marriages too often have blamed our gayness on the breakup of the marriage. No. They broke up because marriage is a contract which smothers both people, denies needs, and places impossible demands on both people. And we had the strength, again, to refuse to capitulate to the roles which were demanded of us.

Gay people must stop gauging their self respect by how well they mimic straight marriages. Gay marriages will not have the same problems as straight ones except in burlesque. For the usual legitimacy and pressures which kept straight marriages together are absent, e.g., kids, what parents think, what neighbours say.

To accept that happiness comes through finding a groovy spouse and settling down, showing the world that "we're just the same as you" is avoiding the real issues, and is an expression of self-hatred.

Alternatives to marriage: People want to get married for lots of good reasons, although marriage won't often meet those needs or desires. We're all looking for security, a flow of love, and a feeling of belonging and being needed.

These needs can be met through a number of social relationships and living situations. Things we want to get away from are: 1. exclusiveness, propertied attitudes toward each other, a mutual pact against the rest of the world; 2. promises about the future, which we have no right to make and which prevent us from, or make us feel guilty about, growing; 3. inflexible roles, roles which do not reflect us at the moment but are inherited through mimicry and inability to define equalitarian relationships.

We have to define for ourselves a new pluralistic, role-free social structure for ourselves. It must contain both the freedom and physical space for people to live alone, live together for a while, live together for a long time, either as couples or in larger numbers; and the ability to flow easily from one of these states to another as our needs change.

Liberation for gay people is defining for ourselves how and with whom we live, instead of measuring our relationship in comparison to straight ones, with straight values.

Gay "stereotypes": The straights' image of the gay world is defined largely by those of us who have violated straight roles. There is a tendency among "homophile" groups to deplore gays who play visible roles —the queens and the nellies. As liberated gays, we must take a clear stand. 1. Gays who stand out have become our first martyrs. They came out and withstood disapproval before the rest of us did. 2. If they have suffered from being open, it is straight society which we must indict, not the queen.

Closet queens: This phrase is becoming analogous to "Uncle Tom." To pretend to be straight sexually, or to pretend to be straight socially, is probably the most harmful pattern of behavior in the ghetto. . . .

If we are liberated we are open with our sexuality. Closet queenery must end. *Come out.*

But, in saying come out, we have to have our heads clear about a few things: 1) closet queens are our brothers, and must be defended against attack by straight people; 2) the fear of coming out is not paranoia; the stakes are high: loss of family ties, loss of job, loss of straight friends—these are all reminders that the oppression is not just in our heads. It's real. Each of us must make the steps toward openness at our own speed and on our own impulses. Being open is the foundation of freedom: it has to be built solidly. 3) "Closet queen" is a broad term covering a multitude of forms of defense, self-hatred, lack of strength, and habit. We are all closet queens in some ways, and all of us had to come out—very few of us were "flagrant" at the age of seven! We must afford our brothers and sisters the same patience we afforded ourselves. And while their closet queenery is part of our oppression, it's more a part of theirs. They alone can decide when and how.

On Oppression

It is important to catalog and understand the different facets of our oppression. There is no future in arguing about degrees of oppression. A lot of "movement" types come on with a line of shit about homosexuals not being oppressed as much as blacks or Vietnamese or workers or women. We don't happen to fit into their ideas of class or caste. Bull! When people feel oppressed, they act on that feeling. We feel oppressed. Talk about the priority of Black Liberation or ending imperialism over and above gay liberation is just anti-gay propaganda.

Physical attacks: We are attacked, beaten, castrated and left dead time and time again. There are half a dozen known unsolved slayings in San Francisco parks in the last few years. "Punks," often of minority groups who look around for someone under them socially, feel encouraged to beat up on "queens" and cops look the other way. That used to be called lynching.

.   .   .

Psychological warfare: Right from the beginning we have been subjected to a barrage of straight propaganda. Since our parents don't know any homosexuals, we grow up thinking that we're alone and different and perverted. Our school friends identify "queer" with any nonconformist or bad behavior. Our elementary school teachers tell us not to talk to strangers or accept rides. Television, billboards and magazines put forth a false idealization of male/female relationships, and make us wish we were different, wish we were "in." In family living class we're taught how we're supposed to turn out. And all along, the best we hear, if anything, about homosexuality is that it's an unfortunate problem.

Self-oppression: As gay liberation grows, we will find our uptight brothers and sisters, particularly those who are making a buck off our ghetto, coming on strong to defend the status quo. This is self-oppression: "don't rock the boat"; "things in SF are OK"; "gay people just aren't together"; "I'm not oppressed." These lines are right out of the mouths of the straight establishment. A large part of our oppression would end if we would stop putting ourselves and our pride down.

Institutional: Discrimination against gays is blatant, if we open our eyes. Homosexual relationships are illegal, and even if these laws are not regularly enforced, they encourage and enforce closet queenery. The bulk of the social work/psychiatric field looks upon homosexuality as a problem, and treats us as sick. Employers let it be known that our skills are acceptable only as long as our sexuality is hidden. Big business and government are particularly notorious offenders.

On Sex

What sex is: It is both creative expression and communication: good when it is either, and better when it is both. Sex can also be aggression, and usually is when those involved do not see each other as equals; and it can also be perfunctory, when we are distracted or preoccupied. These uses spoil what is good about it.

.   .   .

Objectification: In this scheme, people are sexual objects, but they are also subjects, and are human beings who appreciate themselves as object and subject. This use of human bodies as objects is legitimate (not harmful) only when it is reciprocal. If one person is always object and the other subject, it stifles the human being in both of them. Objectification must also be open and frank. By silence we often assume or let the other person assume that sex means commitments: if it does, ok; but if not, say it. (Of course, it's not all that simple: our capabilities for manipulation are unfathomed—all we can do is try.)

.   .   .

On positions and role: Much of our sexuality has been perverted through mimicry of straights, and warped from self-hatred. . . . We strive for democratic, mutual, reciprocal sex. This does not mean that we are all mirror images of each other in bed, but that we break away from roles which enslave us. We already do better in bed than straights do, and we can be better to each other than we have been.

Chickens and Studs: Face it, nice bodies and young bodies are attributes, they're groovy. They are inspiration for art, for spiritual elevation, for good sex. The problem arises only in the inability to relate to people of the same age, or people who don't fit the plastic stereotypes of a good body. At that point, objectification eclipses people, and expresses self-hatred: "I hate gay people, and I don't like myself, but if a stud (or chicken) wants to make it with me, I can pretend I'm someone other than me."

A note on exploitation of children: kids can take care of themselves, and are sexual beings way earlier than we'd like to admit. Those of us who began cruising in early adolescence know this, and we were doing the cruising, not being debauched by dirty old men. Scandals such as the one in Boise, Idaho—blaming a "ring" of homosexuals for perverting their youth are the fabrications of press and police and politicians. And as for child molesting, the overwhelming amount is done by straight guys to little girls: it is not particularly a gay problem, and is caused by the frustration resulting from anti-sex puritanism.

.   .   .

On Our Ghetto

We are refugees from Amerika. So we came to the ghetto—and as other ghettos, it has its negative and positive aspects. Refugee camps are better than what preceded them, or perhaps never would have come. But they are still enslaving, if only that we are limited to being ourselves there and only there.

Ghettos breed self-hatred. We stagnate here, accepting the status quo. The status quo is rotten. We are all warped by our oppression, and in the isolation of the ghetto we blame ourselves rather than our oppressors.

Ghettos breed exploitation: Landlords find they can charge exorbitant rents and get away with it, because of the limited area which is safe to live in openly. Mafia control of bars and baths in NYC is only one example of outside money controlling our institutions for their profit. In San Francisco the Tavern Guild favors maintaining the ghetto, for it is through ghetto culture that they make a buck. We crowd their bars not because of their merit but because of the absence of any other social institution. The Guild has refused to let us collect defense funds or pass out gay liberation literature in their bars—need we ask why?

Police or con men who shake down the straight guy in return for not revealing him; the bookstores and movie makers who keep raising prices because they are the only outlet for pornography; heads of "modeling" agencies and other pimps who exploit both the hustlers and the johns— these are parasites who flourish in the ghetto.

SAN FRANCISCO—Ghetto or Free Territory: Our ghetto certainly is more beautiful and larger and more diverse than most ghettos, and is certainly freer than the rest of Amerika. That's why we're here. But it isn't ours. Capitalists make money off us, cops patrol us, government tolerates us as long as we shut up, and daily work for and pay taxes to those who oppress us.

To be a free territory, we must govern ourselves, set up our own institutions, defend ourselves, and use our own energies to improve our lives. The emergence of gay liberation communes, and our own paper is a good start. The talk about a gay liberation coffee shop/dance hall should be acted upon. Rural retreats, political action offices, food cooperatives, a free school, unalienating bars and after hours places—they must be developed if we are to have even the shadow of a free territory.

. . .

On Coalition

Right now the bulk of our work has to be among ourselves—self education, fending off attacks, and building free territory. Thus basically we have to have a gay/straight vision of the world until the oppression of gays is ended.

But not every straight is our enemy. Many of us have mixed identities, and have ties with other liberation movements: women, blacks, other minority groups; we may also have taken on an identity which is vital to us; ecology, dope, ideology. And face it: we can't change Amerika alone:

Who do we look to for coalition?

Women's Liberation: Summarizing earlier statements, 1) they are our closest ally; we must try hard to get together with them; 2) a lesbian caucus is probably the best way to attack gay guys' male chauvinism, and challenge the straightness of women's liberation; 3) as males we must be sensitive to their developing identities as women, and respect that; if we know what *our* freedom is about, *they* certainly know what's best for *them.*

Black Liberation: This is tenuous right now because of the uptightness and supermasculinity of many black men (which is understandable). Despite that, we must support their movement, particularly when they are under attack from the establishment; we must show them that we mean business, and we must figure out which our common enemies are: police, city hall, capitalism.

Chicanos: Basically the same problem as with blacks: trying to overcome mutual animosity and fear, and finding ways to support them. The extra problem of super up-tightness and machismo among Latin cultures, and the traditional pattern of Mexicans beating up "queers," can be overcome: we're both oppressed, and by the same people at the top.

White radicals and ideologues: We're not, as a group, Marxist or communist. We haven't figured out what kind of political/economic system is good for us gays. Neither capitalist or socialist countries have treated us as anything other than *non grata* so far.

But we know we are radical, in that we know the system that we're under now is a direct source of oppression, and it's not a question of getting our share of the pie. The pie is rotten.

We can look forward to coalition and mutual support with radical groups if they are able to transcend their anti-gay and male chauvinist patterns. We support radical and militant demands when they arise, e.g., Moratorium, People's Park; but only as a group; we can't compromise or soft-pedal our gay identity.

Problems: because radicals are doing somebody else's thing, they tend to avoid issues which affect them directly, and see us as jeopardizing their "work" with other groups (workers, blacks). Some years ago a dignitary of SDS on a community organization project announced at an initial staff meeting that there would be no homosexuality (or dope) on the project. And recently in New York, a movement group which had a coffee-house get-together after a political rally told the gays to leave when they started dancing together. (It's interesting to note that in this case, the only two groups which supported us were Women's Liberation and the Crazies.)

Perhaps most fruitful would be to broach with radicals their stifled homosexuality and the issues which arise from challenging sexual roles.

Hip and street people: A major dynamic of rising gay lib sentiment is the hip revolution within the gay community. Emphasis on love, dropping out, being honest, expressing yourself through hair and clothes, and smoking dope are all attributes of this. The gays who are the least vulnerable to attack by the establishment have been the freest to express themselves on gay liberation.

We can make a direct appeal to young people, who are not so up tight about homosexuality. One kid, after having his first sex with a male, said, "I don't know what all the fuss is about, making it with a girl just isn't that different."

The hip/street culture has led people into a lot of freeing activities: encounter/sensitivity, the quest for reality, freeing territory for the people, ecological consciousness, communes. These are real points of agreement and probably will make it easier for them to get their heads straight about homosexuality, too.

Homophile groups: 1) Reformist or pokey as they sometimes are, they are our brothers. They'll grow as we have grown and grow. Do not attack them in straight or mixed company. 2) Ignore their attack on us. 3) Cooperate where cooperation is possible without essential compromise of our identity.

Conclusion: An Outline of Imperatives for Gay Liberation

1. Free ourselves: come out everywhere; initiate self defense and political activity; initiate counter community institutions.

2. Turn other gay people on: talk all the time; understand, forgive, accept.

3. Free the homosexual in everyone: we'll be getting a good bit of shit from threatened latents: be gentle, and keep talking and acting free.

4. We've been playing an act for a long time, so we're consummate actors. Now we can begin *to be*, and it'll be a good show!

The New Generation

CHARLES A. REICH (1928–   ), born in New York City, received a B.A. from Oberlin in 1949, and an LL.B. at Yale three years later. After practicing law in New York and Washington during the 1950s, he joined the faculty of the Yale Law School in 1960. Hailed as an apostle of peaceful revolution, damned as the Norman Vincent Peale of the youth culture, Reich in **The Greening of America** describes Consciousness I, II, and III. Consciousness I, the dog-eat-dog mentality of the nineteenth century had yielded by the 1930s to Consciousness II, the creeds of the modern corporate state, with its faith in institutions, welfarism, and the virtues of organization. Consciousness III, the product of the 1960s, is described in this selection.

. . . The foundation of Consciousness III is liberation. It comes into being the moment the individual frees himself from automatic acceptance of the imperatives of society and the false consciousness which society imposes. For example, the individual no longer accepts unthinkingly the personal goals proposed by society; a change of personal goals is one of the first and most basic elements of Consciousness III. The meaning of liberation is that the individual is free to build his own philosophy and values, his life-style, and his own culture from a new beginning.

Consciousness III starts with self. In contrast to Consciousness II, which accepts society, the public interest, and institutions as the primary reality, III declares that the individual self is the only true reality. Thus it returns to the earlier America: "Myself I sing." The first commandment is: thou shalt not do violence to thyself. It is a crime to allow oneself to become an instrumental being, a projectile designed to accomplish some extrinsic end, a part of an organization or a machine. It is a crime to be alienated from oneself, to be a divided or schizophrenic being, to defer meaning to the future. One must live completely at each moment, not with the frenzied "nowness" of advertising, but with the utter *wholeness* that Heidegger expresses. The commandment is: be true to oneself.

To start from self does not mean to be selfish. It means to start from premises based on human life and the rest of nature, rather than premises that are the artificial products of the Corporate State, such as power or status. It is not an "ego trip" but a radical subjectivity designed to find genuine values in a world whose official values are false and distorted. It is not egocentricity, but honesty, wholeness, genuineness in all things. It starts from self because human life is found as individual units, not as corporations and institutions; its intent is to start from life.

Consciousness III postulates the absolute worth of every human being—every self. Consciousness III does not believe in the antagonistic or competitive doctrine of life. Competition, within the limits of a sport like tennis or swimming, is accepted for its own pleasure, although even as athletes III's are far less competitive (and sometimes, but not always, poorer athletes as a result). But III's do not compete "in real life." They do not measure others, they do not see others as something to struggle against. People are brothers, the world is ample for all. In consequence, one never hears the disparagements, the snickers, the judgments that are so common among I's and II's. A boy who was odd in some way used to suffer derision all through his school days. Today there would be no persecution; one might even hear one boy speak, with affection, of "my freaky friend." Instead of insisting that everyone be measured by given standards, the new generation values what is unique and different in each self; there is no pressure that anyone be an athlete unless he wants to; a harpsichord player is accepted on equal terms. No one judges anyone else. This is a second commandment.

.   .   .

A third commandment is: be wholly honest with others, use no other person as a means. It is equally wrong to alter oneself for someone else's sake; by being one's true self one offers others the most; one offers them something honest, genuine, and, more important, something for them to respond to, to be evoked by. A work of art is not valued because it changes itself for each person who views it, it retains its own integrity and thus means something unique and marvelous to those who see it. Being true to oneself is, so Consciousness III says, the best and only way to relate to others. Consciousness III rejects most of what happens between people in our world: manipulation of others, forcing anyone to do anything against his wish, using others for one's own purposes, irony and sarcasm, defensive stand-offishness. III also rejects relationships of authority and subservience. It will neither give commands nor follow them; coercive relations between people are wholly unacceptable. And III also rejects any relationships based wholly on role, relationships limited along strictly impersonal and functional lines. There is no situation in which one is entitled to act impersonally, in a stereotyped fashion, with another human being; the relationship of businessman to clerk, passenger to conductor, student to janitor must not be impersonal.

But to observe duties toward others, after the feelings are gone, is no virtue and may even be a crime. Loyalty is valued but not artificial duty. Thus the new generation looks with suspicion on "obligations" and contractual relations between people, but it believes that honesty can produce far more genuine relationships than the sterile ones it observes among the older generation. To most people, there is something frightening about the notion that no oath, no law, no promise, no indebtedness holds people together when the feeling is gone. But for the new generation that is merely recognition of the truth about human beings. Moreover, getting rid of what is artificial is essential to make way for what is real, and Consciousness III considers genuine relationships with others, friendship, companionship, love, the human community, to be among the highest values of life.

The premise of self and of values based on human life leads directly to a radical critique of society. Many people are puzzled by the radicalism of Consciousness III—have they been infiltrated by communists, are they influenced by "a few left-wing agitators," have they been reading Marx? It does indeed seem astonishing that naïve young people, without political experience, should come up with a critique of society that seems to have escaped the most scholarly as well as the most astute and experienced of their elders. But there is no mystery, no conspiracy, and very little reading of Marx. Older people begin by assuming that much of the structure of the Corporate State is necessary and valid; starting there they never get very far. The young people start with entirely different premises, and all is revealed to them.

What Consciousness III sees, with an astounding clarity that no ideology could provide, is a society that is unjust to its poor and its minorities, is run for the benefit of a privileged few, is lacking in its proclaimed democracy and liberty, is ugly and artificial, that destroys environment and self, and is, like the wars it spawns, "unhealthy for children and other living things." It sees a society that is deeply untruthful and hypocritical; one of the gifts of the young is to see through phoniness and cant, and Consciousness III sees through the Establishment verities of our society with corrosive ease.

.   .   .

Because it accepts no imposed system, the basic stance of Consciousness III is one of openness to any and all experience. It is always in a state of becoming. It is just the opposite of Consciousness II, which tries to force all new experience into a pre-existing system, and to assimilate all new knowledge to principles already established. Although we can attempt to describe the specific content of Consciousness III at a given moment, its lasting essence is constant change, and constant growth of each individual.

One quality unites all aspects of the Consciousness III way of life: energy. It is the energy of enthusiasm, of happiness, of hope. Some people assume that what they are seeing is merely the energy of youth, but it is greater than this; other generations never had such energy even in their youth. Consciousness III draws energy from new sources: from the group, the community, from eros, from the freedom of technology, from the uninhibited self.

A good place to begin is clothes, for the dress of the new generation expresses a number of the major themes of Consciousness III in a very vivid and immediate way. The first impression the clothes give is of uniformity and conformity—as if everyone felt obliged to adopt the same style. We shall try to show that this is an erroneous impression—that there is agreement on certain principles, but great individuality within those principles. Another first impression is of drabness—browns, greens, blue jeans. This is an accurate observation and for a reason. They are a deliberate rejection of the neon colors and plastic, artificial look of the affluent society. They are inexpensive to buy, inexpensive to maintain. They suggest that neither individuality nor distinction can be bought in a clothing store; clothes are primarily functional. The clothes are earthy and sensual. They express an affinity with nature; the browns, greens, and blues are nature's colors, earth's colors, not the colors of the machine, and the materials are rough and tactile. The clothes are like architecture that does not clash with its natural surroundings but blends in. And the clothes have a functional affinity with nature too; they don't show dirt, they are good for lying on the ground.

These clothes express freedom. Expensive clothes enforce social constraints; a grease spot on an expensive suit is a social error, so is a rip in a tailored ladies' coat, or a missing button. A man in an expensive suit must be careful of every move he makes, where he sits, what he leans against. A well-dressed woman is hardly able to walk or move. The new clothes give the wearer freedom to do anything he wants. He can work in them, read in them, roll down a hill in them, ride a bike in them, play touch football, dance, sit on the floor, go on a camping trip, sleep in them. Above all, they are comfortable.

The freedom of new clothes expresses a second principle as well: a wholeness of self, as against the schizophrenia of Consciousness II. There is not one set of clothes for the office; another for social life, a third for play. The same clothes can be used for every imaginable activity, and so they say: it is the same person doing each of these things, not a set of different masks or dolls, but one many-sided, *whole*, individual. We do not have another, secret life outside the office; as we are here, we are always. At the same time, these clothes say: a single individual may do many different things in the course of a day, he is not limited to a single role or a role-plus-recreation; each individual is truly protean, with unlimited possibilities including the possibility of whatever new and spontaneous thing may come along. Consciousness III is extremely reluctant to go to a restaurant or hotel where it is necessary to "dress up"—this would require a loss of wholeness and self; a dishonest constraint.

One reason the clothes are not "uniform," as people think, is that they are extremely expressive of the human body, and each body is different and unique. Men's suits really *are* uniform; they look the same on a man as they do on the rack in the clothing store; they hide the fact that one man may be muscular, another flabby, one soft, one bony, one hairy, another smooth. The pants give no hint of a man's legs, and when they wrinkle along body lines, they are quickly taken to the dry cleaners to be pressed back into straight lines. Jeans express the shape of legs, heavy or thin, straight or bowed. As jeans get more wrinkled, they adapt even more to the particular legs that are wearing them. Sitting across from a man in a business suit, it is as if he did not have a body at all, just a face and a voice. Jeans make one conscious of the body, not as something separate from the face but as part of the whole individual; Consciousness III believes that a person's body is one of the essential parts of his self, not something to be ignored while one carries on a conversation with his face and mind. Also the new clothes make the wearer conscious of his own body; a man's suit is at odds with his body all day long. The new clothes are a declaration of sensuality, not sensuality-for-display as in Madison Avenue style, but sensuality as a part of the natural in man. There is no masculinity or femininity hang-up. A boy does not feel he has to dress in a certain way or "he will not be a man"; he is not that anxious or concerned about his own masculinity.

If the individual wishes, he can add touches to his clothes that make them a costume, expressing whatever he feels at the moment. With the magic deftness of stage sorcery, a headband can produce an Indian, a black hat a cowboy badman. When a high fashion woman wears a costume, say a "matador" suit, it seems to have been imposed on her, mask-like, by her designer. She is an object that has been decorated. But the costumes of the young are not masks, they are expressions of an inner, perhaps momentary state of mind. The individual is free to be inventive, playful, humorous. A boy can wear a military dress jacket, all buttons and brass, and both mock the military establishment and at the same time express his small-boy's love of uniforms, and parade-ground pomp. Likewise with a Mexican peasant's blanket-shawl, or a David Copperfield hat, boots of all descriptions, gangster suits, phantom-of-the-opera cloaks. These costumes do not hide the real person as role-dress does, they show a state of mind and thus reveal him to us, and they add to the gaiety and humor of the world. Costumes raise existential questions for the person wearing them. For they confront a person, whenever he dresses, with questions that are never posed in our society—questions of identity and self. They allow experimentation and changes of mood that are characteristic of, and essential to youth. But they nudge the wearer with deep questions, because their very freedom reminds him that he does have choice.

Bell bottoms have to be worn to be understood. They express the body, as jeans do, but they say much more. They give the ankles a special freedom as if to invite dancing right on the street. They bring dance back into our sober lives. A touch football game, if the players are wearing bell bottoms, is like a folk dance or a ballet. Bell bottoms, on girls or boys, are happy and comic, rollicking. No one can take himself entirely seriously in bell bottoms. Imagine a Consciousness II university professor, or even a college athlete, in bell bottoms, and all of his pretensions become funny; he has to laugh at himself.

. . .

When we turn to the music of Consciousness III, we come to the chief medium of expression, the chief means by which inner feelings are communicated. Consciousness III has not yet developed a widely accepted written poetry, literature, or theatre; the functions of all of these have so far been assumed by music and the lyrics that go with it.

The new music was built out of materials already in existence: blues, rock 'n' roll, folk music. But although the forms remained, something wholly new and original was made out of these older elements—more original, perhaps, than even the new musicians themselves yet realize. The transformation took place in 1966–1967. Up to that time, the blues had been an essentially black medium. Rock 'n' roll, a blues derivative, was rhythmic, raunchy, teen-age dance music. Folk music, old and modern, was popular among college students. The three forms remained musically and culturally distinct, and even as late as 1965, none of them were expressing any radically new states of consciousness. Blues expressed black soul; rock, as made famous by Elvis Presley, was the beat of youthful sensuality; and folk music, with such singers as Joan Baez, expressed antiwar sentiments as well as the universal themes of love and disillusionment.

In 1966–1967 there was a spontaneous transformation. In the United States, it originated with youthful rock groups playing in San Francisco. In England, it was led by the Beatles, who were already established as an extremely fine and highly individual rock group. What happened, as well as it can be put into words, was this. First, the separate musical traditions were brought together. Bob Dylan and the Jefferson Airplane played folk rock, folk ideas with a rock beat. White rock groups began experimenting with the blues. Of course, white musicians had always played the blues, but essentially as imitators of the Negro style; now it began to be the white bands' own music. And all of the groups moved toward a broader eclecticism and synthesis. They freely took over elements from Indian ragas, from jazz, from American country music, and as time went on from even more diverse sources (one group seems recently to have been trying out Gregorian chants). What developed was a protean music, capable of an almost limitless range of expression.

The second thing that happened was that all the musical groups began using the full range of electric instruments and the technology of electronic amplifiers. The twangy electric guitar was an old country-western standby, but the new electronic effects were altogether different —so different that a new listener in 1967 might well feel that there had never been any sounds like that in the world before. The high, piercing, unearthly sounds of the guitar seemed to come from other realms. Electronics did, in fact, make possible sounds that no instrument up to that time could produce. And in studio recordings, multiple tracking, feedback, and other devices made possible effects that not even an electronic band could produce live. Electronic amplification also made possible a fantastic increase in volume, the music becoming as loud and penetrating as the human ear could stand, and thereby achieving a "total" effect, so that instead of an audience of passive listeners, there were now audiences of total participants, feeling the music in all of their senses and all of their bones.

Third, the music becomes a multimedia experience; a part of a total environment. In the Bay Area ballrooms, the Fillmore, the Avalon, or Pauley Ballroom at the University of California, the walls were covered with fantastic changing patterns of light, the beginning of the new art of the light show. And the audience did not sit, it danced. With records at home, listeners imitated these lighting effects as best they could, and heightened the whole experience by using drugs. Often music was played out of doors, where nature—the sea or tall redwoods—provided the environment.

Fourth, each band began to develop a personality; often they lived together as a commune, and their music expressed their group life. The names of the groups, while often chosen rather casually and for public effect, nevertheless expressed the anti-Establishment, "outsider" identity of the groups. One way to gauge this is to imagine congressmen from the House Internal Security Committee (formerly HUAC) trying to grasp the derivations and nuances of such names as Notes From Underground, Loading Zone, Steppenwolf, the Cleanliness and Godliness Skiffle Band. A name such as the Grateful Dead, with its implications of atomic holocaust, Hiroshima, bitter alienation from society, and playful, joking don't-give-a-damnness, would baffle the security investigators for a long time. The name may have been chosen for the band's own esoteric reasons. But it suggests the idea that in our society the living are really dead, and only the "dead" are really alive; this idea would probably escape the investigators altogether. In short, the bands, by achieving a high degree of individual identity, and being clearly "outsiders," members of the youth culture themselves, became groups with which young audiences could feel a great closeness and rapport. By contrast, Consciousness II people have little identification with band members or the musicians in a symphony orchestra.

Fifth, musician-listener rapport has been heightened by two other kinds of participation: an enormous number of the young listeners had instruments or even bands and played the new music themselves, and both bands and listeners considered drugs to be an integral part of the musical experience. Consciousness II people may love Mozart, or jazz, but comparatively few of them spend much time playing an instrument. The use of drugs, especially because they are illegal, establishes a blood-brotherhood before the musicians even begin to play. And drugs, as we shall point out later, add a whole new dimension to creativity and to experience.

Sixth, a pulsing new energy entered into all the forms of music. Not even the turbulent fury of Beethoven's Ninth Symphony can compete for sheer energy with the Rolling Stones. Compared to the new music, earlier popular songs seem escapist and soft, jazz seems cerebral, classical music seems dainty or mushy; these epithets are surely undeserved but the driving, screaming, crying, bitter-happy-sad heights and depths and motion of the new music adds a dimension unknown in any earlier western music. The older music was essentially intellectual; it was located in the mind and in the feelings known to the mind; the new music rocks the whole body, and penetrates the soul.

Seventh, the new music, despite its apparently simple form and beat, gradually evolved a remarkably complex texture. It has a complexity unknown to classical music, even to symphonies written for full orchestra. Beethoven seems like a series of parallel lines, sometimes vertical, sometimes diagonal; Mozart a flow of rounded forms, but as few as three rock musicians, such as the Cream, or Crosby, Stills & Nash can set up a texture of rhythms, timbres, kinds of sounds, emotions that create a world by contrast to which the classical composers seem to have lived in a world of simple verities, straightforward emotions, and established, reassuring conventions. It is no criticism of the eighteenth- or nineteenth-century geniuses to say that today's music has found a world they never knew.

Eighth, not only did many young people play the new music in one form or another, a great many, amateur and professional alike, began composing it. Nearly all of the successful rock groups of today write most of their own words and music. The distinction between composer and performer as professions has virtually disappeared. Thus songs are highly personal to the singer, not a mere "interpretation" of someone else's thought. Also, what is undeniably a mass culture is at the same time a genuine folk culture, because it is not imposed upon the people but written by them. And the writing is not limited to professional musicians; amateur and casual groups also compose some of their own material. And when one group does play another person's song, the group freely adds to it. There is no such thing, then, as the musician who tries in all things to be faithful to some remote composer, reserving for himself a display of skill and subtlety, spirit and nuance. The new music is a music of unrestrained creativity and self-expression.

Ninth, the new music, most notably through the poetry of its songs, has succeeded in expressing an understanding of the world, and of people's feelings, incredibly far in advance of what other media have been able to express. Journalists, writers for opinion journals, social scientists, novelists have all tried their hand at discussing the issues of the day. But almost without exception, they have been far more superficial than writers of rock poetry, and what is even more striking, several years behind the musicians. Compare a writer for *The New York Times*, or for *The New Republic,* talking about contemporary political and social ills, with Dylan's "It's All Right Ma (I'm only Bleeding)" or "Subterranean Homesick Blues." Compare a sociologist talking about alienation with the Beatles' "Eleanor Rigby" or "Strawberry Fields Forever." But more important than comparisons is the fact that rock music has been able to give critiques of society at a profound level ("Draft Morning," by the Byrds, "Tommy," by The Who) and at the same time express the longings and aspirations of the new generation ("I Feel Free," by the Cream, "Wooden Ships," by Crosby, Stills & Nash, "Stand," by Sly and the Family Stone). The music has achieved a relevance, an ability to penetrate to the essence of what is wrong with society, a power to speak to man "in his condition" that is perhaps the deepest source of its power.

. . .

What the new music has become is a medium that expresses the whole range of the new generation's experiences and feelings. The complex, frantic, disjointed machinelike experiences of modern urban existence were presented, with piercing notes of pain, and dark notes of anger, by the Cream. The mystical transcendence of ordinary experience achieved by the hippies, the drug world, and the spiritual realm, soaring fantasy and brilliant patterns of rhythm and sound, are the domain of the San Francisco acid rock of the Jefferson Airplane, and the psychedelic meditations of the early music of Country Joe and the Fish. Irony, satire, mockery of the Establishment and of rational thought were the specialty of the Mothers of Invention. A uniquely personal but universal view of the world has been achieved by the Beatles, gentle, unearthly, the world transformed. Another highly personal view of the world, but one close to the experiences of young listeners, is that of Bob Dylan. Dylan has gone through a whole cycle of experience, from folk music to social protest and commentary, next to folk rock, then to the extraordinary personal world of the ballad "Sad-Eyed Lady of the Lowlands," and finally to the serene, but achieved, innocence of the country music of the album "Nashville Skyline." Perhaps more than any other individual in the field of music, Dylan has been, from the very beginning, a true prophet of the new consciousness.

. . .

Questions for Discussion and Writing

1. Treating Morton and Bradford as differing "eyewitnesses" present an account of Merry Mount and its dissolution in which you (a) give as "objective" a description as possible of the participants and proceedings, and (b) compare the different values of Morton and Bradford.

2. How does Hawthorne's statement that "the whipping-post . . . might be termed the Puritan Maypole" illuminate his overall view of the Puritans and the hedonists?

3. Two types of imagery—flowers and iron—pervade Hawthorne's story. How do they function symbolically?

4. When Hawthorne writes that at Merry Mount "Jollity and gloom were contending for an empire," what is he suggesting about the symbolic importance of the events to the future of American history?

5. At the conclusion of "The Maypole of Merry Mount," Endicott tosses a wreath of roses over the heads of the Lord and Lady of the May. What is the meaning of this symbolic gesture?

6. Is Whitman's view of the "soul" the conventional Christian one? Does he advocate "free love"? homosexuality?

7. Is "Comstockery" the same as "puritanism"?

8. Can Cowley's description of the "consumption ethic" and "salvation by the child" be applied to the 1960s? Compare his views of the 1920s with Reich's views of the 1960s.

9. Is Rubin's writing properly defined as poetry or prose? Compare it with Whitman's poetry, noting similarities and differences.

10. Compare the attitudes of Whitman, Rubin, and Wittman toward sex.

11. Are you persuaded by Wittman's argument that heterosexuality is sick?

12. Merle Miller has said, "A 'fag' is a homosexual gentleman who has just left the room." Discuss the role of language, slang or otherwise, in enforcing conformity to social norms.

13. Discuss the following as they are defined in the readings, *and* as you believe they ought correctly to be defined: love, nature or natural, individual freedom, wholeness, "real" things.

Essay Topics

1. According to Jerzy Kosinski, "The phrase 'doing one's own thing' is really no more than a mockery uttered by people whose own thing is to be part of an amorphous supergang." Is this a fair summary of past attempts to realize personal freedom? of recent attempts?
2. Who would you wish to keep from reading any of the above selections? younger brothers or sisters? parents? grandparents? Explain.
3. "Can you separate politics from sex?" Discuss the answers to this question stated or implied in several of the readings in this section.
4. To what degree has the situation of the homosexual in this country been comparable to that of racial and ethnic minorities?

Suggestions for Further Reading

PRIMARY

SHERWOOD ANDERSON, *Winesburg, Ohio* (1919). A group portrait of the residents of a small town who, freed of their inhibitions by Anderson, reveal a longing for liberation, and the forces that frustrate this desire.

RANDOLPH BOURNE, "Youth," *Atlantic Monthly,* 109 (1912), 433–41. An analysis of the role of youth in realizing a richer spiritual life in America.

WARNER BROWN, "Why 'Hair' Has Become Our Four Letter Word," *Avant-Garde,* No. 12 (1970), 49–53. An essay suggesting that present-day battles over hair-length reflect a perennial struggle of "self-actualizing" and "self-strangling" personalities.

P. CURTISS, "Morality's New Threat," *Harper's,* 155 (1927), 118–21. A semihumorous account of neo-puritanism among youth in the Roaring Twenties, with contemporary implications.

ALLEN GINSBERG, *Howl* (1956). A Whitmanesque catalog of the horrors of modern life by a leading member of the Beat Generation of the 1950's.

CHRISTOPHER ISHERWOOD, *A Single Man* (1964). A fictional re-creation of one day in the life of a homosexual professor of English; his perceptions and reflections concerning American society.

SECONDARY

PAUL GOODMAN, "Art, Pornography, and Censorship," *Commentary,* 31 (1961), 203–12. An indictment of the methods and principles governing censorship.

ERAZIN KOHAK, "Turning on for Freedom," *Dissent,* 16 (1959), 437–43. A critical assessment of the cult of personal freedom on the New Left by a Czech who wants "socialism with clothes."

JULES SIEGEL, "West of Eden," *Playboy,* 17 (1970), 173–74, 240–53. A description of communal life in the present-day Southwest.

ALEXIS DE TOCQUEVILLE, *Democracy in America* (1831). A classic analysis of American society by a sympathetic but not uncritical French observer; a starting point for all discussions of manners and morals.

FRANCES TROLLOPE, *Domestic Manners of the Americans* (1832). A spirited critique of American manners and morals by the mother of the English novelist Anthony Trollope.

Marriage, Motherhood, and the Family

Before the Birth of One of Her Children

ANNE BRADSTREET (1612–1672), the daughter of Thomas Dudley, a steward of the Earl of Lincoln, was born in Northampton, England, and educated amidst considerable wealth. Married at age sixteen to Simon Bradstreet, she came in 1630 to the Massachusetts Bay Colony, of which her husband and father were eventually governors. A busy hostess and loving wife, she had eight children. Her book **Tenth Muse** (1650) contained the first poetry of any merit to be written by an English-woman in America.

All things within this fading world hath end,
Adversity doth still our joys attend;
No ties so strong, no friends so dear and sweet,
But with death's parting blow is sure to meet.
The sentence past is most irrevocable,
A common thing, yet oh, inevitable.
How soon, my Dear, death may my steps attend,
How soon't may be thy lot to lose thy friend,
We both are ignorant, yet love bids me
These farewell lines to recommend to thee,
That when that knot's untied that made us one,
I may seem thine, who in effect am none.
And if I see not half my days that's due,
What nature would, God grant to yours and you;
The many faults that well you know I have
Let be interred in my oblivious grave;
If any worth or virtue were in me,
Let that live freshly in thy memory
And when thou feel'st no grief, as I no harms,
Yet love thy dead, who long lay in thine arms.

BEFORE THE BIRTH OF ONE OF HER CHILDREN. Reprinted by permission of the publishers from Jeannine Hensley, editor, *The Works of Anne Bradstreet,* Cambridge, Mass.: The Belknap Press of Harvard University Press, Copyright, 1967, by the President and Fellows of Harvard College.

And when thy loss shall be repaid with gains
Look to my little babes, my dear remains.
And if thou love thyself, or loved'st me,
These O protect from step-dame's injury.
And if chance to thine eyes shall bring this verse,
With some sad sighs honour my absent hearse;
And kiss this paper for thy love's dear sake,
Who with salt tears this last farewell did take.

The Prologue

1

To sing of wars, of captains, and of kings,
Of cities founded, commonwealths begun,
For my mean pen are too superior things:
Or how they all, or each their dates have run
Let poets and historians set these forth,
My obscure lines shall not so dim their worth.

2

But when my wond'ring eyes and envious heart
Great Bartas' sugared lines do but read o'er,
Fool I do grudge the Muses did not part
'Twixt him and me that overfluent store;
A Bartas can do what a Bartas will
But simple I according to my skill.

3

From schoolboy's tongue no rhet'ric we expect,
Nor yet a sweet consort from broken strings,
Nor perfect beauty where's a main defect:

THE PROLOGUE.   From Anne Bradstreet, *Tenth Muse* (1650).

My foolish, broken, blemished Muse so sings,
And this to mend, alas, no art is able,
'Cause nature made it so irreparable.

4

Nor can I, like that fluent sweet tongued Greek,
Who lisped at first, in future times speak plain.
By art he gladly found what he did seek,
A full requital of his striving pain.
Art can do much, but this maxim's most sure:
A weak or wounded brain admits no cure.

5

I am obnoxious to each carping tongue
Who says my hand a needle better fits,
A poet's pen all scorn I should thus wrong,
For such despite they cast on female wits:
If what I do prove well, it won't advance,
They'll say it's stol'n, or else it was by chance.

6

But sure the antique Greeks were far more mild
Else of our sex, why feigned they those nine
And poesy made Calliope's own child;
So 'mongst the rest they placed the arts divine:
But this weak knot they will full soon untie,
The Greeks did nought, but play the fools and lie.

7

Let Greeks be Greeks, and women what they are
Men have precedency and still excel,
It is but vain unjustly to wage war;
Men can do best, and women know it well.

Preeminence in all and each is yours;
Yet grant some small acknowledgement of ours.

8

And oh ye high flown quills that soar the skies,
And ever with your prey still catch your praise,
If e'er you deign these lowly lines your eyes,
Give thyme or parsley wreath, I ask no bays;
This mean and unrefined ore of mine
Will make your glist'ring gold but more to shine.

The Great Lawsuit

MARGARET FULLER (1810–1850), born in Cambridgeport, Massachusetts, ranks unquestionably among America's most brilliant and scholarly women. As a youth, she suffered the rule of a father whose tyrannical masculinity amounted almost to sadism. In 1840, after teaching school for several years, she joined Emerson and others in publishing the **Dial,** the literary and philosophic organ of the Transcendentalists. "The Great Lawsuit," appearing initially in July 1843, was subsequently expanded in **Woman in the Nineteenth Century** (1845). Damned almost universally as immoral, hypocritical, and absurd, this piece marked a turning point in the life of its author. In December 1844, Miss Fuller moved to New York to write literary criticism for the **Tribune.** Two years later she sailed for Europe, settling in Italy where, to the distress of many of her Boston allies, she married Giovanni Ossoli, a Marquis and follower of the Italian democrat Mazzini. Caught up in the excitement of the revolution of 1848–49, Miss Fuller sailed for America in 1850 with her husband and infant son. All three of them were killed when their ship wrecked off the coast of Fire Island. Her flamboyant career provoked Hawthorne's portrait of Zenobia in the **Blithedale Romance** (1852), and later provided Henry James with a model for the **Bostonians** (1886). Inspiration and enigma, she excited in

THE GREAT LAWSUIT. From *Dial*, 4 (July 1843).

her time no less passion than the most fervid advocates of "women's liberation" today.

. . . It is worthy of remark, that, as the principle of liberty is better understood and more nobly interpreted, a broader protest is made in behalf of woman. As men become aware that all men have not had their fair chance, they are inclined to say that no women have had a fair chance. The French revolution, that strangely disguised angel, bore witness in favor of woman, but interpreted her claims no less ignorantly than those of man. Its idea of happiness did not rise beyond outward enjoyment, unobstructed by the tyranny of others. The title it gave was Citoyen, Citoyenne, and it is not unimportant to woman that even this species of equality was awarded her. Before, she could be condemned to perish on the scaffold for treason, but not as a citizen, but a subject. The right, with which this title then invested a human being, was that of bloodshed and license. The Goddess of Liberty was impure. Yet truth was prophesied in the ravings of that hideous fever induced by long ignorance and abuse. Europe is conning a valued lesson from the blood-stained page. The same tendencies, farther unfolded, will bear good fruit in this country.

Yet, in this country, as by the Jews, when Moses was leading them to the promised land, everything has been done that inherited depravity could, to hinder the promise of heaven from its fulfilment. The cross, here as elsewhere, has been planted only to be blasphemed by cruelty and fraud. The name of the Prince of Peace has been profaned by all kinds of injustice towards the Gentile whom he said he came to save. But I need not speak of what has been done towards the red man, the black man. These deeds are the scoff of the world; and they have been accompanied by such pious words, that the gentlest would not dare to intercede with, "Father forgive them, for they know not what they do."

Here, as elsewhere, the gain of creation consists always in the growth of individual minds, which live and aspire, as flowers bloom and birds sing, in the midst of morasses; and in the continual development of that thought, the thought of human destiny, which is given to eternity to fulfil, and which ages of failure only seemingly impede. Only seemingly, and whatever seems to the contrary, this country is as surely destined to elucidate a great moral law, as Europe was to promote the mental culture of man.

Though the national independence be blurred by the servility of individuals; though freedom and equality have been proclaimed only to leave room for a monstrous display of slave dealing and slave keeping; though the free American so often feels himself free, like the Roman, only to pamper his appetites and his indolence through the misery of his fellow beings, still it is not in vain, that the verbal statement has been made, "All men are born free and equal." There it stands, a golden certainty, wherewith to encourage the good, to shame the bad.

.   .   .

Of all its banners, none has been more steadily upheld, and under none has more valor and willingness for real sacrifices been shown, than that of the champions of the enslaved African. And this band it is, which, partly in consequence of a natural following out of principles, partly because many women have been prominent in that cause, makes, just now, the warmest appeal in behalf of woman.

Though there has been a growing liberality on this point, yet society at large is not so prepared for the demands of this party, but that they are, and will be for some time, coldly regarded as the Jacobins of their day.

"Is it not enough," cries the sorrowful trader, "that you have done all you could to break up the national Union, and thus destroy the prosperity of our country, but now you must be trying to break up family union, to take my wife away from the cradle, and the kitchen hearth, to vote at polls, and preach from a pulpit? Of course, if she does such things, she cannot attend to those of her own sphere. She is happy enough as she is. She has more leisure than I have, every means of improvement, every indulgence."

"Have you asked her whether she was satisfied with these indulgences?"

"No, but I know she is. She is too amiable to wish what would make me unhappy, and too judicious to wish to step beyond the sphere of her sex. I will never consent to have our peace disturbed by any such discussions."

" 'Consent'—you? it is not consent from you that is in question, it is assent from your wife."

"Am I not the head of my house?"

"You are not the head of your wife. God has given her a mind of her own."

"I am the head and she the heart."

"God grant you play true to one another then. If the head represses no natural pulse of the heart, there can be no question as to your giving your consent. Both will be of one accord, and there needs but to present any question to get a full and true answer. There is no need of precaution, of indulgence, or consent. But our doubt is whether the heart consents with the head, or only acquiesces in its decree; and it is to ascertain the truth on this point, that we propose some liberating measures."

Thus vaguely are these questions proposed and discussed at present. But their being proposed at all implies much thought, and suggests more. Many women are considering within themselves what they need that they have not, and what they can have, if they find they need it. Many men are considering whether women are capable of being and having more than they are and have, and whether, if they are, it will be best to consent to improvement in their condition.

The numerous party, whose opinions are already labelled and adjusted too much to their mind to admit of any new light, strive, by lectures on some model-woman of bridal-like beauty and gentleness, by writing or lending little treatises, to mark out with due precision the limits of woman's sphere, and woman's mission, and to prevent other than the rightful shepherd from climbing the wall, or the flock from using any chance gap to run astray.

Without enrolling ourselves at once on either side, let us look upon the subject from that point of view which to-day offers. No better, it is to be feared, than a high housetop. A high hill-top, or at least a cathedral spire, would be desirable.

It is not surprising that it should be the Anti-Slavery party that pleads for woman, when we consider merely that she does not hold property on equal terms with men; so that, if a husband dies without a will, the wife, instead of stepping at once into his place as head of the family, inherits only a part of his fortune, as if she were a child, or ward only, not an equal partner.

We will not speak of the innumerable instances, in which profligate or idle men live upon the earnings of industrious wives; or if the wives leave them and take with them the children, to perform the double duty of mother and father, follow from place to place, and threaten to rob them of the children, if deprived of the rights of a husband, as they call them, planting themselves in their poor lodgings, frightening them into paying tribute by taking from them the children, running into debt at the expense of these otherwise so overtasked helots. Though such instances abound, the public opinion of his own sex is against the man, and when cases of extreme tyranny are made known, there is private action in the wife's favor. But if woman be, indeed, the weaker party, she ought to have legal protection, which would make such oppression impossible.

And knowing that there exists, in the world of men, a tone of feeling towards women as towards slaves, such as is expressed in the common phrase, "Tell that to women and children;" that the infinite soul can only work through them in already ascertained limits; that the prerogative of reason, man's highest portion, is allotted to them in a much lower degree; that it is better for them to be engaged in active labor, which is to be furnished and directed by those better able to think, &c. &c.; we need not go further, for who can review the experience of last week, without recalling words which imply, whether in jest or earnest, these views, and views like these? Knowing this, can we wonder that many reformers think that measures are not likely to be taken in behalf of women, unless their wishes could be publicly represented by women?

That can never be necessary, cry the other side. All men are privately influenced by women; each has his wife, sister, or female friends, and is too much biassed by these relations to fail of representing their interests. And if this is not enough, let them propose and enforce their wishes with the pen. The beauty of home would be destroyed, the delicacy of the sex be violated, the dignity of halls of legislation destroyed, by an attempt to introduce them there. Such duties are inconsistent with those of a mother; and then we have ludicrous pictures of ladies in hysterics at the polls, and senate chambers filled with cradles.

But if, in reply, we admit as truth that woman seems destined by nature rather to the inner circle, we must add that the arrangements of civilized life have not been as yet such as to secure it to her. Her circle, if the duller, is not the quieter. If kept from excitement, she is not from drudgery. Not only the Indian carries the burdens of the camp, but the favorites of Louis the Fourteenth accompany him in his journeys, and the washerwoman stands at her tub and carries home her work at all seasons, and in all states of health.

As to the use of the pen, there was quite as much opposition to woman's possessing herself of that help to free-agency as there is now to her seizing on the rostrum or the desk; and she is likely to draw, from a permission to plead her cause that way, opposite inferences to what might be wished by those who now grant it.

As to the possibility of her filling, with grace and dignity, any such position, we should think those who had seen the great actresses, and heard the Quaker preachers of modern times, would not doubt, that woman can express publicly the fulness of thought and emotion, without losing any of the peculiar beauty of her sex.

As to her home, she is not likely to leave it more than she now does for balls, theatres, meetings for promoting missions, revival meetings, and others to which she flies, in hope of an animation for her existence, commensurate with what she sees enjoyed by men. Governors of Ladies' Fairs are no less engrossed by such a charge, than the Governor of the State by his; presidents of Washingtonian societies, no less away from home than presidents of conventions. If men look straitly to it, they will find that, unless their own lives are domestic, those of the women will not be. The female Greek, of our day, is as much in the street as the male, to cry, What news? We doubt not it was the same in Athens of old. The women, shut out from the market-place, made up for it at the religious festivals. For human beings are not so constituted, that they can live without expansion; and if they do not get it one way, must another, or perish.

And, as to men's representing women fairly, at present, while we hear from men who owe to their wives not only all that is comfortable and graceful, but all that is wise in the arrangement of their lives, the frequent remark, "You cannot reason with a woman," when from those of delicacy, nobleness, and poetic culture, the contemptuous phrase, "Women and children," and that in no light sally of the hour, but in works intended to give a permanent statement of the best experiences, when not one man in the million, shall I say, no, not in the hundred million, can rise above the view that woman was made *for man,* when such traits as these are daily forced upon the attention, can we feel that man will always do justice to the interests of woman? Can we think that he takes a sufficiently discerning and religious view of her office and destiny, ever to do her justice, except when prompted by sentiment; accidentally or transiently, that is, for his sentiment will vary according to the relations in which he is placed. The lover, the poet, the artist, are likely to view her nobly. The father and the philosopher have some chance of liberality; the man of the world, the legislator for expediency, none.

Under these circumstances, without attaching importance in themselves to the changes demanded by the champions of woman, we hail them as signs of the times. We would have every arbitrary barrier thrown down. We would have every path laid open to woman as freely as to man. Were this done, and a slight temporary fermentation allowed to subside, we believe that the Divine would ascend into nature to a height unknown in the history of past ages, and nature, thus instructed, would regulate the spheres not only so as to avoid collision, but to bring forth ravishing harmony.

Yet then, and only then, will human beings be ripe for this, when inward and outward freedom for woman, as much as for man, shall be acknowledged as a right, not yielded as a concession. As the friend of the negro assumes that one man cannot, by right, hold another in bondage, should the friend of woman assume that man cannot, by right, lay even well-meant restrictions on woman. If the negro be a soul, if the woman be a soul, apparelled in flesh, to one master only are they accountable. There is but one law for all souls, and, if there is to be an interpreter of it, he comes not as man, or son of man, but as Son of God.

Were thought and feeling once so far elevated that man should esteem himself the brother and friend, but nowise the lord and tutor of woman, were he really bound with her in equal worship, arrangements as to function and employment would be of no consequence. What woman needs is not as a woman to act or rule, but as a nature to grow, as an intellect to discern, as a soul to live freely, and unimpeded to unfold such powers as were given her when we left our common home. If fewer talents were given her, yet, if allowed the free and full employment of these, so that she may render back to the giver his own with usury, she will not complain, nay, I dare to say she will bless and rejoice in her earthly birth-place, her earthly lot.

Let us consider what . . . signs give reason to hope that [this good era] draws near. . . .

Where the thought of equality has become pervasive, it shows itself in four kinds.

The household partnership. In our country the woman looks for a "smart but kind" husband, the man for a "capable, sweet-tempered" wife.

The man furnishes the house, the woman regulates it. Their relation is one of mutual esteem, mutual dependence. Their talk is of business, their affection shows itself by practical kindness. They know that life goes more smoothly and cheerfully to each for the other's aid; they are grateful and content. The wife praises her husband as a "good provider," the husband in return compliments her as a "capital housekeeper." This relation is good as far as it goes.

Next comes a closer tie which takes the two forms, either of intellectual companionship, or mutual idolatry. The last, we suppose, is to no one a pleasing subject of contemplation. The parties weaken and narrow one another; they lock the gate against all the glories of the universe that they may live in a cell together. To themselves they seem the only wise, to all others steeped in infatuation, the gods smile as they look forward to the crisis of cure, to men the woman seems an unlovely syren, to women the man an effeminate boy.

The other form, of intellectual companionship, has become more and more frequent. Men engaged in public life, literary men, and artists have often found in their wives companions and confidants in thought no less than in feeling. And, as in the course of things the intellectual development of woman has spread wider and risen higher, they have, not unfrequently, shared the same employment.

.   .   .

[But] we do not mean to imply that community of employment is an essential to union of this sort, more than to the union of friendship. Harmony exists no less in difference than in likeness, if only the same key-note govern both parts. Woman the poem, man the poet; woman the heart, man the head; such divisions are only important when they are never to be transcended. If nature is never bound down, nor the voice of inspiration stifled, that is enough. We are pleased that women should write and speak, if they feel the need of it, from having something to tell; but silence for a hundred years would be as well, if that silence be from divine command, and not from man's tradition.

.   .   .

I have not spoken of the higher grade of marriage union, the religious, which may be expressed as pilgrimage towards a common shrine. This includes the others; home sympathies, and household wisdom, for these pilgrims must know how to assist one another to carry their burdens along the dusty way; intellectual communion, for how sad it would be on such a journey to have a companion to whom you could not communicate thoughts and aspirations, as they sprang to life, who would have no feeling for the more and more glorious prospects that open as we advance, who would never see the flowers that may be gathered by the most industrious traveler.

.   .   .

Another sign of the time is furnished by the triumphs of female authorship. These have been great and constantly increasing. They have taken possession of so many provinces for which men had pronounced them unfit, that though these still declare there are some inaccessible to them, it is difficult to say just *where* they must stop.

.   .   .

In this regard, of self-dependence and a greater simplicity and fulness of being, we must hail as a preliminary the increase of the class contemptuously designated as old maids.

We cannot wonder at the aversion with which old bachelors and old maids have been regarded. Marriage is the natural means of forming a sphere, of taking root on the earth: it requires more strength to do this without such an opening, very many have failed of this, and their imperfections have been in every one's way. They have been more partial, more harsh, more officious and impertinent than others. Those, who have a complete experience of the human instincts, have a distrust as to whether they can be thoroughly human and humane, such as is hinted at in the saying, "Old maids' and bachelors' children are well cared for," which derides at once their ignorance and their presumption.

Yet the business of society has become so complex, that it could now scarcely be carried on without the presence of these despised auxiliaries, and detachments from the army of aunts and uncles are wanted to stop gaps in every hedge. They rove about, mental and moral Ishmaelites, pitching their tents amid the fixed and ornamented habitations of men.

They thus gain a wider, if not so deep, experience. They are not so intimate with others, but thrown more upon themselves, and if they do not there find peace and incessant life, there is none to flatter them that they are not very poor and very mean.

A position, which so constantly admonishes, may be of inestimable benefit. The person may gain, undistracted by other relationships, a closer communion with the One. Such a use is made of it by saints and sibyls. Or she may be one of the lay sisters of charity, or more humbly only the useful drudge of all men, or the intellectual interpreter of the varied life she sees.

Or she may combine all these. Not "needing to care that she may please a husband," a frail and limited being, all her thoughts may turn to the centre, and by steadfast contemplation enter into the secret of truth and love, use it for the use of all men, instead of a chosen few, and interpret through it all the forms of life.

Saints and geniuses have often chosen a lonely position, in the faith that, if undisturbed by the pressure of near ties they could give themselves up to the inspiring spirit, it would enable them to understand and reproduce life better than actual experience could.

How many old maids take this high stand, we cannot say; it is an unhappy fact that too many of those who come before the eye are gossips rather, and not always good-natured gossips. But, if these abuse, and none make the best of their vocation, yet, it has not failed to produce some good fruit. It has been seen by others, if not by themselves, that beings likely to be left alone need to be fortified and furnished within themselves, and education and thought have tended more and more to regard beings as related to absolute Being, as well as to other men. It has been seen that as the loss of no bond ought to destroy a human being, so ought the missing of none to hinder him from growing. And thus a circumstance of the time has helped to put woman on the true platform. Perhaps the next generation will look deeper into this matter, and find that contempt is put on old maids, or old women at all, merely because they do not use the elixir which will keep the soul always young.

．　　　．　　　．

Male and female represent the two sides of the great radical dualism. But, in fact, they are perpetually passing into one another. Fluid hardens to solid, solid rushes to fluid. There is no wholly masculine man, no purely feminine woman.

History jeers at the attempts of physiologists to bind great original laws by the forms which flow from them. They make a rule; they say from observation what can and cannot be. In vain! Nature provides exceptions to every rule. She sends women to battle, and sets Hercules spinning; she enables women to bear immense burdens, cold, and frost; she enables the man, who feels maternal love, to nourish his infant like a mother. . . .

Man partakes of the feminine in the Apollo, woman of the masculine as Minerva.

Let us be wise and not impede the soul. Let her work as she will. Let us have one creative energy, one incessant revelation. Let it take what form it will, and let us not bind it by the past to man or woman, black or white. Jove sprang from Rhea, Pallas from Jove. So let it be.

If it has been the tendency of the past remarks to call woman rather to the Minerva side,—if I, unlike the more generous writer, have spoken from society no less than the soul,—let it be pardoned. It is love that has caused this, love for many incarcerated souls, that might be freed could the idea of religious self-dependence be established in them, could the weakening habit of dependence on others be broken up.

Every relation, every gradation of nature, is incalculably precious, but only to the soul which is poised upon itself, and to whom no loss, no change, can bring dull discord, for it is in harmony with the central soul.

If any individual live too much in relations, so that he becomes a stranger to the resources of his own nature, he falls after a while into a distraction, or imbecility, from which he can only be cured by a time of isolation, which gives the renovating fountains time to rise up. With a society it is the same. Many minds, deprived of the traditionary or instinctive means of passing a cheerful existence, must find help in self-impulse or perish. It is therefore that while any elevation, in the view of union, is to be hailed with joy, we shall not decline celibacy as the great fact of the time. It is one from which no vow, no arrangement, can at present save a thinking mind. For now the rowers are pausing on their oars, they wait a change before they can pull together. All tends to illustrate the thought of a wise contemporary. Union is only possible to those who are units. To be fit for relations in time, souls, whether of man or woman, must be able to do without them in the spirit.

It is therefore that I would have woman lay aside all thought, such as she habitually cherishes, of being taught and led by men. I would have her, like the Indian girl, dedicate herself to the Sun, the Sun of Truth, and go no where if his beams did not make clear the path. I would have her free from compromise, from complaisance, from helplessness, because I would have her good enough and strong enough to love one and all beings, from the fulness, not the poverty of being.

Men, as at present instructed, will not help this work, because they also are under the slavery of habit.

.   .   .

[Men] do *not* look at both sides, and women must leave off asking them and being influenced by them, but retire within themselves, and explore the groundwork of being till they find their peculiar secret. Then when they come forth again, renovated and baptized, they will know how to turn all dross to gold, and will be rich and free though they live in a hut, tranquil, if in a crowd. Then their sweet singing shall not be from passionate impulse, but the lyrical overflow of a divine rapture, and a new music shall be elucidated from this many-chorded world.

Grant her then for a while the armor and the javelin. Let her put from her the press of other minds and meditate in virgin loneliness. The same idea shall reappear in due time as Muse, or Ceres, the all-kindly, patient Earth-Spirit.

.   .   .

A profound thinker has said "no married woman can represent the female world, for she belongs to her husband. The idea of woman must be represented by a virgin."

But that is the very fault of marriage, and of the present relation between the sexes, that the woman does belong to the man, instead of forming a whole with him. Were it otherwise there would be no such limitation to the thought.

Woman, self-centred, would never be absorbed by any relation; it would be only an experience to her as to man. It is a vulgar error that love, *a* love to woman is her whole existence; she also is born for Truth and Love in their universal energy. Would she but assume her inheritance, Mary would not be the only Virgin Mother. . . . The soul is ever young, ever virgin.

And will not she soon appear? The woman who shall vindicate their birthright for all women; who shall teach them what to claim, and how to use what they obtain? Shall not her name be for her era Victoria, for her country and her life Virginia? Yet predictions are rash; she herself must teach us to give her the fitting name.

The Ethics of Sex

M. A. HARDAKER contributed articles on sociology, philosophy, and the question of women's role in society to the **Atlantic Monthly,** the **North American Review,** and the **Popular Science Monthly** in the early 1880s. In forceful prose, she discussed with some sophistication the implications of science, especially the new developments in biology, for social and ethical questions. Identified only as "Miss Hardaker," she left no traces in the usual biographical sources, a victim perhaps of the social order she here explains.

The main psychological distinction between men and women is that men *think* more than women, and that their thinking is of a better

THE ETHICS OF SEX. From the *North American Review*, 131 (1880).

quality, because it is carried on chiefly in the form of reasoning, and is drawn from a wider field of facts. This is not a random inference, but may be scientifically verified by any observer who will approach this question in the same impartially critical spirit which should guide investigation upon every subject. Brain-activity is a constant phenomenon in both sexes during waking hours; but much of this activity is merely emotional in women. A great part of the conversation of women is a helpless playing with facts, a bringing of them together like the words of a dictionary, with little endeavor to found any conclusions upon them; and it is among women that we hear the most positive expressions of approval, condemnation, or pity. An intense personality modifies their decisions on most questions. The scientific spirit which desires to possess the truth and the philosophic spirit which impels to reason upon that truth are rarely found in women.

Nature has exacted the penalty for this constitutional narrowness by keeping their activity within narrow bounds. To verify this, we have only to take the testimony found in the records of modern civilization. Wherever we look we find woman caring for the *individual*, while man has cared for the individual and for the community. General interests have fallen into his hands, while personal ones have been left to hers. This division of labor has been so strictly based upon natural facts that we see that those facts must hold a fundamental cause of such results. In many of the processes of civilization we get the combined influence of the sexes; but we have one institution which shows the record of unmixed masculine activity; and this institution is the state. The moral evolution of national life has been shared by women; but the intellectual bases of all governments have been devised by men. The modern state, in its two forms of republic and constitutional monarchy, covers a vast variety of relations, and attempts the orderly adjustment of the needs and duties of immense communities, all agreeing or endeavoring to live in accordance with its requirements. These requirements are called laws —the constitution being the soil out of which laws grow to answer special needs. Not only is the plan of the modern state an emanation from the masculine mind, but its administration has been wholly in the hands of men. Queens have leaned upon masculine advisers so completely as to have left their reigns practically to masculine guidance.

Now, the course of history does not show any deliberate exclusion of woman from the affairs of government; but it does show, most clearly, that her want of participation in governments has been due to her defective reasoning powers, and to her incapacity for judging of general interests. Her small brain has limited her to a small field of activity; and her activity in this narrow field has been so intense as to give great perfection to those departments of life which have fallen under her care. She has ruled well in her small realm, and has shown a fine ability in organizing and applying her small forces.

Women have made four important contributions to modern civilization: they have cared for the body in its immediate needs by the preparation of food and clothing, and by ministration to the sick; they have been the conservers of moral forces, and have insisted on special standards of conduct in society and in the home; they have guided the rudimentary intellectual training of children; and they have contributed to the æsthetic development of the race by creating and combining beautiful forms and colors in dress, in decoration, and in household art. These four departments have been mainly controlled by women, and the comfort and beauty of every-day life proclaim their success.

Moral claims or rights exist only in the fitness of the claimant to do the work involved in such rights. Man's right to found states was in his comprehension of the immense interests involved in them. Women could not possibly have organized any modern state. There has never been any body of women of sufficient largeness of mind and inductive reasoning power to have grasped and dealt with the facts and principles which go to the making of any one of our better national constitutions. In every civilized community it has always been possible to select a larger number of intellectual men than of women equally endowed; and it is safe to say that, if nation-making had been left to women, the elements would still have been in seething confusion. But, now that the wild horse is caught and tamed, answers obediently to word, bit, and bridle, we may all take a holiday ride! We may even hold the reins and guide him over the smooth road. The owner is at hand to relieve us if he grows restless, and it is our *right* to take advantage of a holiday prepared for us by the foresight of generations of thoughtful men. It is not true that men have legislated for themselves alone. If they have fought for their altars and firesides, they have also legislated for them. Nothing is so plain to the scientific student of history as that the inconspicuous position of women in the state has been due to a natural lack of power to deal with great questions. Small brains can not give birth to great thoughts. Certainly there can have been no conspiracy on the part of man throughout the centuries to lessen the amount of woman's brain. Men lay far-reaching plans; they project undertakings which are to cover wide territories and affect large communities. Women's plans rarely extend beyond the few immediately about them. It is true that the modern movement for woman suffrage has been originated and mainly carried on by women; but this is the only project of great magnitude which they have originated. Putting the man's share in creating civilization beside woman's, the latter shrinks to a mere speck in contrast with the mighty achievements of men. This contrast has rarely been stated and dwelt upon with the emphasis which it deserves. Woman's work has been temporary in character, accomplished, expended, and repeated day by day. Much of man's work has been permanent. The principles of mathematics and optics, the invention of machinery, the immense industrial enterprises which feed millions, systems of trade, voyages of discovery, the art of printing, the creations of architecture, temples, palaces, bridges, ships, the great accumulation of facts in natural science, marine geography, meteorology, medicine, jurisprudence, musical composition, sculpture, creative painting, and literature are, with slight exceptions, the work of men. The only one of these departments to which women have considerably contributed is literature; here their creations have been mostly of poetry and fiction. In history, philosophy, criticism, and the drama, they have done nothing of great value or amount.

.   .   .

Although the claim of women to intellectual equality with men is childish, and their excited denials of masculine preëminence still more so, there is a claim which may be fairly made for them, the granting of which would lessen the inequality. They have a right to the most favorable conditions for intellectual development; but, as no advantages can atone for a defective natural endowment, so women must mainly climb intellectual steeps by means of scaling-ladders which men have put in place. It is true that individual men may be met every day who would show inferiority to individual women in power of independent thought; but, if the comparisons be made from those reared in the same social and educational ranks, our statement will hold. The great distinction between boy and girl in grammar and high schools is that, while the girl is dreaming, the boy is thinking.

There is no discouragement in facing and accepting scientific truths. There is no humiliation in it: and it is a finer and more honorable thing to see and admit one's true position in the great drama of human evolution than to contend by defiant assertion that we possess something which in the nature of things can never be ours. Women will have given proof of candor and will have made a step toward that intellectual power which they long to attain, when they can see and acknowledge that a decree of Nature has made them permanently inferior to men in intellect. If Nature had given them brains as large and as finely constituted as those of men, they might hope for the same results by exposing themselves to the same developing influences; but, while the physiological fact remains, the psychological one must keep it company. There is nothing disheartening in a great truth evolved from an immense accumulation of facts. When we have put our feet upon an eternal truth, the desire of growth and the power of growth are born in

us like strong twins of one blood. Shall we neglect music because we
can not compose like Beethoven, or sing like Parepa? When we have
repented and confessed our sins, we are ready for amendment.

.   .   .

In arguments upon the sex question it is usually claimed that women
have a finer moral development than men; that the ethical idea, or
conception of duty, controls them more powerfully. Applying the scientific method to this inquiry, and looking at facts, we do find a more
frequent solicitude to conform to fixed standards of conduct, determined by society, law, and religion, a more intense anxiety to secure
the approval of others, and a greater reluctance to refuse any individual
appeal for aid. Women give sympathy as freely as the clouds give rain;
and, when human hearts have been jarred or wounded, nothing is more
necessary than sympathy. But a thought which will mend the hurt by
preventing its repetition is of more value than a tear which expresses
sympathetic suffering. Women have a preëminent power of putting
themselves in the place of others, and of carefully considering every
weakness and sparing any infliction of pain. This kindliness and consideration for the individual explain their exquisite power of ministering to
the happiness of others. What is called conscientiousness—the careful,
painstaking balancing of different courses of conduct—is very native to
them; and this dealing with the minutiæ of morals makes them the
rightful guides of children in the school and home. Wherever the question has been one of immediate relief and of present comfort, women
have been natural ministers. In many cases their benevolence has extended to a thoughtful removal of causes; but great plans of philanthropy which have involved the bettering of the condition of whole
nations have originated with men. This has been due to a no less intense
desire for general good upon the part of women, but from their slighter
power of seeing wide ranges of facts and reasoning from them to general
remedies. While the woman is ministering to the needs of one sick
family, the man is organizing a plan of action which shall improve the
sanitary condition of the whole village. Women have in many instances
appropriated fortunes to philanthropies founded upon the thought of
men; but they have seldom originated such schemes. They have been far
behind in thinking upon philanthropies and reforms, though they have
been prompt to feel and to act. This feeling and action are most valuable
in supplementing thought, but, from their great amount, their relative
value has been overrated. The one who conceives a great plan is always
greater than those who execute it. He is the master, and they who
follow are his servants.

.   .   .

The strong and constant demands which wifehood and motherhood
make upon the physical, the emotional, and the moral forces, seem to

constitute a reason for the checking of intellectual growth. Yet, in the cases of women upon whom no such demands are made, we see no higher degree of development; and this certainly helps to show that their general contentment, with emotional gratification, is an inherent trait. What sufficient cause can there be for this relatively lower development than the relatively smaller bodies and brains of those who exhibit the effect?

There is a direct ethical value in the exercise of the intellect. Its most healthful action can occur only where the moral nature is perfectly sound. We can not acquire facts or reason to conclusions under emotional excitement, or when we are devising some social stratagem. If there is any reason for concealment of motives or of conduct, the necessity for keeping up that concealment will so employ the brain as to render any except this low form of action impossible. The attainment of moral purity, in the sense of a strong desire for the right and true, is the clearing of the field and preparation of the soil for intellectual harvests. The motive to self-preservation and the very general dependence of women upon men for the means of life have fostered moral disease. We know a woman who, for the last quarter of a century, has habitually taken money from her husband's purse while he was asleep, and this has been done to supply reasonable needs and social requirements which he ignored. To be free from the temptation to deceive men, women must be independent of them in respect to the means of life, and they must gain such an intellectual culture as shall lift them out of their exclusive indulgence of the emotions. At present, women seem obliged to marry for two reasons: one, that they can not win social independence without it; and the other, that their emotional natures crave constant exercise. How much the severe culture of the intellect will do toward the moral redemption of women by making them less dependent upon men, and less solicitous for their favor, is one of the problems of our future civilization.

One perplexing aspect of the sex question has grown into considerable importance in America, the so-called free-love philosophy. The very great majority of women, with their inability to take in facts in their larger relations, have nothing but utter condemnation for a movement which attempts the destruction of the family in the name of a reform. The majority of advocates of this social theory are men who show that they have thought upon the question, but that their conclusions have neglected some of the most influential facts. One of the fundamental arguments against the present solution of sex relations is that monogamic marriage is a failure: it has not solved the problem of human happiness. Instead of this rotten social institution, in which men and women give pledges and promises under legal and ecclesiastical sanction, it is proposed to substitute absolute personal control of these relations.

Neither church nor state, it is claimed, has any more moral right to interfere with individual freedom to form and to dissolve sexual ties than to interfere with the choice, purchase, or sale of a house or of a suit of clothes. The history of civil liberty, it is said, is a history of the enlargement of the rights of the individual; as he has grown more intelligent, he has continually wrested from the state more and more liberty to control his own actions. It is the policy of governing organizations, like church and state, to keep men in vassalage as long as possible. People can not be freed from irksome matrimonial bondage without the expense and delay of legal processes. So long as people must submit judgment and inclination to statute laws, on such questions they are children or slaves instead of freemen. Such is the general argument of these reformers.

It is not hard to discover the sources of such a social theory. The plan of government in the United States favors the largest possible individualism. It was to give the freest possible play to individual rights that the men of the Revolution fought their battles and framed their laws. The easy conditions of divorce and the yearly augmenting number of divorces under state legislation is a further movement toward strengthening individualism. If anything goes wrong, the spirit of our legislation is to right it, as far as practicable, by altering the conditions for the individual. This extreme liberality of the state toward her citizens is analogous to the indulgence of a mother to her children who insist on trying some experiment which the mother foresees will not help them. Yet the wise mother knows that the scientific method of developing her child is to let it see for itself what is helpful and hurtful. Changed conditions sometimes increase the happiness of sexual relations; but, as the reason for unhappy associations is found in the imperfect moral development or lack of judgment of those forming them, the way to insure happier results is *to improve human nature*. Happy unions are always voluntary, not only at the beginning, but as long as life lasts. Love can not be made free by a change of statutes. It can not be bound or loosed under any circumstances. If the state should listen to the petitions of those who ask that sex relations be exempted from control, the experience of a quarter of a century would convince the world that the old, long-tried, monogamic solution of the sex question is the wise one. There are evident reasons why such a result would come. In all the past emotional experience of the race it has been found impossible to create an intense idealization of more than one object at one time; it has been found, too, that when such idealization has been tested by knowledge and time it does not diminish, but deepen; and that the effect of this long-continued idealization is to create the best conditions of development, both for those who exercise it and for those toward whom it is directed. Now, if the best conditions of happiness are once secured they should be maintained. It is not possible to bring out all the results of this mutual sex idealization in any short period of association. The very fact that the association is a permanent one gives it earnestness and dignity. It would not be possible to extract from a half-dozen associations, extending over twenty-five years, the same amount of fine character-development that would come from one fortunate association lasting for the same time. When we are once sure of the wisdom, integrity, and affection of some friend through long experience, we spend no more brain-activity in learning his peculiarities of character and in adapting ourselves to them. The association of husband and wife is rather moral and affectional than intellectual. It is a rest, a certainty, a point of departure for all other activities. Once settled, and safely settled, we waste no power in readjusting these relations, but take the fruit as it ripens, without the need of uprooting the old and planting new trees. There is abundance of unanswerable scientific proof of better results in character and in happiness from long-continued sexual association than from transient and varied connections. For the state to grant to individuals the power of forming and dissolving such associations at will would be to grant them a power of injuring themselves by an unwholesome experiment. If the facts be carefully studied they will convince any fair-minded observer of the true solution of this question, without a resort to such a dangerous legislation. A wiser development of human nature in all directions is the real key to human happiness.

Men Versus Women: An Indictment

IDA HUSTED HARPER (1851–1931), born in Fairfield, Indiana, attended Indiana University and Stanford, and joined the National American Women's Suffrage Association in 1898. "Official reporter" of the movement, in which she was also an active participant, she prepared a three-volume **Life** (1898–1908) of Susan B. Anthony, a leading suffragette of the nineteenth century, and subsequently wrote the final volumes of Anthony's **History of Woman Suffrage** (1900–22).

MEN VERSUS WOMEN: AN INDICTMENT. From *Independent*, 64 (April 2, 1908).

From the time that Eve created in Adam a taste for cider by giving him a bite of her apple, women have been cautioned that they must not do this, that or the other, lest they drive men to drink. They must be everlastingly on their good behavior or they will be responsible for all sorts of dreadful things which men never would have dreamed of doing had they not been driven to it. Now, at this beginning of a new century, it looks as if men had conspired to drive women to extremes in every possible direction. That impudent action of the New York Board of Aldermen in passing an ordinance forbidding women to smoke in hotels and cafés was enough to make every woman look for a cigaret and a public place to smoke it in. When Alderman Sullivan was told that his ordinance was not constitutional, he is reported to have said: "That doesn't make a particle of difference." And so it doesn't when it affects only women. The courts of New York and other States have decided that no hotel or restaurant need give food to a woman after six o'clock unless she brings some man to share it with her, and by the same law she may be refused a night's lodging. The lawmaking power is entirely in the hands of men, and when they choose to enact a statute that women shall not eat at all except in the privacy of home they can do it without fear of the consequences. Neither the national nor State constitutions protect women in their rights as citizens, and not in one State in the Union are the laws exactly as fair to women as to men.

The young men follow in the footsteps of their fathers. A girl student at Cornell University, in a fair contest, with unprejudiced professors as judges, is selected to represent that institution at the intercollegiate debate. Instantly the students of the other two universities, Columbia and Pennsylvania, declare she shall not do it. Why? Because she is a woman. They would not have dared make an objection to the meanest man Cornell might have chosen of whatever creed or color, but, with their fathers' example before them, they do not hesitate to strike at the rights of a woman.

When the women of Chicago University won more than their share of the honors, the president put them off to one side in separate classes where they could not compete with the men. Why was it not the men themselves who were "segregated" until they were smart enough to hold their own? With the number of women at Tufts College now threatening to exceed the number of men, the president sends out an appeal for somebody to build another college for the women. Why not for the men, if they are to be in the minority?

Dr. G. Stanley Hall and other college presidents are advocating a special course of study which women must take to fit them for wifehood and motherhood. What right has a university to compel any class of students to prepare themselves for a certain vocation? On this hand are presidents and professors objecting to the higher education of women because it is apt to delay marriage or defer it altogether. On the other hand are those who decry the expenditure of time and money on this education because women take it only for general culture and do not adopt professions or go into research work; and yet either of these occupations would operate directly against marriage.

School boards composed wholly of men make regulations that no married woman shall teach; the general Government rules that women in its employ shall lose their positions when they marry. Then all join in a chorus of disapprobation because educated and competent women are showing a disinclination for marriage.

The wage-earning men denounce women because they accept less pay and lower the standard of wages. Then they bar women out of their trade unions, the most potent means of keeping up the standard, and deprive them of the ballot, the strongest weapon which labor has for the protection of its rights.

Women have tried for sixty years to get the suffrage, only to be met with the jeering assertion by those who can give or withhold it: "You'll have to prove that you want it as much as women in other countries do." Then, when it is proposed to adopt the tactics of those women, the cry is, "Oh, no, such methods are not at all suited to this country." "Convert your own sex; there are not enough women asking for it," is the universal taunt. And then the metropolitan dailies print big caricatures of a great mob of English "suffragettes" clamoring for their rights, and put over them the sarcastic caption, "Will New York Women Ever Do This?"

Yes, it is probable they will, and a great deal worse if they are driven to it; that is for the men of this country to determine. The present generation of women has moved on a long way from the patience, submission and supineness of the one preceding. It is logical to believe that the next will be still more spirited, independent and determined to have fair play and a square deal. The past generation were thinking of this fair play and square deal; the present are talking about them; the next will get them. As long as women were without education, without property, without voice, without organization, they were compelled to occupy an inferior position and accept whatever was dealt out to them. Now they have all four of these requisites to obtain equality of rights, but have not fully learned how to use them. That is the lesson for those of the present to master and pass on for the younger generation to apply in whatever way will accomplish the purpose.

When the pioneer women suffragists started out on their fifty years' war, among the other epithets hurled at them was that of "man-hater." As a matter of fact they loved the men of their own families and circles of friends quite as well as other women did, but they were the first to run counter to the general scheme of things as fixt by men, and the latter made a personal affair of it. The women said, "Give us better laws"; and the men answered, "You don't love us or you would be satisfied with the laws we have made." Finally the women demanded, "Give us the chance to make the laws ourselves or to help choose those who do this"; and the men replied, "You must positively hate us or you never would insult us by such a request, but we love you too much to grant it." And so they have continued up to the present day, on the same principle that parents punish children, "for their own good." Children reach an age after a while when they decide for themselves as to their well-being, and women feel that they, too, have about arrived at this point.

There should be no antagonism between men and women. The problems and struggles of life are very much the same for both, and they should stand together. Both are equally interested in the welfare of the family and the community, and this can be secured much more easily by their united effort. From every point of view it is highly desirable that they should dwell together in peace and harmony, but this is wholly impossible on any other basis than equality of rights.

When girls in college are stigmatized as "co-eds" by boys who are just as much co-eds themselves; and when they are made continually to feel that they are interlopers because they are less in numbers, and have a constant struggle for their rights in the student body, a burning resentment is engendered which it will take years to eradicate; and this is the situation today in nearly every co-educational institution. When, for the very reason that girls have proved their superiority in scholarship, they are set aside in "annexes" or in classes by themselves, with the stigma of "segregation" placed upon them, is it to be wondered at that their hearts are filled with bitterness and that they carry this out into life?

The principal of a New York public school said not long ago: "When we have our teachers' meetings and we women sit there and look at those male principals, who do exactly the same amount of work as we do and often not so well, and yet get nearly twice the salary, we hate them with all the intensity we are capable of." They would be saints if they did not feel exactly this way, and yet this hostile atmosphere must influence unfavorably the teachers' meetings and the work in the schools.

A woman who is rendering a great educational service to other women and is frequently brought into contact with the members of Congress, often says, "I cannot put into words how I loathe those men as legislators." Women in all parts of the country, whose efforts to better conditions take them with bills to the Legislatures, invariably come away with a most profound contempt for the cowardice, double-dealing and treachery which they meet with from many of the members. This lessens their respect for the whole body and arouses the feeling that, whatever the sacrifice, women must secure some power over the lawmakers and the laws of the State.

From time too far back to reckon, men have had their clubs and societies and banquets from which women were rigorously excluded. After generations of loneliness and resentment, the women have now gone headlong into these entertainments themselves, and are creating a life in which men have no part. Each year sees the gulf between them widen, the women thinking less about the men, caring less for them, and this is very far from the ideal state for both sexes—but it did not originate with the women.

It cannot be denied that there is a growing disinclination for marriage on the part of women. Their anxiety to marry used to be a standing joke that couldn't have the changes on it rung too often, and every man, in his own estimation, ranked with the horse that had taken first prize at the races. Now the most of them are entered as sweepstakes, with very few takers. Why? The nature of women has not changed. Their desire for a home and their love of children are just as strong as they ever were. The change lies in their having learned that they can maintain a fairly comfortable home without a husband, and have something more than a life interest in one-third of it. While nothing entirely compensates for the lack of children, they have found many substitutes which give a satisfactory fulness and completeness of existence. Unequal laws as to property, children, etc., made by men; the rules of the Church requiring obedience, and its refusal of divorce, even for just cause, are strongly discouraging to matrimony. They did not matter so much when it was marriage or nothing for a woman, but they matter a great deal now that she is comparatively a free agent to order her life to her own liking. The woman also whose education and ability give her a good earning power hesitates about seeing this obliterated by marriage. The fact that two-thirds of the divorces are granted on complaint of women may also cause the unmarried to ponder. Men themselves, in every capacity—legal, clerical, official and domestic—have put all these obstacles in the way of marriage. While women in constantly increasing numbers have too much pride and good sense to accept the conditions, none the less they have a feeling of regret and disappointment that, because of them, they must forego the possible pleasures of married life, and this creates a sentiment of dislike toward those who are responsible.

The wage-earning women have their special grievance, for into their homes, where once they were busy all day long with tasks that had been their own undisputed possession since the beginning of time, men entered and took them all away, carried every one to the great factories; and when they followed their occupations, their very own and their mothers' and their grandmothers', men met them with the question, "How do you dare come here and steal our work?" And so in their hearts too is a sense of deep wrong and cruel injustice.

And then when women at last find courage to protest at the universal injustice practiced against them they are met with the injunction: "Now mind that you don't say one word against men. Vinegar never catches flies. If you want any more concessions be sure to express your gratitude for past kindnesses. Men can only be won over by soft words and sweet womanly actions. Speak low, look pretty and don't ask anything as a right, but only as a great favor."

Women would like to recognize a higher standard than this for men. Notwithstanding the evidence of all the past ages to the contrary, they still wish to believe that men have a strong sense of justice and equity to which women can appeal in a manner that would be creditable to both of them. It is men themselves who say: "If you want to get anything from us it will have to be thru flattery, blandishment and cajolery." For some reason, perhaps higher education, perhaps financial independence, perhaps a knowledge of the little of real worth that has been gained by such means, women of high purposes are beginning to rebel against them. A class also has been developed who have studied the results of years of dignified, orderly methods on the part of still other women to secure needed legislation and have found them exprest in one word—failure. And so they have determined not to appeal to either masculine vanity or masculine reason. The tactics of this class are finding their first expression in the new phase of the movement for the suffrage.

Exactly twenty years ago Elizabeth Cady Stanton said in one of her matchless arguments before the United States Senate Committee on Woman Suffrage:

> You have now the power to settle this question by wise legislation, but, if you cannot be aroused to its serious consideration, like every other step in progress, it will be settled by violence. The wild enthusiasm of woman can be used for evil as well as good. Today you have the power to direct and guide it into channels of true patriotism, but in the future, with all the elements of discontent now gathering from foreign countries, you will have the scenes of the French Commune repeated in our land.

The beginning of the fulfilment of this prophecy is seen in the open-air meetings now taking place in Madison Square. The forum is changed from legislative halls, where two generations of women have made their pleadings to selected representatives of one-half the people, to this great public thorofare, where delicate women face the rigors of the weather to plead their case before a promiscuous crowd of loafers, aliens and the former occupants of workhouses and prison cells. To this action do one portion of the women feel that they have been driven. And now they promise that in the near future vast processions of the women of New York shall parade its streets to emphasize in this public and unpleasant way their demand for a sacred right which has been given without the asking to all the hundreds of thousands of men who will line the gutters and jeer them as they pass.

It is for men to decide how long this contest shall be kept up and what extremes it shall eventually reach, for it will never cease until its object is attained, and no one can foretell what form it will assume when it is reinforced by women of less self-restraint and stronger personal grievances than those who have directed it in the past. It is for men to say whether the antagonism of women, which now is plainly on the increase, shall grow stronger or diminish and die out because the cause for it has been removed. Women of the future will be satisfied with nothing less than exact justice.

When Mrs. Rose Pastor Stokes said a short time ago, "Much as I love the Stars and Stripes I love the red flag better," there was a loud outcry from the newspapers. In editorials and letters from the people it was iterated and reiterated that the flag of the United States guarantees the fullest liberty and opportunity for every citizen, and for this reason it deserves the strongest loyalty from all. It does not guarantee these rights to the women over whom it floats, but it flaunts its Stars and Stripes around the whole world as the symbol of a country whose written Constitution denies absolutely to one-half its citizens a voice or a vote in their own government.

Marriage

CHARLES ERSKINE SCOTT WOOD (1852–1944), born in Erie, Pennsylvania, graduated from West Point in 1874, and subsequently served in several campaigns against the Indians in the Northwest. Resigning his commission, he took a law degree at Columbia in 1883, and practiced law in Portland, Oregon until 1919. **Heavenly Discourse** first appeared during the First World War in the **Masses,**

MARRIAGE. Reprinted by permission of the publisher, The Vanguard Press, from "Heavenly Discourse" by Charles Erskine Scott Wood. Copyright, 1927, 1955, by Sara Bard Field Wood.

a periodical that led in the literary and political radicalism of the "innocent rebellion" of the 1910s.

(GOD and JESUS *are strolling through the universe, stepping from star to star.*)

JESUS   Father, how small the earth is in the infinity of space, among stars, bewildering in magnitude.

GOD   Yes. A speck. Why are you so fond of it?

JESUS   I don't know. Because they crucified me, I guess.

GOD   Well, yes, I can understand that.

JESUS   We love where we forgive, and we never forget where we have suffered.

GOD   No, I suppose not. I never suffered.

JESUS   Didn't you suffer when Aaron set up the golden calf?

GOD   No. I made him suffer.

JESUS   Father, am I the only son you ever had?

GOD   No, my son. I have had many sons, but you are the only son I ever had by a Jewess.

JESUS   Father, were you and mother ever married?

GOD   Ever what?

JESUS   Married. Holy matrimony. Holy wedlock.

GOD   Holy smoke! what are you talking about?

JESUS   On earth when a man and a woman love and want to unite their lives, they have first to get leave or license from somebody— then they have to stand before a priest or some other man and say something, and he tells them all right they may love. They are married. But when you are married, it is for forever and you can never go apart, even though you grow out of love and are very unhappy.

GOD   My son, your earth-visits are beginning to affect your mind.

JESUS   I don't say this. But they say it is your law.

GOD   Who says so?

JESUS   The priests and the county clerk.

GOD   When you want to know my law come to me—or look around you. You don't see or hear this foolishness anywhere else, do you?

JESUS   No, only where there are men and priests.

GOD   My laws are universal. Your mother and I loved each other and you were born as flowers are born.

JESUS   Then I am a bastard?

GOD   What do you mean?

JESUS   On earth, if the father and mother are not married, the child is a bastard. And I was born on earth.

GOD   You don't seem to be able to get away from that perfectly absurd earth.

JESUS   No, it's not that, but now in the midst of this war to end war, they want to get more babies for soldiers in the next war and there will be a lot of poor little innocent bastards. The Church——

GOD   Don't mention it. We have nothing to do with it.

JESUS   And the State——

GOD   What's that?

JESUS   The rich few who govern the people.

GOD   O, gods?

JESUS   Yes, in a way. The Church and the State, in order to have more men for more wars, are urging a lot of young men and women to take out permission papers for leave to love and have babies.

GOD   That's marriage?

JESUS   Yes.

GOD   Holy matrimony?

JESUS   Yes.

GOD   What makes it holy?

JESUS   The love of the pair for each other.

GOD   What has the Church or the State to do with that?

JESUS   Nothing. But as I was saying, the Church and the State urged the young people to get babies; certificates, I mean, so that they could get more babies for more wars.

GOD   Couldn't they get any babies without this certificate?

JESUS   Certainly, and that's the trouble. A lot of young people are doing it, but the children will be bastards.

GOD   Won't they be just as good babies?

JESUS   Yes.

GOD   Did the babies insist on certificates?

JESUS   No.

GOD   Won't they make just as good soldiers and mothers of soldiers? The boys can be killed just the same?

JESUS   O, yes.

GOD   Then what's the trouble?

JESUS   I don't know. Only, if the parents are not legally married, the babies are bastards.

GOD   So they punish the babies? Is it marked on them?

JESUS   No.

GOD   Does it hurt their health?

JESUS   No, Father, but Christians look down on them. They say such births are not lawful.

GOD   Christians look down on most everything that is loving and sensible. Has this loving and pairing without permission been going on very long?

JESUS   Ever since creation.

GOD   My! My! How awful!

JESUS   Father, you are mocking.

GOD   I have to—in order not to send an affliction on your stupid, silly pismires and blot them out. But they will do that themselves. Why not kill the unlawfuls as soon as born? Why let them be born?

JESUS   O, the State and the Church can use them; but the idea is this: the parents are rebels, in a way. They didn't have leave from Church and State to get these babies.

GOD   Well, I'll be—no, of course, I couldn't be. Listen. Won't these babies grow up to be men and women?

JESUS   Yes. But the Church and the State will call them bastards. They'll be forever disgraced.

GOD   Who? The Church and the State?

JESUS   No, the babies.

GOD   Are you disgraced?

JESUS   No, Father. I am your beloved son.

GOD   My beloved son. Who was never smirched by Church or State. Leave to love. Let us go home. Your talk has made me just a little tired. I can endure anything but stupidity. My law is—The stupid shall pass away.

The Crisis in Woman's Identity

BETTY FRIEDAN (1921–   ), born in Peoria, Illinois, received a B.A. **summa cum laude** from Smith College in 1942. A reseach fellow in psychology at Berkeley for a year, she later assisted in experiments in group dynamics at the University of Iowa. The mother of three children, she has contributed to **Harper's,** the **Reader's Digest,** the **Ladies Home Journal,** and other magazines.

I discovered a strange thing, interviewing women of my own generation over the past ten years. When we were growing up, many of us could not see ourselves beyond the age of twenty-one. We had no image of our own future, of ourselves as women.

THE CRISIS IN WOMAN'S IDENTITY. Reprinted from *The Feminine Mystique* by Betty Friedan. By permission of W. W. Norton & Company, Inc. Copyright © 1963 by Betty Friedan.

I remember the stillness of a spring afternoon on the Smith campus in 1942, when I came to a frightening dead end in my own vision of the future. A few days earlier, I had received a notice that I had won a graduate fellowship. During the congratulations, underneath my excitement, I felt a strange uneasiness; there was a question that I did not want to think about.

"Is this really what I want to be?" The question shut me off, cold and alone, from the girls talking and studying on the sunny hillside behind the college house. I thought I was going to be a psychologist. But if I wasn't sure, what did I want to be? I felt the future closing in —and I could not see myself in it at all. I had no image of myself, stretching beyond college. I had come at seventeen from a Midwestern town, an unsure girl; the wide horizons of the world and the life of the mind had been opened to me. I had begun to know who I was and what I wanted to do. I could not go back now. I could not go home again, to the life of my mother and the women of our town, bound to home, bridge, shopping, children, husband, charity, clothes. But now that the time had come to make my own future, to take the deciding step, I suddenly did not know what I wanted to be.

I took the fellowship, but the next spring, under the alien California sun of another campus, the question came again, and I could not put it out of my mind. I had won another fellowship that would have committed me to research for my doctorate, to a career as professional psychologist. "Is this really what I want to be?" The decision now truly terrified me. I lived in a terror of indecision for days, unable to think of anything else.

The question was not important, I told myself. No question was important to me that year but love. We walked in the Berkeley hills and a boy said: "Nothing can come of this, between us. I'll never win a fellowship like yours." Did I think I would be choosing, irrevocably, the cold loneliness of that afternoon if I went on? I gave up the fellowship, in relief. But for years afterward, I could not read a word of the science that once I had thought of as my future life's work; the reminder of its loss was too painful.

I never could explain, hardly knew myself, why I gave up this career. I lived in the present, working on newspapers with no particular plan. I married, had children, lived according to the feminine mystique as a suburban housewife. But still the question haunted me. I could sense no purpose in my life, I could find no peace, until I finally faced it and worked out my own answer.

I discovered, talking to Smith seniors in 1959, that the question is no less terrifying to girls today. Only they answer it now in a way that my generation found, after half a lifetime, not to be an answer at all. These girls, mostly seniors, were sitting in the living room of the college house, having coffee. It was not too different from such an evening when I was a senior, except that many more of the girls wore rings on their left hands. I asked the ones around me what they planned to be. The engaged ones spoke of weddings, apartments, getting a job as a secretary while husband finished school. The others, after a hostile silence, gave vague answers about this job or that, graduate study, but no one had any real plans. A blonde with a ponytail asked me the next day if I had believed the things they had said. "None of it was true," she told me. "We don't like to be asked what we want to do. None of us know. None of us even like to think about it. The ones who are going to be married right away are the lucky ones. They don't have to think about it."

.   .   .

The feminine mystique permits, even encourages, women to ignore the question of their identity. The mystique says they can answer the question "Who am I?" by saying "Tom's wife . . . Mary's mother." But I don't think the mystique would have such power over American women if they did not fear to face this terrifying blank which makes them unable to see themselves after twenty-one. The truth is—and how long it has been true, I'm not sure, but it was true in my generation and it is true of girls growing up today—an American woman no longer has a private image to tell her who she is, or can be, or wants to be.

The public image, in the magazines and television commercials, is designed to sell washing machines, cake mixes, deodorants, detergents, rejuvenating face creams, hair tints. But the power of that image, on which companies spend millions of dollars for television time and ad space, comes from this: American women no longer know who they are. They are sorely in need of a new image to help them find their identity. As the motivational researchers keep telling the advertisers, American women are so unsure of who they should be that they look to this glossy public image to decide every detail of their lives. They look for the image they will no longer take from their mothers.

In my generation, many of us knew that we did not want to be like our mothers, even when we loved them. We could not help but see their disappointment. Did we understand, or only resent, the sadness, the emptiness, that made them hold too fast to us, try to live our lives, run our fathers' lives, spend their days shopping or yearning for things that never seemed to satisfy them, no matter how much money they cost? Strangely, many mothers who loved their daughters—and mine was one —did not want their daughters to grow up like them either. They knew we needed something more.

But even if they urged, insisted, fought to help us educate ourselves, even if they talked with yearning of careers that were not open to them, they could not give us an image of what we could be. They could only tell us that their lives were too empty, tied to home; that children, cooking, clothes, bridge, and charities were not enough. A mother might tell her daughter, spell it out, "Don't be just a housewife like me." But that daughter, sensing that her mother was too frustrated to savor the love of her husband and children, might feel: "I will succeed where my mother failed, I will fulfill myself as a woman," and never read the lesson of her mother's life.

Recently, interviewing high-school girls who had started out full of promise and talent, but suddenly stopped their education, I began to see new dimensions to the problem of feminine conformity. These girls, it seemed at first, were merely following the typical curve of feminine adjustment. Earlier interested in geology or poetry, they now were interested only in being popular; to get boys to like them, they had concluded, it was better to be like all the other girls. On closer examination, I found that these girls were so terrified of becoming like their mothers that they could not see themselves at all. They were afraid to grow up. They had to copy in identical detail the composite image of the popular girl—denying what was best in themselves out of fear of femininity as they saw it in their mothers. . . .

. . . A college junior from South Carolina told me:

> I don't want to be interested in a career I'll have to give up.
>
> My mother wanted to be a newspaper reporter from the time she was twelve, and I've seen her frustration for twenty years. I don't want to be interested in world affairs. I don't want to be interested in anything beside my home and being a wonderful wife and mother. Maybe education is a liability. Even the brightest boys at home want just a sweet, pretty girl. Only sometimes I wonder how it would feel to be able to stretch and stretch and stretch, and learn all you want, and not have to hold yourself back.

Her mother, almost all our mothers, were housewives, though many had started or yearned for or regretted giving up careers. Whatever they told us, we, having eyes and ears and mind and heart, knew that their lives were somehow empty. We did not want to be like them, and yet what other model did we have?

The only other kind of women I knew, growing up, were the old-maid high-school teachers; the librarian; the one woman doctor in our town, who cut her hair like a man; and a few of my college professors. None of these women lived in the warm center of life as I had known it at home. Many had not married or had children. I dreaded being like them, even the ones who taught me truly to respect my own mind and use it, to feel that I had a part in the world. I never knew a woman, when I was growing up, who used her mind, played her own part in the world, and also loved, and had children.

I think that this has been the unknown heart of woman's problem in America for a long time, this lack of a private image. Public images that defy reason and have very little to do with women themselves have had the power to shape too much of their lives. These images would not have such power, if women were not suffering a crisis of identity.

The strange, terrifying jumping-off point that American women reach—at eighteen, twenty-one, twenty-five, forty-one—has been noticed for many years by sociologists, psychologists, analysts, educators. But I think it has not been understood for what it is. It has been called a "discontinuity" in cultural conditioning; it has been called woman's "role crisis." It has been blamed on the education which made American girls grow up feeling free and equal to boys—playing baseball, riding bicycles, conquering geometry and college boards, going away to college, going out in the world to get a job, living alone in an apartment in New York or Chicago or San Francisco, testing and discovering their own powers in the world. All this gave girls the feeling they could be and do whatever they wanted to, with the same freedom as boys, the critics said. It did not prepare them for their role as women. The crisis comes when they are forced to adjust to this role. Today's high rate of emotional distress and breakdown among women in their twenties and thirties is usually attributed to this "role crisis." If girls were educated for their role as women, they would not suffer this crisis, the adjusters say.

But I think they have seen only half the truth.

What if the terror a girl faces at twenty-one, when she must decide who she will be, is simply the terror of growing up—growing up, as women were not permitted to grow before? What if the terror a girl faces at twenty-one is the terror of freedom to decide her own life, with no one to order which path she will take, the freedom and the necessity to take paths women before were not able to take? What if those who choose the path of "feminine adjustment"—evading this terror by marrying at eighteen, losing themselves in having babies and the details of housekeeping—are simply refusing to grow up, to face the question of their own identity?

Mine was the first college generation to run head-on into the new mystique of feminine fulfillment. Before then, while most women did indeed end up as housewives and mothers, the point of education was to discover the life of the mind, to pursue truth and to take a place in the world. There was a sense, already dulling when I went to college, that we would be New Women. Our world would be much larger than home. Forty per cent of my college class at Smith had career plans. But I remember how, even then, some of the seniors, suffering the pangs of that bleak fear of the future, envied the few who escaped it by getting married right away.

The ones we envied then are suffering that terror now at forty. "Never have decided what kind of woman I am. Too much personal life in college. Wish I'd studied more science, history, government, gone deeper into philosophy," one wrote on an alumnae questionnaire, fifteen years later. "Still trying to find the rock to build on. Wish I had finished college. I got married instead." "Wish I'd developed a deeper and more creative life of my own and that I hadn't become engaged and married at nineteen. Having expected the ideal in marriage, including a hundred-per-cent devoted husband, it was a shock to find this isn't the way it is," wrote a mother of six.

Many of the younger generation of wives who marry early have never suffered this lonely terror. They thought they did not have to choose, to look into the future and plan what they wanted to do with their lives. They had only to wait to be chosen, marking time passively until the husband, the babies, the new house decided what the rest of their lives would be. They slid easily into their sexual role as women before they knew who they were themselves. It is these women who suffer most the problem that has no name.

It is my thesis that the core of the problem for women today is not sexual but a problem of identity—a stunting or evasion of growth that is perpetuated by the feminine mystique. It is my thesis that as the Victorian culture did not permit women to accept or gratify their basic sexual needs, our culture does not permit women to accept or gratify their basic need to grow and fulfill their potentialities as human beings, a need which is not solely defined by their sexual role.

Biologists have recently discovered a "youth serum" which, if fed to young caterpillars in the larva state, will keep them from ever maturing into moths; they will live out their lives as caterpillars. The expectations of feminine fulfillment that are fed to women by magazines, television, movies, and books that popularize psychological half-truths, and by parents, teachers and counselors who accept the feminine mystique, operate as a kind of youth serum, keeping most women in the state of sexual larvae, preventing them from achieving the maturity of which they are capable. And there is increasing evidence that woman's failure to grow to complete identity has hampered rather than enriched her sexual fulfillment, virtually doomed her to be castrative to her husband and sons, and caused neuroses, or problems as yet unnamed as neuroses, equal to those caused by sexual repression.

There have been identity crises for man at all the crucial turning points in human history, though those who lived through them did not give them that name. It is only in recent years that the theorists of psychology, sociology and theology have isolated this problem, and given it a name. But it is considered a man's problem. It is defined, for man, as the crisis of growing up, of choosing his identity, "the decision as to what one is and is going to be," in the words of the brilliant psycho-analyst Erik H. Erikson:

> I have called the major crisis of adolescence the identity crisis; it occurs in that period of the life cycle when each youth must forge for himself some central perspective and direction, some working unity, out of the effective remnants of his childhood and the hopes of his anticipated adulthood; he must detect some meaningful resemblance between what he has come to see in himself and what his sharpened awareness tells him others judge and expect him to be. . . . In some people, in some classes, at some periods in history, the crisis will be minimal; in other people, classes and periods, the crisis will be clearly marked off as a critical period, a kind of "second birth," apt to be aggravated either by widespread neuroticisms or by pervasive ideological unrest.

In this sense, the identity crisis of one man's life may reflect, or set off, a rebirth, or new stage, in the growing up of mankind. "In some periods of his history, and in some phases of his life cycle, man needs a new ideological orientation as surely and sorely as he must have air and food," said Erikson, focusing new light on the crisis of the young Martin Luther, who left a Catholic monastery at the end of the Middle Ages to forge a new identity for himself and Western man.

The search for identity is not new, however, in American thought—though in every generation, each man who writes about it discovers it anew. In America, from the beginning, it has somehow been understood that men must thrust into the future; the pace has always been too rapid for man's identity to stand still. In every generation, many men have suffered misery, unhappiness, and uncertainty because they could not take the image of the man they wanted to be from their fathers. The search for identity of the young man who can't go home again has always been a major theme of American writers. And it has always been considered right in America, good, for men to suffer these agonies of growth, to search for and find their own identities. The farm boy went to the city, the garment-maker's son became a doctor, Abraham Lincoln taught himself to read—these were more than rags-to-riches stories. They were an integral part of the American dream. The problem for many was money, race, color, class, which barred them from choice—not what they would be if they were free to choose.

Even today a young man learns soon enough that he must decide who he wants to be. If he does not decide in junior high, in high school, in college, he must somehow come to terms with it by twenty-five or thirty, or he is lost. But this search for identity is seen as a greater problem now because more and more boys cannot find images in our culture —from their fathers or other men—to help them in their search. The old frontiers have been conquered, and the boundaries of the new are not so clearly marked. More and more young men in America today suffer an identity crisis for want of any image of man worth pursuing, for want of a purpose that truly realizes their human abilities.

But why have theorists not recognized this same identity crisis in women? In terms of the old conventions and the new feminine mystique women are not expected to grow up to find out who they are, to choose their human identity. Anatomy is woman's destiny, say the theorists of femininity; the identity of woman is determined by her biology.

But is it? More and more women are asking themselves this question. As if they were waking from a coma, they ask, "Where am I . . . what am I doing here?" For the first time in their history, women are becoming aware of an identity crisis in their own lives, a crisis which began many generations ago, has grown worse with each succeeding generation, and will not end until they, or their daughters, turn an unknown corner and make of themselves and their lives the new image that so many women now so desperately need.

In a sense that goes beyond any one woman's life, I think this is the crisis of women growing up—a turning point from an immaturity that has been called femininity to full human identity. I think women had to suffer this crisis of identity, which began a hundred years ago, and have to suffer it still today, simply to become fully human.

Passage to More Than India

GARY SNYDER (1930–   ), born in San Francisco, spent most of his youth on his parents' farm north of Seattle. As an undergraduate at Reed College (B.A., 1951) he majored in anthropology and literature, and later took graduate work in oriental languages. He has published numerous volumes of poetry and was active in the "beat movement" with Allen Ginsberg and Jack Kerouac. Twice divorced, he told one interviewer that his favorite living women are "a score of West Coast hippies." He is a confirmed Buddhist, and since 1959 has claimed Japan as his principal residence.

"It will be a revival, in higher form, of the liberty, equality, and fraternity of the ancient gentes."

—LEWIS HENRY MORGAN

The Tribe

The celebrated human Be-In in San Francisco, January of 1967, was called "A Gathering of the Tribes." The two posters: one based on a photograph of a Shaivite sadhu with his long matted hair, ashes and beard; the other based on an old etching of a Plains Indian approaching a powwow on his horse—the carbine that had been cradled in his left arm replaced by a guitar. The Indians, and the Indian. The tribes were Berkeley, North Beach, Big Sur, Marin County, Los Angeles, and the host, Haight-Ashbury. Outriders were present from New York, London and Amsterdam. Out on the polo field that day the splendidly clad ab/originals often fell into clusters, with children, a few even under banners. These were the clans.

Large old houses are rented communally by a group, occupied by couples and singles (or whatever combinations) and their children. In some cases, especially in the rock-and-roll business and with light-show groups, they are all working together on the same creative job. They might even be a legal corporation. Some are subsistence farmers out in the country, some are contractors and carpenters in small coast towns. One girl can stay home and look after all the children while the other girls hold jobs. They will all be cooking and eating together and they may well be brown-rice vegetarians. There might not be much alcohol or tobacco around the house, but there will certainly be a stash of marijuana and probably some LSD. If the group has been together for some time it may be known by some informal name, magical and natural. These house-holds provide centers in the city and also out in the country for loners and rangers; gathering places for the scattered smaller hip families and havens for the questing adolescent children of the neighborhood. The clan sachems will sometimes gather to talk about larger issues —police or sheriff department harassments, busts, anti-Vietnam projects, dances and gatherings.

All this is known fact. The number of committed total tribesmen is not so great, but there is a large population of crypto-members who move through many walks of life undetected and only put on their beads and feathers for special occasions. Some are in the academies, others in the legal or psychiatric professions—very useful friends indeed. The number of people who use marijuana regularly and have experienced LSD is (considering it's all illegal) staggering. The impact of all this on the cultural and imaginative life of the nation—even the politics—is enormous.

And yet, there's nothing very new about it, in spite of young hippies just in from the suburbs for whom the "beat generation" is a kalpa away. For several centuries now Western Man has been ponderously preparing himself for a new look at the inner world and the spiritual realms. Even in the centers of nineteenth-century materialism there were dedicated seekers—some within Christianity, some in the arts, some within the occult circles. Witness William Butler Yeats. My own opinion is that we are now experiencing a surfacing (in a specifically "American" incarnation) of the Great Subculture which goes back as far perhaps as the late Paleolithic.

This subculture of illuminati has been a powerful undercurrent in all higher civilizations. In China it manifested as Taoism, not only Lao-tzu but the later Yellow Turban revolt and medieval Taoist secret societies; and the Zen Buddhists up till early Sung. Within Islam the Sufis; in India the various threads converged to produce Tantrism. In the West it has been represented largely by a string of heresies starting with the Gnostics, and on the folk level by "witchcraft."

Buddhist Tantrism, or Vajrayana as it's also known, is probably the finest and most modern statement of this ancient shamanistic-yogic-gnostic-socioeconomic view: that mankind's mother is Nature and Nature should be tenderly respected; that man's life and destiny is growth and enlightenment in self-disciplined freedom; that the divine has been made flesh and that flesh is divine; that we not only should but *do* love one another. This view has been harshly suppressed in the past as threatening to both Church and State. Today, on the contrary, these values seem almost biologically essential to the survival of humanity.

The Family

Lewis Henry Morgan (d. 1881) was a New York lawyer. He was asked by his club to reorganize it "after the pattern of the Iroquois confederacy." His research converted him into a defender of tribal rights and started him on his career as an amateur anthropologist. His major contribution was a broad theory of social evolution which is still useful. Morgan's *Ancient Society* inspired Engels to write *Origins of the Family, Private Property and the State* (1884, and still in print in both Russia and China), in which the relations between the rights of women, sexuality and the family, and attitudes toward property and power are tentatively explored. The pivot is the revolutionary implications of the custom of matrilineal descent, which Engels learned from Morgan; the Iroquois are matrilineal.

A schematic history of the family:

Hunters and gatherers—a loose monogamy within communal clans usually reckoning descent in the female line, i.e., matrilineal.

Early agriculturalists—a tendency toward group and polyandrous marriage, continued matrilineal descent and smaller-sized clans.

Pastoral nomads—a tendency toward stricter monogamy and patrilineal descent; but much premarital sexual freedom.

Iron-Age agriculturalists—property begins to accumulate and the family system changes to monogamy or polygyny with patrilineal descent. Concern with the legitimacy of heirs.

Civilization so far has implied a patriarchal, patrilineal family. Any other system allows too much creative sexual energy to be released into channels which are "unproductive." In the West, the clan, or gens, disappeared gradually, and social organization was ultimately replaced by political organization, within which separate male-oriented families compete: the modern state.

Engels' Marxian classic implies that the revolution cannot be completely achieved in merely political terms. Monogamy and patrilineal descent may well be great obstructions to the inner changes required for a people to truly live by "communism." Marxists after Engels let these questions lie. Russia and China today are among the world's staunchest supporters of monogamous, sexually turned-off families. Yet Engels' insights were not entirely ignored. The Anarcho-Syndicalists showed a sense for experimental social reorganization. American anarchists and the I.W.W. lived a kind of communalism, with some lovely stories handed down of free love—their slogan was more than just words: "Forming the new society within the shell of the old." San Francisco poets and gurus were attending meetings of the "Anarchist Circle"— old Italians and Finns—in the 1940's.

.   .   .

The Heretics

"When Adam delved and Eve span,
Who was then a gentleman?"

The memories of a Golden Age—the Garden of Eden—the Age of the Yellow Ancestor—were genuine expressions of civilization and its discontents. Harking back to societies where women and men were more free with each other; where there was more singing and dancing; where there were no serfs and priests and kings.

Projected into future time in Christian culture, this dream of the

Millennium became the soil of many heresies. It is a dream handed down right to our own time—of ecological balance, classless society, social and economic freedom. It is actually one of the possible futures open to us. To those who stubbornly argue "it's against human nature," we can only patiently reply that you must know your own nature before you can say this. Those who have gone into their own natures deeply have, for several thousand years now, been reporting that we have nothing to fear if we are willing to train ourselves, to open up, explore and grow.

One of the most significant medieval heresies was the Brotherhood of the Free Spirit, of which Hieronymus Bosch was probably a member. The Brotherhood believed that God was immanent in everything, and that once one had experienced this God-presence in himself he became a Free Spirit; he was again living in the Garden of Eden. The brothers and sisters held their meetings naked, and practiced much sharing. They "confounded clerics with the subtlety of their arguments." It was complained that "they have no uniform . . . sometimes they dress in a costly and dissolute fashion, sometimes most miserably, all according to time and place." The Free Spirits had communal houses in secret all through Germany and the Lowlands, and wandered freely among them. Their main supporters were the well-organized and affluent weavers.

When brought before the Inquisition they were not charged with witchcraft, but with believing that man was divine, and with making love too freely, with orgies. Thousands were burned. There are some who have as much hostility to the adepts of the subculture today. This may be caused not so much by the outlandish clothes and dope, as by the nutty insistence on "love." The West and Christian culture on one level deeply wants love to win—and having decided (after several sad tries) that love can't, people who still say it will are like ghosts from an old dream.

Love begins with the family and its network of erotic and responsible relationships. A slight alteration of family structure will project a different love-and-property outlook through a whole culture . . . thus the communism and free love of the Christian heresies. This is a real razor's edge. Shall the lion lie down with the lamb? And make love even? The Garden of Eden.

White Indians

The modern American family is the smallest and most barren family that has ever existed. Each newly-married couple moves to a new house or apartment—no uncles or grandmothers come to live with them.

There are seldom more than two or three children. The children live with their peers and leave home early. Many have never had the least sense of family.

I remember sitting down to Christmas dinner eighteen years ago in a communal house in Portland, Oregon, with about twelve others my own age, all of whom had no place they wished to go home to. That house was my first discovery of harmony and community with fellow beings. This has been the experience of hundreds of thousands of men and women all over America since the end of World War II. Hence the talk about the growth of a "new society." But more; these gatherings have been people spending time with each other—talking, delving, making love. Because of the sheer amount of time "wasted" together (without TV) they know each other better than most Americans know their own family. Add to this the mind-opening and personality-revealing effects of grass and acid, and it becomes possible to predict the emergence of groups who live by mutual illumination—have seen themselves as of one mind and one flesh—the "single eye" of the heretical English Ranters; the meaning of sahajiya, "born together"—the name of the latest flower of the Tantric community tradition in Bengal.

Industrial society indeed appears to be finished. Many of us are, again, hunters and gatherers. Poets, musicians, nomadic engineers and scholars; fact-diggers, searchers and re-searchers scoring in rich foundation territory. Horse-traders in lore and magic. The super hunting-bands of mercenaries like Rand or CIA may in some ways belong to the future, if they can be transformed by the ecological conscience, or acid, to which they are very vulnerable. A few of us are literally hunters and gatherers, playfully studying the old techniques of acorn flour, seaweed-gathering, yucca-fiber, rabbit snaring and bow hunting. The densest Indian population in pre-Columbian America north of Mexico was in Marin, Sonoma and Napa Counties, California.

And finally, to go back to Morgan and Engels, sexual mores and the family are changing in the same direction. Rather than the "breakdown of the family" we should see this as the transition to a new form of family. In the near future, I think it likely that the freedom of women and the tribal spirit will make it possible for us to formalize our marriage relationships in any way we please—as groups, or polygynously or polyandrously, as well as monogamously. I use the word "formalize" only in the sense of make public and open the relationships, and to sacramentalize them; to see family as part of the divine ecology. Because it is simpler, more natural, and breaks up tendencies toward property accumulation by individual families, matrilineal descent seems ultimately indicated. Such families already exist. Their children are different in personality structure and outlook from anybody in the history of Western culture since the destruction of Knossos.

The American Indian is the vengeful ghost lurking in the back of the troubled American mind. Which is why we lash out with such ferocity and passion, so muddied a heart, at the black-haired young peasants and soldiers who are the "Viet Cong." That ghost will claim the next generation as its own. When this has happened, citizens of the USA will at last begin to be Americans, truly at home on the continent, in love with their land. The chorus of a Cheyenne Indian Ghost dance song—"hiniswa' vita'ki'ni"—"We shall live again."

> Passage to more than India!
> Are thy wings plumed indeed for such far flights?
> O soul, voyagest thou indeed on voyages like those?

Theory of Sexual Politics

KATE MILLETT (1934–   ), born in St. Paul, Minnesota, educated at the University of Minnesota and Oxford, emerged during 1970 as a leading theorist of the Women's Liberation Movement. Originally a doctoral dissertation, **Sexual Politics** won her a Ph.D. with distinction at Columbia. ("All it is," she has remarked, "is my goddam Ph.D. thesis.") In the book, she traces the delineation of male and female roles in history, psychology, biology, anthropology, religion, and literature. Criticizing the male chauvinism of such writers as Norman Mailer, D. H. Lawrence, and Henry Miller, she argues that our entire social system is premised on the oppression of the female. In the selection below she considers the role of traditional mythology, exemplified in the story of Adam and Eve, in defining this oppressive relationship.

. . . In introducing the term "sexual politics," one must first answer the inevitable question "Can the relationship between the sexes be viewed in a political light at all?" The answer depends on how one defines politics. This essay does not define the political as that relatively narrow and exclusive world of meetings, chairmen, and parties. The term "politics" shall refer to power-structured relationships, arrangements whereby one group of persons is controlled by another.

.   .   .

The word "politics" is enlisted here when speaking of the sexes primarily because such a word is eminently useful in outlining the real nature of their relative status, historically and at the present. It is opportune, perhaps today even mandatory, that we develop a more relevant psychology and philosophy of power relationships beyond the simple conceptual framework provided by our traditional formal politics. Indeed, it may be imperative that we give some attention to defining a theory of politics which treats of power relationships on grounds less conventional than those to which we are accustomed. I have therefore found it pertinent to define them on grounds of personal contact and interaction between members of well-defined and coherent groups: races, castes, classes, and sexes. For it is precisely because certain groups have no representation in a number of recognized political structures that their position tends to be so stable, their oppression so continuous.

In America, recent events have forced us to acknowledge at last that the relationship between the races is indeed a political one which involves the general control of one collectivity, defined by birth, over another collectivity, also defined by birth. Groups who rule by birthright are fast disappearing, yet there remains one ancient and universal scheme for the domination of one birth group by another—the scheme that prevails in the area of sex. The study of racism has convinced us that a truly political state of affairs operates between the races to perpetuate a series of oppressive circumstances. The subordinated group has inadequate redress through existing political institutions, and is deterred thereby from organizing into conventional political struggle and opposition.

Quite in the same manner, a disinterested examination of our system of sexual relationship must point out that the situation between the sexes now, and throughout history, is a case of that phenomenon Max Weber defined as *herrschaft*, a relationship of dominance and subordinance. What goes largely unexamined, often even unacknowledged (yet is institutionalized nonetheless) in our social order, is the birthright priority whereby males rule females. Through this system a most ingenious form of "interior colonization" has been achieved. It is one which tends moreover to be sturdier than any form of segregation, and more rigorous than class stratification, more uniform, certainly more enduring. However muted its present appearance may be, sexual dominion obtains nevertheless as perhaps the most pervasive ideology of our culture and provides its most fundamental concept of power.

This is so because our society, like all other historical civilizations, is a patriarchy. The fact is evident at once if one recalls that the military, industry, technology, universities, science, political office, and finance—in short, every avenue of power within the society, including the coercive force of the police, is entirely in male hands. As the essence of politics is power, such realization cannot fail to carry impact. What lingers of supernatural authority, the Deity, "His" ministry, together with the ethics and values, the philosophy and art of our culture—its very civilization—as T. S. Eliot once observed, is of male manufacture.

.   .   .

Evidence from anthropology, religious and literary myth all attests to the politically expedient character of patriarchal convictions about women. One anthropologist refers to a consistent patriarchal strain of assumption that "woman's biological differences set her apart . . . she is essentially inferior," and since "human institutions grow from deep and primal anxieties and are shaped by irrational psychological mechanisms . . . socially organized attitudes toward women arise from basic tensions expressed by the male." Under patriarchy the female did not herself develop the symbols by which she is described. As both the primitive and the civilized worlds are male worlds, the ideas which shaped culture in regard to the female were also of male design. The image of women as we know it is an image created by men and fashioned to suit their needs. These needs spring from a fear of the "otherness" of woman. Yet this notion itself presupposes that patriarchy has already been established and the male has already set himself as the human norm, the subject and referent to which the female is "other" or alien. Whatever its origin, the function of the male's sexual antipathy is to provide a means of control over a subordinate group and a rationale which justifies the inferior station of those in a lower order, "explaining" the oppression of their lives.

The feeling that woman's sexual functions are impure is both worldwide and persistent. One sees evidence of it everywhere in literature, in myth, in primitive and civilized life. It is striking how the notion persists today. The event of menstruation, for example, is a largely clandestine affair, and the psycho-social effect of the stigma attached must have great effect on the female ego. There is a large anthropological literature on menstrual taboo; the practice of isolating offenders in huts at the edge of the village occurs throughout the primitive world. Contemporary slang denominates menstruation as "the curse." There is considerable evidence that such discomfort as women suffer during their period is often likely to be psychosomatic, rather than physiological, cultural rather than biological, in origin. That this may also be true to some extent of labor and delivery is attested to by the recent experiment with "painless childbirth." Patriarchal circumstances and beliefs seem to have the effect of poisoning the female's own sense of physical self until it often truly becomes the burden it is said to be.

Primitive peoples explain the phenomenon of the female's genitals in terms of a wound, sometimes reasoning that she was visited by a bird or snake and mutilated into her present condition. Once she was wounded, now she bleeds. Contemporary slang for the vagina is "gash." The Freudian description of the female genitals is in terms of a "castrated" condition. The uneasiness and disgust female genitals arouse in patriarchal societies is attested to through religious, cultural, and literary proscription. In preliterate groups fear is also a factor, as in the belief in a castrating *vagina dentata*. The penis, badge of the male's superior status in both preliterate and civilized patriarchies, is given the most crucial significance, the subject both of endless boasting and endless anxiety.

Nearly all patriarchies enforce taboos against women touching ritual objects (those of war or religion) or food. In ancient and preliterate societies women are generally not permitted to eat with men. Women eat apart today in a great number of cultures, chiefly those of the Near and Far East. Some of the inspiration of such custom appears to lie in fears of contamination, probably sexual in origin. In their function of domestic servants, females are forced to prepare food, yet at the same time may be liable to spread their contagion through it. A similar situation obtains with blacks in the United States. They are considered filthy and infectious, yet as domestics they are forced to prepare food for their queasy superiors. In both cases the dilemma is generally solved in a deplorably illogical fashion by segregating the act of eating itself, while cooking is carried on out of sight by the very group who would infect the table. With an admirable consistency, some Hindu males do not permit their wives to touch their food at all. In nearly every patriarchal group it is expected that the dominant male will eat first or eat better, and even where the sexes feed together, the male shall be served by the female.

All patriarchies have hedged virginity and defloration in elaborate rites and interdictions. Among preliterates virginity presents an interesting problem in ambivalence. On the one hand, it is, as in every patriarchy, a mysterious good because a sign of property received intact. On the other hand, it represents an unknown evil associated with the mana of blood and terrifyingly "other." So auspicious is the event of defloration that in many tribes the owner-groom is willing to relinquish breaking the seal of his new possession to a stronger or older personality who can neutralize the attendant dangers. Fears of defloration appear to originate in a fear of the alien sexuality of the female. Although any physical suffering endured in defloration must be on the part of the female (and most societies cause her—bodily and mentally—to suffer anguish), the social interest, institutionalized in patriarchal ritual and custom, is exclusively on the side of the male's property interest, prestige, or (among preliterates) hazard.

Patriarchal myth typically posits a golden age before the arrival of women, while its social practices permit males to be relieved of female company. Sexual segregation is so prevalent in patriarchy that one encounters evidence of it everywhere. Nearly every powerful circle in contemporary patriarchy is a men's group. But men form groups of their own on every level. Women's groups are typically auxiliary in character, imitative of male efforts and methods on a generally trivial or ephemeral plane. They rarely operate without recourse to male authority, church or religious groups appealing to the superior authority of a cleric, political groups to male legislators, etc.

In sexually segregated situations the distinctive quality of culturally enforced temperament becomes very vivid. This is particularly true of those exclusively masculine organizations which anthropology generally refers to as men's house institutions. The men's house is a fortress of patriarchal association and emotion. Men's houses in preliterate society strengthen masculine communal experience through dances, gossip, hospitality, recreation, and religious ceremony. They are also the arsenals of male weaponry.

.   .   .

Considerable sexual activity does take place in the men's house, all of it, needless to say, homosexual. But the taboo against homosexual behavior (at least among equals) is almost universally of far stronger force than the impulse and tends to effect a rechanneling of the libido into violence. This association of sexuality and violence is a particularly militaristic habit of mind. The negative and militaristic coloring of such men's house homosexuality as does exist, is of course by no means the whole character of homosexual sensibility. Indeed, the warrior caste of mind with its ultravirility, is more *incipiently* homosexual, in its exclusively male orientation, than it is *overtly* homosexual. (The Nazi experience is an extreme case in point here.) And the heterosexual roleplaying indulged in, and still more persuasively, the contempt in which the younger, softer, or more "feminine" members are held, is proof that the actual ethos is misogynist, or perversely rather than positively heterosexual. The true inspiration of men's house association therefore comes from the patriarchal situation rather than from any circumstances inherent in the homo-amorous relationship.

.   .   .

Primitive society practices its misogyny in terms of taboo and mana which evolve into explanatory myth. In historical cultures, this is transformed into ethical, then literary, and in the modern period, scientific rationalizations for the sexual politic. Myth is, of course, a felicitous advance in the level of propaganda, since it so often bases its arguments on ethics or theories of origins. The two leading myths of Western culture are the classical tale of Pandora's box and the Biblical story of the

Fall. In both cases earlier mana concepts of feminine evil have passed through a final literary phase to become highly influential ethical justifications of things as they are.

.   .   .

The myth of the Fall[,] . . . [a] mythic version of the female as the cause of human suffering, knowledge, and sin is still the foundation of sexual attitudes, for it represents the most crucial argument of the patriarchal tradition in the West. . . .

The tale of Adam and Eve is, among many other things, a narrative of how humanity invented sexual intercourse. Many such narratives exist in preliterate myth and folk tale. Most of them strike us now as delightfully funny stories of primal innocents who require a good deal of helpful instruction to figure it out. There are other major themes in the story: the loss of primeval simplicity, the arrival of death, and the first conscious experience of knowledge. All of them revolve about sex. Adam is forbidden to eat of the fruit of life or of the knowledge of good and evil, the warning states explicitly what should happen if he tastes of the latter: "in that day that thou eatest thereof thou shalt surely die." He eats but fails to die (at least in the story), from which one might infer that the serpent told the truth.

But at the moment when the pair eat of the forbidden tree they awake to their nakedness and feel shame. Sexuality is clearly involved, though the fable insists it is only tangential to a higher prohibition against disobeying orders in the matter of another and less controversial appetite—one for food. Róheim points out that the Hebrew verb for "eat" can also mean coitus. Everywhere in the Bible "knowing" is synonymous with sexuality, and clearly a product of contact with the phallus, here in the fable objectified as a snake. To blame the evils and sorrows of life —loss of Eden and the rest—on sexuality, would all too logically implicate the male, and such implication is hardly the purpose of the story, designed as it is expressly in order to blame all this world's discomfort on the female. Therefore it is the female who is tempted first and "beguiled" by the penis, transformed into something else, a snake. Thus Adam has "beaten the rap" of sexual guilt, which appears to be why the sexual motive is so repressed in the Biblical account. Yet the very transparency of the serpent's universal phallic value shows how uneasy the mythic mind can be about its shifts. Accordingly, in her inferiority and vulnerability the woman takes and eats, simple carnal thing that she is, affected by flattery even in a reptile. Only after this does the male fall, and with him, humanity—for the fable has made him the racial type, whereas Eve is a mere sexual type and, according to tradition, either expendable or replaceable. And as the myth records the original sexual adventure, Adam was seduced by woman, who was seduced by a penis. "The woman whom thou gavest to be with me, she gave me of the fruit and I did eat" is the first man's defense. Seduced by the phallic snake, Eve is convicted for Adam's participation in sex.

Adam's curse is to toil in the "sweat of his brow," namely the labor the male associates with civilization. Eden was a fantasy world without either effort or activity, which the entrance of the female, and with her sexuality, has destroyed. Eve's sentence is far more political in nature and a brilliant "explanation" of her inferior status. "In sorrow thou shalt bring forth children. And thy desire shall be to thy husband. And he shall rule over thee." Again, . . . a proprietary father figure is punishing his subjects for adult heterosexuality. It is easy to agree with Róheim's comment on the negative attitude the myth adopts toward sexuality: "Sexual maturity is regarded as a misfortune, something that has robbed mankind of happiness . . . the explanation of how death came into the world."

What requires further emphasis is the responsibility of the female, a marginal creature, in bringing on this plague, and the justice of her suborned condition as dependent on her primary role in this original sin. The connection of woman, sex, and sin constitutes the fundamental pattern of western patriarchal thought thereafter.

.   .   .

Questions for Discussion and Writing

1. Did Bradstreet accept what Friedan calls the "feminine mystique," seventeenth-century style?
2. Does Fuller's assertion that there exists a natural alliance between antislavery and women's rights forces hold true for present day movements to "liberate" women and blacks?
3. Is Fuller opposed to marriage? How do her opinions on this subject compare with those of the other writers represented in this section?
4. Hardaker contends that men, by their political acumen, have sustained the orderly development of civilization. In what ways, other than the political, have women truly supported and provided the continuity for the development of societies?
5. Discuss the use of "science" in Hardaker's essay.
6. Does the Harper article justify the conclusion that although suffragettes claimed to speak for *all* women their characteristic concerns were those of the well-to-do middle and professional classes? Is it true of later defenders of women's rights?

7. Compare and contrast Wood's attitudes toward the state and the marriage relationship with those of the writers of other selections in this section.
8. Discuss the following, as they pertain to women in America today: image, identity, role crisis, patriarchy, matrilinear descent.
9. Discuss Snyder's uses of history in describing the new tribalism.
10. Is the "feminine mystique" an aspect of "sexual politics"? How would you relate the two concepts?
11. Have women a "special role" to play, even under conditions of "equality"?

Essay Topics

1. Are changes in the "role" and "image" of women possible without fundamental social and political change?
2. Analyze the "image" of women in several television serials, and television commercials. Compare your analysis to those presented in the selections in this section.
3. Assess the importance of physiological-psychological versus social-cultural factors in determining the relation of the sexes.
4. Are defenders of "women's rights" necessarily antimale?

Suggestions for Further Reading

PRIMARY

EDWARD ALBEE, *The American Dream* (1961). A playwright's attack on complacency, cruelty, emasculation, and vacuity in the life of one man's family.

EVAN CONNELL, *Mrs. Bridge* (1959). An ironic look at the deadening routines of a suburban matron.

ROBERT GRANT, *Unleavened Bread* (1900). A popular novel of the turn of the century, chronicling the empty success of an unscrupulous young woman.

SINCLAIR LEWIS, *Main Street* (1920). The story of a young wife's battles against the stifling conventions of Midwestern life.

FERDINAND LUNDBERG and MARYNIA FARNHAM, *Modern Woman: The*

Lost Sex (1946). A diagnosis of the evils flowing from the displacement of women from their maternal role; attacks feminists as neurotics seeking to imitate men.

MARY MCCARTHY, *The Company She Keeps* (1942). A novel dealing with a seemingly "liberated" young woman's attempts to define and discover herself.

SECONDARY

ARTHUR W. CALHOUN, *A Social History of the American Family* (3 vols., 1917–20). A comprehensive history of the American family from Puritan times to the 1920s by a sociologist sympathetic to the woman's rights movement of his day.

SIDNEY DITZION, *Marriage, Morals and Sex in America* (1953). A history of ideas about American sexual behavior from the time of Columbus to Kinsey.

EILEEN KRADITOR, *Ideas of the Woman's Suffrage Movement 1890–1920* (1966). An analysis of the ideas of feminists and their opponents, revealing the roots, strengths, and weaknesses of the movement.

EDMUND MORGAN, *The Puritan Family,* rev. ed. (1966). A social history of the Puritan family that suggests interesting contrasts with the present.

WILLIAM O'NEILL, *Divorce in the Progressive Era* (1967). A challenging account, which argues that divorce provided a safety valve necessary to the preservation of marriage and the family in a time of rapid change.

——, *Everyone Was Brave* (1969). A survey of feminism that argues that the movement failed.

ROBERT RIEGEL, *American Feminists* (1963). Historical sketches of leading feminists of the nineteenth century.

ANDREW SINCLAIR, *The Better Half* (1965). A sympathetic history of the feminist movement from Puritan times to the 1920s.

The
Melting
Pot

The American People

ANDREW CARNEGIE (1835–1919), perhaps America's most celebrated immigrant, was born in Dunfermline, Scotland, the son of
a weaver. Moving to Allegheny, Pennsylvania, in 1848, Carnegie
began his rise to fortune by investing in railroads and oil, but in
1873 concentrated in steel. One of the most literate of nineteenth-
century American businessmen, and the richest, he preached socially enlightened capitalism in numerous articles and several
books. In **Triumphant Democracy,** written before a major strike at
his steel plant in Homestead signaled the unrest of the 1890s, he
expressed the optimism with which he viewed every facet of the
national life.

Fortunately for the American people they are essentially British. I
trust they are evermore to remain truly grateful for this crowning
mercy. The assertion of the historian of the Norman Conquest that the
chief difference between the Briton and the American is that the
former has crossed but one ocean, the latter two, is something more
than a mere dictum; it is capable of actual demonstration.

> .   .   .

[The] American of to-day is certainly more than four-fifths British
in his ancestry. The other fifth is principally German; for more than
three millions of these educated, thrifty, and law-abiding citizens were
received between 1840 and 1880, almost as many as from Ireland. From
all countries other than Britain and Germany, the immigration is
scarcely worth taking into account; for during the forty years noted the
total number was little more than a million; France and Sweden and
Norway contributed about three hundred thousand each. But this non-
British blood has even less than its proportional influence in forming the
national character, especially in its political phase; because the language,
literature, laws, and institutions are English. It may, however, safely be
averred that the small mixture of foreign races is a decided advantage to
the new race, for even the British race is improved by a slight cross.

> .   .   .

THE AMERICAN PEOPLE. From Andrew Carnegie, *Triumphant Democracy*
(1886).

The American fortunately has, in the German, French, and other races which have contributed to his make-up, the lacking ingredients which confer upon him a much less savage and more placable nature than that of the original Briton. To this slight strain of foreign blood, and to the more stimulating effects of his brighter climate (which caused an English friend once to remark that temperance is no virtue in the American since he breathes champagne), together with the more active play of forces in a new land under political institutions which make the most of men, we must attribute the faculty observed in him by Matthew Arnold, of thinking straighter and seeing clearer, and also of acting more promptly than the original stock, for the American is nothing if not logical. He gets hold of the underlying principle, and, reasoning from that, he goes ahead to conclusion. He wants everything laid down by square and compass, and in political institutions something that is "fair all around," neither advantages nor disadvantages, but universal equality.

.   .   .

The generally diffused love of music which characterizes America is largely the outcome of the German and Continental contingent for, with all the phlegm of the Briton, there is in the German a part of his nature "touched to fine issues." He loves music, is highly sociable, very domestic at home, and at his best in the bosom of his family. Most valuable of all he is well educated and has excellent habits, is patient, industrious, peaceful, and law-abiding. Another important characteristic of this race is the alacrity with which they adopt American ideas. The vast majority have already done so ere they sailed westward. The German loves his native country, but hates its institutions. Prince Bismarck's yoke is neither light nor easy. Universal military service, the blood-tax of monarchies, is calculated to set the best minds among the bone and sinew to thinking over the political situation, and O, America! how bright and alluring you appear to the down-trodden masses of Europe, with your equal laws, equal privileges and the halo of peace surrounding your brow! What a bribe you offer to the most loyal-minded man to renounce his own country, to share a heritage so fair! The emigrant may not succeed in the new land, or succeed as the Irishman did, who replied to the inquiry of his friend as to whether the Republic was the country for the poor man: "It is, indade; look at me, when I came I hadn't a rag to my back, and now I'm just covered with them." Many new arrivals fail, many would succeed better in their old homes. America is only a favored land for the most efficient; drones have no place in her hive, but in whatever the emigrant may fail, whether in securing wealth, or home, whether he remain poor or lose health, whether his lot be happy or miserable, there remains one great prize which cannot escape him, one blessing so bright, so beneficent, as to shed upon the darkest career the glory of its entrancing rays and compensate for the absence of material good. Upon every exile from home falls the boon of citizenship, equal with the highest. The Republic may not give wealth, or happiness; she has not promised these, it is the freedom to pursue these, not their realization, which the Declaration of Independence claims; but, if she does not make the emigrant happy or prosperous, this she can do and does do for every one, she makes him a citizen, a *man*.

The Frenchman is not a migrating animal. It is much to the credit of America that it has attracted even three hundred thousand of these home-keeping Gauls. Their number is so small that their influence upon the national character cannot be otherwise than trifling. They are the cooks and the epicures of the world and to them America may well be grateful for the standard maintained by the "Delmonicos," the French restaurants of the principal cities. No country has experienced so clearly as this, till recently, that while God sent the victuals, the cooks came from another source. These were not from France, nor under French influence in the former days. Even yet, west of Chicago, the cookery is shameful, but thanks to the Frenchman, the better modes travel westward rapidly. Nature never furnished to any nation so great a variety of food, yet no civilized people ever cooked so badly.

In women's dress, for the few male "dudes" affect English fashions, our Gallic brethren give evidence of their influence in the direction of good taste. The verdict of my English friends invariably is that the American woman dresses so well—so much better than her English sister. We must credit the French citizen with this flattering verdict.

.   .   .

The value to the country of the annual foreign influx . . . is very great indeed. This is more apt to be under than overestimated. During the ten years between 1870 and 1880 the number of immigrants averaged two hundred and eighty thousand per annum. . . . [The] average yearly augmentation of the Republic's wealth from immigrants, who seek its shores to escape the enormous taxation and military laws of monarchical governments, and to obtain under Republican institutions entire political equality, is now more than twice as great as the total product of all the silver and gold mines in the world. Were the owners of every gold and silver mine in the world compelled to send to the Treasury at Washington, at their own expense, every ounce of the precious metals produced, the national wealth would not be enhanced one-half as much as it is from the golden stream which flows into the country every year through immigration.

But the value of these peaceful invaders does not consist solely in their numbers or in the wealth which they bring. To estimate them aright we must take into consideration also the superior character of those who immigrate. . . . The emigrant is the capable, energetic, ambitious, discontented man—the sectary, the refugee, the persecuted, the exile from despotism—who, longing to breathe the air of equality, resolves to tear himself away from the old home with its associations to found in hospitable America a new home under equal and just laws, which insure to him, and what, perhaps, counts with him and his wife for more, insure also to their children the full measure of citizenship, making them free men in a free state, possessed of every right and privilege.

.   .   .

The capacity of America to absorb the population which is flowing into her, as well as the great natural increase of her people, cannot be more strikingly illustrated than by a comparison. Belgium has four hundred and eighty-two inhabitants to the square mile, Britain two hundred and ninety, the United States, exclusive of Alaska, less than fourteen. In the ten years from 1870 to 1880, eleven and a half millions were added to the population of America. Yet these only added three persons to each square mile of territory; and should America continue to double her population every thirty years instead of every twenty-five years as hitherto, seventy years must elapse before she will attain the density of Europe. The population will then reach two hundred and ninety millions. If the density of Britain ever be attained, there will be upwards of a thousand million Americans, for at the present every Briton has two acres and every American forty-four acres of land as his estate.

.   .   .

In view of these startling probabilities, it would seem advisable that the statesmen of the old home, instead of bestowing so much of their attention on the petty States of Europe, should look thoughtfully westward sometimes to the doings of their own kith and kin, who are rapidly building up a power which none can hope to rival.

We must not pass without mention, our fellow-citizens of African descent, who, as we have seen, are equal in number to the entire foreign population—one-eighth of the whole. . . .

Grave apprehensions were entertained that freedom suddenly granted to these poor slaves would be abused. Those best acquainted with their habits, the Southern slave-holders, predicted, as a result of freedom, universal idleness, riot, and dissipation. It was asserted that the negro would not work save under the lash of the overseer. None of these gloomy predictions have been fulfilled—every one of them has been falsified. There is now more cotton grown than ever, and at less cost. Under the reign of freedom the material resources of the South have increased faster than ever before. Indeed, so surprised were most Americans by the result of the last census that it was insisted mistakes had been made: the figures could not be right, and in some districts the enumeration was made a second time, with the result of verifying the former figures. The number of Congressmen to each State is determined every ten years by the population shown by the census. When the census of 1880 was made the general expectation was that the Northern States would increase their proportionate representation; but the Southern States not only held their own, but actually gained. The ninety-eight Southern representatives were increased by thirteen, while the one hundred and ninety-five Northern representatives gained only eighteen—only half the Southern ratio of increase. Even the unexampled growth of the North-western States was insufficient to give the Northern States a proportionately increased legislative power. So much for freedom versus slavery!

.   .   .

The proportion of the colored to the white element steadily grows less and less. In 1790 it was twenty-seven per cent. of the whole, in 1830 it had fallen to eighteen per cent., in 1880 it was only thirteen per cent. While the total white population of the country has risen from ten and a half to forty-three and a half millions in fifty years, the number of the colored population has only risen from two and a quarter to six and a half millions. This steady decrease results from two causes. First, the colored race receives no immigrants, but is restricted wholly to native increase for its growth; and, second, it has been proved that although their birth-rate is greater than that of the whites, it is more than balanced by their higher death-rate. The increase of colored people from 1860 to 1880 was but forty-eight per cent., against sixty-one per cent. increase of the whites.

It is too soon yet to judge whether, with superior knowledge and more provident habits flowing from freedom, this excessive death rate will not be considerably reduced; but the conclusion seems unavoidable that the colored race cannot hold its own numerically against the whites and must fall farther and farther behind. Adaptive as man is, we can scarcely expect the hotter climate of the Southern States, in which the colored people live, to produce as hardy a race as that of the cooler States of the North.

We close, then, showing in the Republic a race essentially British in origin, but fast becoming more and more American in birth, the foreign-born elements sinking into insignificance and destined soon to become of no greater relative magnitude, perhaps, in proportion to the native-born American than the foreign-born residents of Britain are at present to the native born. The American republican can never be other in his blood and nature than a true Briton, a real chip of the old block, a new edition of the original work, and, as is the manner of new editions, revised and improved, and, like his prototype in the thousand and one ways, some of them grotesque in their manifestations, which link the daughter to the mother, who, seen together, impress beholders not so much as two separate and distinct individualities as two members of the one grand family.

The Melting Pot

ISRAEL ZANGWILL (1864–1926), an English Jew, gained a wide audience in America for his books and plays, beginning with **Children of the Ghetto** (1892). An active Jewish nationalist, he bolted from the Zionists over the issue of whether Jews should accept any land other than Palestine in the settlement after the First World War. Although **The Melting Pot** was written by an Englishman, its popularity during the progressive era in America suggests that it captured an important aspect of the American mood after two decades of the so-called "new immigration." The following is a condensed version that appeared in the popular monthly magazine **Current Literature.**

The first act takes us to the living room in the house of the Quixanos in a non-Jewish district of New York. The effect of the furniture is described as a curious blend of shabbiness, Americanism, Jewishness and music. These elements are combined in the figure of Mendel Quixano, master of the household, in his black skull cap, red carpet slippers and seedy velvet jacket. He is an elderly music master with a fine Jewish face pathetically furrowed by misfortunes, and a short grizzled beard. He is not an orthodox Jew, but his hopes and ideals are anchored in the past of his race. There is a tragic element in the character of Frau Quixano, his mother. She is an orthodox Jewess, unable to understand the New World or its language. Mendel's nephew, David Quixano, the hero of Zangwill's play, is a young Jewish musician with unabounded faith in this country that has hospitably received him coming, as it were, from the blood-stained pavements of Kishineff. Vera Revendal, daughter of a Russian official, who is devoted to settlement work in New York, having been disowned by her father for her anti-bureaucratic opinions,

THE MELTING POT.   From *Current Literature*, 47 (August 1909).

appears on the scene in order to ask David for his cooperation in a settlement concert. When incidentally she learns of his being a Jew, she is taken aback. "A Jew," she exclaims, "this wonderful boy a Jew! But then so was David the shepherd youth with his harp and psalms, the sweetest singer in Israel." She hesitates, but finally makes her request. David gladly accepts, waiving the possibility of a fee. "A fee! I'd pay a fee to see those happy immigrants you gather together. I love going to Ellis Island," he goes on to explain, "to watch the ships coming in from Europe, and to think that all those weary sea-tossed wanderers are feeling what *I* felt when America first stretched out her mother hand to *me!*"

VERA   (*Softly.*) Were you very happy?
DAVID   It was Heaven. You must remember that all my life I had heard of America. Everybody in our town had friends there or was going there or got money-orders from there. The earliest game I played at was selling off my toy furniture and setting up in America. All my life America was waiting, beckoning, shining, the place where God would wipe away tears from off all faces.
MENDEL (*Rises, as in terror.*) Now, now, David, don't get excited.
DAVID   To think that the same great torch of liberty which threw its light across all the broad seas and lands into my little garret in Russia is shining also for all those other weeping millions of Europe, shining wherever men hunger and are oppressed!
MENDEL (*Soothingly.*) Yes, yes, David. (*Lays hand on his shoulder.*) Now sit down and calm yourself.
DAVID   (*Unheeding.*) Shining over the starving villages of Italy and Ireland, over the swarming stony cities of Poland and Galicia, over the ruined farms of Roumania, over the shambles of Russia!
MENDEL (*Pleadingly.*) David!
DAVID   Oh, Miss Revendal, when I look at our statue of Liberty I seem to hear the voice of America crying: "Come unto me all ye that labor and are heavy laden and I will give you rest."
MENDEL Don't talk any more. You know it is bad for you.
DAVID   But Miss Revendal asked, and I want to explain to her what America means to me.
MENDEL You can explain it in your American Symphony.
VERA   (*Rising eagerly, to David.*) You compose?
DAVID   Oh, uncle, why did you talk of my music? It is so thin and tinkling. When I am writing my American Symphony it seems like thunder crashing through a forest full of bird songs. But next day, oh, next day! (*Laughs dolefully.*)
VERA   So your music finds inspiration in America?

DAVID   Yes, in the seething of the Crucible.

VERA   The Crucible? I don't understand!

DAVID   Not understand! You, the spirit of the Settlement! Not understand that America is God's crucible where all the races of Europe are rising and re-forming! Here you stand, good folk, think I, when I see them at Ellis Island, here you stand in your fifty groups with your fifty languages and histories and your fifty hatreds and rivalries. But you won't be long like that, brothers, for these are the fires of God you've come to, these are the fires of God! A fig for your feuds and vendettas! German and Frenchman, Irishman and Englishman, Jews and Russians—into the Melting Pot with you all! God is making the American.

MENDEL   I should have thought the American was made already, eighty millions of him.

DAVID   Eighty millions over a continent! Why that cockle-shell of a Britain holds forty millions! No, uncle, the real American has not yet arrived. He is only in the Crucible, I tell you—he will be the fusion of all races, the coming superman. Ah, what a glorious finale for my symphony, if I can only write it.

VERA   But you have written some of it already. May I not see it?

DAVID   (*Relapsing to boyish shyness.*) Please, please, don't ask me. (*Moves over to his desk and nervously shuts it down and turns keys of drawers as tho protecting his MSS.*)

VERA   Won't you give a bit of it at our concert?

DAVID   Oh, it needs an orchestra.

VERA   But you at the violin and I at the piano—

MENDEL   You didn't tell me you played, Miss Revendal!

VERA   I told you less commonplace things.

DAVID   Miss Revendal plays quite like a professional.

VERA   (*Smiling.*) I don't feel so complimented as you expect. You see I did have a professional training. I went to Petersburg—

DAVID   (*Dazed.*) To Petersburg?

VERA   (*Smiling.*) Naturally. To the conservatoire. There wasn't much music to be had at Kishineff.

DAVID   Kishineff! (*He begins to tremble.*)

VERA   (*Still smiling.*) My birth place.

MENDEL   Calm yourself, David.

DAVID   Yes, yes! So you are a Russian! (*Shudders violently, staggers.*)

VERA   (*Alarmed.*) You are ill!

DAVID   It is nothing, I—not much music at Kishineff! No, only the Death March! Mother! Father! Ah, cowards, murderers! And you! (*Shakes fist at air.*) You looking on with your cold butcher's face! Oh, God! Oh, God! (*Bursts into hysterical sobs and runs shamefacedly out.*)

VERA (*Wildly.*) What have I said? What have I done?

MENDEL Oh, I was afraid of this, I was afraid of this.

FRAU QUIXANO (*Who has fallen asleep over her book, wakes as if with a sense of horror and gazes dazedly around, adding to the thrill of the moment.*) David! Wo ist David? Es scheint mir—

MENDEL (*Pressing her back to her slumbers.*) Du träumst, Mutter! Schlaf! (*She sinks back to sleep.*)

VERA (*In hoarse whisper.*) His father and mother were massacred?

MENDEL (*In same tense tone.*) Before his eyes. Father, mother, sister, down to the youngest babe, whose skull was battered in by a ruffian's heel.

VERA How did he escape?

MENDEL He was shot in the shoulder and fell unconscious. As he wasn't a girl, the mob left him for dead and hurried to fresh sport.

VERA Terrible! Terrible! (*Almost in tears.*)

MENDEL (*Shrugging shoulders hopelessly.*) It is only Jewish history! David belongs to the species of pogrom orphans. They arrive by almost every ship.

VERA Poor boy! Poor boy! And he looked so happy!

MENDEL So he is most of the time. A sunbeam took human shape when he was born. But naturally that dreadful scene left a scar on his brain, as the bullet left a scar on his shoulder and he is always liable to see red when Kishineff is mentioned.

VERA I will never mention my miserable birthplace to him again.

MENDEL But you see every few months the newspapers tell us of another *pogrom* and then he screams out against what he calls that butcher's face so that I tremble for his reason. I tremble even when I see him writing that crazy music about America, for it only means he is brooding over the difference between America and Russia.

VERA But perhaps all the terrible memory will pass peacefully away in his music.

MENDEL There will always be the scar on his shoulder to remind him. Whenever the wound twinges it brings up these terrible faces and visions.

VERA And it's on his right shoulder?

MENDEL No, on his left. For a violinist that is even worse.

VERA Ah, of course, the weight and the fingering. (*Half unconsciously places and fingers an imaginary violin.*)

MENDEL That is why I·fear so for his future. He will never be strong enough for the feats of bravura that the public demands.

VERA The wild beasts! I feel more ashamed of my country than ever. But there's his symphony.

MENDEL And who will look at that amateurish stuff? He knows so little of harmony and counterpoint. He breaks all the rules. I've

tried to give him a few pointers, but he ought to have gone to
Germany.

VERA   Perhaps it's not too late.

MENDEL   (*Passionately.*) Ah, if you and your friends could help him!

VERA   My father loves music. Perhaps he—but no! He lives in Kishineff. But I will think. There are people here. I will write to you.

MENDEL   (*Fervently.*) Thank you! Thank you!

The second act takes place on the day of Purim, the Jewish
Carnival. Old Dame Quixano has bought false noses and other
paraphernalia of fun sanctified by tradition. David is playing a
merry tune on the fiddle, when Vera appears to redeem her
promise, accompanied by Quincy Davenport, Jr., an "unemployed millionaire," and his private orchestra conductor, the celebrated Herr Pappelmeister. Davenport, altho married, is actuated
by his unreciprocated love for Vera to take an interest in the
young Jewish musician. Pappelmeister examines the score of the
symphony critically and declares it to be a masterpiece. Davenport at once proposes to produce it at one of his private concerts,
and the shy young David is summoned from the kitchen, where
he had hidden himself, to receive the tidings. When the identity
of Davenport is divulged to him, the lad overcomes his bashful-
ness and turns to cross-examine his prospective protector.

DAVID   Are all the stories the papers tell about you true?

QUINCY   All the stories? That's a tall order. Ha! Ha! Ha!

DAVID   Well, anyhow, is it true that—?

VERA   Mr. Quixano! What are you driving at?

QUINCY   Oh, it's rather fun to hear what the masses read about me.
Fire ahead. Is what true?

DAVID   That you were married in a balloon?

QUINCY   Ha! Ha! Ha! That's true enough. Marriage in high life, they
said, didn't they? Ha! Ha! Ha!

DAVID   And is it true you live in America only two months in the year
and then only to entertain Europeans who wander to these wild
parts?

QUINCY   Lucky for you, young man. You'll have an Italian prince
and a British Duke to hear your scribblings.

DAVID   And the palace where they will hear my scribblings, it is true
that—?

VERA   (*Who has been on pins and needles.*) Mr. Quixano, what possible—

DAVID   (*Entreatingly holds up hand.*) Miss Revendal! (*To Quincy*

Davenport.) Is this palace the same whose grounds were turned into Venetian canals where the guests ate in gondolas?

QUINCY   Ah, Miss Revendal, what a pity you refused that invitation! It was a fairy scene of twinkling lights and delicious darkness. Each couple had their own gondola to sup in, and their own side-canal to slip down.

DAVID   And the same night women and children died of hunger in New York!

QUINCY   Eh?

DAVID   And these are the sort of people you would invite to hear my symphony, these gondola-guzzlers!

VERA   Mr. Quixano!

DAVID   These magnificent animals who went into the gondolas two by two, to feed and flirt!

QUINCY   Sir!

DAVID   I should be a new freak for you, for a new freak evening—I and my dreams and my music!

QUINCY   You low-down, ungrateful—

DAVID   Not for you and such as you have I sat here writing and dreaming, not for you who are killing my America!

QUINCY   Your America? you Jew-immigrant!

DAVID   Yes, Jew-immigrant! But a Jew who knows that your Pilgrim Fathers came straight out of his Old Testament and that our Jew-immigrants are prouder of the glory of this great Commonwealth than some of you sons of the soil. Look around at our Jew-immigrants, how they have climbed from the pack or the push-cart to equality with you idle inheritors of easy gold! How they stand before America, white men of Wall Street, incorruptible Judges, honest politicians, scrupulous traders, princely philanthropists, scholars, thinkers, artists, a growing army of grateful patriots anxious to repay America's hospitality by making her still greater among the nations! It is you, freak fashionables, who are undoing the work of Washington and Lincoln, vulgarizing your high heritage and turning the last and noblest hope of humanity into a caricature.

QUINCY   You never told me your Jew-scribbler was a socialist!

DAVID   I am nothing but a simple artist, but I come from Europe, one of her victims, and I know that she is a failure; that her palaces and peerages are outworn toys of the human spirit, and that the only hope of mankind lies in a new world. And here, in the land of to-morrow, you are bringing back all the follies and fetishes of yesterday, trying to bring back Europe, Europe with her comic opera coronets and her worm-eaten stage decorations and her pomp and chivalry built on a morass of crime and misery. But you shall not kill my dream! There shall come a fire round the Crucible that will melt you and your breed like wax in a blowpipe.

PAPPELMEISTER   (*Who has remained imperturbable throughout all this dialog springs up and waves his umbrella hysterically.*) Hoch, Quixano! Hoch! Hoch! Es lebe Quixano! Hoch!

QUINCY   Poppy! You're dismissed!

PAPPELMEISTER   (*Snaps fingers at Quincy. Goes to David with out-stretched hand.*) Danks. (*They grip hands. Pappelmeister turns to Quincy Davenport.*) Comic operas! Ouf!

QUINCY   (*Goes to street door at white heat.*)

Vera, instead of reproaching the lad, expresses her admiration for him. In a sudden wave of tenderness, he passionately takes her hand and she suffers him to embrace her.

DAVID   You cannot care for me. You so far above me!

VERA   Above you, you simple boy? Your genius lifts you to the stars.

DAVID   No, no, it is you who lift me.

VERA   And to think that I was brought up to despise your race.

DAVID   (*Sadly.*) Yes, all Russians are.

VERA   But we of the nobility in particular.

DAVID   (*Amazed, half releasing her.*) You are noble?

VERA   My father is Baron Revendal, but I have long since carved out a life of my own.

DAVID   Then he will not separate us?

VERA   No. (*Re-embraces him.*) Nothing can separate us. (*A knock at the street door. They separate. Sound of an automobile clattering off.*)

DAVID   It is my uncle coming back.

VERA   (*In low tense tones.*) Then I shall slip out. I could not bear a third. I will write. (*Goes to door.*)

DAVID   Yes, yes, Vera. (*Follows her to door. He opens it and she slips out.*)

MENDEL   (*Half seen, expostulating.*) You, too, Miss Revendal? (*Enters.*) Oh, David, you have driven away all your friends.

DAVID   Not all, uncle. (*Throws his arms boyishly round his uncle.*) I am so happy.

MENDEL   Happy?

DAVID   She loves me. Vera loves me.

MENDEL   Vera?

DAVID   Miss Revendal.

MENDEL   Miss Revendal? Have you lost your wits?

DAVID   I don't wonder you're amazed. Do you think I wasn't? It is as if an angel should stoop down.

MENDEL (*Hoarsely.*) This is true? This is not some stupid Purim joke?

DAVID True and sacred as the sunrise.

MENDEL But you are a Jew!

DAVID Yes, and just think! She was brought up to despise Jews. Her father was a Russian Baron.

MENDEL If she was the daughter of fifty Barons you cannot marry her.

DAVID Then your hankering after the synagog was serious after all?

MENDEL It is not so much the synagog; it is the call of our blood through immemorial generations.

DAVID You say that! You who have come to the heart of the Crucible, where the roaring fires of God are fusing our race with all the others.

MENDEL Not our race, not your race and mine.

DAVID What immunity has our race? The pride and the prejudice, the dreams and the sacrifices, the traditions and the superstitions, the fasts and the feasts, things noble and things sordid, they must all into the Crucible.

MENDEL The Jew has been tried in a thousand fires and only tempered and annealed.

DAVID Fires of hate, not fires of love. That is what melts.

MENDEL So I see.

DAVID Your sneer is false. The love that melted me was not Vera's. It was the love America showed me the day she gathered me to her breast.

MENDEL Many countries have gathered us. Holland took us when we were driven from Spain, but we did not become Dutchmen. Turkey took us when Germany oppressed us, but we have not become Turks.

DAVID Those countries were not in the making. They were old civilizations stamped with the seal of creed. Here in this new secular Republic we must look forward.

MENDEL We must look backwards, too.

DAVID To what? To Kishineff. To that Butcher's face directing the slaughter? To those—?

MENDEL Hush! Calm yourself.

DAVID Yes, I will calm myself, but how else shall I calm myself save by forgetting all that nightmare of religions and races, save by holding out my hands with prayer and music towards the Republic of Man and the Kingdom of God? The Past I cannot mend.

MENDEL You are mad! Your dreams are mad. The Jew is hated here as everywhere. You are false to your race.

DAVID I keep faith with America. I have faith America will keep faith with us.

MENDEL Go! You have cast off the God of our fathers!

DAVID And the God of our children? Does He demand no service? (*Quieter.*) But I must go away. You were right. I do need a wider world. (*Expands his lungs.*)

MENDEL Go, then. I'll hide the truth. She must never suspect, lest she mourn you as dead.

FRAU QUIXANO (*Outside in kitchen.*) Ha! Ha! Ha! Ha! Ha! (*Both men turn toward the kitchen and listen.*)

MENDEL (*Bitterly.*) A merry Purim.

FRAU QUIXANO (*Hilariously.*) *Nu spiel noch!*

MENDEL (*Putting out a protesting hand.*) No, no, David. I couldn't bear it.

DAVID But I must! You said she mustn't suspect, and it may be the last time I shall ever play for her. (*Changes to mock merry laugh.*) *Gewiss, Mumme!* (*Starts a merry old jig.*)

FRAU QUIXANO (*Childishly pleased.*) He! He! He! (*Claps on a false nose from her pocket.*)

DAVID (*Half between laughter and tears.*) Ha! Ha! Ha! Ha!

MENDEL (*Shocked.*) *Mutter!*

FRAU QUIXANO *Und du auch!* (*Claps another false nose on Mendel, laughing merrily at the effect.*)

Davenport, still bent on marrying Vera after divorcing his wife, informs her father of the impending marriage of his daughter with the Jewish fiddler. The Baron, a Russian of the most orthodox type and a convinced anti-semite, hastens to New York to rejoin his rebellious child, to whom his heart still goes out in affection. The Baron is a great music lover, and Vera, in an intensely dramatic interview, reminds him that Rubinstein was a Jew. He goes out to quiet his commotion and promises to meet David on his return. It appears that David has left the Mendel home and is living in a garret not far from Vera's abode. She quickly summons him and tells him that her father has weakened in his opposition. "Dear little father," she exclaims, "if only he were not so narrow about Holy Russia!"

DAVID If only my folks were not so narrow about Holy Judea! But the ideals of the fathers shall not be foisted on the children. Each generation must live and die for its own dream.

VERA Yes, David, yes. You are the prophet of the living present. I am so happy. Kiss me. (*He kisses her gently.*) It is all too wonderful. You are happy, too?

DAVID I cannot realize that all our troubles have melted away.

VERA You, David, who always see everything in such rosy colors?

Now that the whole horizon is one great splendid rose you almost seem as if gazing out towards a blackness.

DAVID   We Jews are cheerful in gloom, mistrustful in joy. It is our tragic history.

VERA   But you have come to end the tragic history, to throw off the coils of the centuries.

DAVID   Yes, yes, Vera. You bring back my sunnier self. I must be a pioneer on the lost road of happiness. Today shall be all joy, all lyric ecstasy. (*Takes up his violin.*) Yes, I will make my old fiddle-strings burst with joy! (*At this moment the face of Baron Revendal appears at the door.*)

DAVID   (*Hoarsely.*) The face! The face!

VERA   David, my dearest!

DAVID   (*His eyes closed.*) Don't be anxious. I shall be better soon. I oughtn't to have talked about it, the hallucination has never been so complete!

VERA   Don't speak. Rest against Vera's heart, till it has passed away. (*The Baron comes dazedly forward, half with a shocked sense of Vera's impropriety, half to relieve her of her burden. She motions him back.*) This is the work of your Holy Russia.

BARON   (*Harshly.*) What is the matter with him? (*David's violin falls from his grasp. Only the bow remains in his hand.*)

DAVID   The voice! (*He opens his eyes, stare frenziedly at the Baron, then struggles out of Vera's arms.*)

VERA   (*Trying to hold him.*) Dearest!

DAVID   Let me go. (*He moves like a sleep-walker towards the paralyzed Baron, puts out his left hand and testingly touches his face.*)

BARON   (*Shuddering back.*) Hands off!

DAVID   (*Shrieking.*) A-a-a-h! It is flesh and blood. No, it is stone, the man of stone! Monster! (*Raises the bow frenziedly.*)

BARON   (*Whipping out his pistol.*) Back, dog!

DAVID   Ha! You want my life, too! Is the cry not yet loud enough?

BARON   The cry?

DAVID   (*Mystically.*) Can you not hear it? The voice of the blood of my brothers crying out against you from the ground? Oh, how can you bear not to turn that pistol against yourself and execute upon yourself the justice which Russia denies you?

BARON   Tush! (*Pockets the pistol a little shamefacedly.*)

VERA   Justice on himself? For what?

DAVID   For crimes beyond human penalty, for obscenities beyond human utterance, for—

VERA   You are raving.

DAVID   Would to heaven I were.

VERA   But this is my father.

DAVID   Your father! God! (*Staggers back, drops bow.*)

BARON   Come, Vera, I told you—

VERA   (*Frenziedly, shrinking back.*) Don't touch me!

BARON   (*Starting back in amaze.*) Vera!

VERA   (*Hoarsely.*) Say it's not true.

BARON   What is not true?

VERA   What David said. It was the mob that massacred. You had no hand in it?

BARON   (*Sullenly.*) I was there with my soldiers.

DAVID   (*Pale, leaning against a chair, hisses.*) And you looked on with that cold face of hate while my mother—

BARON   (*Sullenly.*) I could not see everything.

DAVID   Now and again you ordered your soldiers to fire.

VERA   (*In joyous relief.*) Ah, he did check the mob; he did tell his soldiers to fire!

DAVID   At any Jew who tried to defend himself.

VERA   God! (*Falls on the sofa, buries her head on the cushion, moans.*)

BARON   It was the people avenging itself, Vera. The people rose like a flood. It had centuries of spoliation to wipe out. The voice of the people is the voice of God.

VERA   (*Moaning.*) But you could have stopped them!

BARON   I had no orders to defend the foes of Christ and the Czar. The people—

VERA   (*Moaning.*) But you could have stopped them!

BARON   Who can stop a flood? I did my duty. A soldier's duty is not so pretty as a musician's.

VERA   (*Moaning.*) But you could have stopped them!

BARON   Silence! You talk like an ignorant girl, blinded by passion. The pogrom is a holy crusade. Are we Russians the first people to crush down the Jew? No, from the dawn of history the nations have had to stamp upon him, the Egyptians, the Assyrians, the Persians, the Babylonians, the Greeks, the Romans—

DAVID   Yes, it is true. Even Christianity did not invent hatred. But not till Holy Church arose were we burnt at the stake, and not till Holy Russia arose were our babes torn limb from limb. Oh, it is not much! Delivered from Egypt four thousand years ago to be slaves to the Russian Pharaoh today. (*Falls as if kneeling on a chair, leans his head on the rail*) O God, shall we always be broken on the wheel of history? How long, O Lord, how long?

BARON   (*Savagely.*) Till you are all stamped out, ground into your dirt. (*Tenderly.*) Look up, little Vera! You saw how your little father loves you; how he was ready to hold out his hand and how

this cur tried to bite it. Be calm; tell him a daughter of Russia cannot mate with dirt.

VERA   (*Rising.*) Father, I will be calm. I will speak without passion
or blindness. I will tell David the truth. I was never absolutely
sure of my love for him. Perhaps that was why I doubted his love
for me. Often after our enchanted moments there would come a
nameless uneasiness, some vague instinct, relic of the long centuries
of Jew-loathing, some strange shrinking from his Christless creed.

BARON   (*Exultantly.*) She is a Revendal.

VERA   But now— (*Turns to David*) now, David. I come to you and
say in the words of Ruth, thy people shall be my people and thy
God my God! (*Stretches out her hands to David.*)

BARON   You shameless— (*His pistol rises in his hand almost of itself,
then lowers, as he perceives that David remains impassive.*)

VERA   (*With agonized cry.*) David!

DAVID   (*In low icy tone.*) You cannot come to me. There is a river
of blood between us.

VERA   Were it seven seas our love must cross them.

DAVID   Easy words to you. You never saw that red flood bearing the
mangled breasts of women and the spattered brains of babes and
sucklings. Oh! (*Covers eyes with hands.*) It was your Easter and
the air was full of holy bells and the streets of holy processions,
priests in black and girls in white, and waving palms and crucifixes,
and everybody exchanging Easter eggs and kissing one another three
times on the mouth in token of peace and good-will, and even the
Jew-boy felt the spirit of love brooding over the earth, tho he did
not then know that this Christ, whom holy chants proclaimed re-
risen, was born in the form of a brother Jew. And what added to
the peace and holy joy was that our own Passover was shining before us. My mother had already made the raisin wine and my greedy
little brother Solomon had sipped it on the sly that very morning.
We were all at home, all except my father. He was away in a little
synagog at which he was cantor. I was playing my cracked little
fiddle. Little Miriam was making her doll dance to it. Ah! that
decrepit old china doll! We were all laughing to see it caper to my
music. Suddenly my father flies in through the door desperately,
clasping to his breast the Holy Scroll. We cry out to him to explain,
and then we see that in that beloved mouth of song there is no longer
a tongue! He tries to bar the door. The mob breaks in. We dash out
through the back into the street. There are the soldiers and the
Face!

VERA   (*Who has listened tensely, gives a low spasmodic sob.*) O God!
(*Baron turns away slowly.*)

DAVID   When I came to myself I saw lying beside me a strange shape-less something. By the crimson doll in what seemed a hand I knew it must be little Miriam. The doll was a dream of beauty and per-fection beside all that remained of my sister, of my mother, of greedy little Solomon! Oh, you Christians can only see that rosy splendor on the horizon of happiness. And the Jew didn't see rosily enough for you. Ha! Ha! Ha! The Jew who gropes in one great crimson mist.

VERA   Hush, David! Your laughter hurts more than tears. Let Vera comfort you. (*Kneels by his chair, tries to put arms round him.*)

DAVID   (*Shuddering.*) Take them away! Don't you feel the cold dead pushing between us?

VERA   (*Unfalteringly moving his face towards her lips.*) Kiss me!

DAVID   I should feel the blood on my lips.

VERA   My love shall wipe it out.

DAVID   (*Unwinds her clinging arms and springs up.*) Love! Christian love! (*Laughs frenziedly.*) Ha! Ha! Ha! Ha! For this I gave up my people, darkened the home that sheltered me. There was always a still voice at my heart calling me back, but I heeded nothing, only the voice of the butcher's daughter! (*Brokenly.*) Let me go home, let me go home! (*Begins tottering towards the door with dazed pauses, but never looking at Vera. The door closes behind him.*)

Act four transpires on the fourth of July. David has joined Pappelmeister's new orchestra and his symphony is being per-formed for the first time before the immigrants of all nations banded together under the guidance of the settlement workers. He scores a musical triumph, but his heart is dead to the praise showered upon him. Even when Vera adds her voice to the gen-eral chorus he is not consoled. "The irony in all the congratula-tions," he bitterly exclaims. "How can I ever endure them, when I know what a terrible failure I have made."

VERA   Failure! You have produced something real and new.

DAVID   Every bar of my music cried, "Failure! Failure! Failure!"

VERA   (*Vehemently, coming still nearer.*) Oh no! no! I watched the faces, those faces of toil and sorrow, those faces from many lands. In some strange beautiful way the inner meaning of your music stole into all those simple souls.

DAVID   (*Springing up.*) And *my* soul! What of *my* soul? False to its own mission, its own dream. That is what I mean by failure, Vera. I preached of God's Crucible, this great new continent that could melt up all race differences and vendettas, and God tried me with his supremest test. He gave me a heritage from the Old World, hate and vengeance and blood, and said: "Cast it all into my Crucible." And I said: "Even thy Crucible cannot melt this hate, cannot drink up this blood." And so I sat crooning over the dead past, the prophet of the God of our children. Oh, how my music mocked me! And you, so fearless, so high above fate, how you must despise me!

VERA I? Ah no!

DAVID You must. You do. Your words still sting. Were it seven seas between us, you said, our love must cross them. And I, I who have prated of seven seas!

VERA Not seas of blood! (*Shudders and covers her eyes.*)

DAVID There lies my failure, to have brought it to your eyes, instead of blotting it from my own.

VERA No man could have blotted it out.

DAVID Yes, by faith in the Crucible. From the blood of battlefields spring daisies and buttercups. But in the supreme moment my faith was found wanting. You came to me, and I thrust you away.

VERA I ought not to have come to you. We must not meet again.

DAVID Ah, you cannot forgive me!

VERA Forgive? It is I that should go down on my knees for my father's sin. (*She is half sinking to her knees. He stops her by a gesture and a cry.*)

DAVID No! The sins of the fathers shall not be visited on the children.

VERA My brain follows you, but not my heart. It is heavy with the sense of unpaid debts, debts that can only cry for forgiveness.

DAVID You owe me nothing.

VERA But my father, my people, my country— (*Breaks down, recovers herself.*) My only consolation is, you need nothing.

DAVID (*Dazed.*) I need nothing?

VERA Nothing but your music, your dreams.

DAVID And your love. Do I not need that?

VERA (*Shaking her head sadly.*) No.

DAVID Your love for me is dead?

VERA No, it is my love for myself that is dead.

DAVID You torture me. What do you mean?

VERA I used to be jealous of your music, your prophetic visions. I wanted to come first, before them all! Now, dear David, I only pray that they may fill your life to the brim.

DAVID But they cannot.

VERA They will. Have faith in yourself, in your mission! Good-by. (*The music from below surges up softly, sad and sweet.*)

DAVID (*Dazed.*) You love me and you leave me?

VERA What else can I do? Shall the shadow of Kishineff hang over all your years to come? Shall I kiss you and leave blood upon your lips, cling to you and be pushed away by all those cold dead hands?

DAVID   (*Taking her hands with a great cry.*) Yes, cling to me despite them all, cling to me till all these ghosts are exorcised, cling to me till our love triumphs over death. Kiss me, kiss me now.

VERA   (*Resisting, drawing back.*) I dare not! It will make you remember.

DAVID   It will make me forget. Kiss me. (*A slight pause of hesitation, filled up by the Cathedral music from Faust coming softly from below.*)

VERA   (*Slowly.*) I will kiss you as we Russians kiss at Easter, the three kisses of peace. (*Kisses him three times on the mouth as in ritual solemnity.*)

DAVID   (*Very calmly.*) Easter was the date of the massacre. See! I am at peace.

VERA   God grant it endure! (*They stand quietly hand in hand.*) How beautiful the sunset is after the storm! (*David turns. The sunset, which has begun to grow beautiful just after Vera's entrance, has now reached its most magnificent moment. Below there are narrow lines of saffron and gold, and above the sky is one glory of burning flame.*)

DAVID   (*Prophetically exalted by the spectacle.*) It is the fires of God round His Crucible. (*Drops her hand and points downwards.*) There she lies, the great melting-pot. Listen! Can't you hear the roaring and the bubbling? There gapes her mouth (*Points East.*), the harbor where a thousand mammoth feeders come from the ends of the world to pour in their human freight. Ah, what a stirring and seething! Celt and Latin, Slav and Teuton, Greek and Syrian, black and yellow.

VERA   (*Softly, nestling to him.*) Jews and Gentile—

DAVID   Yes, East and West and North and South, the palm and the pine, the pole and the equator, the Crescent and the Cross, how the great Alchemist melts and fuses them with His purging flame! (*Raises his hands in benediction over the shining city.*) Ah, all ye unborn millions, fated to fill this giant continent, the God of our children give you peace! (*An instant's solemn pause. Then from below comes up the sound of voices and instruments joining in "My Country, 'Tis of Thee"; the sunset sinks to a more restful golden glory, the curtain falls slowly.*)

Trans-National America

RANDOLPH S. BOURNE (1886–1918), born in suburban Bloomfield, New Jersey, was, in the parlance of his time, an "Anglo-Saxon." Physically deformed, he was further handicapped by a reversal in family fortune that kept him from attending college until his twenty-third year. His career, following his graduation from Columbia in 1913, was as brief as it was brilliant. An apostle of "Youth," the subject of his first published essay, he contributed frequently to such magazines as the **New Republic** and the **Seven Arts.** In **The Gary Schools** (1916) and **Education and Living** (1917), he championed the educational principles of John Dewey, but the event of the First World War caused him to repudiate many of Dewey's views. Deepening in radicalism, growing in power, Bourne opposed the war, hawkish intellectuals, and all excesses of "Americanism." He fell victim to influenza in 1918.

No reverberatory effect of the great war has caused American public opinion more solicitude than the failure of the "melting-pot." The discovery of diverse nationalistic feelings among our great alien population has come to most people as an intense shock. It has brought out the unpleasant inconsistencies of our traditional beliefs. We have had to watch hard-hearted old Brahmins virtuously indignant at the spectacle of the immigrant refusing to be melted, while they jeer at patriots like Mary Antin who write about "our forefathers." We have had to listen to publicists who express themselves as stunned by the evidence of vigorous nationalistic and cultural movements in this country among Germans, Scandinavians, Bohemians, and Poles, while in the same breath they insist that the alien shall be forcibly assimilated to that Anglo-Saxon tradition which they unquestioningly label "American."

As the unpleasant truth has come upon us that assimilation in this country was proceeding on lines very different from those we had marked out for it, we found ourselves inclined to blame those who were thwarting our prophecies. The truth became culpable. We blamed the war, we blamed the Germans. And then we discovered with a moral shock that these movements had been making great headway

TRANS-NATIONAL AMERICA. From *Atlantic Monthly*, 118 (1916).

before the war even began. We found that the tendency, reprehensible and paradoxical as it might be, has been for the national clusters of immigrants, as they became more and more firmly established and more and more prosperous, to cultivate more and more assiduously the literatures and cultural traditions of their homelands. Assimilation, in other words, instead of washing out the memories of Europe, made them more and more intensely real. Just as these clusters became more and more objectively American, did they become more and more German or Scandinavian or Bohemian or Polish.

To face the fact that our aliens are already strong enough to take a share in the direction of their own destiny, and that the strong cultural movements represented by the foreign press, schools, and colonies are a challenge to our facile attempts, is not, however, to admit the failure of Americanization. It is not to fear the failure of democracy. It is rather to urge us to an investigation of what Americanism may rightly mean. It is to ask ourselves whether our ideal has been broad or narrow—whether perhaps the time has not come to assert a higher ideal than the "melting-pot." Surely we cannot be certain of our spiritual democracy when, claiming to melt the nations within us to a comprehension of our free and democratic institutions, we fly into panic at the first sign of their own will and tendency. We act as if we wanted Americanization to take place only on our own terms, and not by the consent of the governed. All our elaborate machinery of settlement and school and union, of social and political naturalization, however, will move with friction just in so far as it neglects to take into account this strong and virile insistence that America shall be what the immigrant will have a hand in making it, and not what a ruling class, descendant of those British stocks which were the first permanent immigrants, decide that America shall be made. This is the condition which confronts us, and which demands a clear and general readjustment of our attitude and our ideal.

.   .   .

We are all foreign-born or the descendants of foreign-born, and if distinctions are to be made between us they should rightly be on some other ground than indigenousness. The early colonists came over with motives no less colonial than the later. They did not come to be assimilated in an American melting-pot. They did not come to adopt the culture of the American Indian. They had not the smallest intention of "giving themselves without reservation" to the new country. They came to get freedom to live as they wanted to. They came to escape from the stifling air and chaos of the old world; they came to make their fortune in a new land. They invented no new social framework. Rather they brought over bodily the old ways to which they had been accustomed. Tightly concentrated on a hostile frontier, they were conservative beyond belief. Their pioneer daring was reserved for the objective conquest of material resources. In their folkways, in their social and political institutions, they were, like every colonial people, slavishly imitative of the mother-country. So that, in spite of the "Revolution," our whole legal and political system remained more English than the English, petrified and unchanging, while in England law developed to meet the needs of the changing times.

It is just this English-American conservatism that has been our chief obstacle to social advance. We have needed the new peoples— the order of the German and Scandinavian, the turbulence of the Slav and Hun—to save us from our own stagnation. I do not mean that the illiterate Slav is now the equal of the New Englander of pure descent. He is raw material to be educated, not into a New Englander, but into a socialized American along such lines as those thirty nationalities are being educated in the amazing schools of Gary. I do not believe that this process is to be one of decades of evolution. The spectacle of Japan's sudden jump from mediævalism to post-modernism should have destroyed that superstition. We are not dealing with individuals who are to "evolve." We are dealing with their children, who, with that education we are about to have, will start level with all of us. Let us cease to think of ideals like democracy as magical qualities inherent in certain peoples. Let us speak, not of inferior races, but of inferior civilizations. We are all to educate and to be educated. These peoples in America are in a common enterprise. It is not what we are now that concerns us, but what this plastic next generation may become in the light of a new cosmopolitan ideal.

.   .   .

The non-English American can scarcely be blamed if he sometimes thinks of the Anglo-Saxon predominance in America as little more than a predominance of priority. The Anglo-Saxon was merely the first immigrant, the first to found a colony. He has never really ceased to be the descendant of immigrants, nor has he ever succeeded in transforming that colony into a real nation, with a tenacious, richly woven fabric of native culture. Colonials from the other nations have come and settled down beside him. They found no definite native culture which should startle them out of their colonialism, and consequently they looked back to their mother-country, as the earlier Anglo-Saxon immigrant was looking back to his. What has been offered the newcomer has been the chance to learn English, to become a citizen, to salute the flag. And those elements of our ruling classes who are responsible for the public schools, the settlements, all the organizations for amelioration in the cities, have every reason to be proud of the care and labor which they have devoted to absorbing the immigrant. His opportunities the immigrant has taken to gladly, with almost a pathetic eagerness to make his way in the new land without friction or disturbance. The common language has made not only for the necessary communication, but for all the amenities of life.

If freedom means the right to do pretty much as one pleases, so long as one does not interfere with others, the immigrant has found freedom, and the ruling element has been singularly liberal in its treatment of the invading hordes. But if freedom means a democratic coöperation in determining the ideals and purposes and industrial and social institutions of a country, then the immigrant has not been free, and the Anglo-Saxon element is guilty of just what every dominant race is guilty of in every European country: the imposition of its own culture upon the minority peoples. The fact that this imposition has been so mild and, indeed, semi-conscious does not alter its quality. And the war has brought out just the degree to which that purpose of "Americanizing," that is, "Anglo-Saxonizing," the immigrant has failed.

For the Anglo-Saxon now in his bitterness to turn upon the other peoples, talk about their "arrogance," scold them for not being melted in a pot which never existed, is to betray the unconscious purpose which lay at the bottom of his heart. It betrays too the possession of a racial jealousy similar to that of which he is now accusing the so-called "hyphenates." Let the Anglo-Saxon be proud enough of the heroic toil and heroic sacrifices which moulded the nation. But let him ask himself, if he had had to depend on the English descendants, where he would have been living to-day. To those of us who see in the exploitation of unskilled labor the strident red *leit-motif* of our civilization, the settling of the country presents a great social drama as the waves of immigration broke over it.

Let the Anglo-Saxon ask himself where he would have been if these races had not come? Let those who feel the inferiority of the non-Anglo-Saxon immigrant contemplate that region of the States which has remained the most distinctively "American," the South. Let him ask himself whether he would really like to see the foreign hordes Americanized into such an Americanization. Let him ask himself how superior this native civilization is to the great "alien" states of Wisconsin and Minnesota, where Scandinavians, Poles, and Germans have self-consciously labored to preserve their traditional culture, while being outwardly and satisfactorily American. . . . The foreign cultures have not been melted down or run together, made into some homogeneous Americanism, but have remained distinct but coöperating to the greater glory and benefit, not only of themselves but of all the native "Americanism" around them.

What we emphatically do not want is that these distinctive qualities should be washed out into a tasteless, colorless fluid of uniformity. Already we have far too much of this insipidity,—masses of people who are cultural half-breeds, neither assimilated Anglo-Saxons nor nationals of another culture. Each national colony in this country seems to retain in its foreign press, its vernacular literature, its schools, its intellectual and patriotic leaders, a central cultural nucleus. From this nucleus the colony extends out by imperceptible gradations to a fringe where national characteristics are all but lost. Our cities are filled with these half-breeds who retain their foreign names but have lost the foreign savor. This does not mean that they have actually been changed into New Englanders or Middle Westerners. It does not mean that they have been really Americanized. It means that, letting slip from them whatever native culture they had, they have substituted for it only the most rudimentary American—the American culture of the cheap newspaper, the "movies," the popular song, the ubiquitous automobile. The unthinking who survey this class call them assimilated, Americanized. The great American public school has done its work. With these people our institutions are safe. We may thrill with dread at the aggressive hyphenate, but this tame flabbiness is accepted as Americanization. The same moulders of opinion whose ideal is to melt the different races into Anglo-Saxon gold hail this poor product as the satisfying result of their alchemy.

Yet a truer cultural sense would have told us that it is not the self-conscious cultural nuclei that sap at our American life, but these fringes. It is not the Jew who sticks proudly to the faith of his fathers and boasts of that venerable culture of his who is dangerous to America, but the Jew who has lost the Jewish fire and become a mere elementary, grasping animal. It is not the Bohemian who supports the Bohemian schools in Chicago whose influence is sinister, but the Bohemian who has made money and has got into ward politics. Just so surely as we tend to disintegrate these nuclei of nationalistic culture do we tend to create hordes of men and women without a spiritual country, cultural outlaws, without taste, without standards but those of the mob. We sentence them to live on the most rudimentary planes of American life. The influences at the centre of the nuclei are centripetal. They make for the intelligence and the social values which mean an enhancement of life. And just because the foreign-born retains this expressiveness is he likely to be a better citizen of the American community. The influences at the fringe, however, are centrifugal, anarchical. They make for detached fragments of peoples. Those who came to find liberty achieve only license. They become the flotsam and jetsam of American life, the downward undertow of our civilization with its leering cheapness and falseness of taste and spiritual outlook, the absence of mind and sincere feeling which we see in our slovenly towns, our vapid moving pictures, our popular novels, and in the vacuous faces of the crowds on the city street. This is the cultural wreckage of our time, and it is from the fringes of the Anglo-Saxon as well as the other stocks that it falls. America has as yet no impelling integrating force. It makes too easily for this detritus of cultures. In our loose, free country, no constraining national purpose, no tenacious folk-tradition and folk-style hold the people to a line.

.   .   .

The failure of the melting-pot, far from closing the great American democratic experiment, means that it has only just begun. Whatever American nationalism turns out to be, we see already that it will have a color richer and more exciting than our ideal has hitherto encompassed. In a world which has dreamed of internationalism, we find that we have all unawares been building up the first international nation. The voices which have cried for a tight and jealous nationalism of the European pattern are failing. From that ideal, however valiantly and disinterestedly it has been set for us, time and tendency have moved us further and further away. What we have achieved has been rather a cosmopolitan federation of national colonies, of foreign cultures, from whom the sting of devastating competition has been removed. America is already the world-federation in miniature, the continent where for the first time in history has been achieved that miracle of hope, the peaceful living side by side, with character substantially preserved, of the most heterogeneous peoples under the sun. Nowhere else has such contiguity been anything but the breeder of misery. Here, notwithstanding our tragic failures of adjustment, the outlines are already too clear not to give us a new vision and a new orientation of the American mind in the world.

It is for the American of the younger generation to accept this cosmopolitanism, and carry it along with self-conscious and fruitful purpose. In his colleges, he is already getting, with the study of modern history and politics, the modern literatures, economic geography, the privilege of a cosmopolitan outlook such as the people of no other nation of to-day in Europe can possibly secure. If he is still a colonial, he is no longer the colonial of one partial culture, but of many. He is a colonial of the world. Colonialism has grown into cosmopolitanism, and his mother-land is no one nation, but all who have anything life-enhancing to offer to the spirit.

.   .   .

Only America, by reason of the unique liberty of opportunity and traditional isolation for which she seems to stand, can lead in this cosmopolitan enterprise. Only the American—and in this category I include the migratory alien who has lived with us and caught the pioneer spirit and a sense of new social vistas—has the chance to become that citizen of the world. America is coming to be, not a nationality but a trans-nationality, a weaving back and forth, with the other lands, of many threads of all sizes and colors. Any movement which attempts to thwart this weaving, or to dye the fabric any one color, or disentangle the threads of the strands, is false to this cosmopolitan vision. I do not mean that we shall necessarily glut ourselves with the raw product of humanity. It would be folly to absorb the nations faster than we could weave them. We have no duty either to admit or reject. It is purely a question of expediency. What concerns us is the fact that the strands are here. We must have a policy and an ideal for an actual situation. Our question is, What shall we do with our America? How are we likely to get the more creative America—by confining our imaginations to the ideal of the melting-pot, or broadening them to some such cosmopolitan conception as I have been vaguely sketching?

The war has shown America to be unable, though isolated geographically and politically from a European world-situation, to remain aloof and irresponsible. She is a wandering star in a sky dominated by two colossal constellations of states. Can she not work out some position of her own, some life of being in, yet not quite of, this seething and embroiled European world? This is her only hope and promise. A transnationality of all the nations, it is spiritually impossible for her to pass into the orbit of any one. It will be folly to hurry herself into a premature and sentimental nationalism, or to emulate Europe and play fast and loose with the forces that drag into war. No Americanization will fulfill this vision which does not recognize the uniqueness of this trans-nationalism of ours. . . .

Is it a wild hope that the undertow of opposition to metaphysics in international relations, opposition to militarism, is less a cowardly provincialism than a groping for this higher cosmopolitan ideal? One can understand the irritated restlessness with which our proud pro-British colonists contemplate a heroic conflict across the seas in which they have no part. It was inevitable that our necessary inaction should evolve in their minds into the bogey of national shame and dishonor. But let us be careful about accepting their sensitiveness as final arbiter. Let us look at our reluctance rather as the first crude beginnings of assertion on the part of certain strands in our nationality that they have a right to a voice in the construction for the American ideal. Let us face realistically the America we have around us. Let us work with the forces that are at work. Let us make something of this trans-national spirit instead of outlawing it. Already we are living this cosmopolitan America. What we need is everywhere a vivid consciousness of the new ideal. Deliberate headway must be made against the survivals of the melting-pot ideal for the promise of American life.

We cannot Americanize America worthily by sentimentalizing and moralizing history. When the best schools are expressly renouncing the questionable duty of teaching patriotism by means of history, it is not the time to force shibboleth upon the immigrant. This form of Americanization has been heard because it appealed to the vestiges of our old sentimentalized and moralized patriotism. This has so far held the field as the expression of the new American's new devotion. The inflections of other voices have been drowned. They must be heard. We must see if the lesson of the war has not been for hundreds of these later Americans a vivid realization of their trans-nationality, a new consciousness of what America meant to them as a citizenship in the world. It is the vague historic idealisms which have provided the fuel for the European flame. Our American ideal can make no progress until we do away with this romantic gilding of the past.

All our idealisms must be those of future social goals in which all can participate, the good life of personality lived in the environment of the Beloved Community. No mere doubtful triumphs of the past, which redound to the glory of only one of our trans-nationalities, can satisfy us. It must be a future America, on which all can unite, which pulls us irresistibly toward it, as we understand each other more warmly.

To make real this striving amid dangers and apathies is work for a younger *intelligentsia* of America. Here is an enterprise of integration into which we can all pour ourselves, of a spiritual welding which should make us, if the final menace ever came, not weaker, but infinitely strong.

The Melting Pot Mistake

HENRY PRATT FAIRCHILD (1880–1956), a professional sociologist, was born in Dundel, Illinois, and took his B.A. at Doane College in Crete, Nebraska. After teaching in Turkey, he completed his Ph.D. at Yale in 1909, writing a thesis on Greek immigration to the United States. He taught for nine years at Yale, then joined the faculty of New York University in 1919. **The Melting Pot Mistake** (1926), a popularization of views held widely if in varying degree among sociologists, represented a high-water mark of the learned nativism

THE MELTING POT MISTAKE. From *The Melting Pot Mistake* by Henry Pratt Fairchild. Little, Brown and Company, 1926.

that helped produce the Immigration Restriction Bill two years earlier.

1. Symbols

If "an evil generation seeketh a sign" a mentally harassed and over-taxed generation seeks a symbol. The mind that is wearied with multitudinous demands for judgment upon programs and policies yearns for a simplication of its problems.

.   .   .

We simply can not get all the facts on all the problems. If we are to form independent judgments at all we must of necessity be guided largely by labels and symbols. It is fundamentally important, then, that the interpreters be both honest and acute, and that the symbols be authentic as well as realistic.

These were the facts which gave to Israel Zangwill's little drama, "The Melting-Pot", when it appeared in 1909, a significance quite disproportionate to its literary importance. For one hundred years and more a stream of immigration had been pouring into the United States in constantly increasing volume. At first this movement had attracted little attention, and such feelings as it aroused were mainly those of complacency and satisfaction. As the decades rolled by certain features of the movement created considerable consternation and a demand sprang up for some form of governmental relief. In time this relief was granted, and the popular concern died down. In general, however, during practically the whole of the nineteenth century the attitude of the American people toward immigration was one of easy-going, tolerant indifference when it was not actually welcome. But as the century drew to a close evidences of popular uneasiness and misgiving began to display themselves. These were due in part to changes in the social and economic situation in the United States, in part to changes in the personal and social characteristics of the immigrants, and in part to repeated warnings issued by those whose professional activities and opportunities gave them a wider access to the facts of immigration than was possible to the average citizen. In particular the American people began to ponder about the ultimate effect upon its own vitality and solidarity of this stupendous injection of foreign elements. Could we stand it, and if so, how long? Were not the foundations of our cherished institutions already partially undermined by all these alien ideas, habits, and customs? What kind of a people were we destined to become physically? Was the American nation itself in danger? Immigration became a great public problem, calling for judgment.

Then came the symbol, like a portent in the heavens. America is a Melting-Pot. Into it are being poured representatives of all the world's peoples. Within its magic confines there is being formed something that is not only uniform and homogeneous but also finer than any of the separate ingredients. The nations of the world are being fused into a new and choicer nation, the United States.

The figure was a clever one—picturesque, expressive, familiar, just the sort of thing to catch the popular fancy and lend itself to a thousand uses. It swept over this country and other countries like wild fire. As always, it was welcomed as a substitute for both investigation and thought. It calmed the rising wave of misgiving. Few stopped to ask whether it fitted the phenomena of assimilation. Few inquired whether Mr. Zangwill's familiarity with the intricate facts of immigration were such as to justify him in assuming the heavy responsibility of interpreter. America was a Melting-Pot, the apparent evidences of national disintegration were illusions, and that settled it.

It would be hard to estimate the influence of the symbol of the melting pot in staving off the restriction of immigration. It is certain that in the popular mind it offsets volumes of laboriously compiled statistics and carefully reasoned analyses. It is virtually beyond question that restriction would have come in time in any case. How soon it would have come without the Great War must remain a matter of conjecture. Be that as it may, when the concussions of that conflict had begun to die down the melting pot was discovered to be so badly cracked that it is not likely ever to be dragged into service again. Its day was over. But this did not mean that the real facts of immigration had suddenly become public property. Our symbol had been shattered, but we had not yet, as a people, been able to undertake the extensive investigation necessary to reveal the true nature of the case. The history of post-war movements is replete with evidences of the gross misconceptions of the meaning and processes of assimilation which characterized many even of those who devoted themselves directly to the problem. Even to-day, in spite of the fact that there is perhaps no other great public problem on which the American people is so well educated as on immigration, there is yet great need of a clearer understanding of the tremendous task that still confronts us. We know now that the Melting-Pot did not melt, but we are not entirely sure why. We suspect that that particular figure of speech was an anomaly, but we have not yet found a more appropriate one to take its place. We are a little in doubt as to whether so complicated a phenomenon as assimilation can be adequately represented by any symbol at all. Perhaps there is no short cut to a comprehension of this great problem, and he who would form a sound independent judgment must resign himself to the laborious methods of investigation and thought.

There is a general agreement that in connection with its great immigration movement the United States tried to do something and failed. What was this thing that it tried to do? Why did it fail? Is there still a menace in the results of that failure? Was there ever a possibility of success under the old conditions? Is there hope of escaping the consequences of failure under present conditions? If so, by what means may that hope be realized? These are some of the questions intimately bound up with the fallacy of the Melting-Pot.

12. The Duty of America

. . . There can be only one conclusion. The eventual effect of an unrestricted immigration movement, governed only by the economic self-interest of the migrating individuals, must under modern conditions be a progressive depression of the standard of living of mankind as a whole. It is therefore contrary to the liberal spirit, and the label so vigorously exploited, and so confidently flaunted in the face of the American public, is found to have been falsely applied.

But there is more to the question than this. Other interests than the economic call for consideration.

It has been repeatedly stated that the consequence of nonassimilation is the destruction of nationality. This is the central truth of the whole problem of immigration and it cannot be overemphasized. An immigration movement that did not involve nonassimilation might be tolerated, though it might have other evil consequences which would condemn it. But an immigration movement that does involve nonassimilation—like the movement to the United States during the last fifty years at least—is a blow at the very heart of nationality and can not be endured if nationality is conceived to have any value whatsoever. The American nationality has already been compared to a plant. There is, indeed, a striking parallelism between a nation and a noble tree—for instance, one of our own incomparable redwoods—which may be followed a little further, not with any expectation or desire of popularizing a new symbol, but merely for the clarification that it affords.

A nation, like a tree, is a living vital thing. Growth is one of its conditions of life, and when it ceases to grow there is good reason to fear that it is about to decay and die. Every nation, like every tree, belongs to a certain general type, but it is also uniquely individual within that type. Its peculiar form is determined by various forces, some of which are internal and some external. No nation need fear the changes which come as the result of the operation of natural, wholesome internal forces, that is to say, the ideas and activities of its own true members. These forces may, in the course of time, produce a form and character wholly different from the original, just as the mature plant may have an entirely different aspect from the seedling. This is nothing to be dreaded or opposed. No change that represents the natural evolution of internal forces need be dreaded. But there are other forces which originate without which threaten not only the form and character but also the vigor and perhaps the very life of the nation. Some of these are the forcible attacks of other nations, like the crowding of trees upon each other, or the unwholesome influence of alien ideas which may be compared with harsh and uncongenial winds which blow upon trees, dwarfing and distorting them.

Most dangerous of all however, are those foreign forces which, among trees, are represented by minute hostile organisms that make their way into the very tissue of the tree itself and feed upon its life substances, and among nations by alien individuals who are accepted as immigrants and by a process of "boring from within" (in something much more than a mere trade-union sense) sap the very vitality of their host. In so doing the immigrants may be merely following out their natural and defensible impulses without any hostility toward the receiving nation, any more than the parasites upon a tree may be considered to have any hostility to the tree. Nor can the immigrants, any more than the parasites, be expected to foresee that their activities will eventually destroy the very organism upon which they depend for their existence. The simple fact is that they are alien particles, not assimilated, and therefore wholly different from the foreign particles which the tree takes in the form of food, and transforms into cells of its own body.

. . .

There are, it should be noted, a few foreigners whose attitude toward the United States is more positively destructive than that of those who simply can not understand America because they are not Americans. Among this number are those, very few altogether, who make it their business to launch direct attacks upon the fundamental form and institutions of the American government. To them the deportation acts may most appropriately be applied. But much more dangerous are those who insolently regard the United States as a mere economic catch basin, to which they have come to get out of it what they can, confessing no obligation to it, recognizing no claim on its part to the preservation of its own identity, displaying no intention to contribute to its development or to remain permanently as a part of it. One type of this group looks forward to a return to the native land as soon as America has been bled of all it has to offer. Another type looks upon America as a sort of no man's land, or every man's land, upon which they can develop a separate group existence along any lines that they see fit. For instance, we are told upon the best of authority that there has already developed in the United States a distinct Polish-American society, which is neither truly Polish nor truly American, but which has a vigorous and distinct character and existence of its own.

More dangerous, however, than any foreign elements, are certain individuals of native birth who in an excess of zeal for the foreigner, emanating, it may be presumed, from a misguided and sentimental though well-meaning reaction from the attitude of ethno-centric superiority so characteristic of many Americans, go to the extreme of denying any merit in American institutions, and ignoring any claim on the part of America to the perpetuation of its peculiar existence. They are ready to throw any and all distinctly American characteristics into the discard if only we can absorb the "dear foreigners" into our midst. They applaud any expression of national pride on the part of a foreigner as an evidence of sturdy and commendable patriotism, but condemn a similar expression on the part of an American as narrow bigotry. A representative of this type, apparently of native extraction, was talking at an Americanization meeting called by a prominent commercial organization in one of our great cities. Working herself up to a fine pitch of emotionalism she finally exclaimed, "The noblest and finest persons I ever knew in my life were newly arrived immigrants, and the meanest, the lowest, the most contemptible were descendants of the old New England stock!" This was the keynote of the meeting, and called forth a tumult of applause.

The central factor in the world organization of the present is nationalism. Strong, self-conscious nationalities are indispensable to the efficient ordering and peaceful promotion of international relations. Every well-developed nationality is a priceless product of social evolution. Each has its peculiar contribution to make to future progress. The destruction of any one would be an irreparable loss to mankind.

Among the nations of the world America stands out unique, and in many ways preëminent. Favored by Nature above all other nations in her physical endowment, favored by history in the character of her people and the type of her institutions, she has a rôle to play in the development of human affairs which no other nation can play. Foremost in this rôle is the development of true democracy. In America the stage is set more favorably than anywhere else for the great drama of the common man. Here if anywhere the conditions are auspicious for the upward movement of the masses. If democracy fails in America, where shall we look for it to succeed? Any program or policy which interferes in the slightest degree with the prosecution of this great enterprise must be condemned as treason to our high destiny. Any yielding to a specious and superficial humanitarianism which threatens the material, political, and social standards of the average

American must be branded as a violation of our trust. The highest service of America to mankind is to point the way, to demonstrate the possibilities, to lead onward to the goal of human happiness. Any force that tends to impair our capacity for leadership is a menace to mankind and a flagrant violation of the spirit of liberalism.

Unrestricted immigration was such a force. It was slowly, insidiously, irresistibly eating away the very heart of the United States. What was being melted in the great Melting Pot, losing all form and symmetry, all beauty and character, all nobility and usefulness, was the American nationality itself. Let the justification for checking this force for all time be voiced in the words of two distinguished foreigners. First, Rabbi Joel Blau: "The chief duty that a people owes both itself and the world is reverence for its own soul, the mystic centre of its being." Then, Gustave LeBon: "A preponderating influence of foreigners is a sure solvent of the existence of States. It takes away from a people its most precious possession—its soul."

McCarran Act

MARYA MANNES (1904–   ), author and social critic, was born and privately educated in New York City. A feature editor for **Vogue** in the 1930s, she served with the government during the Second World War, and from 1952 to 1963 was a staff writer for the **Reporter**, a liberal journal of news and opinion. "McCarran Act," a sample of the political satire she frequently contributed to the **Reporter**, lampoons the McCarran-Walter Act of 1952, a codification of the restrictionist immigration laws of the 1920s which added provisions to prevent "subversives" from entering America. In books and essays, speeches and television appearances, Mannes has surveyed American life and culture with intelligence and wit. Her published works include **Message from a Stranger** (1948), a novel; **More in Anger** (1958), a collection of essays; and **But Will It Sell?** (1966), a warning that business values are corrupting the American spirit.

The blood that made this nation great
Will now be tested at the gate
To see if it deserves to be
Admitted to democracy,
Or rather to that small elite
Whose hemoglobin counts can meet
Requirements of purity
Consistent with security
And with that small and rabid mind
That thinks itself above mankind.

The Need for a Cultural Base
to Civil Rites & Bpower
Mooments

LeROI JONES (1934–   ), now known also as Imamu Ameer Ba-
raka, born in Newark, New Jersey, has fought numerous battles to
free himself from the domination of white culture. Entering Rut-
gers, he left after one year for the more congenial atmosphere of
Howard where he received a B.A. in 1954. He initially married a
white woman, but divorced her to marry a black. A playwright and
poet, he began his career with a book of poems, **Preface to a
Twenty Volume Suicide Note** (1961). He elaborates his social views
in the essays in **Home** (1966).

The civilrighter is usually an american, otherwise he would know,
if he is colored, that that concept is meaningless fantasy. Slaves
have no civil rights. On the other hand, even integration is into the
mobile butcher shop of the devil's mind. To be an american one
must be a murderer. A white murderer of colored people. Anywhere
on the planet. The colored people, negroes, who *are* Americans, and
there are plenty, are only colored on their skin. They are white mur-

THE NEED FOR A CULTURAL BASE TO CIVIL RITES & BPOWER MOOMENTS.
From Le Roi Jones, *The Black Power Revolt*. Copyright © 1967 by LeRoi
Jones. Reprinted by permission of The Sterling Lord Agency Inc.

derers of colored people. Themselves were the first to be murdered by
them, in order to qualify.

The blackpower seeker, if connected to civilrights mooment can
be bourgeois meaning. He wants the same civilrights/power white
people have. He wants to be a capitalist, a live-gooder, and a death-
freak. In whatever order. There is the difference Frantz Fanon implies
in *BlkSkin-WhiteMask*. Black Bourgeoisie can be white or black. The
difference is critical only if Black Black Bourgeoisie can be used for
good, possibly. White ones are examples of shadow worship, and are
deathfreaks and American.

Black Power cannot mean ONLY a black sheriff in the sovereign
state of Alabama. But that is a start, a road, a conceptualizing on
heavier bizness. Black Power, the power to control our lives ourselves.
All of our lives. Our laws. Our culture. Our children. Their lives.
Our total consciousness, black oriented. We do not speak of the need
to live in peace or universal humanity, since we are peaceful humanists
seeking the spiritual resolution of the world. The unity of all men will
come with the evolution of the species that recognizes the need for
such. The black man does. The black man is a spirit worshiper as
well. The religious-science and scientific-religion is the black man's
special evolutional province. He will reorder the world, as he finds his
own rightful place in it. The world will be reordered by the black
man's finding such place. Such place is, itself, the reordering. Black
Power. Power of the majority is what is meant. The actual majority in
the world of colored people.

Census

BLACK PEOPLE BLACK PEOPLE BLACK PEOPLE
YELLOW PEOPLE YELLOW PEOPLE YELLOW PEOPLE
BROWN PEOPLE BROWN PEOPLE BROWN
RED PEOPLE RED PEOPLE RED PEOPLE
POOR PEOPLE POOR PEOPLE POOR PEOPLE POOR
PEOPLE POOR PEOPLE POOR PEOPLE POOR PEOPLE
· · · · · · ·
& others.

Bourgeois black power seeks mostly to get in on what's going
down now. The implication or murderermembership is clear. Of course
the form of Bourgeois black power can be harnessed for heavier ends.
The control by black people for their own benefit CAN BE set up
similar to bourgeois black power, but if the ends are actually to be
realized, you are talking again about nationalism, nationalization. Finally the only black power that can exist is that established by black
nationalism. We want power to control our lives, as separate from

what americans, white and white oriented people, want to do with their lives. That simple. We ain't with yuall. Otherwise you are talking tricknology and lieconjuring. Black power cannot exist WITHIN white power. One or the other. There can only be one or the other. They might exist side by side as separate entities, but never in the same space. Never. They are mutually exclusive.

"Might exist," because that is theoretically possible, except the devils never want to tolerate any power but their own. In such cases they want to destroy what is not them. However, the power of the majority on the planet will exist, this is an evolutional fact. The adjustment, what the world must go through because of this, is current events.

The socio-political workers for black power must realize this last fact. That the black and white can never come to exist as equals within the same space. Side by side perhaps, if the devils are cool, but the definition of devil is something uncool.

This means that any agitation within the same space for Black Power is for control of the space you *can* control called part of the society, but in reality in black enclaves, cities, land, black people are usually already in control in terms of population. Further control must be nationalization, separation. Black power cannot exist except as itself, power, to order, to control, to legalize, to define. There are wars going on now to stop black power, whether in Sinai, Vietnam, Angola, or Newark, New Jersey. The difference is that in Newark, New Jersey, many colored people do not even *know* they are in this war (tho they might realize, on whatever level of consciousness, that they are losing).

Black power is nationalization. Absolute control of resources beneficial to a national group. It cannot come to exist in areas of white control. Neither Harlem nor Hough nor Watts &c. are really America. They are controlled by America . . . this is the sickness. Black power is the cure for this sickness. But it must be the alternative to what already exists, i.e., white power. And to be an actual alternative it must be complete.

Black power cannot be complete unless it is the total reflection of black people. Black power must be spiritually, emotionally, and historically in tune with black people, as well as serving their economic and political ends. To be absolutely in tune, the seekers of black power must know what it is they seek. They must know what is this power-culture alternative through which they bring to focus the world's energies. They must have an understanding and grounding in the cultural consciousness of the nation they seek to bring to power. And this is what is being done, bringing to power a nation that has been weak and despised for 400 years.

That is, to provide the alternative, the new, the needed strength for this nation, they must proceed by utilizing the complete cultural consciousness of this black nation's people. We should not cry black power unless we know what that signifies. We must know full well what it is we are replacing white power with, in all its implications. We are replacing not only a white sheriff, for the values that sheriff carries with him are, in fact, an extension of the white culture. *That black sheriff had better be an extension of black culture, or there is NoChange!* (In the sense that Edward Brooke, so-called Negro Senator from Massachusetts, as a representative of white culture, could never signify in any sense, Black Power. He is, for all intents and purposes, a white man.)

There are people who might cry BlackPower, who are representatives, extensions of white culture. So-called BlackPower advocates who are mozartfreaks or Rolling Stones, or hypnotized by Joyce or Hemingway or Frank Sinatra, are representatives, extensions, of white culture, and can never therefore signify black power. Black power, as black, must be, is in reality, the total realization of that nation's existence on this planet from the year one until this moment. All those experiences which have been this lost nation's must be brought to bear upon all its righteous workings; especially for Power. (And with Power will come Freedom.) Black Power is the Power first to be Black. It is better, in America, to be white. So we leave America, or we never even go there. (It could be twelve miles from New York City (or two miles) and it would be the black nation you found yourself in. That's where yourself was, all the time.)

The very failure of the civil rights and blackpower organizations (collecting memberships on strictly socio-political grounds) to draw more membership is due to the fact that these organizations make very little reference to the totality of black culture. The reason Mr. Muhammad's Nation of Islam has had such success gathering black people from the grass roots is that Mr. Muhammad offers a program that reflects a totality of black consciousness. Islam is a form of spirit worship (a moral guide) as well as a socio-economic and political program. Religion as the total definer of the world. (This is as old as the world, and finally will be the only Renewal possible for any of us to submit to the Scientific-Reiigious reordering of the world, through black eyes and black minds.) It must be a culture, a way of feeling, a way of living, that is replaced with a culture, feeling, way of living and being, that is black, and, yes, finally, more admirable.

Hence, the socio-political must be wedded to the cultural. The socio-political must be a righteous extension of the cultural, as it is, legitimately, with National groups. The american negro's culture, as it is, is a diphthong with the distortions of the master's hand always in back or front ground, not real but absolutely concrete and there; . . .

the culture, the deepest black and the theoretical . . . socio-politico (and art &c.) must be wedded. A culturally aware black politics would use all the symbols of the culture, all the keys and images out of the black past, out of the black present, to gather the people to it, and energize itself with their strivings at conscious blackness. The Wedding . . . the conscious-unconscious. The politics and the art and the religion all must be black. The social system. The entirety of the projection. Black Power must mean a black people with a past clear back to the beginning of the planet, channeling the roaring energies of black to revive black power. If you can dig it???. Not to discover it now . . . but to revive. Our actual renaissance (Like the devils pulled themselves out of their "dark ages" by re-embracing the "classics," or Classicism: what they could see as the strengths and beauties of a certain kind of "pure" Europeanism (whiteness). And with that went to the source! Eastern Thought . . . black african-middle eastern, also the re-embracing of the Far East via Marco Polo, &c., like *Trade*.)

So that no man can be "cultured" without being *consciously* Black. Which is what we're talking about all the time, in any Rising (Evolutional) Pitch. *Consciousness.*

The Civil Righters are not talking about exchanging a culture. They are, no matter what moves they make, layin' in the same place, making out. Black Power, as an actuality, will only exist in a Black-oriented, Black-controlled space. It is White Culture that rules us with White Guns. Our only freedom will be in bringing a Black Culture to Power. We Cannot Do This Unless We Are Cultured. That is, Consciously Black. (The Consciousness of Black Consciousness must know & Show itself as well.)

The erection of large schools teaching Black Consciousness. Wherever there are Black People in America. This should be one definite earnest commitment of any Black Power group. Even the rundown schools full of black children deep in the ghettos are white schools. The children are taught to value white things more than themselves. All of them are white-controlled, and the quality of education suffers because white people want the quality of our education to suffer, otherwise something else would be the case. We will have no quality education for our children until we administer it ourselves. You *must* know this!

There is no black power without blackness conscious of itself. "Negro History" is not what we must mean, but the absolute re-ordering of our Education Systems. In other words the philosophy of blackness, the true consciousness of our world, is what is to be taught. The understanding of the world as felt and analyzed by men and women of soul.

The Black Student Union of San Francisco State College has started moving toward a "Black Studies Program" at that school. A Black Studies Program on departmental status at the school, where students could spend all of their time recreating our black past, and understanding, and creating the new strong black nation we all must swear to bring into existence.

The black power groups must help to create the consciousness of who we black people are, and then we will be driven to take power, and be faithful to our energies as black people with black minds and hearts, quite a *different* people from the species that now rules us.

Afro-American History, African History, Realistic World History, Eastern Philosophies—Religion, Islam-Arabic-African Religion and Languages, Black Art—past and contemporary, The Evolving Patterns of the Colored World, Black Psychology, Revolutionary Consciousness, Socio-Political Evolution of Afro-Americans, Africans, Colored Peoples, War, The Placement of the New Culture, Eastern Science, Black Science, Community Workshops (How To) in Black Power, Business and Economics: Keys to a new black world, given the strengths our studies into times of the black man's power will build for us. Black Studies is to make us cultured, i.e., consciously black.

The so-called Negro Colleges ought to be the first to be forced into Blackness. The consciousness of the self, without which no righteous progress is possible. Instead the Negro Colleges are "freak factories," places where black children are turned into white-oriented schizophrenic freaks of a dying society. But many of the students have already shown that they are not willing to be misused by the whiteminds of their puppet professors.

A cultural base, a black base, is the completeness the black power movement must have. We must understand that we are *Replacing* a dying culture, and we must be prepared to do this, and be absolutely conscious of what we are replacing it with.

We are sons and daughters of the most ancient societies on this planet. The reordering of the world that we are moving toward cannot come unless we are completely aware of this fact, and are prepared to make use of it in our day-to-day struggle with the devil.

E.G.: Black Art—The recreation of our lives, as black . . . to inspire, educate, delight and move black people.

It is easier to get people into a consciousness of black power, what it is, by emotional example than through dialectical lecture. Black people seeing the recreation of their lives are struck by what is wrong or missing in them.

Programmatic application of what is learned through black art is centrally the black power movement's commitment.

The teaching of colored people's languages, including the ones we speak automatically, moves the student's mind to other psychological horizons. European language carries the bias of its inventors & users. *You must be* anti-black, speaking in their language, except by violent effort. The masses of black people, for instance, have never spoken the European's languages. Or let me say, they have never spoken them to such degree that the complete bias of that "competence" would dull their natural tuning.

The teaching of Black History (African and African-American) would put our people absolutely in touch with themselves as a nation, and with the reality of their situation. You want them to move to take power, they must know how they can deserve this power.

Black Power must be a program of Consciousness. The consciousness to Act. (Maulana Ron Karenga and the US group in Los Angeles work very successfully at making black consciousness cultural and of course socio-political.) It should all be one thing. Blackness.

Voting nor picketing nor for that matter fighting in the streets means anything unless it is proposed by a black consciousness for the aggrandizement and security of the Black culture and Black people. Each of our "acts of liberation" must involve the liberation of the Black man in every way imaginable.

Black Power movements not grounded in Black culture cannot move beyond the boundaries of Western thought. The paramount value of Western thought is the security and expansion of Western culture. Black Power is inimical to Western culture as it has manifested itself within black and colored majority areas anywhere on this planet. Western culture is and has been destructive to Colored People all over the world. No movement shaped or contained by Western culture will ever benefit Black people. Black power must be the actual force and beauty and wisdom of Blackness . . . reordering the world.

Portnoy, the Pumpkin, and the Pilgrim

PHILIP ROTH (1933–   ), one year older than Jones, was also born in Newark, that seething caldron of race and nationality. A graduate of Bucknell (B.A., 1954) and the University of Chicago

PORTNOY, THE PUMPKIN, AND THE PILGRIM. From *Portnoy's Complaint,* by Philip Roth. Copyright © 1967, 1968, 1969 by Philip Roth. Reprinted by permission of Random House, Inc.

(M.A., 1955), he has taught at the universities of Iowa and Pennsylvania, and at Princeton. He won the National Book Award for **Goodbye, Columbus** (1959), which, like **Portnoy's Complaint** (1969), was made into a popular movie.

In 1950, just seventeen, and Newark two and a half months behind me (well, not exactly "behind": in the mornings I awake in the dormitory baffled by the unfamiliar blanket in my hand, and the disappearance of one of "my" windows; oppressed and distraught for minutes on end by this unanticipated transformation given my bedroom by my mother)—I perform the most openly defiant act of my life: instead of going home for my first college vacation, I travel by train to Iowa, to spend Thanksgiving with The Pumpkin and her parents. Till September I had never been farther west than Lake Hopatcong in New Jersey—now I am off to Ioway! And with a blondie! Of the Christian religion! Who is more stunned by this desertion, my family or me? What daring! Or was I no more daring than a sleepwalker?

The white clapboard house in which The Pumpkin had grown up might have been the Taj Mahal for the emotions it released in me. Balboa, maybe, knows what I felt upon first glimpsing the swing tied up to the ceiling of the front porch. *She was raised in this house. The girl who has let me undo her brassiere and dry-hump her at the dormitory door, grew up in this white house. Behind those* goyische *curtains! Look, shutters!*

"Daddy, Mother," says The Pumpkin, when we disembark at the Davenport train station, "this is the weekend guest, this is the friend from school whom I wrote you about—"

I am something called "a weekend guest"? I am something called "a friend from school"? What tongue is she speaking? I am "the *bonditt*," "the *vantz*," I am the insurance man's son. I am Warshaw's ambassador! "How do you do, Alex?" To which of course I reply, "Thank you." Whatever anybody says to me during my first twenty-four hours in Iowa, I answer, "Thank you." Even to inanimate objects. I walk into a chair, promptly I say to it, "Excuse me, thank you." I drop my napkin on the floor, lean down, flushing, to pick it up, "Thank you," I hear myself saying to the napkin—or is it the floor I'm addressing? Would my mother be proud of her little gentleman! Polite even to the furniture!

Then there's an expression in English, "Good morning," or so I have been told; the phrase has never been of any particular use to me. Why should it have been? At breakfast at home I am in fact known to the other boarders as "Mr. Sourball," and "The Crab." But suddenly, here in Iowa, in imitation of the local inhabitants, I am transformed into a veritable geyser of good mornings. That's all anybody around that place knows how to say—they feel the sunshine on their faces, and it just sets off some sort of chemical reaction: Good *morning! Good* morning! Good *mor*ning! sung to half a dozen different tunes! Next they all start asking each other if they had "a good night's sleep." And asking me! Did I have a good night's sleep? I don't really know, I have to think—the question comes as something of a surprise. Did I Have A Good Night's Sleep? Why, yes! I think I did! Hey—did you? "Like a log," replies Mr. Campbell. And for the first time in my life I experience the full force of a simile. This man, who is a real estate broker and an alderman of the Davenport town council, says that he slept like a log, and I actually *see* a log. *I* get it! Motionless, heavy, *like a log!* "Good *morning*," he says, and now it occurs to me that the word "morning," as he uses it, refers specifically to the hours between eight A.M. and twelve noon. I'd never thought of it that way before. He wants the hours between eight and twelve to be *good,* which is to say, enjoyable, pleasurable, beneficial! We are all of us wishing each other four hours of pleasure and accomplishment. Why, that's terrific! Hey, that's very nice! Good morning! And the same applies to "Good afternoon"! And "Good evening"! And "Good night"! My God! The English language is *a form of communication!* Conversation isn't just crossfire where you shoot and get shot at! Where you've got to duck for your life and aim to kill! Words aren't only bombs and bullets— no, they're little gifts, containing *meanings!*

Wait, I'm not finished—as if the experience of being on the inside rather than the outside of these *goyische* curtains isn't overwhelming enough, as if the incredible experience of my wishing hour upon hour of pleasure to a houseful of *goyim* isn't sufficient source for bewilderment, there is, to compound the ecstasy of disorientation, the name of the street upon which the Campbell house stands, the street where *my* girl friend grew up! skipped! skated! hop-scotched! sledded! all the while I dreamed of her existence some fifteen hundred miles away, in what they tell me is the same country. The street name? Not Xanadu, no, better even than that, oh, more preposterous by far: *Elm.* Elm! It is, you see, as though I have walked right through the orange celluloid station band of our old Zenith, directly into "One Man's Family." Elm. Where trees grow—which must be elms!

To be truthful, I must admit that I am not able to draw such a conclusion first thing upon alighting from the Campbell car on Wednesday night: after all, it has taken me seventeen years to recognize an oak, and even there I am lost without the acorns. What I see first in a landscape isn't the flora, believe me—it's the fauna, the human opposition, who is screwing and who is getting screwed. Greenery I leave to the birds and the bees, they have their worries, I have mine. At home who knows the name of what grows from the pavement at the front of our house? It's a tree—and that's it. The kind is of no consequence, who cares what kind, just as long as it doesn't fall down on your head. In the autumn (or is it the spring? Do you know this stuff? I'm pretty sure it's not the winter) there drop from its branches long crescent-shaped pods containing hard little pellets. Okay. Here's a scientific fact about our tree, comes by way of my mother, Sophie Linnaeus: If you shoot those pellets through a straw, you can take somebody's eye out and make him blind for life. (SO NEVER DO IT! NOT EVEN IN JEST! AND IF ANYBODY DOES IT TO YOU, YOU TELL ME INSTANTLY!) And this, more or less, is the sort of botanical knowledge I am equipped with, until that Sunday afternoon when we are leaving the Campbell house for the train station, and I have my Archimedean experience: Elm Street . . . . . then . . . . . elm *trees!* How simple! I mean, you don't *need* 158 points of I.Q., you don't *have* to be a genius to make sense of this world. It's really all so very simple!

A memorable weekend in my lifetime, equivalent in human history, I would say, to mankind's passage through the entire Stone Age. Every time Mr. Campbell called his wife "Mary," my body temperature shot into the hundreds. There I was, eating off dishes that had been touched by the hands of a woman named *Mary*. . . . Please, I pray on the train heading west, let there be no pictures of Jesus Christ in the Campbell house. Let me get through this weekend without having to see his pathetic *punim*—or deal with anyone wearing a cross! When the aunts and uncles come for the Thanksgiving dinner, please, let there be no anti-Semite among them! Because if someone starts in with "the pushy Jews," or says "kike" or "jewed him down"— Well, I'll jew them down all right, I'll jew their fucking teeth down their throat! No, no violence (as if I even had it in me), let *them* be violent, that's *their* way. No, I'll rise from my seat—and (*vuh den?*) make a speech! I will shame and humiliate them in their bigoted hearts! Quote the Declaration of Independence over their candied yams! Who the fuck are they, I'll ask, to think they own Thanksgiving!

Then at the railroad station her father says, "How do you do, young man?" and I of course answer, "Thank you." Why is *he* acting so nice? Because he has been forewarned (which I don't know whether to take as an insult or a blessing), or because he doesn't know yet? Shall I say it then, before we even get into the car? Yes, I must! I can't go on living a lie! "Well, it sure is nice being here in Davenport, Mr. and Mrs. Campbell, what with my being Jewish and all." Not quite ringing enough perhaps. "Well, as a friend of Kay's, Mr. and Mrs. Campbell, and a Jew, I do want to thank you for inviting me—"

Stop pussyfooting! What then? Talk Yiddish? *How?* I've got twenty-five words to my name—half of them dirty, and the rest mispronounced! Shit, just shut up and get in the car. "Thank you, thank you," I say, picking up my own bag, and we all head for the station wagon.

Kay and I climb into the back seat, *with the dog.* Kay's dog! To whom she talks as though he's human! Wow, she really *is* a *goy.* What a stupid thing, to talk to a dog—except Kay isn't stupid! In fact, I think she's smarter really than I am. And yet talks to a dog? "As far as dogs are concerned, Mr. and Mrs. Campbell, we Jews by and large—" Oh, forget it. Not necessary. You are ignoring anyway (or trying awfully hard to) that eloquent appendage called your nose. Not to mention the Afro-Jewish hairpiece. Of course they know. Sorry, but there's no escaping destiny, *bubi,* a man's cartilage is his fate. *But I don't want to escape!* Well, that's nice too—because you can't. *Oh, but yes I can—if I should want to!* But you said you don't want to. *But if I did!*

As soon as I enter the house I begin (on the sly, and somewhat to my own surprise) to sniff: what will the odor be like? Mashed potatoes? An old lady's dress? Fresh cement? I sniff and I sniff, trying to catch the scent. There! is *that* it, is that Christianity I smell, or just the dog? Everything I see, taste, touch, I think, *"Goyish!"* My first morning I squeeze half an inch of Pepsodent down the drain rather than put my brush where Kay's mother or father may have touched the bristles with which they cleanse their own *goyische* molars. True! The soap on the sink is bubbly with foam from somebody's hands. Whose? *Mary's?* Should I just take hold of it and begin to wash, or should I maybe run a little water over it first, just to be safe. But safe from *what?* Schmuck, maybe you want to get a piece of soap to wash the soap with! I tiptoe to the toilet, I peer over into the bowl: "Well, there it is, boy, a real *goyische* toilet bowl. The genuine article. Where your girl friend's father drops his gentile turds. What do you think, huh? Pretty impressive." Obsessed? Spellbound!

Next I have to decide whether or not to line the seat. It isn't a matter of hygiene, I'm sure the place is clean, spotless in its own particular antiseptic *goy* way: the question is, what if it's warm yet from a Campbell behind—from her mother! *Mary!* Mother also of Jesus Christ! If only for the sake of my family, maybe I should put a little paper around the rim; it doesn't cost anything, and who will ever know?

I will! *I* will! So down I go—and it *is* warm! Yi, seventeen years old and I am rubbing asses with the enemy! How far I have traveled since September! *By the waters of Babylon, there we sat down, yea, we wept when we remembered Zion!* And yea is right! On the can I am besieged by doubt and regret, I am suddenly languishing with all my heart for home . . . When my father drives out to buy "real apple cider" at the roadside farmer's market off in Union, I won't be with him! And how can Hannah and Morty go to the Weequahic-Hillside game Thanksgiving morning without me along to make them laugh? Jesus, I hope we win (which is to say, lose by less than 21 points). Beat Hillside, you bastards! Double U, Double E, Q U A, H I C! Bernie, Sidney, Leon, "Ushie," come on, backfield, FIGHT!

> Aye-aye ki-ike-us,
> Nobody likes us,
> We are the boys of Weequahic High—
> Aye-aye ki-ucch-us,
> *Kish mir in tuchis,*
> We are the boys of Weequahic High!

Come on—hold that line, make that point, kick 'em in the *kishkas,* go team go!

See, I'm missing my chance to be clever and quick-witted in the stands! To show off my sarcastic and mocking tongue! And after the game, missing the historical Thanksgiving meal prepared by my mother, that freckled and red-headed descendant of Polish Jews! Oh, how the blood will flow out of their faces, what a deathly silence will prevail, when she holds up the huge drumstick, and cries, "Here! For guess who!" and Guess-who is found to be AWOL! Why have I deserted my family? Maybe around the table we don't look like a painting by Norman Rockwell, but we have a good time, too, don't you worry! We don't go back to the Plymouth Rock, no Indian ever brought maize to any member of our family as far as we know—but just smell that stuffing! And look, cylinders of cranberry sauce at *either* end of the table! And the turkey's name, "Tom"! Why then can't I believe I am eating my dinner in America, that America is where *I* am, instead of some other place to which I will one day travel, as my father and I must travel every November out to that hayseed and his wife in Union, New Jersey (the *two* of them in overalls), for real Thanksgiving apple cider.

.   .   .

Another gentile heart broken by me belonged to the Pilgrim, Sarah Abbott Maulsby—New Canaan, Foxcroft, and Vassar (where she had as companion, stabled in Poughkeepsie, that other flaxen beauty, her palomino). A tall, gentle, decorous twenty-two-year-old, fresh from college, and working as a receptionist in the office of the Senator from Connecticut when we two met and coupled in the fall of 1959.

I was on the staff of the House subcommittee investigating the television quiz scandals. Perfect for a closet socialist like myself: commercial deceit on a national scale, exploitation of the innocent public, elaborate corporate chicanery—in short, good old capitalist greed. And then of course that extra bonus, Charlatan Van Doren. Such character, such brains and breeding, that candor and schoolboyish charm—the ur-WASP, wouldn't you say? And turns out he's a fake. Well, what do you know about that, Gentile America? Supergoy, a *gonif!* Steals money. Covets money. Wants money, will do anything for it. Goodness gracious me, almost as bad as Jews—you sanctimonious WASPs!

Yes, I was one happy yiddel down there in Washington, a little Stern gang of my own, busily exploding Charlie's honor and integrity, while simultaneously becoming lover to that aristocratic Yankee beauty whose forebears arrived on these shores in the seventeenth century. Phenomenon known as Hating Your Goy And Eating One Too.

Why didn't I marry that beautiful and adoring girl? I remember her in the gallery, pale and enchanting in a navy blue suit with gold buttons, watching with such pride, with such love, as I took on one afternoon, in my first public cross-examination, a very slippery network P.R. man . . . and I was impressive too, for my first time out: cool, lucid, persistent, just the faintest hammering of the heart—and only twenty-six years old. Oh yeah, when I am holding all the moral cards, watch out, you crooks you! I am nobody to futz around with when I know myself to be four hundred per cent in the right.

Why didn't I marry the girl? Well, there was her cutesy-wootsy boarding school argot, for one. Couldn't bear it. "Barf" for vomit, "ticked off" for angry, "a howl" for funny, "crackers" for crazy, "teeny" for tiny. Oh, and "*divine*." (What Mary Jane Reed means by "groovy"—I'm always telling these girls how to talk right, me with my five-hundred-word New Jersey vocabulary.) Then there were the nicknames of her friends; there were the friends themselves! Poody and Pip and Pebble, Shrimp and Brute and Tug, Squeek, Bumpo, Baba— it sounded, I said, as though she had gone to Vassar with Donald Duck's nephews . . . But then my argot caused her some pain too. The first time I said fuck in her presence (and the presence of friend Pebble, in her Peter Pan collar and her cablestitch cardigan, and tanned like an Indian from so much tennis at the Chevy Chase Club), such a look of agony passed over The Pilgrim's face, you would have thought I had just branded the four letters on her flesh. Why, she asked so plaintively once we were alone, why *had* I to be so "unattractive"? What possible pleasure had it given me to be so "ill-mannered"? What on earth had I "proved"? "Why did you have to be so pus-y like that? It was so un*called*-for." Pus-y being Debutante for disagreeable.

In bed? Nothing fancy, no acrobatics or feats of daring and skill; as we screwed our first time, so we continued—I assaulted and she surrendered, and the heat generated on her mahogany fourposter (a

Maulsby family heirloom) was considerable. Our one peripheral delight was the full-length mirror on the back of the bathroom door. There, standing thigh to thigh, I would whisper, "Look, Sarah, look." At first she was shy, left the looking to me, at first she was modest and submitted only because I wished her to, but in time she developed something of a passion for the looking glass, too, and followed the reflection of our joining with a certain startled intensity in her gaze. Did she see what I saw? *In the black pubic hair, ladies and gentlemen, weighing one hundred and seventy pounds, at least half of which is still undigested halvah and hot pastrami, from Newark, NJ, The Shnoz, Alexander Portnoy! And his opponent, in the fair fuzz, with her elegant polished limbs and the gentle maidenly face of a Botticelli, that ever-popular purveyor of the social amenities here in the Garden, one hundred and fourteen pounds of Republican refinement, and the pertest pair of nipples in all New England, from New Canaan, Connecticut, Sarah Abbott Maulsby!*

What I'm saying, Doctor, is that I don't seem to stick my dick up these girls, as much as I stick it up their backgrounds—as though through fucking I will discover America. *Conquer* America—maybe that's more like it. Columbus, Captain Smith, Governor Winthrop, General Washington—now Portnoy. As though my manifest destiny is to seduce a girl from each of the forty-eight states. As for Alaskan and Hawaiian women, I really have no feelings either way, no scores to settle, no coupons to cash in, no dreams to put to rest—who are they to me, a bunch of Eskimos and Orientals? No, I am a child of the forties, of network radio and World War Two, of eight teams to a league and forty-eight states to a country. I know all the words to "The Marine Hymn," and to "The Caissons Go Rolling Along"—and to "The Song of the Army Air Corps." I know the song of the *Navy* Air Corps: "Sky anchors aweigh/ We're sailors of the air/ We're sailing everywhere—" I can even sing you the song of the Seabees. Go ahead, name your branch of service, Spielvogel, I'll sing you your song! Please, allow me—it's my money. We used to sit on our coats, I remember, on the concrete floor, our backs against the sturdy walls of the basement corridors of my grade school, singing in unison to keep up our morale until the all-clear signal sounded—"Johnny Zero." "Praise the Lord and Pass the Ammunition." "The sky-pilot said it/ You've got to give him credit/ For a son of a gun of a gunner was he-e-e-e!" You name it, and if it was in praise of the Stars and Stripes, I know it word for word! Yes, I am a child of air raid drills, Doctor, I remember Corregidor and "The Cavalcade of America," and that flag, fluttering on its pole, being raised at that heartbreaking angle over bloody Iwo Jima. Colin Kelly went down in flames when I was eight, and Hiroshima and Nagasaki went up in a puff, one week when I was twelve, and that was the heart of my boyhood, four years of hating Tojo, Hitler, and Mussolini, and loving this brave determined republic! Rooting my little Jewish heart out for our American democracy! Well, we won, the enemy is dead in an alley back of the Wilhelmstrasse, and dead because I *prayed* him dead—and now I want what's coming to me. *My* G.I. bill—real American ass! The cunt in country-'tis-of-thee! I pledge allegiance to the twat of the United States of America—and to the republic for which it stands: Davenport, Iowa! Dayton, Ohio! Schenectady, New York, and neighboring Troy! Fort Myers, Florida! New Canaan, Connecticut! Chicago, Illinois! Albert Lea, Minnesota! Portland, Maine! Moundsville, West Virginia! Sweet land of *skikse*-tail, of thee I sing!

From the mountains,

To the prairies,

To the oceans, white-with-my-fooaahhh-mmm!

God bless A-me-ri-cuuuuhhhh!

My home, SWEET HOOOOOHHHH-M!

The Decline of the Wasp

PETER SCHRAG (1931–   ), born in Karlsruhe, Germany, came to the United States at age ten. After receiving a B.A. at Amherst in 1953, he spent two years as a reporter on the El Paso **Herald-Post** before returning for graduate work at Amherst and the University of Massachusetts. In the early 1960s he taught American Studies at Amherst, but later devoted full time to his literary work. Much of his writing has dealt with American education, including **Voices in the Classroom** (1965) and **Village School Downtown** (1967). **The Decline of the Wasp** (1972) is an expansion of the essay printed here. In 1969 he became the editor of **Change,** a magazine concerned with the problems of higher education. He has also published sprightly and penetrating essays on race, poverty, and the environment is such journals as the **Saturday Review,** the **New Republic, Commonweal,** and **Harper's.**

For most of us who were born before World War II, America was a place to be discovered; it was imperfect, perhaps—needed some re-

THE DECLINE OF THE WASP. Reprinted by permission of Curtis Brown, Ltd. Copyright © 1971 by Peter Schrag. Published in *Harper's,* April, 1970.

form, some shaping up—but it did not need to be reinvented. It was all given, like a genetic code, waiting to unfold. We all wanted to learn the style, the proper accent, agreed on its validity, and while our interpretations and our heroes varied, they were all cut from the same stock. Cowboys, pioneers, athletes, entrepreneurs, men of letters: whatever we were offered we took pretty much as our own. Whether we were small-town boys or the children of urban immigrants, we shared an eagerness to become apprentices in the great open democracy, were ready to join up, wanting only to be accepted according to the terms that history and tradition had already established. It never occurred to us to think otherwise.

What held that world together was not just a belief in some standardized version of textbook Americanism, a catalogue of accepted values, but a particular class of people and institutions that we identified with our vision of the country. The people were white and Protestant: the institutions were English; American culture was WASP. We paid lip service to the melting pot, but if, for instance, one's grandmother asked, "Is it good for the Jews?" there wasn't any question in her mind about who was running the country. The critics, the novelists, the poets, the social theorists, the men who articulated and analyzed American ideas, who governed our institutions, who embodied what we were or hoped to be—nearly all of them were WASPs. . . . The American mind was the WASP mind.

We grew up with them; they surrounded us: they were the heroes of the history we studied and of the fantasy life we sought in those Monday-through-Friday radio serials. Even Hollywood, after all the creation of Jewish producers, never did much for pluralism. The stars were often ethnics—show business and sports constituting two major avenues for "outsiders" to make it into the mainstream—but their names and the roles they played rarely, if ever, acknowledged the existence of anything beyond that mainstream. The Hyman Kaplans were lovable jerks, immigrant Sambos; Rochester said, "Yassuh, Mr. Benny" (did we realize that Benny was a Jew?) and anything beginning with Mike, Pat, or Abie was set up for a laugh. Hollywood's Jews sold the American dream strictly in WASP terms.

They—the WASPs—never thought of themselves as anything but Americans, nor did it occur to others to label them as anything special until, about twenty-five years ago, their influence began to decline and they started to lose their cultural initiative and preeminence. There were, to be sure, regional distinctions, but whatever was "American" was WASP. Indeed, there was no "other"—was, that is, no domestic base of social commentary, no voice except their voice, for the discussion of "American" problems. The ethnics had their place and their strong loyalties, but insofar as that place was *American* it was defined by WASPs. We could distinguish Jews, Irishmen, Italians, Catholics, Poles, Negroes, Indians, Mexican-Americans, Japanese-Americans, but not WASPs. When WASPs were alienated it was because, as in the case of Henry Adams, the country had moved away from them, not because, as with the others, they regarded themselves as alien in heritage or tradition. (Southerners who had lost their war and their innocence were—in that respect—alien, ethnically WASPs but also in some sense unwilling immigrants; they were among the first to be out of place in their own country.) For most WASPs, their complaints were proprietary. That is, the old place was going down because the tenants weren't keeping it up properly. They were the landlords of our culture, and their values, with rare exceptions, were those that defined it: hard work, perseverance, self-reliance, puritanism, the missionary spirit, and the abstract rule of law.

They are, of course, still with us—in corporations and clubs, in foundations and universities, in government and the military, maintaining the interlocking directorates that make sociologists salivate and that give the Establishment its ugly name: the Power Structure, the Military-Industrial Complex; the rulers of America. But while they still hold power, they hold it with less assurance and with less legitimacy than at any time in history. They are hanging on, men living off their cultural capital, but rarely able or willing to create more. One can almost define their domains by locating the people and institutions that are chronically on the defensive: university presidents and trustees; the large foundations; the corporations; government; the military. They grew great as initiators and entrepreneurs. They invented the country, its culture and its values; they shaped the institutions and organizations. Then they drew the institutions around themselves, moved to the suburbs, and became org-men.

.   .   .

One of the major attributes of the WASP idiom was its self-confidence in its own Americanism. In following the ethic of the small town, in trying to make it, the WASP was operating in a system designed by his people, operated by his people, and responsive to his people. He wasn't trying to stand somebody else's ground or beat somebody else's game. But what is there for a nation that is urban (or suburban), in which the majority has (presumably) already made it, and where size and technology are rendering much of the system impersonal and unresponsive? It is no longer possible for anyone to control the country (or the world) as we once believed we could. With the exception of the balanced ticket (in politics or employment) we have no urban ethic. And so somewhere the self-confidence froze: what in the national spirit and imagery was expansive became conservative and restrictive, enterprise turned to management, ebullience to caution. Most of all, it tended to become dull.

.   .   .

A lot of people, needless to say, have only barely made it, or haven't made it at all: prominent among them Negroes, Puerto Ricans, Poles, Irishmen, Italians, and a good number of underclass WASPs.

For them the decline in confidence tends to be traumatic. At the very moment that they are persuaded, or forced to believe, that the system will work for them—that they can make it, that their children must go to college, and all the rest—the signals from headquarters become confused and indistinct, and the rules seem to change. The children of the affluent march in the streets; long hair and at least the outward signals of sexual freedom are acceptable; hard work, stoicism, and perseverance aren't the ultimate values; individual initiative is not sufficient; the schools are "in trouble." The cultural colonies, forced by "modernization" (the supermarket, urban renewal, automated equipment, Vatican II) to abandon their own styles of life—the hierarchical family, ward politics, closed unions, old neighborboods, religion, language, food—become witnesses to behavior indicating that the (perhaps mythic) mainstream has begun to stagnate, that a lot of people no longer believe in it, or no longer believe in the old ways of getting there. Those on the move upward and outward have, in other words, no attractive place to go. Which is to say that the underclass tenants have discovered the neglect of the landlord.

Blacks are alienated because they have been kept out of the running. The white ethnics are frustrated because public attention, in defiance of the rhetoric of individual initiative and equality, has gone to blacks. (And because affluent WASPs, who had discriminated against all minorities, are trying to shift the burden of blame on the white underclass.) All of them, sensing the decline of WASP self-confidence and leadership, are left with choices among law and order (meaning militant normalcy, the old ethic), a return to their own cultural and political resources, or exotic combinations of the two. Following the lead, and to their eyes, success, of Black Power and Black Studies, a lot of minorities are trying to redevelop or to invent some exactly corresponding form of ethnic consciousness for themselves. Most of the whites, however, are or in the end will be content to cheer on the cops. For the first time we have Polish vigilantes and a Hebrew posse (the Jewish Defense League). Blacks and honkies, talking like frontiersmen, are buying guns. If the old WASP ethic was the ethic of making it, it isn't surprising that the most militant contemporary exponents of that ethic—those inclined to take its legends of force and action literally—should be among people outside the system trying to break in.

.   .   .

The enervation of WASP culture may derive, more than anything, from a loss of place. The geographic and psychic worlds of the old mainstream become less distinct, but certain special neighborhoods, even if they are a generation away, survive as regions of the mind. The sense of place: Salem and Boston and Concord; Zenith and Winesburg; Yoknapatawpha County. It produced people with accents and fashions and biases—personalities—that they carried around as overtly as parasols and walking sticks. And because they knew who they were, they were quite willing to be eccentric and crazy. Now much of that material is gone. The black ghetto still remains as a real place, and so does the memory, if not the fact, of South Boston, of Brooklyn, of rural Mississippi and small-town Texas. But how much of a sense of place can grow in a bedroom suburb? What is the inner sense of Bronxville or Winnetka?

Because WASPs regarded themselves as the proprietors of history and the managers of destiny, there was a double displacement. While they were losing their regions they also began to lose their special role as the intrinsic Americans. When we discovered that the country and the world were no longer easily manageable—when we lost our innocence—it was the WASP role which was most affected. No matter how enthusiastically the ethnics waved the flag, they had always been partial outsiders. (Or perhaps better to say that they enjoyed dual citizenship.) In any case, their culture never depended on the assurance that they were running the show. They were tenants, had learned to survive as minorities. Obviously this produced problems, but it also created the tensions and identities of which modern literature (for example) is made. And these conditions of tenancy haven't yet been destroyed, may, indeed, have been strengthened through the mass media, which have nationalized isolated pockets of minority culture. Moreover, the media help create new minorities, new constituencies: students, for example, and women. What kids or blacks do in one town is now immediately communicated to others. Normalcy doesn't make good television, happenings do. The greatest effect of the melting pot, ironically, may not have been on immigrants and minorities, but on the mainstream.

The vacuum left by the old arbiters of the single standard—Establishment intellectuals, literary critics, English professors, museum directors, and all the rest—has produced a sort of cultural prison break. And not only by ethnics, by blacks and Indians, or by kids, but by a lot of others, including all sorts of WASPs themselves, who behave as if they have been waiting for this freedom all their lives. That a lot of what results from this new breakout is bad (and who, these days, can get away with saying that?), and that a lot will be transitory is hardly surprising. In a decade hundreds of thousands of "creative" people proclaimed themselves artists and poets, a million amateurs entered the culture biz, and God knows how many gurus, cultists, swamis, and T-group trainers hung out their shingles. No one could expect most of them to be good, or perhaps even to be serious. The wildcatters are working new territory and a lot are going to go bust. But for the moment they're thriving: the Stones and the Beatles, the groups and groupies, Polish Power and Black Studies, liberation schools and free universities, Norman Mailer's ego and Alexander Portnoy's mother, *The Graduate* and *Alice's Restaurant,* rebellious nuns and protesting priests, *Rat* and *Screw* and a hundred other underground papers, mixed-media shows and the Living Theater, bookstores of the occult, Tarot cards and freaks and hipsters, miniskirts and maxi coats, beads and joss sticks . . . all coexisting (barely, uneasily) with Lyndon Johnson's cornpone, Norman Vincent Peale's sermons, *I Love Lucy, Reader's Digest,* and Apollo 12. If the 1960s produced the beginning of any sort of renaissance, its characteristic instruments are the hand-held movie camera, the electric guitar, and the mimeograph machine, and if its efforts survive in nothing else, they will undoubtedly be remembered by the greatest outpouring of poster art in all history: peace doves and protest proclamations, the face of John Lennon, the pregnant Girl Scout over the motto "Be Prepared," and the pregnant black woman over the 1968 campaign slogan, "Nixon's The One." This is a counter culture—not high, not low or middle—but eclectic.

Until recently, when encounter groups, public therapy, and other psychic ceremonies became fashionable, reason had been more or less successfully keeping the dark night of the soul within the hidden closets of the mind. And WASPs were the most reasonable people of all. There were, obviously, advantages in that. Most people, I suspect, prefer dispassionate men for airplane pilots, surgeons, and commanders of nuclear-armed strategic bombers. Moreover, we may have survived the last twenty-five years precisely because we kept hot men from taking charge. But their style didn't do much for cultural enrichment. Now everything that a graying, nervous civilization kept jammed in those closets is coming out, whether it deserves to or not: sex in all forms, feelings, emotions, self-revelation, and forms of religion and ritual long condemned as superstition. "Honesty" replaces stoicism, and "love," however understood, overwhelms "work." It may well be that the kids are mining McLuhan's non-linear culture, that print and cool reason (and WASPs) will go under together. So far there is no way of knowing. What is certain is that the old media—books, newspapers, magazines—can no longer claim a monopoly on urgent cultural articulation, and that people who work the new territories have moved a long way from the old mainstream.

WASPs seem to have been crippled by their own sanity. They have become too levelheaded. Having confused their particular social order with the Immutability of Things (and with their own welfare), they have defaulted on their birthright of cussedness and irreverence. "This took courage, this took prudence, this took stoutheartedness," thinks Arthur Winner, Jr., James Gould Cozzens' hero, at the end of *By Love Possessed*. (He has just covered up—to his and Cozzens' satisfaction—some $200,000 worth of ledger-de-main perpetrated by one of his partners.) "In this life we cannot have everything for ourselves we might like to have. . . . Victory is not in reaching certainties or solving mysteries: victory is making do with uncertainties, in supporting mysteries." WASPs are willing to be "sick"—meaning that they can have their neuroses and their "reason" too—but never crazy. People who are willing to be crazy are almost invariably Something Else. We no longer have, or seem to have the possibility of having, a figure like Bertrand Russell; we no longer even have an Everett Dirksen or a John L. Lewis.

WASP crimes these days are invariably dull—price fixing, antitrust capers, tax fraud—which is why we are so fascinated by Jimmy Hoffa, Roy Cohn, and the Mafia, why we need the Mafia, would have to invent it were we ever to suspect (as has Daniel Bell) that it doesn't really exist.

Beyond the formal institutions of business and government—the banks, the corporations, the State Department, and Congress—the unique provinces of of WASP domination tend to be conservative (in the pure sense) and mediating. WASPs, I think, still regard themselves as the principal heirs of an estate in which the streams flowed clear, the air was clean, and the language pure. In the growing number of conservation societies, and in their almost exclusive dominion over libraries, dictionary-making, and (surprising as it may seem to those familiar with only the current "celebrities" in the profession) the teaching of English, they are trying to preserve some of that estate. But as "the environment" becomes a national issue, they are going to lose ground (you should pardon the pun) even as conservationists. There are going to be new men—technicians, population planners, engineers —who will move in on the Audubon Society, the Sierra Club, and the Izaak Walton League. The urban environment (John Lindsay *vs.* the New York legislature and Nelson Rockefeller) will demand parity with the environment of Daniel Boone and the bald eagle. On some issues urban and rural conservationists can make common cause, but on others (mass transit, housing, street cleaning, and garbage collection) they cannot.

But it would be unfortunate, perhaps even fatal, if the WASP's mediating function (through courts and other institutions) were also to be seriously eroded. It is inconceivable that America could ever be integrated on ethnic terms. Can one imagine this country as essentially Negro or Italian or Polish; or believe that the Republican party would nominate anyone named Spiro Agnopopoulos for Vice President; or visualize a trial in which the defendant is white and all the other participants—judge, jurors, lawyers, witnesses—are black? (It did, in fact, happen—in the preliminary proceedings against the Klansmen charged with plotting to murder Charles Evers, the black mayor of Fayette, Mississippi—but it may never happen again.) For if the minorities no longer accept the new style of the mainstream, they are even further from accepting each other. And somebody is going to have to help keep them from tearing each other apart: cops and kids, blacks and blue-collar whites, freaks and squares. Robert Kennedy, I think, recognized this need before he was killed (significantly by a crazy ethnic resenting Kennedy's sympathy with other ethnics). This is also what made the reelection of John Lindsay possible—and significant. The Jews and Negroes of New York may have distrusted him, but they trusted the Italians even less.

Even mediation, however, is no longer feasible on the old standard rigid WASP terms. For the first time, any sort of settlement among competing group interests is going to have to do more than pay lip service to minorities and to the pluralism of styles, beliefs, and cultures. The various commissions on violence and urban riots struggled with that problem but couldn't see beyond their assumptions to the logical conclusion. America is not on the verge of becoming two separate societies, one rich and white, the other poor and black. It is becoming, in all its dreams and anxieties, a nation of outsiders for whom no single style or ethic remains possible. The Constitutional prohibition against an established state religion was adopted because the Jeffersonians understood the destructive consequences of imposing a single set of cultural beliefs beyond the guarantees of freedom and due process.

The Establishment in America has, in part, lost its grip because it devoted itself too much to the management of its game, rather than to the necessary objective of making it possible for everyone to play his own. Minorities—cultural, ethnic, even minorities of one—are fighting over the wreckage of the WASP-abandoned cities and the WASP-forsaken culture. If the WASP Establishment is to act as umpire in this contest—and if we are not to become a police state—it will have to recognize the legitimacy of the contenders. One of the reasons that growing up in America is absurd and chaotic is that the current version of Americanization—what the school people call socializing children—has lost its appeal. We will now have to devise ways of recognizing and assessing the alternatives. The mainstream is running thin.

Questions for Discussion and Writing

1. Was Andrew Carnegie's melting pot in reality Anglo-Saxon cultural imperialism? Discuss.
2. What sort of revisions would be necessary were you to undertake a production of Zangwill's play that would be palatable to modern audiences?
3. In Bourne's view what forces were working toward the "new cosmopolitan ideal" at the time of the First World War? Do you find evidence in other selections in this book that similar forces were operating in the 1960s?
4. Do Carnegie and Bourne differ concerning the effect of American life on immigrants?
5. Discuss the relation of the melting pot to "democracy," taking into account the opinions of Carnegie, Zangwill, Fairchild, and Mannes on the subject.
6. Is Jones's "Black Power" compatible with Bourne's "transnationalism"?
7. Debate Jones's contention that the only alternative to white power is exclusive and total black power.
8. Was America a melting pot for Portnoy and his family? Is there any evidence that they tried to assimilate into the American culture?
9. Contrast the different uses Zangwill and Roth make of the melting-pot ideal.
10. Does Schrag's notion of a WASP "mediating role" constitute an abandonment of the melting-pot ideal?
11. According to Zangwill what factors were eroding the melting-pot ideal by 1909? What factors did Bourne cite in 1915? Fairchild in 1926? Schrag in 1970?
12. Define: Americanism, WASP, transnationality, integration, black nation, counter-culture, pluralism.

Essay Topics

1. Does the preservation of ethnic or cultural differences require the dispersion of economic and political power to neighborhood or racial groups?
2. Discuss the impact of war on the melting-pot ideal in the twentieth century.
3. Discuss the idea that ethnic and racial stereotypes, caricatures of the groups they purport to describe, are usually mirror images of the values of the dominant culture, often reflecting its deepest fears about itself.
4. One might conclude that the failure of the melting pot is finally the failure of men to escape history. Discuss evidences of this in the selections in this section, and in current events.
5. Discuss the changing definitions of the term "dangerous foreigners" since the 1880s, and its implications for the melting-pot ideal.

Suggestions for Further Reading

PRIMARY

MARY ANTIN, *The Promised Land* (1913). The memoirs of an immigrant who became a successful author, reaffirming the melting-pot ideal in the face of criticism of the New Immigration.

J. HECTOR ST. JOHN DE CREVECOEUR, "What Is an American?" *Letters from an American Farmer* (1782). A classic statement of the melting-pot ideal by a Frenchman living in America in the earliest days of the Republic.

HAROLD CRUSE, *The Crisis of the Negro Intellectual* (1967). A provocative and controversial analysis of America's racial impasse, by a black intellectual.

NATHAN GLAZER, *Beyond the Melting Pot* (1963). A sociological analysis of the blacks, Puerto Ricans, Jews, Irish, and Italians of New York City, arguing that ethnic divisions are a permanent feature of American life despite the melting-pot ideal.

MIKE GOLD, *Jews Without Money* (1930). A semiautobiographical account of life in a New York ghetto by one of the leading Communist writers of the 1930s.

HORACE M. KALLEN, "Democracy Versus the Melting Pot," *Nation*, 100 (1915), 190–94, 217. An early statement of the cultural pluralist position in response to concern over "hyphenated-Americans" during the First World War.

THEODORE ROOSEVELT, "What Americanization Means," *Forum*, 17 (1894), 196–206. A definition by the future President, mirroring a growing concern over the New Immigration, and the "patriotism" that would inspire later attempts to Americanize the immigrant.

UPTON SINCLAIR, *The Jungle* (1906). A vivid account of immigrant life in Chicago, in a "muckraking" novel that is often also credited with inspiring the reform of the meat-packing industry.

SECONDARY

S. P. FULLINWIDER, *The Mind and Mood of Black America* (1969). A survey of black thought since the Civil War that dissects assumptions behind proposals for both integration and black separatism.

OSCAR HANDLIN, *Race and Nationality in American Life* (1957). A collection of essays that contains a challenging account of the Dillingham Commission Report of 1910, the basis of later immigration restriction laws.

EDWARD G. HARTMANN, *The Movement to Americanize the Immigrant* (1948). A history of the individuals, voluntary organizations, and state and federal agencies that advocated Americanization before and during the First World War.

JOHN HIGHAM, *Strangers in the Land* (1955). A profile of American nativist reaction to immigrants in the period from the 1880s to 1920, relating opposition to broader tensions within the society.

BARBARA SOLOMON, *Ancestors and Immigrants* (1956). A study of the rationale for immigration restrictions of the 1850s through the 1920s.

Success

The Art of Money Getting

P. T. Barnum (1810–1891), America's master showman, began his climb to success in 1835 when he purchased and displayed for profit an aged black woman, allegedly George Washington's nurse. A Connecticut Yankee, he combined native shrewdness with a keen sense of publicity in operating an American museum, complete with "freak" shows, and in managing the American tour of the Swedish actress Jenny Lind. A sometime politician, he served briefly as mayor of Bridgeport, Connecticut, and in that state's legislature. His greatest success, however, began in 1871 when he launched his famous circus. A decade later he merged his circus with that of a leading competitor to form the Barnum & Bailey Circus, "The Greatest Show on Earth."

In the United States, where we have more land than people, it is not at all difficult for persons in good health to make money. In this comparatively new field there are so many avenues of success open, so many vocations which are not crowded, that any person of either sex who is willing, at least for the time being, to engage in any respectable occupation that offers, may find lucrative employment.

Those who really desire to attain an independence, have only to set their minds upon it, and adopt the proper means, as they do in regard to any other object which they wish to accomplish, and the thing is easily done. But however easy it may be found to make money, I have no doubt many of my hearers will agree it is the most difficult thing in the world to keep it. The road to wealth is, as Dr. Franklin truly says, "as plain as the road to mill." It consists simply in expending less than we earn; that seems to be a very simple problem. Mr. Micawber, one of those happy creations of the genial Dickens, puts the case in a strong light when he says that to have an income of twenty pounds, per annum, and spend twenty pounds and sixpence, is to be the most miserable of men; whereas, to have an income of only twenty pounds, and spend but nineteen pounds and sixpence, is to be the happiest of mortals. Many of my hearers may say, "we understand this; this is

THE ART OF MONEY GETTING. From P. T. Barnum, *Struggles and Triumphs* (1869).

economy, and we know economy is wealth; we know we can't eat our cake and keep it also." Yet I beg to say that perhaps more cases of failure arise from mistakes on this point than almost any other. The fact is, many people think they understand economy when they really do not.

. . .

True economy consists in always making the income exceed the out-go. Wear the old clothes a little longer if necessary; dispense with the new pair of gloves; mend the old dress; live on plainer food if need be; so that under all circumstances, unless some unforeseen accident occurs, there will be a margin in favor of the income. A penny here, and a dollar there, placed at interest, goes on accumulating, and in this way the desired result is attained. It requires some training, perhaps, to accomplish this economy, but when once used to it, you will find there is more satisfaction in rational saving, than in irrational spending. Here is a recipe which I recommend; I have found it to work an excellent cure for extravagance and especially for mistaken economy: When you find that you have no surplus at the end of the year, and yet have a good income, I advise you to take a few sheets of paper and form them into a book and mark down every item of expenditure. Post it every day or week in two columns, one headed "necessaries" or even "comforts," and the other headed "luxuries," and you will find that the latter column will be double, treble, and frequently ten times greater than the former. The real comforts of life cost but a small portion of what most of us can earn. Dr. Franklin says "it is the eyes of others and not our own eyes which ruin us. If all the world were blind except myself I should not care for fine clothes or furniture."

. . .

The foundation of success in life is good health; that is the substratum of fortune; it is also the basis of happiness. A person cannot accumulate a fortune very well when he is sick. He has no ambition; no incentive; no force. Of course, there are those who have bad health and cannot help it; you cannot expect that such persons can accumulate wealth; but there are a great many in poor health who need not be so.

If, then, sound health is the foundation of success and happiness in life, how important it is that we should study the laws of health, which is but another expression for the laws of nature! . . .

Many persons knowingly violate the laws of nature against their better impulses, for the sake of fashion. For instance, there is one thing that nothing living except a vile worm ever naturally loved, and that is tobacco; yet how many persons there are who deliberately train an unnatural appetite, and overcome this implanted aversion for tobacco, to such a degree that they get to love it. They have got hold of a poisonous, filthy weed, or rather that takes a firm hold of them. Here are married men who run about spitting tobacco juice on the carpet and floors, and sometimes even upon their wives besides. They do not kick their wives out of doors like drunken men, but their wives, I have no doubt, often wish they were outside of the house. Another perilous feature is that this artificial appetite, like jealousy, "grows by what it feeds on"; when you love that which is unnatural, a stronger appetite is created for the hurtful thing than the natural desire for what is harmless. There is an old proverb which says that "habit is second nature," but an artificial habit is stronger than nature. Take for instance an old tobacco-chewer; his love for the "quid" is stronger than his love for any particular kind of food. He can give up roast beef easier than give up the weed.

.   .   .

These remarks apply with ten-fold force to the use of intoxicating drinks. To make money, requires a clear brain. A man has got to see that two and two make four; he must lay all his plans with reflection and forethought, and closely examine all the details and the ins and outs of business. As no man can succeed in business unless he has a brain to enable him to lay his plans, and reason to guide him in their execution, so, no matter how bountifully a man may be blessed with intelligence, if the brain is muddled, and his judgment warped by intoxicating drinks, it is impossible for him to carry on business successfully. How many good opportunities have passed, never to return, while a man was sipping a "social glass," with his friend! How many foolish bargains have been made under the influence of the "nervine," which temporarily makes its victim think he is rich. How many important chances have been put off until to-morrow, and then forever, because the wine cup has thrown the system into a state of lassitude, neutralizing the energies so essential to success in business. Verily "wine is a mocker." The use of intoxicating drinks as a beverage, is as much an infatuation, as is the smoking of opium by the Chinese, and the former is quite as destructive to the success of the business man as the latter. It is an unmitigated evil, utterly indefensible in the light of philosophy, religion, or good sense. It is the parent of nearly every other evil in our country.

Don't mistake your vocation: The safest plan, and the one most sure of success for the young man starting in life, is to select the vocation which is most congenial to his tastes.

.   .   .

Unless a man enters upon the vocation intended for him by nature, and best suited to his peculiar genius, he cannot succeed. I am glad to believe that the majority of persons do find the right vocation. Yet we see many who have mistaken their calling, from the blacksmith up (or down) to the clergyman. You will see for instance, that extraordinary linguist the "learned blacksmith," who ought to have been a teacher of languages; and you may have seen lawyers, doctors and clergymen who were better fitted by nature for the anvil or the lapstone.

·   ·   ·

Avoid debt: Young men starting in life should avoid running into debt. There is scarcely anything that drags a person down like debt. It is a slavish position to get in, yet we find many a young man hardly out of his "teens" running in debt. He meets a chum and says, "Look at this; I have got trusted for a new suit of clothes." He seems to look upon the clothes as so much given to him; well, it frequently is so, but, if he succeeds in paying and then gets trusted again, he is adopting a habit which will keep him in poverty through life. Debt robs a man of his self respect, and makes him almost despise himself. Grunting and groaning and working for what he has eaten up or worn out, and now when he is called upon to pay up, he has nothing to show for his money; this is properly termed "working for a dead horse." I do not speak of merchants buying and selling on credit, or of those who buy on credit in order to turn the purchase to a profit. The old Quaker said to his farmer son, "John, never get trusted; but if thee gets trusted for anything, let it be for 'manure,' because that will help thee pay it back again."

·   ·   ·

Persevere: When a man is in the right path, he must persevere. I speak of this because there are some persons who are "born tired"; naturally lazy and possessing no self reliance and no perseverance. But, they can cultivate these qualities, as Davy Crockett said:

> "This thing remember, when I am dead,
> Be sure you are right, then go ahead."

It is this go-aheaditiveness, this determination not to let the "horrors" or the "blues" take possession of you, so as to make you relax your energies in the struggle for independence, which you must cultivate.

How many have almost reached the goal of their ambition, but losing faith in themselves have relaxed their energies, and the golden prize has been lost forever.

It is, no doubt, often true, as Shakespeare says:

> "There is a tide in the affairs of men,
> Which taken at the flood, leads on to fortune."

If you hesitate, some bolder hand will stretch out before you and get the prize. Remember the proverb of Solomon: "He becometh poor that dealeth with a slack hand; but the hand of the diligent maketh rich."

.   .   .

Whatever you do, do with all your might: Work at it, if necessary, early and late, in season and out of season, not leaving a stone unturned, and never deferring for a single hour that which can be done just as well *now*. The old proverb is full of truth and meaning, "Whatever is worth doing at all, is worth doing well." Many a man acquires a a fortune by doing his business thoroughly, while his neighbor remains poor for life because he only half does it. Ambition, energy, industry, perseverance, are indispensable requisites for success in business.

.   .   .

Depend upon your own personal exertions: The eye of the employer is often worth more than the hands of a dozen employees. In the nature of things, an agent cannot be so faithful to his employer as to himself. Many who are employers will call to mind instances where the best employees have overlooked important points which could not have escaped their own observation as a proprietor. No man has a right to expect to succeed in life unless he understands his business, and nobody can understand his business thoroughly unless he learns it by personal application and experience. A man may be a manufacturer; he has got to learn the many details of his business personally; he will learn something every day, and he will find he will make mistakes nearly every day. And these very mistakes are helps to him in the way of experiences if he but heeds them. He will be like the Yankee tin-peddler, who, having been cheated as to quality in the purchase of his merchandise, said: "All right, there's a little information to be gained every day; I will never be cheated in that way again." Thus a man buys his experience, and it is the best kind if not purchased at too dear a rate.

.   .   .

There is no such thing in the world as luck. There never was a man who could go out in the morning and find a purse full of gold in the street to-day, and another to-morrow, and so on, day after day. He may do so once in his life; but so far as mere luck is concerned, he is as liable to lose it as to find it. "Like causes produce like effects." If a man adopts the proper methods to be successful, "luck" will not prevent him. If he does not succeed, there are reasons for it, although perhaps, he may not be able to see them.

.   .   .

Learn something useful: Every man should make his son or daughter learn some trade or profession, so that in these days of changing fortunes—of being rich to-day and poor to-morrow,—they may have something tangible to fall back upon. This provision might save many persons from misery, who by some unexpected turn of fortune have lost all their means.

Let hope predominate, but be not too visionary: Many persons are always kept poor, because they are too visionary. Every project looks to them like certain success, and therefore they keep changing from one business to another, always in hot water, always "under the harrow." The plan of "counting the chickens before they are hatched" is an error of ancient date, but it does not seem to improve by age.

Do not scatter your powers: Engage in one kind of business only, and stick to it faithfully until you succeed, or until your experience shows that you should abandon it. A constant hammering on one nail will generally drive it home at last, so that it can be clinched. When a man's undivided attention is centered on one object, his mind will constantly be suggesting improvements of value, which would escape him if his brain was occupied by a dozen different subjects at once. Many a fortune has slipped through a man's fingers because he was engaging in too many occupations at a time. There is good sense in the old caution against having too many irons in the fire at once.

Be systematic: Men should be systematic in their business. A person who does business by rule, having a time and place for everything, doing his work promptly, will accomplish twice as much and with half the trouble of him who does it carelessly and slipshod. By introducing system into all your transactions, doing one thing at a time, always meeting appointments with punctuality, you find leisure for pastime and recreation; whereas the man who only half does one thing, and then turns to something else and half does that, will have his business at loose ends, and will never know when his day's work is done, for it never will be done. Of course there is a limit to all these rules. We must try to preserve the happy medium, for there is such a thing as being too systematic. There are men and women, for instance, who put away things so carefully that they can never find them again. It is too much like the "red tape" formality at Washington, and Mr. Dickens' "Circumlocution Office,"—all theory and no result.

.   .   .

Advertise your business: We all depend, more or less, upon the public for our support. We all trade with the public,—lawyers, doctors, shoemakers, artists, blacksmiths, showmen, opera singers, railroad presidents, and college professors. Those who deal with the public must be careful that their goods are valuable; that they are genuine, and will give satisfaction. When you get an article which you know is going to please your customers, and that when they have tried it, they will feel they have got their money's worth, then let the fact be known that you have got it. Be careful to advertise it in some shape or other, because it is evident that if a man has ever so good an article for sale, and nobody knows it, it will bring him no return. In a country like this, where nearly everybody reads, and where newspapers are issued and circulated in editions of five thousand to two hundred thousand, it would be very unwise if this channel was not taken advantage of to reach the public in advertising. A newspaper goes into the family and is read by wife and children, as well as the head of the house; hence hundreds and thousands of people may read your advertisement, while you are attending to your routine business. Many, perhaps, read it while you are asleep. The whole philosophy of life is, first "sow," then "reap." That is the way the farmer does; he plants his potatoes and corn, and sows his grain, and then goes about something else, and the time comes when he reaps. But he never reaps first and sows afterwards. This principle applies to all kinds of business, and to nothing more eminently than to advertising. If a man has a genuine article, there is no way in which he can reap more advantageously than by "sowing" to the public in this way. He must, of course, have a really good article, and one which will please his customers; anything spurious will not succeed permanently, because the public is wiser than many imagine. Men and women are selfish, and we all prefer purchasing where we can get the most for our money; and we try to find out where we can most surely do so.

You may advertise a spurious article, and induce many people to call and buy it once, but they will denounce you as an imposter and swindler, and your business will gradually die out, and leave you poor. This is right. Few people can safely depend upon chance custom. You all need to have your customers return and purchase again. A man said to me, "I have tried advertising, and did not succeed; yet I have a good article."

I replied, "My friend, there may be exceptions to a general rule. But how do you advertise?"

"I put it in a weekly newspaper three times, and paid a dollar and a half for it."

I replied: "Sir, advertising is like learning—'a little is a dangerous thing.'"

.   .   .

Some men have a peculiar genius for writing a striking advertisement, one that will arrest the attention of the reader at first sight. This tact, of course, gives the advertiser a great advantage. Sometimes a man makes himself popular by an unique sign or a curious display in his window. Recently I observed a swing sign extending over the sidewalk in front of a store, on which was the inscription, in plain letters,

"DON'T READ THE OTHER SIDE"

Of course I did, and so did everybody else, and I learned that the man had made an independence by first attracting the public to his business in that way and then using his customers well afterwards.

.   .   .

Be polite and kind to your customers: Politeness and civility are the best capital ever invested in business. Large stores, gilt signs, flaming advertisements, will all prove unavailing if you or your employees treat your patrons abruptly. The truth is, the more kind and liberal a man is, the more generous will be the patronage bestowed upon him. "Like begets like." The man who gives the greatest amount of goods of a corresponding quality for the least sum (still reserving to himself a profit) will generally succeed best in the long run. This brings us to the golden rule, "As ye would that men should do to you, do ye also to them," and they will do better by you than if you always treated them as if you wanted to get the most you could out of them for the least return. Men who drive sharp bargains with their customers, acting as if they never expected to see them again, will not be mistaken. They never will see them again as customers. People don't like to pay and get kicked also.

.   .   .

Be charitable: Of course men should be charitable, because it is a duty and a pleasure. But even as a matter of policy, if you possess no higher incentive, you will find that the liberal man will command patronage, while the sordid, uncharitable miser will be avoided.

Solomon says: "There is that scattereth and yet increaseth; and there is that withholdeth more than meet, but it tendeth to poverty." Of course the only true charity is that which is from the heart.

The best kind of charity is to help those who are willing to help themselves. Promiscuous almsgiving, without inquiring into the worthiness of the applicant, is bad in every sense. But to search out and quietly assist those who are struggling for themselves, is the kind that "scattereth and yet increaseth." But don't fall into the idea that some persons practise, of giving a prayer instead of a potato, and a benediction instead of bread, to the hungry. It is easier to make Christians with full stomachs than empty.

Don't blab: Some men have a foolish habit of telling their business secrets. If they make money they like to tell their neighbors how it was done. Nothing is gained by this, and ofttimes much is lost. Say nothing about your profits, your hopes, your expectations, your intentions. And this should apply to letters as well as to conversation. Goethe makes Mephistopheles say: "never write a letter nor destroy me." Business men must write letters, but they should be careful what they put in them. If you are losing money, be specially cautious and not tell of it, or you will lose your reputation.

Preserve your integrity: It is more precious than diamonds or rubies. The old miser said to his sons: "Get money; get it honestly, if you can, but get money." This advice was not only atrociously wicked, but it was the very essence of stupidity. It was as much as to say, "if you find it difficult to obtain money honestly, you can easily get it dishonestly. Get it in that way." Poor fool! Not to know that the most difficult thing in life is to make money dishonestly! not to know that our prisons are full of men who attempted to follow this advice; not to understand that no man can be dishonest without soon being found out, and that when his lack of principle is discovered, nearly every avenue to success is closed against him forever. . . .

A man who is known to be strictly honest, may be ever so poor, but he has the purses of all the community at his disposal;—for all know that if he promises to return what he borrows, he will never disappoint them. As a mere matter of selfishness, therefore, if a man had no higher motive for being honest, all will find that the maxim of Dr. Franklin can never fail to be true, that "honesty is the best policy."

To get rich, is not always equivalent to being successful. "There are many rich poor men," while there are many others, honest and devout men and women, who have never possessed so much money as some rich persons squander in a week, but who are nevertheless really richer and happier than any man can ever be while he is a transgressor of the higher laws of his being.

The inordinate love of money, no doubt, may be and is "the root of all evil," but money itself, when properly used, is not only a "handy thing to have in the house," but affords the gratification of blessing our race by enabling its possessor to enlarge the scope of human happiness and human influence. The desire for wealth is nearly universal, and none can say it is not laudable, provided the possessor of it accepts its responsibilities, and uses it as a friend to humanity.

The history of money getting, which is commerce, is a history of civilization, and wherever trade has flourished most, there, too, have art and science produced the noblest fruits. In fact, as a general thing, money getters are the benefactors of our race. To them, in a great measure, are we indebted for our institutions of learning and of art, our academies, colleges and churches. It is no argument against the desire for, or the possession of wealth, to say that there are sometimes misers who hoard money only for the sake of hoarding, and who have no higher aspiration than to grasp everything which comes within their reach. As we have sometimes hypocrites in religion, and demagogues in politics, so there are occasionally misers among money getters. These, however, are only exceptions to the general rule. But when, in this country, we find such a nuisance and stumbling block as a miser, we remember with gratitude that in America we have no laws of primogeniture, and that in the due course of nature the time will come when the hoarded dust will be scattered for the benefit of mankind. To all men and women, therefore, do I conscientiously say, make money honestly, and not otherwise, for Shakespeare has truly said, "He that wants money, means and content, is without three good friends."

Life Without Principle

HENRY DAVID THOREAU (1817–1862), probably America's boldest thinker, was born in Concord, Massachusetts. A Harvard graduate, he was by occupation a sometime surveyor and pencil-maker. Challenging tradition, he had little use for conventional wisdom. "No way of thinking or doing, however ancient, can be trusted without proof," he wrote. "I have lived some thirty years on this planet, and I have yet to hear the first syllable of valuable or even earnest advice from my seniors."

Like his friend and mentor Ralph Waldo Emerson, one of the several Transcendentalists with whom he associated, Thoreau found special inspiration in nature. In **Walden** (1854) he translated his experiences during a two-year period of primitive living at Walden Pond outside Concord into a masterpiece that has few rivals in American literature. The empty bustle of Barnum's America, the dreary routines that passed for "busyness," especially disturbed

LIFE WITHOUT PRINCIPLE. From Henry David Thoreau, *The Writings of Henry David Thoreau* (1906).

him. "The mass of men," he wrote in one of the most quoted passages in **Walden,** "lead lives of quiet desperation." In "Life Without Principle," published posthumously in 1863, he developed this theme. "He was," wrote Emerson in his obituary of Thoreau, "a speaker and actor of the truth."

. . . Let us consider the way in which we spend our lives.

This world is a place of business. What an infinite bustle! I am awaked almost every night by the panting of the locomotive. It interrupts my dreams. There is no sabbath. It would be glorious to see mankind at leisure for once. It is nothing but work, work, work. I cannot easily buy a blank-book to write thoughts in; they are commonly ruled for dollars and cents. An Irishman, seeing me making a minute in the fields, took it for granted that I was calculating my wages. If a man was tossed out of a window when an infant, and so made a cripple for life, or scared out of his wits by the Indians, it is regretted chiefly because he was thus incapacitated for—business! I think that there is nothing, not even crime, more opposed to poetry, to philosophy, ay, to life itself, than this incessant business.

There is a coarse and boisterous money-making fellow in the outskirts of our town, who is going to build a bank-wall under the hill along the edge of his meadow. The powers have put this into his head to keep him out of mischief, and he wishes me to spend three weeks digging there with him. The result will be that he will perhaps get some more money to hoard, and leave for his heirs to spend foolishly. If I do this, most will commend me as an industrious and hardworking man; but if I choose to devote myself to certain labors which yield more real profit, though but little money, they may be inclined to look on me as an idler. Nevertheless, as I do not need the police of meaningless labor to regulate me, and do not see anything absolutely praiseworthy in this fellow's undertaking any more than in many an enterprise of our own or foreign governments, however amusing it may be to him or them, I prefer to finish my education at a different school.

If a man walk in the woods for love of them half of each day, he is in danger of being regarded as a loafer; but if he spends his whole day as a speculator, shearing off those woods and making earth bald before her time, he is esteemed an industrious and enterprising citizen. As if a town had no interest in its forests but to cut them down!

Most men would feel insulted if it were proposed to employ them in throwing stones over a wall, and then in throwing them back, merely that they might earn their wages. But many are no more worthily employed now. For instance: just after sunrise, one summer morning,

I noticed one of my neighbors walking beside his team, which was slowly drawing a heavy hewn stone swung under the axle, surrounded by an atmosphere of industry,—his day's work begun,—his brow commenced to sweat,—a reproach to all sluggards and idlers,—pausing abreast the shoulders of his oxen, and half turning round with a flourish of his merciful whip, while they gained their length on him. And I thought, Such is the labor which the American Congress exists to protect,—honest, manly toil,—honest as the day is long,—that makes his bread taste sweet, and keeps society sweet,—which all men respect and have consecrated; one of the sacred band, doing the needful but irksome drudgery. Indeed, I felt a slight reproach, because I observed this from a window, and was not abroad and stirring about a similar business. The day went by, and at evening I passed the yard of another neighbor, who keeps many servants, and spends much money foolishly, while he adds nothing to the common stock, and there I saw the stone of the morning lying beside a whimsical structure intended to adorn this Lord Timothy Dexter's premises, and the dignity forthwith departed from the teamster's labor, in my eyes. In my opinion, the sun was made to light worthier toil than this. I may add that his employer has since run off, in debt to a good part of the town, and, after passing through Chancery, has settled somewhere else, there to become once more a patron of the arts.

The ways by which you may get money almost without exception lead downward. To have done anything by which you earned money *merely* is to have been truly idle or worse. If the laborer gets no more than the wages which his employer pays him, he is cheated, he cheats himself. If you would get money as a writer or lecturer, you must be popular, which is to go down perpendicularly. Those services which the community will most readily pay for, it is most disagreeable to render. You are paid for being something less than a man. The state does not commonly reward a genius any more wisely. Even the poet laureate would rather not have to celebrate the accidents of royalty. He must be bribed with a pipe of wine; and perhaps another poet is called away from his muse to gauge that very pipe. As for my own business, even that kind of surveying which I could do with most satisfaction my employers do not want. They would prefer that I should do my work coarsely and not too well, ay, not well enough. When I observe that there are different ways of surveying, my employer commonly asks which will give him the most land, not which is most correct. I once invented a rule for measuring cord-wood, and tried to introduce it in Boston; but the measurer there told me that the sellers did not wish to have their wood measured correctly,—that he was already too accurate for them, and therefore they commonly got their wood measured in Charlestown before crossing the bridge.

The aim of the laborer should be, not to get his living, to get "a good job," but to perform well a certain work; and, even in a pecuniary sense, it would be economy for a town to pay its laborers so well that they would not feel that they were working for low ends, as for a livelihood merely, but for scientific, or even moral ends. Do not hire a man who does your work for money, but him who does it for love of it.

It is remarkable that there are few men so well employed, so much to their minds, but that a little money or fame would commonly buy them off from their present pursuit. I see advertisements for *active* young men, as if activity were the whole of a young man's capital. Yet I have been surprised when one has with confidence proposed to me, a grown man, to embark in some enterprise of his, as if I had absolutely nothing to do, my life having been a complete failure hitherto. What a doubtful compliment this to pay me! As if he had met me half-way across the ocean beating up against the wind, but bound nowhere, and proposed to me to go along with him! If I did, what do you think the underwriters would say? No, no! I am not without employment at this stage of the voyage. To tell the truth, I saw an advertisement for ablebodied seamen, when I was a boy, sauntering in my native port, and as soon as I came of age I embarked.

The community has no bribe that will tempt a wise man. You may raise money enough to tunnel a mountain, but you cannot raise money enough to hire a man who is minding *his own* business. An efficient and valuable man does what he can, whether the community pay him for it or not. The inefficient offer their inefficiency to the highest bidder, and are forever expecting to be put into office. One would suppose that they were rarely disappointed.

Perhaps I am more than usually jealous with respect to my freedom. I feel that my connection with and obligation to society are still very slight and transient. Those slight labors which afford me a livelihood, and by which it is allowed that I am to some extent serviceable to my contemporaries, are as yet commonly a pleasure to me, and I am not often reminded that they are a necessity. So far I am successful. But I foresee that if my wants should be much increased, the labor required to supply them would become a drudgery. If I should sell both my forenoons and afternoons to society, as most appear to do, I am sure that for me there would be nothing left worth living for. I trust that I shall never thus sell my birthright for a mess of pottage. I wish to suggest that a man may be very industrious, and yet not spend his time well. There is no more fatal blunderer than he who consumes the greater part of his life getting his living. All great enterprises are self-supporting. The poet, for instance, must sustain his body by his poetry, as a steam planing-mill feeds its boilers with the shavings it makes. You must get your living by loving. But as it is said of the merchants that ninety-seven in a hundred fail, so the life of men generally, tried by this standard, is a failure, and bankruptcy may be surely prophesied.

Merely to come into the world the heir of a fortune is not to be born, but to be still-born, rather. To be supported by the charity of friends, or a government pension,—provided you continue to breathe, —by whatever fine synonyms you describe these relations, is to go into the almshouse. On Sundays the poor debtor goes to church to take an account of stock, and finds, of course, that his outgoes have been greater than his income. In the Catholic Church, especially, they go into chancery, make a clean confession, give up all, and think to start again. Thus men will lie on their backs, talking about the fall of man, and never make an effort to get up.

As for the comparative demand which men make on life, it is an important difference between two, that the one is satisfied with a level success, that his marks can all be hit by point-blank shots, but the other, however low and unsuccessful his life may be, constantly elevates his aim, though at a very slight angle to the horizon. I should much rather be the last man,—though, as the Orientals say, "Greatness doth not approach him who is forever looking down; and all those who are looking high are growing poor."

It is remarkable that there is little or nothing to be remembered written on the subject of getting a living; how to make getting a living not merely honest and honorable, but altogether inviting and glorious; for if *getting* a living is not so, then living is not. One would think, from looking at literature, that this question had never disturbed a solitary individual's musings. Is it that men are too much disgusted with their experience to speak of it? The lesson of value which money teaches, which the Author of the Universe has taken so much pains to teach us, we are inclined to skip altogether. As for the means of living, it is wonderful how indifferent men of all classes are about it, even reformers, so called,—whether they inherit, or earn, or steal it. I think that Society has done nothing for us in this respect, or at least has undone what she has done. Cold and hunger seem more friendly to my nature than those methods which men have adopted and advise to ward them off.

The title *wise* is, for the most part, falsely applied. How can one be a wise man, if he does not know any better how to live than other men?—if he is only more cunning and intellectually subtle? Does Wisdom work in a tread-mill? or does she teach how to succeed *by her example?* Is there any such thing as wisdom not applied to life? Is she merely the miller who grinds the finest logic? It is pertinent to ask if Plato got his *living* in a better way or more successfully than his contemporaries,—or did he succumb to the difficulties of life like other men? Did he seem to prevail over some of them merely by indifference, or by assuming grand airs? or find it easier to live, because his aunt remembered him in her will? The ways in which most men get their living, that is, live, are mere makeshifts, and a shirking of the real business of life,—chiefly because they do not know, but partly because they do not mean, any better. . . .

Success Is Counted Sweetest

EMILY DICKINSON (1830–1886) was born in Amherst, Massachusetts where she lived almost all of her secluded life. Entering South Hadley seminary (later Mount Holyoke) she was, as she said, "cramped, curbed and repressed in every natural desire or impulse," and soon quit her formal education. A brief and mysterious love affair, during a winter in Washington, D.C., in 1853, changed a bright and witty young girl into the mystical poetess who turned the soul of her generation inside-out. "Success," written in 1859 and published in 1878, was one of the few of her poems to appear during her lifetime.

Success is counted sweetest
By those who ne'er succeed.
To comprehend a nectar
Requires sorest need.

Not one of all the purple Host
Who took the Flag today
Can tell the definition
So clear of Victory

As he defeated—dying—
On whose forbidden ear

SUCCESS IS COUNTED SWEETEST. From Emily Dickinson, *Poems* (1890). Reprinted by permission of the publishers and the Trustees of Amherst College from Thomas H. Johnson, editor, *The Poems of Emily Dickinson*, Cambridge, Mass.: The Belknap Press of Harvard University Press, Copyright, 1951, 1955, by The President and Fellows of Harvard College.

The distant strains of triumph
Burst agonized and clear!

Richard Cory

EDWIN ARLINGTON ROBINSON (1869–1935), born and raised in Maine, numbered among his colonial ancestors the poetess Anne Bradstreet (who is represented in the second section of this book). After attending Harvard for two years he was summoned home permanently to find the family fortune dissipated, his father slowly dying, and his two brothers stricken with incurable diseases. His poetry, dark and sardonic in its view of human life, echoed this personal experience. A master of form and technique, especially in blank verse, he gained recognition slowly. Impressed by his early poems, President Theodore Roosevelt appointed him to a minor position in the customs service, allowing him to pursue his writing. Robinson won national acclaim for **The Man Against the Sky** (1916), a book of verse, and subsequently received the Pulitzer prize for his **Collected Poems** (1922).

Whenever Richard Cory went down town,
We people on the pavement looked at him:
He was a gentleman from sole to crown,
Clean favored, and imperially slim.

And he was always quietly arrayed,
And he was always human when he talked;
But still he fluttered pulses when he said,
"Good-morning," and he glittered when he walked.

And he was rich—yes, richer than a king—
And admirably schooled in every grace:
In fine, we thought that he was everything
To make us wish that we were in his place.

RICHARD CORY. From Edwin Arlington Robinson, *Children of the Night* (1897).

So on we worked, and waited for the light,
And went without the meat, and cursed the bread;
And Richard Cory, one calm summer night,
Went home and put a bullet through his head.

The Trees in the Garden
Rained Flowers

STEPHEN CRANE (1871–1900), novelist and journalist, was born in Newark, New Jersey, and attended Lafayette College and Syracuse University. Considered a member of the Naturalist school, he scandalized many Americans with **Maggie: A Girl of the Street** (1894), and won fame with **The Red Badge of Courage** (1895) and **The Open Boat and Other Stories** (1899). His interest in the success myth, a favorite theme of the Naturalists, is apparent in "A Self Made Man," a parody in his **Midnight Sketches** (1899), and in **George's Mother** (1896), a novelette dealing with the Temperance question.

The trees in the garden rained flowers.
Children ran there joyously.
They gathered the flowers
Each to himself.
Now there were some
Who gathered great heaps—
Having opportunity and skill—
Until, behold, only chance blossoms
Remained for the feeble.
Then a little spindling tutor
Ran importantly to the father, crying:
"Pray, come hither!
See this unjust thing in your garden!"
But when the father had surveyed,

THE TREES IN THE GARDEN RAINED FLOWERS.   From Stephen Crane, *War Is Kind* (1899).

He admonished the tutor:
"Not so, small sage!
This thing is just.
For, look you,
Are not they who possess the flowers
Stronger, bolder, shrewder
Than they who have none?
Why should the strong—
The beautiful strong—
Why should they not have the flowers?"
Upon reflection, the tutor bowed to the ground,
"My lord," he said,
"The stars are displaced
By this towering wisdom."

Sowing and Reaping

BOOKER T. WASHINGTON (1856–1915), born in slavery in Franklin County, Virginia, achieved success that rivaled that of the "rags to riches" heroes. After working his way through Hampton Institute, he became president of the newly founded Tuskegee Institute in Alabama in 1881. Within a decade he emerged as the leading spokesman for black America. **Sowing and Reaping**, published a year before his autobiographical **Up from Slavery** (1901), reveals the perennial appeal of "black capitalism." During the final years of his life, Washington came under sharp attack from a younger generation of black professionals who found this program inadequate.

1

"Be not deceived; God is not mocked; for whatsoever a man soweth that shall he also reap." Again: "He which soweth sparingly shall also reap sparingly; and he which soweth bountifully shall reap also bountifully." (II. Cor. ix. 6.)

From Booker T. Washington, *Sowing and Reaping* (1900).

These quotations are applicable to man in all the activities of life, both spiritual and material. Our harvest is always in proportion to the amount of earnest labour that we put into our work. A farmer who puts earnest effort into his field work will reap a profitable harvest. The student who puts earnest effort into a lesson will get pleasure and satisfaction from it; he need not, however, be a student only in the closet, but in the great world as well, where practice takes the place of theory. In either case, when he has performed his duty, his conscience will be clear; he will be free from any restraint; he will have courage to face the obligations which confront all of us in the battle of life. A man gets knowledge and lays the basis of substantial influence in so far and no farther as he applies himself to the mastery of the thing to which he is most inclined.

Take, for example, the man engaged in business pursuits. His profits are always in proportion to the amount of money, the skill and the labour that he puts into his business. If he fails to keep his eyes open to the main chance, if he does not know when to advance and when to reduce the price of his goods, he will have no profit; his rivals will get the best of him, and he may have to go out of business. And this is true of all the pursuits of life. We get out of every venture just what we put into it; no more, no less. To attain success we must put forth hard and honest labour. At the back of all success there is hard, persistent labour. There is no royal road. Those who think there is always fail. No man ever reaped any success in life who did not sow wisely. As each man takes up the serious business of life he must do something,—he must labour and wait. In order to reap something, something must be done. Value for value, is the real standard of life's exchange of benefits.

Show me a man who is always grumbling, always finding fault with his condition, never satisfied with his opportunities, and I will show you a man who does not appreciate the opportunities in the environment in which he is to work out his weal or woe. Hard labour is the key-note to success. One of the wisest things ex-Senator B. K. Bruce ever said was that "luck is a fool." So it is. There is no luck; it is all labour and patience.

And every man who wants to succeed must learn the process of overlapping. That is, no man who wishes to succeed should be afraid of doing just a little more than lies in the direct line of his duty. He must be interested in his work.

No man lives to himself. He is a related creature. He cannot confine himself to himself. He is his brother's keeper, because his brother is his keeper in more ways than one. We lean one upon the other. When we do this we establish a feeling of confidence, of appreciation, of helpfulness, in the estimation of a neighbour, that nothing can destroy. If a person asks us to do a certain thing which is fair and honest, do that thing; not only do that, but do more. Combine your force with his, and win his undivided confidence. This process of over-lapping establishes the greatest happiness, since it creates a community of feeling and interest, without which no man can hope to succeed.

In every pursuit of life, it may be accepted as an axiom that we get out of every effort just what we put into it of hard, honest labour. That is to say: "Whatsoever a man soweth that shall he also reap."

7

The Negro race must recognise that their condition is, in a large measure, different from that of the white race. Now, this difference in condition demands a certain difference in education. It is true that the Negro labours under a great many disadvantages; still, he is in a position to profit by the mistakes of the white race. The white race has been two or three centuries learning that they have made a mistake in simply cultivating the head,—in not coupling education of the head with education of the hand. They have only discovered their mistake in the closing years of the nineteenth century. Most that has been done in the development of industrial education has been done in the past three decades. While the white race was three thousand years discovering this fundamental error in education, the Negro was born right into a condition of activity in industrial and scientific education, in which he can take advantage of the mistakes the white race has been making.

Negro children have educational advantages that thousands of white children never had. Take the President of the United States. The smallest black boy on the grounds of the Tuskegee Institute has four or five times the advantages in education that the President had when he was a boy. Speak to a white man who is forty or fifty years of age about kindergartens, about learning the alphabet without going through the old humdrum method, and he will tell you that he knows nothing about the subject. Now, Negro as well as white children are born into the kindergarten system.

But, in spite of all the educational and other advantages that the Negro enjoys, his condition is not the same as that of other people. Why? Because, as I have often said, the whole race is hungry. I was talking to the president of Alcorn College, at Rodney, Miss., recently, about the condition of the Negroes in Mississippi and Louisiana, and he said those people were hungry. I have letters from South Carolina and other States which contain the one general piece of information that the people are hungry. If you will agree that the Negro race is hungry,—hungry morally, mentally, spiritually, and materially,—then you will also agree with me that the most sensible thing to do is to give most of our time and strength toward supplying for the masses the thing they most stand in need of.

I am not now, and never have been, opposed to any man or woman getting all the education he or she can. The more the better. It does not matter where or how they get it; the main question is, What are they going to do with it when they have got it? The system of education is false the whole strength of which shall not be applied during the next fifty or one hundred years to preparing the masses to wring from our social conditions the means to supply their hunger with the food of life.

And are not the masses of all races in all lands hungry? Are they not waiting and crying for the sort of education that will enable them to conquer their hunger by conquering the forces of nature and the ignorance which wastes more than it utilises?

I may appropriately conclude this little volume, as I began it, with the words from the Inspired Book, which were intended more for the educated few than for the ignorant many:

"Be not deceived; God is not mocked; for whatsoever a man soweth that shall he also reap."

The Big Secret of Dealing with People

DALE CARNEGIE (1888–1955), born in Maryville, Missouri, studied for his highly successful lecturing career at a Missouri teachers college, dramatic and journalism schools, and at the Baltimore School of Commerce and Finance (B.C.S., 1917). Between 1912 and 1945 his classes, radio broadcasts, and writings on effective speaking and applied psychology attracted millions of Americans interested in "making it" in the complex world of modern business.

THE BIG SECRET OF DEALING WITH PEOPLE. From Dale Carnegie, *How to Win Friends and Influence People*. Copyright © 1936 by Dale Carnegie. Renewed Copyright © 1969 by Dorothy Carnegie. Reprinted by permission of Simon & Schuster, Inc.

There is only one way under high Heaven to get anybody to do anything. Did you ever stop to think of that? Yes, just one way. And that is by making the other person want to do it.

Remember, there is no other way.

Of course, you can make a man want to give you his watch by sticking a revolver in his ribs. You can make an employee give you co-operation—until your back is turned—by threatening to fire him. You can make a child do what you want it to do by a whip or a threat. But these crude methods have sharply undesirable repercussions.

The only way I can get you to do anything is by giving you what you want.

What do you want?

The famous Dr. Sigmund Freud of Vienna, one of the most distinguished psychologists of the twentieth century, says that everything you and I do springs from two motives: the sex urge and the desire to be great.

Professor John Dewey, America's most profound philosopher, phrases it a bit differently. Dr. Dewey says the deepest urge in human nature is "the desire to be important." Remember that phrase: "the desire to be important." It is significant. You are going to hear a lot about it in this book.

What do you want? Not many things, but the few things that you do wish, you crave with an insistence that will not be denied. Almost every normal adult wants—

1. Health and the preservation of life.
2. Food.
3. Sleep.
4. Money and the things money will buy.
5. Life in the hereafter.
6. Sexual gratification.
7. The well-being of our children.
8. A feeling of importance.

Almost all these wants are gratified—all except one. But there is one longing almost as deep, almost as imperious, as the desire for food or sleep which is seldom gratified. It is what Freud calls "the desire to be great." It is what John Dewey calls the "desire to be important."

.　　.　　.

It was this desire for a feeling of importance that led an uneducated, poverty-stricken grocery clerk to study some law books that he found in the bottom of a barrel of household plunder that he had bought for fifty cents. You have probably heard of this grocery clerk. His name was Lincoln.

It was this desire for a feeling of importance that inspired Dickens to write his immortal novels. This desire inspired Sir Christopher Wren to design his symphonies in stone. This desire made Rockefeller amass millions that he never spent! And this same desire made the richest man in your town build a house far too large for his requirements.

This desire makes you want to wear the latest styles, drive the latest car, and talk about your brilliant children.

It is this desire which lures many boys into becoming gangsters and gunmen. "The average young criminal of today," says E. P. Mulrooney, former Police Commissioner of New York, "is filled with ego, and his first request after arrest is for those lurid newspapers that make him out a hero. The disagreeable prospect of taking a 'hot squat' in the electric chair seems remote, so long as he can gloat over his likeness sharing space with pictures of Babe Ruth, LaGuardia, Einstein, Lindbergh, Toscanini, or Roosevelt."

If you tell me how you get your feeling of importance, I'll tell you what you are. That determines your character. That is the most significant thing about you. For example, John D. Rockefeller gets his feeling of importance by giving money to erect a modern hospital in Peking, China, to care for millions of poor people whom he has never seen and never will see. Dillinger, on the other hand, got his feeling of importance by being a bandit, a bank robber and killer. When the G-men were hunting him, he dashed into a farmhouse up in Minnesota and said, "I'm Dillinger!" He was proud of the fact that he was Public Enemy Number One. "I'm not going to hurt you, but I'm Dillinger!" he said.

Yes, the one significant difference between Dillinger and Rockefeller is how they got their feeling of importance.

.   .   .

Some authorities declare that people may actually go insane in order to find, in the dreamland of insanity, the feeling of importance that has been denied them in the harsh world of reality. There are more patients suffering from mental diseases in the hospitals in the United States than from all other diseases combined. One student out of every sixteen in our high schools today will spend part of his life in an insane asylum. If you are over fifteen years of age and residing in New York State, the chances are one out of twenty that you will be confined to an insane asylum for seven years of your life.

What is the cause of insanity?

Nobody can answer such a sweeping question as that, but we know that certain diseases, such as syphilis, break down and destroy the brain cells and result in insanity. In fact, about one-half of all mental diseases can be attributed to such physical causes as brain lesions, alcohol, toxins, and injuries. But the other half—and this is the appalling part of the story—the other half of the people who go insane apparently have nothing organically wrong with their brain cells. In post-mortem examinations, when their brain tissues are studied under the highest-powered microscopes, they are found to be apparently just as healthy as yours and mine.

Why do these people go insane?

I recently put that question to the head physician of one of our most important hospitals for the insane. This doctor, who has received the highest honors and the most coveted awards for his knowledge of insanity, told me frankly that he didn't know why people went insane. Nobody knows for sure. But he did say that many people who go insane find in insanity a feeling of importance that they were unable to achieve in the world of reality.

.   .   .

If some people are so hungry for a feeling of importance that they actually go insane to get it, imagine what miracles you and I can achieve by giving people honest appreciation.

There is only one man in the world who has ever been given a salary of a million dollars a year, so far as I know; and in spite of all the Scotch jokes, he was paid that staggering sum by a Scotsman.

Andrew Carnegie paid Charles Schwab a million dollars a year. Because Schwab is a genius? No. Because he knew more about the manufacture of steel than other people? Nonsense. Charles Schwab told me himself that he had many men working for him who knew more about the manufacture of steel than he did. Schwab truly responded to people. He knew instinctively that they hungered for recognition; so he gave them praise and appreciation.

Schwab says that he was paid this salary largely because of his ability to deal with people. And what is his secret? Here it is in his own words—words that ought to be cast in eternal bronze and hung in every home and school, every shop and office in the land—words that children ought to memorize instead of wasting their time memorizing the declension of Latin verbs or the amount of the annual rainfall in Brazil—words that will all but transform your life and mine if we will only live them:

"I consider my ability to arouse enthusiasm among the men," said Schwab, "the greatest asset I possess, and the way to develop the best that is in a man is by appreciation and encouragement.

"There is nothing else that so kills the ambitions of a man as criticisms from his superiors. I never criticize anyone. I believe in giving a man incentive to work. So I am anxious to praise but loath to find fault. If I like anything, I am hearty in my approbation and lavish in my praise."

That is what Schwab does. But what does the average man do? The exact opposite. If he doesn't like a thing, he raises the Old Harry; if he does like it, he says nothing.

"In my wide association in life, meeting with many and great men in various parts of the world," Schwab declared, "I have yet to find the man, however great or exalted his station, who did not do better work and put forth greater effort under a spirit of approval than he would ever do under a spirit of criticism."

That he said, frankly, was one of the outstanding reasons for the phenomenal success of Andrew Carnegie. Carnegie praised his associates publicly as well as privately.

Carnegie wanted to praise his assistants even on his tombstone. He wrote an epitaph for himself which read: "Here lies one who knew how to get around him men who were cleverer than himself."

Sincere appreciation was one of the secrets of Rockefeller's success in handling men. For example, when one of his partners, Edward T. Bedford, pulled a boner and lost the firm a million dollars by a bad buy in South America, John D. might have criticized; but he knew Bedford had done his best—and the incident was closed. So Rockefeller found something to praise; he congratulated Bedford because he had been able to save sixty per cent of the money he had invested. "That's splendid," said Rockefeller. "We don't always do as well as that upstairs."

.   .   .

Some readers are saying right now as they read these lines: "Old stuff! Soft soap! Bear oil! Flattery! I've tried that stuff. It doesn't work—not with intelligent people."

Of course, flattery seldom works with discerning people. It is shallow, selfish, and insincere. It ought to fail and it usually does. True, some people are so hungry, so thirsty, for appreciation that they will swallow anything, just as a starving man will eat grass and fish worms.

Why, for example, were the much-married Mdivani brothers such flaming successes in the matrimonial market? Why were these so-called "Princes" able to marry two beautiful and famous screen stars and a world-famous prima donna and Barbara Hutton with her five-and-ten-cent-store millions? Why? How did they do it?

"The Mdivani charm for women," said Adela Rogers St. Johns, in an article in the magazine *Liberty,* ". . . has been among the mysteries of the ages to many.

"Pola Negri, a woman of the world, a connoisseur of men, and a great artist, once explained it to me. She said, 'They understand the art of flattery as do no other men I have ever met. And the art of flattery is almost a lost one in this realistic and humorous age. That, I assure you, is the secret of the Mdivani charm for women. I know.'"

Even Queen Victoria was susceptible to flattery. Disraeli confessed that he put it on thick in dealing with the Queen. To use his exact words, he said he "spread it on with a trowel." But Disraeli was one of the most polished, deft, and adroit men who ever ruled the far-flung British Empire. He was a genius in his line. What would work for him wouldn't necessarily work for you and me. In the long run, flattery will do you more harm than good. Flattery is from the teeth out. Sincere appreciation is from the heart out. No! No! No! I am not suggesting flattery! Far from it. I'm talking about a new way of life. Let me repeat. *I am talking about a new way of life.*

King George V had a set of six maxims displayed on the walls of his study at Buckingham Palace. One of these maxims said: "Teach me neither to proffer nor receive cheap praise." That's all flattery is: cheap praise.

"Use what language you will," said Ralph Waldo Emerson, "you can never say anything but what you are."

If all we had to do was to use flattery, everybody would catch on to it and we should all be experts in human relations.

When we are not engaged in thinking about some definite problem, we usually spend about 95 per cent of our time thinking about ourselves. Now, if we stop thinking about ourselves for awhile and begin to think of the other man's good points, we won't have to resort to flattery so cheap and false that it can be spotted almost before it is out of the mouth.

Emerson said: "Every man I meet is my superior in some way. In that, I learn of him."

If that was true of Emerson, isn't it likely to be a thousand times more true of you and me? Let's cease thinking of our accomplishments, our wants. Let's try to figure out the other man's good points. Then forget flattery. Give honest, sincere appreciation. Be "hearty in your approbation and lavish in your praise," and people will cherish your words and treasure them and repeat them over a lifetime—repeat them years after you have forgotten them.

The Pot of Gold

JOHN CHEEVER (1912–   ), born in Quincy, Massachusetts, has devoted most of his talents to chronicling life among suburban WASPs. Expelled from Thayer Academy at age seventeen, he joined a writers' colony, and for several years wrote television scripts, including "Life with Father." In 1958 he received the National Book Award for **The Wapshot Chronicle** (1957). His other works include **The Way Some People Live** (1943), **Wapshot Scandal** (1964), and **Bullet Park** (1969).

You could not say fairly of Ralph and Laura Whittemore that they had the failings and the characteristics of incorrigible treasure hunters, but you could say truthfully of them that the shimmer and the smell, the peculiar force of money, the promise of it, had an untoward influence on their lives. They were always at the threshold of fortune; they always seemed to have something on the fire. Ralph was a fair young man with a tireless commercial imagination and an evangelical credence in the romance and sorcery of business success, and although he held an obscure job with a clothing manufacturer, this never seemed to him anything more than a point of departure.

The Whittemores were not importunate or overbearing people, and they had an uncompromising loyalty to the gentle manners of the middle class. Laura was a pleasant girl of no particular beauty who had come to New York from Wisconsin at about the same time that Ralph had reached the city from Illinois, but it had taken two years of comings and goings before they had been brought together, late one afternoon, in the lobby of a lower Fifth Avenue office building. So true was Ralph's heart, so well did it serve him then, that the moment he saw Laura's light hair and her pretty and sullen face he was enraptured. He followed her out of the lobby, pushing his way through the crowd, and since she had dropped nothing, since there was no legitimate excuse to speak to her, he shouted after her, *"Louise! Louise! Louise!,"* and the urgency in his voice made her stop. He said he'd made a mistake. He said he was sorry. He said she looked just like a girl named Louise Hatcher. It was a January night and the dark air tasted of smoke, and

THE POT OF GOLD. From *The Enormous Radio* by John Cheever. Copyright 1953 by John Cheever. With permission of Funk & Wagnalls, Publishers.

because she was a sensible and a lonely girl, she let him buy her a drink.

This was in the thirties, and their courtship was hasty. They were married three months later. Laura moved her belongings into a walkup on Madison Avenue, above a pants presser's and a florist's, where Ralph was living. She worked as a secretary, and her salary, added to what he brought home from the clothing business, was little more than enough to keep them going, but they never seemed touched by the monotony of a saving and gainless life. They ate dinners in drugstores. She hung a reproduction of van Gogh's "Sunflowers" above the sofa she had bought with some of the small sum of money her parents had left her. When their aunts and uncles came to town—their parents were dead—they had dinner at the Ritz and went to the theatre. She sewed curtains and shined his shoes, and on Sundays they stayed in bed until noon. They seemed to be standing at the threshold of plenty; and Laura often told people that she was terribly excited because of this wonderful job that Ralph had lined up.

In the first year of their marriage, Ralph worked nights on a plan that promised him a well-paying job in Texas, but through no fault of his own this promise was never realized. There was an opening in Syracuse a year later, but an older man was decided upon. There were many other profitable but elusive openings and projects between these two. In the third year of their marriage, a firm that was almost identical in size and character with the firm Ralph worked for underwent a change of ownership, and Ralph was approached and asked if he would be interested in joining the overhauled firm. His own job promised only meagre security after a series of slow promotions and he was glad of the chance to escape. He met the new owners, and their enthusiasm for him seemed intense. They were prepared to put him in charge of a department and pay him twice what he was getting then. The arrangement was to remain tacit for a month or two, until the new owners had secured their position, but they shook hands warmly and had a drink on the deal, and that night Ralph took Laura out to dinner at an expensive restaurant.

They decided, across the table, to look for a larger apartment, to have a child, and to buy a second-hand car. They faced their good fortune with perfect calm, for it was what they had expected all along. The city seemed to them a generous place, where people were rewarded either by a sudden and deserved development like this or by the capricious bounty of lawsuits, eccentric and peripheral business ventures, unexpected legacies, and other windfalls. After dinner, they walked in Central Park in the moonlight while Ralph smoked a cigar. Later, when Laura had fallen asleep, he sat in the open bedroom window in his pajamas.

The peculiar excitement with which the air of the city seems charged after midnight, when its life falls into the hands of watchmen and drunks, had always pleased him. He knew intimately the sounds of the night street: the bus brakes, the remote sirens, and the sound of water turning high in the air—the sound of water turning a mill wheel—the sum, he supposed, of many echoes, although, often as he had heard the sound, he had never decided on its source. Now he heard all this more keenly because the night seemed to him portentous.

He was twenty-eight years old; poverty and youth were inseparable in his experience, and one was ending with the other. The life they were about to leave had not been hard, and he thought with sentiment of the soiled tablecloth in the Italian restaurant where they usually went for their celebrations, and the high spirits with which Laura on a wet night ran from the subway to the bus stop. But they were drawing away from all this. Shirt sales in department-store basements, lines at meat counters, weak drinks, the roses he brought her up from the subway in the spring, when roses were cheap—these were all unmistakably the souvenirs of the poor, and while they seemed to him good and gentle, he was glad that they would soon be memories.

Laura resigned from her job when she got pregnant. The reorganization and Ralph's new position hung fire, but the Whittemores talked about it freely when they were with friends. "We're *terribly* pleased with the way things are going," Laura would say. "All we need is patience." There were many delays and postponements, and they waited with the patience of people expecting justice. The time came when they both needed clothes, and one evening Ralph suggested that they spend some of the money they had put aside. Laura refused. When he brought up the subject, she didn't answer him and seemed not to hear him. He raised his voice and lost his temper. He shouted. She cried. He thought of all the other girls he could have married—the dark blonde, the worshipful Cuban, the rich and pretty one with a cast in her right eye. All his desires seemed to lie outside the small apartment Laura had arranged. They were still not speaking in the morning, and in order to strengthen his position he telephoned his potential employers. Their secretary told him they were both out. This made him apprehensive. He called several times from the telephone booth in the lobby of the building he worked in and was told that they were busy, they were out, they were in conference with lawyers, or they were talking long distance. This variety of excuses frightened him. He said nothing to Laura that evening and tried to call them the next day. Late in the afternoon, after many tries, one of them came to the phone. "We gave the job to somebody else, sonny," he said. Like a saddened father, he spoke to Ralph in a hoarse and gentle voice. "Don't try and get us on the telephone any more. We've got other things to do besides answer the telephone. This other fellow seemed better suited, sonny. That's all I can tell you, and don't try to get me on the telephone any more."

Ralph walked the miles from his office to his apartment that night, hoping to free himself in this way from some of the weight of his disappointment. He was so unprepared for the shock that it affected him like vertigo, and he walked with an odd, high step, as if the paving were quicksand. He stood downstairs in front of the building he lived in, trying to decide how to describe the disaster to Laura, but when he went in, he told her bluntly. "Oh, I'm sorry, darling," she said softly and kissed him. "I'm terribly sorry." She wandered away from him and began to straighten the sofa cushions. His frustration was so ardent, he was such a prisoner of his schemes and expectations, that he was astonished at the serenity with which she regarded the failure. There was nothing to worry about, she said. She still had a few hundred dollars in the bank, from the money her parents had left her. There was nothing to worry about.

When the child, a girl, was born, they named her Rachel, and a week after the delivery Laura returned to the Madison Avenue walkup. She took all the care of the baby and continued to do the cooking and the housework.

Ralph's imagination remained resilient and fertile, but he couldn't seem to hit on a scheme that would fit into his lack of time and capital. He and Laura, like the hosts of the poor everywhere, lived a simple life. They still went to the theatre with visiting relatives and occasionally they went to parties, but Laura's only continuous contact with the bright lights that surrounded them was vicarious and came to her through a friend she made in Central Park.

She spent many afternoons on a park bench during the first years of Rachel's life. It was a tyranny and a pleasure. She resented her enchainment but enjoyed the open sky and the air. One winter afternoon, she recognized a woman she had met at a party, and a little before dark, as Laura and the other mothers were gathering their stuffed animals and preparing their children for the cold journey home, the woman came across the playground and spoke to her. She was Alice Holinshed, she said. They had met at the Galvins'. She was pretty and friendly, and walked with Laura to the edge of the Park. She had a boy of about Rachel's age. The women met again the following day. They became friends.

Mrs. Holinshed was older than Laura, but she had a more youthful and precise beauty. Her hair and her eyes were black, her pale and perfectly oval face was delicately colored, and her voice was pure. She lighted her cigarettes with Stork Club matches and spoke of the inconvenience of living with a child in a hotel. If Laura had any regrets about her life, they were expressed in her friendship for this pretty woman, who moved so freely through expensive stores and restaurants.

It was a friendship circumscribed, with the exception of the Galvins', by the sorry and touching countryside of Central Park. The women talked principally about their husbands, and this was a game that Laura could play with an empty purse. Vaguely, boastfully, the two women discussed the irons their men had in the fire. They sat together with their children through the sooty twilights, when the city to the south burns like a Bessemer furnace, and the air smells of coal, and the wet boulders shine like slag, and the Park itself seems like a strip of woods on the edge of a coal town. Then Mrs. Holinshed would remember that she was late—she was always late for something mysterious and splendid—and the two women would walk together to the edge of the woods. This vicarious contact with comfort pleased Laura, and the pleasure would stay with her as she pushed the baby carriage over to Madison Avenue and then began to cook supper, hearing the thump of the steam iron and smelling the cleaning fluid from the pants presser's below.

One night, when Rachel was about two years old, the frustration of Ralph's search for the goat track that would let him lead his family to a realm of reasonable contentment kept him awake. He needed sleep urgently, and when this blessing eluded him, he got out of bed and sat in the dark. The charm and excitement of the street after midnight escaped him. The explosive brakes of a Madison Avenue bus made him jump. He shut the window, but the noise of traffic continued to pass through it. It seemed to him that the penetrating voice of the city had a mortal effect on the precious lives of the city's inhabitants and that it should be muffled.

He thought of a Venetian blind whose outer surfaces would be treated with a substance that would deflect or absorb sound waves. With such a blind, friends paying a call on a spring evening would not have to shout to be heard above the noise of trucks in the street below. Bedrooms could be silenced that way—bedrooms, above all, for it seemed to him then that sleep was what everyone in the city sought and only half captured. All the harried faces on the streets at dusk, when even the pretty girls talk to themselves, were looking for sleep. Night-club singers and their amiable customers, the people waiting for taxis in front of the Waldorf on a wet night, policemen, cashiers, window washers—sleep eluded them all.

He talked over this Venetian blind with Laura the following night, and the idea seemed sensible to her. He bought a blind that would fit their bedroom window, and experimented with various paint mixtures.

At last he stumbled on one that dried to the consistency of felt and was porous. The paint had a sickening smell, which filled their apartment during the four days it took him to coat and recoat the outer surface of the slats. When the paint had dried, he hung the blind, and they opened the window for a test. Silence—a relative silence—charmed their ears. He wrote down his formula, and took it during his lunch hour to a patent attorney. It took the lawyer several weeks to discover that a similar formula had been patented some years earlier. The patent owner—a man named Fellows—had a New York address, and the lawyer suggested that Ralph get in touch with him and try to reach some agreement.

The search for Mr. Fellows began one evening when Ralph had finished work, and took him first to the attic of a Hudson Street rooming house, where the landlady showed Ralph a pair of socks that Mr. Fellows had left behind when he moved out. Ralph went south from there to another rooming house and then west to the neighborhood of ship chandlers and marine boarding houses. The nocturnal search went on for a week. He followed the thread of Mr. Fellows' goings south to the Bowery and then to the upper West Side. He climbed stairs past the open doors of rooms where lessons in Spanish dancing were going on, past whores, past women practicing the "Emperor" Concerto, and one evening he found Mr. Fellows sitting on the edge of his bed in an attic room, rubbing the spots out of his necktie with a rag soaked in gasoline.

Mr. Fellows was greedy. He wanted a hundred dollars in cash and fifty per cent of the royalties. Ralph got him to agree to twenty per cent of the royalties, but he could not get him to reduce the initial payment. The lawyer drew up a paper defining's Ralph's and Mr. Fellows' interests, and a few nights later Ralph went over to Brooklyn and got to a Venetian-blind factory after its doors had closed but while the lights of the office were still burning. The manager agreed to manufacture some blinds to Ralph's specifications, but he would not take an order of less than a hundred dollars. Ralph agreed to this and to furnish the compound for the outer surface of the slats. These expenditures had taken more than three-fourths of the Whittemores' capital, and now the problem of money was joined by the element of time. They put a small advertisement in the paper for a housewares salesman, and for a week Ralph interviewed candidates in the living room after supper. He chose a young man who was leaving at the end of the week for the Midwest. He wanted a fifty-dollar advance, and pointed out to them that Pittsburgh and Chicago were just as noisy as New York. A department-store collection agency was threatening to bring them into the small-claims court at this time, and they had come to a place where any illness, any fall, any damage to themselves or to the few clothes they owned would be critical. Their salesman promised to write them from Chicago at the end of the week, and they counted on good news, but there was no news from Chicago at all. Ralph wired the salesman twice, and the wires must have been forwarded, for he replied to them from Pittsburgh: "Can't merchandise blinds. Returning samples express." They put another advertisement for a salesman in the paper and took the first one who rang their bell, an old gentleman with a cornflower in his buttonhole. He had a number of other lines—mirror wastebaskets, orange-juicers—and he said that he knew all the Manhattan housewares buyers intimately. He was garrulous, and when he was unable to sell the blinds, he came to the Whittemores' apartment and discussed their product at length, and with a blend of criticism and charity that we usually reserve for human beings.

Ralph tried to borrow money, but neither his salary nor his patent was considered adequate collateral for a loan at anything but ruinous rates, and one day, at his office, he was served a summons by the department-store collection agency. He went out to Brooklyn and offered to sell the Venetian blinds back to the manufacturer. The man gave him sixty dollars for what had cost a hundred, and Ralph was able to pay the collection agency. They hung the samples in their windows and tried to put the venture out of their minds.

Now they were poorer than ever, and they ate lentils for dinner every Monday and sometimes again on Tuesday. Laura washed the dishes after dinner while Ralph read to Rachel. When the girl had fallen asleep, he would go to his desk in the living room and work on one of his projects. There was always something coming. There was a job in Dallas and a job in Peru. There were the plastic arch preserver, the automatic closing device for ice-box doors, and the scheme to pirate marine specifications and undersell Jane's. For a month, he was going to buy some fallow acreage in upstate New York and plant Christmas trees on it, and then, with one of his friends, he projected a luxury mail-order business, for which they could never get backing. When the Whittemores met Uncle George and Aunt Helen at the Ritz, they seemed delighted with the way things were going. They were terribly excited, Laura said, about a sales agency in Paris that had been offered to Ralph but that they had decided against, because of the threat of war.

The Whittemores were apart for two years during the war. Laura took a job. She walked Rachel to school in the morning and met her at the end of the day. Working and saving, Laura was able to buy herself and Rachel some clothes. When Ralph returned at the end of the war, their affairs were in good order. The experience seemed to have refreshed him, and while he took up his old job as an anchor to windward, as an ace in the hole, there had never been more talk about jobs—jobs in Venezuela and jobs in Iran. They resumed all their old habits and economies. They remained poor.

Laura gave up her job and returned to the afternoons with Rachel in Central Park. Alice Holinshed was there. The talk was the same. The Holinsheds were living in a hotel. Mr. Holinshed was vice-president of a new firm manufacturing a soft drink, but the dress that Mrs. Holinshed wore day after day was one that Laura recognized from before the war. Her son was thin and bad-tempered. He was dressed in serge, like an English schoolboy, but his serge, like his mother's dress, looked worn and outgrown. One afternoon when Mrs. Holinshed and her son came into the Park, the boy was crying. "I've done a dreadful thing," Mrs. Holinshed told Laura. "We've been to the doctor's and I forgot to bring any money, and I wonder if you could lend me a few dollars, so I can take a taxi back to the hotel." Laura said she would be glad to. She had only a five-dollar bill with her, and she gave Mrs. Holinshed this. The boy continued to cry, and his mother dragged him off toward Fifth Avenue. Laura never saw them in the Park again.

Ralph's life was, as it had always been, dominated by anticipation. In the years directly after the war, the city appeared to be immensely rich. There seemed to be money everywhere, and the Whittemores, who slept under their worn overcoats in the winter to keep themselves warm, seemed separated from their enjoyment of this prosperity by only a little patience, resourcefulness, and luck. On Sunday, when the weather was fine, they walked with the prosperous crowds on upper Fifth Avenue. It seemed to Ralph that it might only be another month, at the most another year, before he found the key to the prosperity they deserved. They would walk on Fifth Avenue until the afternoon was ended and then go home and eat a can of beans for dinner and, in order to balance the meal, an apple for dessert.

They were returning from such a walk one Sunday when, as they climbed the stairs to their apartment, the telephone began to ring. Ralph went on ahead and answered it.

He heard the voice of his Uncle George, a man of the generation that remains conscious of distance, who spoke into the telephone as if he were calling from shore to a passing boat. "This is Uncle George, Ralphie!" he shouted, and Ralph supposed that he and Aunt Helen were paying a surprise visit to the city, until he realized that his uncle was calling from Illinois. "Can you hear me?" Uncle George shouted. "Can you hear me, Ralphie? . . . I'm calling you about a job, Ralphie. Just in case you're looking for a job. Paul Hadaam came through—can you hear me, Ralphie?—Paul Hadaam came through here on his way East last week and he stopped off to pay me a visit. He's got a lot of

money, Ralphie—he's rich—and he's starting this business out in the
West to manufacture synthetic wool. Can you hear me, Ralphie? . . .
I told him about you, and he's staying at the Waldorf, so you go and
see him. I saved his life once. I pulled him out of Lake Erie. You go and
see him tomorrow at the Waldorf, Ralphie. You know where that is?
The Waldorf Hotel. . . . Wait a minute, here's Aunt Helen. She
wants to talk with you."

Now the voice was a woman's, and it come to him faintly. All his
cousins had been there for dinner, she told him. They had had a turkey
for dinner. All the grandchildren were there and they behaved very
well. George took them all for a walk after dinner. It was hot, but
they sat on the porch, so they didn't feel the heat. She was interrupted
in her account of Sunday by her husband, who must have seized the
instrument from her to continue his refrain about going to see Mr.
Hadaam at the Waldorf. "You go see him tomorrow, Ralphie—the
nineteenth—at the Waldorf. He's expecting you. Can you hear me?
. . . The Waldorf Hotel. He's a millionaire. I'll say goodbye now."

Mr. Hadaam had a parlor and a bedroom in the Waldorf Towers,
and when Ralph went to see him, late the next afternoon, on his way
home from work, Mr. Hadaam was alone. He seemed to Ralph a very
old man, but an obdurate one, and in the way he shook hands, pulled
at his ear lobes, stretched himself, and padded around the parlor on his
bandy legs Ralph recognized a spirit that was unimpaired, independent,
and canine. He poured Ralph a strong drink and himself a weak one.
He was undertaking the manufacture of synthetic wool on the West
Coast, he explained, and had come East to find men who were experienced in merchandising wool. George had given him Ralph's name, and
he wanted a man with Ralph's experience. He would find the Whittemores a suitable house, arrange for their transportation, and begin
Ralph at a salary of fifteen thousand. It was the size of the salary that
made Ralph realize that the proposition was an oblique attempt to repay his uncle for having saved Mr. Hadaam's life, and the old man
seemed to sense what he was feeling. "This hasn't got anything to do
with your uncle's saving my life," he said roughly. "I'm grateful to
him—who wouldn't be?—but this hasn't got anything to do with your
uncle, if that's what you're thinking. When you get to be as old and as
rich as I am, it's hard to meet people. All my old friends are dead—
all of them but George. I'm surrounded by a cordon of associates and
relatives that's damned near impenetrable, and if it wasn't for George
giving me a name now and then, I'd never get to see a new face. Last
year, I got into an automobile accident. It was my fault. I'm a terrible
driver. I hit this young fellow's car and I got right out and went over
to him and introduced myself. We had to wait about twenty minutes

for the wreckers and we got to talking. Well, he's working for me today and he's one of the best friends I've got, and if I hadn't run into him, I'd never have met him. When you get to be as old as me, that's the only way you can meet people—automobile accidents, fires, things like that."

He straightened up against the back of his chair and tasted his drink. His rooms were well above the noise of traffic and it was quiet there. Mr. Hadaam's breath was loud and steady, and it sounded, in a pause, like the heavy breath of someone sleeping. "Well, I don't want to rush you into this," he said. "I'm going back to the Coast the day after tomorrow. You think it over and I'll telephone you." He took out an engagement book and wrote down Ralph's name and telephone number. "I'll call you on Tuesday evening, the twenty-seventh, about nine o'clock—nine o'clock your time. George tells me you've got a nice wife, but I haven't got time to meet her now. I'll see her on the Coast." He started talking about baseball and then brought the conversation back to Uncle George. "He saved my life. My damned boat capsized and then righted herself and sunk right from underneath me. I can still feel her going down under my feet. I couldn't swim. Can't swim today. Well, goodbye." They shook hands, and as soon as the door closed, Ralph heard Mr. Hadaam begin to cough. It was the profane, hammering cough of an old man, full of bitter complaints and distempers, and it hit him pitilessly for all the time that Ralph was waiting in the hallway for the elevator to take him down.

On the walk home, Ralph felt that this might be it, that this preposterous chain of contingencies that had begun with his uncle's pulling a friend out of Lake Erie might be the one that would save them. Nothing in his experience made it seem unlikely. He recognized that the proposition was the vagary of an old man and that it originated in the indebtedness Mr. Hadaam felt to his uncle—an indebtedness that age seemed to have deepened. He gave Laura the details of the interview when he came in, and his own views on Mr. Hadaam's conduct, and, to his mild surprise, Laura said that it looked to her like the bonanza. They were both remarkably calm, considering the change that confronted them. There was no talk of celebrating, and he helped her wash the dishes. He looked up the site of Mr. Hadaam's factory in an atlas, and the Spanish place name on the coast north of San Francisco gave them a glimpse of a life of reasonable contentment.

Eight days lay between Ralph's interview and the telephone call, and he realized that nothing would be definite until Tuesday, and that there was a possibility that old Mr. Hadaam, while crossing the country, might, under the subtle influence of travel, suffer a change of heart. He might be poisoned by a fish sandwich and be taken off the train in Chicago, to die in a nursing home there. Among the people meeting him in San Francisco might be his lawyer, with the news that he was ruined or that his wife had run away. But eventually Ralph was unable to invent any new disasters or to believe in the ones he had invented.

This inability to persevere in doubting his luck showed some weakening of character. There had hardly been a day when he had not been made to feel the power of money, but he found that the force of money was most irresistible when it took the guise of a promise, and that years of resolute self-denial, instead of rewarding him with reserves of fortitude, had left him more than ordinarily susceptible to temptation. Since the change in their lives still depended upon a telephone call, he refrained from talking—from thinking, so far as possible— about the life they might have in California. He would go so far as to say that he would like some white shirts, but he would not go beyond this deliberately contrite wish, and here, where he thought he was exercising restraint and intelligence, he was, instead, beginning to respect the bulk of superstition that is supposed to attend good fortune, and when he wished for white shirts, it was not a genuinely modest wish so much as it was a memory—he could not have put it into words himself—that the gods of fortune are jealous and easily deceived by false modesty. He had never been a superstitious man, but on Tuesday he scooped the money off his coffee and was elated when he saw a ladybug on the bathroom window sill. He could not remember when he had heard money and this insect associated, but neither could he have explained any of the other portents that he had begun to let govern his movements.

Laura watched this subtle change that anticipation worked on her husband, but there was nothing she could say. He did not mention Mr. Hadaam or California. He was quiet; he was gentle with Rachel; he actually grew pale. He had his hair cut on Wednesday. He wore his best suit. On Saturday, he had his hair cut again and his nails manicured. He took two baths a day, put on a fresh shirt for dinner, and frequently went into the bathroom to wash his hands, brush his teeth, and wet down his cowlick. The preternatural care he gave his body and his appearance reminded her of an adolescent surprised by early love.

The Whittemores were invited to a party for Monday night and Laura insisted that they go. The guests at the party were the survivors of a group that had coalesced ten years before, and if anyone had called the roll of the earliest parties in the same room, like the retreat ceremony of a breeched and decimated regiment, "Missing. . . . Missing. . . . Missing" would have been answered for the squad that had gone into Westchester; "Missing. . . . Missing. . . . Missing" would have been spoken for the platoon that divorce, drink, nervous disorders, and adversity had slain or wounded. Because Laura had gone to the party in indifferent spirits, she was conscious of the missing.

She had been at the party less than an hour when she heard some people coming in, and, looking over her shoulder, saw Alice Holinshed and her husband. The room was crowded and she put off speaking to Alice until later. Much later in the evening, Laura went into the toilet, and when she came out of it into the bedroom, she found Alice sitting on the bed. She seemed to be waiting for Laura. Laura sat down at the dressing table to straighten her hair. She looked at the image of her friend in the glass.

"I hear you're going to California," Alice said.

"We hope to. We'll know tomorrow."

"Is it true that Ralph's uncle saved his life?"

"That's true."

"You're lucky."

"I suppose we are."

"You're lucky, all right." Alice got up from the bed and crossed the room and closed the door, and came back across the room again and sat on the bed. Laura watched her in the glass, but she was not watching Laura. She was stooped. She seemed nervous. "You're lucky," she said. "You're so lucky. Do you know how lucky you are? Let me tell you about this cake of soap," she said. "I have this cake of soap. I mean I had this cake of soap. Somebody gave it to me when I was married, fifteen years ago. I don't know who. Some maid, some music teacher—somebody like that. It was good soap, good English soap, the kind I like, and I decided to save it for the big day when Larry made a killing, when he took me to Bermuda. First, I was going to use it when he got the job in Bound Brook. Then I thought I could use it when we were going to Boston, and then Washington, and then when he got this new job, I thought maybe this is it, maybe *this* is the time when I get to take the boy out of that rotten school and pay the bills and move out of those bum hotels we've been living in. For fifteen years I've been planning to use this cake of soap. Well, last week I was looking through my bureau drawers and I saw this cake of soap. It was all cracked. I threw it out. I threw it out because I knew I was never going to have a chance to use it. Do you realize what that means? Do you know what that feels like? To live for fifteen years on promises and expectations and loans and credits in hotels that aren't fit to live in, never for a single day to be out of debt, and yet to pretend, to feel that every year, every winter, every job, every meeting is going to be the one. To live like this for fifteen years and then to realize that it's never going to end. Do you know what that feels like?" She got up and went over to the dressing table and stood in front of Laura. Tears had risen into her large eyes, and her voice was harsh and loud. "I'm never going to get to Bermuda," she said. "I'm never even going to get to Florida. I'm never going to get out of hock, ever, ever, *ever*. I know that I'm never going to have a decent home and that everything I own that is worn and torn and no good is going to stay that way. I know that for the rest of my life, for the rest of my life, I'm going to wear ragged slips and torn nightgowns and torn underclothes and shoes that hurt me. I know that for the rest of my life nobody is going to come up to me and tell me that I've got on a pretty dress, because I'm not going to be able to afford that kind of a dress. I know that for the rest of my life every taxi-driver and doorman and headwaiter in this town is going to know in a minute that I haven't got five bucks in that black imitation-suède purse that I've been brushing and brushing and brushing and carrying around for ten years. How do you get it? How do you rate it? What's so wonderful about you that you get a break like this?" She ran her fingers down Laura's bare arm. The dress she was wearing smelled of benzine. "Can I rub it off you? Will that make me lucky? I swear to Jesus I'd murder somebody if I thought it would bring us in any money. I'd wring somebody's neck—yours, anybody's—I swear to Jesus I would—"

Someone began knocking on the door. Alice strode to the door, opened it, and went out. A woman came in, a stranger looking for the toilet. Laura lighted a cigarette and waited in the bedroom for about ten minutes before she went back to the party. The Holinsheds had gone. She got a drink and sat down and tried to talk, but she couldn't keep her mind on what she was saying.

The hunt, the search for money that had seemed to her natural, amiable, and fair when they first committed themselves to it, now seemed like a hazardous and piratical voyage. She had thought, earlier in the evening, of the missing. She thought now of the missing again. Adversity and failure accounted for more than half of them, as if beneath the amenities in the pretty room a keen race were in progress, in which the loser's forfeits were extreme. Laura felt cold. She picked the ice out of her drink with her fingers and put it in a flower vase, but the whiskey didn't warm her. She asked Ralph to take her home.

After dinner on Tuesday, Laura washed the dishes and Ralph dried them. He read the paper and she took up some sewing. At a quarter after eight, the telephone, in the bedroom, rang, and he went to it calmly. It was someone with two theatre tickets for a show that was closing. The telephone didn't ring again, and at half past nine he told Laura that he was going to call California. It didn't take long for the connection to be made, and the fresh voice of a young woman spoke to him from Mr. Hadaam's number. "Oh, yes, Mr. Whittemore," she said. "We tried to get you earlier in the evening but your line was busy."

"Could I speak to Mr. Hadaam?"

"No, Mr. Whittemore. This is Mr. Hadaam's secretary. I know he meant to call you, because he had entered this in his engagement book. Mrs. Hadaam has asked me to disappoint as few people as possible, and I've tried to take care of all the calls and appointments in his engagement book. Mr. Hadaam had a stroke on Sunday. We don't expect him to recover. I imagine he made you some kind of promise, but I'm afraid he won't be able to keep it."

"I'm very sorry," Ralph said. He hung up.

Laura had come into the bedroom while the secretary was talking. "Oh, darling!" she said. She put her sewing basket on the bureau and went toward the closet. Then she went back and looked for something in the sewing basket and left the basket on her dressing table. Then she took off her shoes, treed them, slipped her dress over her head and hung it up neatly. Then she went to the bureau, looking for her sewing basket, found it on the dressing table, and took it into the closet, where she put it on a shelf. Then she took her brush and comb into the bathroom and began to run the water for a bath.

The lash of frustration was laid on and the pain stunned Ralph. He sat by the telephone for he did not know how long. He heard Laura come out of the bathroom. He turned when he heard her speak.

"I feel dreadfully about old Mr. Hadaam," she said. "I wish there were something we could do." She was in her nightgown, and she sat down at the dressing table like a skillful and patient woman establishing herself in front of a loom, and she picked up and put down pins and bottles and combs and brushes with the thoughtless dexterity of an experienced weaver, as if the time she spent there were all part of a continuous operation. "It did look like the treasure . . ."

The word surprised him, and for a moment he saw the chimera, the pot of gold, the fleece, the treasure buried in the faint lights of a rainbow, and the primitivism of his hunt struck him. Armed with a sharp spade and a homemade divining rod, he had climbed over hill and dale, through droughts and rain squalls, digging wherever the maps he had drawn himself promised gold. Six paces east of the dead pine, five panels in from the library door, underneath the creaking step, in the roots of the pear tree, beneath the grape arbor lay the bean pot full of doubloons and bullion.

She turned on the stool and held her thin arms toward him, as she had done more than a thousand times. She was no longer young, and more wan, thinner than she might have been if he had found the doubloons to save her anxiety and unremitting work. Her smile, her naked shoulders had begun to trouble the indecipherable shapes and symbols that are the touchstones of desire, and the light from the lamp seemed to brighten and give off heat and shed that unaccountable complacency, that benevolence, that the spring sunlight brings to all kinds of fatigue and despair. Desire for her delighted and confused him. Here it was, here it all was, and the shine of the gold seemed to him then to be all around her arms.

Jobs

PAUL GOODMAN (1911–   ), a gadfly by instinct, emerged in the 1960s as one person over thirty whom youth would trust. Born in New York City, the son of a businessman, he received a B.A. at City College in 1931. During the 1930s, he embraced radical politics while launching a career as novelist, poet, and essayist. Blending anarchism, nonviolence, and decentralization in his social views, he preaches "dropping out" as an acceptable alternative to the dehumanization of modern life. **Growing Up Absurd** (1960), the book that made him a leading prophet of the youth culture, was followed by **The Community of Scholars** (1962), **Compulsory Mis-Education** (1964), and **Like a Conquered Province** (1967).

1

It's hard to grow up when there isn't enough man's work. There is "nearly full employment" (with highly significant exceptions), but there get to be fewer jobs that are necessary or unquestionably useful; that require energy and draw on some of one's best capacities; and that can be done keeping one's honor and dignity. In explaining the widespread troubles of adolescents and young men, this simple objective factor is not much mentioned. Let us here insist on it.

By "man's work" I mean a very simple idea, so simple that it is clearer to ingenuous boys than to most adults. To produce necessary food and shelter is man's work. During most of economic history most men have done this drudging work, secure that it was justified and worthy of a man to do it, though often feeling that the social conditions under which they did it were *not* worthy of a man, thinking,

"It's better to die than to live so hard"—but they worked on. When the environment is forbidding, as in the Swiss Alps or the Aran Islands, we regard such work with poetic awe. In emergencies it is heroic, as when the bakers of Paris maintained the supply of bread during the French Revolution, or the milkman did not miss a day's delivery when the bombs recently tore up London.

.   .   .

Once we turn away from the absolutely necessary subsistence jobs, however, we find that an enormous proportion of our production is not even unquestionably useful. Everybody knows and also feels this, and there has recently been a flood of books about our surfeit of honey, our insolent chariots, the follies of exurban ranch houses, our hucksters and our synthetic demand. Many acute things are said about this useless production and advertising, but not much about the workmen producing it and their frame of mind; and nothing at all, so far as I have noticed, about the plight of a young fellow looking for a manly occupation. The eloquent critics of the American way of life have themselves been so seduced by it that they think only in terms of selling commodities and point out that the goods are valueless; but they fail to see that people are being wasted and their skills insulted. (To give an analogy, in the many gleeful onslaughts on the Popular Culture that have appeared in recent years, there has been little thought of the plight of the honest artist cut off from his audience and sometimes, in public arts such as theater and architecture, from his medium.)

What is strange about it? American society has tried so hard and so ably to defend the practice and theory of production for profit and not primarily for use that now it has succeeded in making its jobs and products profitable and useless.

2

Consider a likely useful job. A youth who is alert and willing but not "verbally intelligent"—perhaps he has quit high school at the eleventh grade (the median), as soon as he legally could—chooses for auto mechanic. That's a good job, familiar to him, he often watched them as a kid. It's careful and dirty at the same time. In a small garage it's sociable; one can talk to the customers (girls). You please people in trouble by fixing their cars, and a man is proud to see rolling out on its own the car that limped in behind the tow truck. The pay is as good as the next fellow's, who is respected.

So our young man takes this first-rate job. But what when he then learns that the cars have a built-in obsolescence, that the manufacturers do not want them to be repaired or repairable? They have lobbied a law that requires them to provide spare parts for only five years (it used to be ten). Repairing the new cars is often a matter of cosmetics, not mechanics; and the repairs are pointlessly expensive— a tail fin might cost $150. The insurance rates therefore double and treble on old and new cars both. Gone are the days of keeping the jalopies in good shape, the artist-work of a proud mechanic. But everybody is paying for foolishness, for in fact the new models are only trivially superior; the whole thing is a sell.

It is hard for the young man now to maintain his feelings of justification, sociability, serviceability. It is not surprising if he quickly becomes cynical and time-serving, interested in a fast buck. And so, on the notorious *Reader's Digest* test, the investigators (coming in with a disconnected coil wire) found that 63 per cent of mechanics charged for repairs they didn't make, and lucky if they didn't also take out the new fuel pump and replace it with a used one (65 per cent of radio repair shops, but *only* 49 per cent of watch repairmen "lied, overcharged, or gave false diagnoses").

. . .

3

Most manual jobs do not lend themselves so readily to knowing the facts and fraudulently taking advantage oneself. In factory jobs the workman is likely to be ignorant of what goes on, since he performs a small operation on a big machine that he does not understand. Even so, there is evidence that he has the same disbelief in the enterprise as a whole, with a resulting attitude of profound indifference.

Semiskilled factory operatives are the largest category of workmen. (I am leafing through the U. S. Department of Labor's *Occupational Outlook Handbook*, 1957.) Big companies have tried the devices of applied anthropology to enhance the loyalty of these men to the firm, but apparently the effort is hopeless, for it is found that a thumping majority of the men don't care about the job or the firm; they couldn't care less and you can't make them care more. But this is *not* because of wages, hours, or working conditions, or management. On the contrary, tests that show the men's indifference to the company show also their (unaware) admiration for the way the company has designed and manages the plant; it is their very model of style, efficiency, and correct behavior. (Robert Dubin, for the U. S. Public Health Service.) Maybe if the men understood more, they would admire less. The union and the grievance committee take care of wages, hours, and conditions; these are the things the workmen themselves fought for and won. (Something was missing in that victory, and we have inherited the failure as well as the success.) The conclusion must be that workmen are indifferent to the job because of its intrinsic nature: it does not enlist worth-while capacities, it is not "interesting"; it is not his, he is not "in" on it; the product is not really useful.

.   .   .

4

Let us go on to the Occupational Outlook of those who are verbally bright. Among this group, simply because they cannot help asking more general questions—e.g., about utility—the problem of finding man's work is harder, and their disillusion is more poignant.

.   .   .

"Teaching," says the *Handbook,* "is the largest of the professions." So suppose our now verbally bright young man chooses for teacher, in the high school system or, by exception, in the elementary schools if he understands that the elementary grades are the vitally important ones and require the most ability to teach well (and of course they have less prestige). Teaching is necessary and useful work; it is real and creative, for it directly confronts an important subject matter, the children themselves; it is obviously self-justifying; and it is ennobled by the arts and sciences. Those who practice teaching do not for the most part succumb to cynicism or indifference—the children are too immediate and real for the teachers to become callous—but, most of the school systems being what they are, can teachers fail to come to suffer first despair and then deep resignation? Resignation occurs psychologically as follows: frustrated in essential action, they nevertheless cannot quit in anger, because the task is necessary; so the anger turns inward and is felt as resignation. (Naturally, the resigned teacher may then put on a happy face and keep very busy.)

.   .   .

5

Next, what happens to the verbally bright who have no zeal for a serviceable profession and who have no particular scientific or artistic bent? For the most part they make up the tribes of salesmanship, entertainment, business management, promotion, and advertising. Here of course there is no question of utility or honor to begin with, so an ingenuous boy will not look here for a manly career. Nevertheless, though we can pass by the sufferings of these well-paid callings, much publicized by their own writers, they are important to our theme because of the model they present to the growing boy.

Consider the men and women in TV advertisements, demonstrating the product and singing the jingle. They are clowns and mannequins, in grimace, speech, and action. And again, what I want to call attention to in this advertising is not the economic problem of synthetic demand, and not the cultural problem of Popular Culture, but the human problem that these are human beings working as clowns; that the writers and designers of it are human beings thinking like idiots; and the broadcasters and underwriters know and abet what goes on—

> *Juicily glubbily*
> Blubber *is dubbily*
> *delicious and nutritious*
> —*eat it, Kitty, it's good.*

Alternately, they are liars, confidence men, smooth talkers, obsequious, insolent, etc., etc.

The popular-cultural content of the advertisements is somewhat neutralized by *Mad* magazine, the bible of the twelve-year-olds who can read. But far more influential and hard to counteract is the *fact* that the workmen and the patrons of this enterprise are human beings. (Highly approved, too.) They are not good models for a boy looking for a manly job that is useful and necessary, requiring human energy and capacity, and that can be done with honor and dignity. They are a good sign that not many such jobs will be available.

The popular estimation is rather different. Consider the following: "As one possible aid, I suggested to the Senate subcommittee that they alert celebrities and leaders in the fields of sports, movies, theater and television to the help they can offer by getting close to these [delinquent] kids. By giving them positive 'heroes' they know and can talk to, instead of the misguided image of trouble-making buddies, they could aid greatly in guiding these normal aspirations for fame and status into wholesome progressive channels." (Jackie Robinson, who was formerly on the Connecticut Parole Board.) Or again: when a mass cross-section of Oklahoma high school juniors and seniors was asked which living person they would like to be, the boys named Pat Boone, Ricky Nelson, and President Eisenhower; the girls chose Debbie Reynolds, Elizabeth Taylor, and Natalie Wood.

.   .   .

7

Yet, economically and vocationally, a very large population of the young people are in a plight more drastic than anything so far mentioned. In our society as it is, there are not enough worthy jobs. But if our society, being as it is, were run more efficiently and soberly, for a majority there would soon not be any jobs at all. There is at present nearly full employment and there may be for some years, yet a vast number of young people are rationally unemployable, useless. This paradox is essential to explain their present temper.

.　　.　　.

Everybody knows this, nobody wants to talk about it much, for we don't know how to cope with it. The effect is that we are living a kind of lie. Long ago, labor leaders used to fight for the shorter work week, but now they don't, because they're pretty sure they don't want it. Indeed, when hours are reduced, the tendency is to get a second, part-time, job and raise the standard of living, *because* the job is meaningless and one must have something; but the standard of living is pretty meaningless, too. Nor is this strange atmosphere a new thing. For at least a generation the maximum sensible use of our productivity could have thrown a vast population out of work, or relieved everybody of a lot of useless work, depending on how you take it. (Consider with how little cutback of useful civilian production the economy produced the war goods and maintained an Army, economically unemployed.) The plain truth is that at present very many of us are useless, not needed, rationally unemployable. It is in this paradoxical atmosphere that young persons grow up. It looks busy and expansive, but it is rationally at a stalemate.

.　　.　　.

9

The majority of young people are [thus] faced with the following alternative: Either society is a benevolently frivolous racket in which they'll manage to boondoggle, though less profitably than the more privileged; or society is serious (and they hope still benevolent enough to support them), but they are useless and hopelessly out. Such thoughts do not encourage productive life. Naturally young people are more sanguine and look for man's work, but few find it. Some settle for a "good job"; most settle for a lousy job; a few, but an increasing number, don't settle.

I often ask, "What do you want to work at? If you have the chance. When you get out of school, college, the service, etc."

Some answer right off and tell their definite plans and projects, highly approved by Papa. I'm pleased for them, but it's a bit boring, because they are such squares.

Quite a few will, with prompting, come out with astounding stereo-typed, conceited fantasies, such as becoming a movie actor when they are "discovered"—"like Marlon Brando, but in my own way."

Very rarely somebody will, maybe defiantly and defensively, maybe diffidently but proudly, make you know that he knows very well what he is going to do; it is something great; and he is indeed already doing it, which is the real test.

The usual answer, perhaps the normal answer, is "I don't know," meaning, "I'm looking; I haven't found the right thing; it's discouraging but not hopeless."

But the terrible answer is, "Nothing." The young man doesn't want to do anything.

—I remember talking to half a dozen young fellows at Van Wagner's Beach outside of Hamilton, Ontario; and all of them had this one thing to say: "Nothing." They didn't believe that what to work at was the kind of thing one *wanted*. They rather expected that two or three of them would work for the electric company in town, but they couldn't care less. I turned away from the conversation abruptly because of the uncontrollable burning tears in my eyes and constriction in my chest. Not feeling sorry for them, but tears of frank dismay for the waste of our humanity (they were nice kids). . . .

Preface to "Making It"

NORMAN PODHORETZ (1930–   ), born in Brooklyn, New York, has good cause for celebrating his success. Educated at Columbia (B.A., 1950), and Cambridge University (B.A., 1952), he joined **Commentary** magazine in 1956 and in two years became editor-in-chief. His published work includes **Doings and Undoings** (1969), a study of the literature and culture of the 1950s.

Let me introduce myself. I am a man who at the precocious age of thirty-five experienced an astonishing revelation: it is better to be a success than a failure. Having been penetrated by this great truth concerning the nature of things, my mind was now open for the first time to a series of corollary perceptions, each one as dizzying in its impact

PREFACE. From *Making It*, by Norman Podhoretz. Copyright © 1967 by Norman Podhoretz. Reprinted by permission of Random House, Inc.

as the Original Revelation itself. Money, I now saw (no one, of course, had ever seen it before), was important: it was better to be rich than to be poor. Power, I now saw (moving on to higher subtleties), was desirable: it was better to give orders than to take them. Fame, I now saw (how courageous of me not to flinch), was unqualifiedly delicious: it was better to be recognized than to be anonymous.

This book represents an effort to explain why it should have taken someone like myself so long to arrive at such apparently elementary discoveries. It is not, in other words, a success story, it is the story of an education; and while it is autobiographical in form, it is not an autobiography in the usual sense, being confined very strictly to those details of my life bearing on the question of career.

To be sure, the story I tell here resembles the traditional success story in tracing the progressive rise of a young man up from poverty and obscure origins. In contrast to the traditional success story, however, its purpose is not to celebrate that rise, but rather to describe certain fine-print conditions that are attached to the successful accomplishment of what the sociologists call "upward mobility" in so heterogeneous a society as our own. There are prices to be paid for the rewards of making it in America, some obvious, some not very well advertised. I try in this book to focus attention on a few of the latter, which are grouped together into the metaphor of "conversions."

My second purpose in telling the story of my own career is to provide a concrete setting for a diagnosis of the curiously contradictory feelings our culture instills in us toward the ambition for success, and toward each of its various goals: money, power, fame, and social position. On the one hand, we are commanded to become successful—that is, to acquire more of these worldly goods than we began with, and to do so by our own exertions; on the other hand, it is impressed upon us by means both direct and devious that if we obey the commandment, we shall find ourselves falling victim to the radical corruption of spirit which, given the nature of what is nowadays called the "system," the pursuit of success requires and which its attainment always bespeaks. On the one hand, "the exclusive worship of the bitch-goddess SUCCESS," as William James put it in a famous remark, "is our national disease"; on the other hand, a contempt for success is the consensus of the national literature for the past hundred years and more. On the one hand, our culture teaches us to shape our lives in accordance with the hunger for worldly things; on the other hand, it spitefully contrives to make us ashamed of the presence of those hungers in ourselves and to deprive us as far as possible of any pleasure in their satisfaction.

Nothing, I believe, defines the spiritual character of American life more saliently than this contradiction, and I doubt that many Amer-

icans, whether they be successes or failures in their careers, can have
escaped its consequences. I myself have tasted enough success of one
kind or another to know something about success, and more than
enough ambition of every kind to know much of what there is to know
about ambition. But these are not the credentials I offer for presuming
to write an autobiographical book about the problem of success in
America. My claim to expertise in this field is simply that I *am* an
American. The fact that I was also born in Brooklyn to East European
Jewish parents and that I have made my career in the wilds of literary
New York does not, I think, disqualify the story of that career from
being considered typical in its underlying contours. On the contrary,
my background and my working life have, if anything, conspired to
render me unusually susceptible to the suasions of both sides of the
contradictory American attitude toward the ambition for and the
pursuit of worldly success.

The immigrant Jewish milieu from which I derive is by now fixed
for all time in the American imagination as having been driven by an
uninhibited hunger for success. This reputation is by no means as justified as we have been led to believe, but certainly on the surface the
"gospel of success" did reign supreme in the world of my childhood.
Success did not necessarily, or even primarily, mean money; just as
often it might mean prestige or popularity. In any case, the concept
always referred, as it was originally intended to do, to the possession
of goods which had value in the eyes of others. These goods might also
have had value in one's own eyes, but that was a secondary consideration, if indeed it was ever considered at all. The main thing was to be
esteemed, and one would no more have questioned the desirability of so
pleasant an estate in life than one would have wondered about the relative merits of illness and good health.

Having grown up with such feelings, I responded with puzzlement
to the discovery first forced upon me in college that something which
might be called a gospel of anti-success, or even a cult of failure, held
as powerful a sway over the spoken attitudes, if not always the behavior, of educated Americans as the opposing creed did over the
minds of the people I had previously known. Most of the books I read
about America assured me—and continue to do so to this day—that
success was the supreme, even the only, American value, and yet at
Columbia College the word "successful" glided automatically into the
judgment "corrupt." The books all said that Americans regarded ambition as a major virtue, and yet a system of manners existed at Columbia which prohibited any expression of worldly ambitiousness. To yearn
for the applause of posterity may have been legitimate, but it was
thought contemptible to dream of the rewards contemporary society
had to offer, and altogether despicable to admit to so low a hunger,

except in tones of irony that revealed one's consciousness of how naughty a thing one was doing.

All this made its mark on me and was to be reinforced by the ethos of New York literary society, where I eventually came both to live and to earn my living as a writer and an editor. Later on, I go into some of the reasons for the special prevalence of the gospel of anti-success among literary people and those involved in the arts in general; here I want only to point out that it *has* a special prevalence in such circles. Thus, as someone who was raised in the most notoriously driving of all American subcultures; who then grew to maturity under the influence of ideas which were in the sharpest possible opposition to the values associated with the worship of success; and whose own experience finally pushed him into rebelling against many of the assumptions behind the oppositionist view—I may perhaps lay claim to a particularly good vantage point from which to report on how the two warring American attitudes toward the pursuit of success are likely to reveal themselves concretely in the details of an individual career.

It is a symptom of the predicament I am concerned with describing that only the immensely successful are permitted to talk about their own careers without becoming vulnerable to the charge of tastelessness. "Good" taste in this area prescribes the denigration of one's achievements, and only the immensely successful can afford, or have the right, to be so modest. The rest of us customarily remain silent, for fear of seeming to inflate our own importance or the importance of the work we do. For taking my career as seriously as I do in this book, I will no doubt be accused of self-inflation and therefore of tastelessness. So be it. There was a time when to talk candidly about sex was similarly regarded as tasteless—a betrayal of what D. H. Lawrence once called "the dirty little secret." For many of us, of course, this is no longer the case. But judging by the embarrassment that a frank discussion of one's feelings about one's own success, or the lack of it, invariably causes in polite company today, ambition (itself a species of lustful hunger) seems to be replacing erotic lust as the prime dirty little secret of the well-educated American soul. And since the natural accompaniments of a dirty little secret are superstition, hypocrisy, and cant, it is no cause for wonder that the theme of success rarely appears in our discourse unattended by at least one of these three dismal Furies inherited from Victorian sex.

To the extent that this book is a confessional work, to the extent that it deliberately exposes an order of feeling in myself, and by implication in others, that most of us usually do our best to keep hidden, from ourselves as well as others, it obviously constitutes the betrayal of a dirty little secret and thereby a violation of certain current standards of tastefulness. There are, however, different standards according to which superstition, hypocrisy, and cant are more damaging to the health of the soul than the admittedly painful offenses against "good" taste that are bound to be committed by a confessional writer bent on bringing the secret out into the open and thus helping to weaken its power to shame. It is on such standards that this book relies, and to them that it makes an appeal.

Questions for Discussion and Writing

1. Does Barnum consider "money getting" the chief aim of life? How does he compare on this point with the other authors represented in this section?

2. How do the ethics and strategies Barnum recommends compare with those of a modern businessman? Are any of them still practiced?

3. In Thoreau's view, would Barnum's "successful" man live a "life without principle"? What precisely are the attitudes and beliefs of nineteenth-century industrial America that Thoreau criticizes?

4. Which other selection best illustrates the point that Dickinson makes in "Success Is Counted Sweetest"? Explain.

5. Compare the criticisms of the success myth in the poems of Crane and Robinson. How might Crane's poem be read as a commentary on Darwin's theory of evolution?

6. In what ways does Washington alter the success myth for the group he addresses? How would a modern black militant respond to his advice?

7. Examine the order in which Carnegie lists man's most compelling wants and speculate about why they are so arranged. Is the primary want the first or last? What would Freud say about the list?

8. Does Ralph Whittemore ignore Barnum's maxims? Why does he "fail" at business? Would any of the other writers judge him a "success"?

9. Define "man's work." Compare Goodman's analysis to Thoreau's "Life Without Principle."

10. Compare Podhoretz's hallmarks of success—Money, Power, Fame —with those suggested in the other writings in this section.

Essay Topics

1. What do you consider the relative importance of the following for achieving success:

hard work	advertising
brains	a college education
luck	ability to cooperate
personality	ambition
"pull"	honesty

2. William James said that "the exclusive worship of the bitch-goddess SUCCESS . . . is our national disease;" Podhoretz avers that "a contempt for success is the consensus of the national literature for the past hundred years and more." Can you reconcile these statements?
3. Which present-day public figures seem to you most successful? Do the values on which you base this assessment differ from those of the students whom Goodman cites?
4. Comparing authorities cited by the various writers represented in this section, discuss changing sources of thought on success, and the significance of the change.

Suggestions for Further Reading

PRIMARY

BRUCE BARTON, *The Man Nobody Knows* (1925). A portrait of Jesus as a dynamic business executive, written by a popular author and member of an important advertising firm.

RUSSELL CONWELL, *Acres of Diamonds* (1880s). Advice on how to find success "in your own backyard" by a Baptist minister from Philadelphia who made his fame and fortune with this popular lecture.

THEODORE DREISER, *The Titan* (1914). A fictional account of the stormy career of Frank Cowperwood, a successful Chicago business-man patterned after traction magnate Charles Yerkes.

F. SCOTT FITZGERALD, *The Great Gatsby* (1925). Gatsby's pursuit of a shabby version of the Franklin creed of success becomes a parable of America's search for her past.

BENJAMIN FRANKLIN, *The Way to Wealth* (1760). The original source of the homey maxims that, often vulgarized and distorted, became the basis of later thought on success.

JOHN P. MARQUAND, *Point of No Return* (1949). A satiric look at the emptiness of success through the life of a banker about to "make it."

COTTON MATHER, *A Christian at His Calling* (1701). A statement of the Protestant ethic by a leading colonial clergyman, showing the roots of the success ideal in Puritan thought.

ARTHUR MILLER, *Death of a Salesman* (1949). A popular dramatization of the blighting effects of the dream of success on Willie Loman, an American Everyman.

NATHANAEL WEST, *A Cool Million* (1934). A sophisticated parody of the "rags to riches" story, written in mock Alger style.

SECONDARY

JOHN G. CAWELTI, *Apostles of the Self-Made Man* (1965). A survey of writings on success from Franklin to the mid-twentieth century.

KENNETH LYNN, *The Dream of Success* (1955). A reassessment of the novels of Theodore Dreiser, Jack London, and other novelists of the progressive era, revealing their ambivalence toward success.

DONALD MEYER, *The Positive Thinkers* (1965). A detailed account of "positive thinking" as related to the quest for personal success in a range of thinkers from Mary Baker Eddy to Norman Vincent Peale.

RICHARD WEISS, *The American Myth of Success* (1969). A history of thought on success since the Gilded Age, relating literature on success in business to inspiration and self-help literature.

LOUIS B. WRIGHT, "Franklin's Legacy to the Gilded Age," *Virginia Quarterly Review*, 22 (1946), 268–79. A description of the secularization of Franklin's ideal during the nineteenth century.

IRVIN WYLLIE, *The Self-Made Man* (1954). An analysis of late nineteenth-century success literature, arguing that it was predominantly Christian in inspiration and moral in nature, not a dog-eat-dog philosophy.

Science,
Technology,
Progress

The Law of Human Progress

CHARLES SUMNER (1811–1874), important American statesman, was born in Boston, and graduated from Harvard College (1830) and Harvard Law School (1833). Active in prison reform and the peace movement, he emerged in the 1840s one of the primary opponents of slavery extension. A leader in the Free Soil party, he later denounced the "Crime Against Kansas" (the Kansas-Nebraska Act— a bill that allowed each territory by majority vote to sanction or ban slavery) from the floor of the United States Senate. During and after the Civil War he was one of the leading Radical Republicans, urging equal suffrage and basic rights for America's freedmen. "The Law of Human Progress," an example of his outstanding oratory, was delivered in 1848, the year of the Free Soil revolt.

Wherever we turn is Progress,—in science, in literature, in knowledge of the earth, in knowledge of the skies, in intercourse among men, in the spread of liberty, in works of beneficence, in the recognition of Human Brotherhood. Thrones, where Authority seemed to sit secure, with the sanction of centuries, are shaken, and new-made constitutions come to restrain the aberrations of unlimited power. Men everywhere, breaking away from the Past, are pressing on to the things that are before.

.   .   .

It is of this that I shall speak to-day. My subject is THE LAW OF HUMAN PROGRESS. In selecting this theme, I would not minister to the pride or gratulation of the Present, nor would I furnish motives for indifference or repose. Rather would I teach how small is the Present and all it contains, compared with the Future, and how duties increase with the grandeur upon which we enter, while we derive new encouragement from knowledge of the law which is our support and guide.

The subject is vast as it is interesting and important. It might well occupy a volume, rather than a brief discourse. In unfolding it, I shall speak *first* of the history of this law, as seen in its origin, gradual

THE LAW OF HUMAN PROGRESS. From Charles Sumner, *Complete Works*, II (1900).

development, and recognition,—and *next* of its character, conditions, and limitations, with the duties it enjoins and the encouragements it affords.

And, first, of its history. The recognition of this law has been reserved for comparatively recent times. Like other general laws governing the course of Nature, it was unknown to Antiquity. The ignorance and prejudice which then prevailed with regard to the earth, the heavenly bodies, and their relations to the universe, found fit companionship with the wild speculations concerning the Human Family. The ignorant live only in the Present, whether of time or place. What they see and observe bounds their knowledge. Thus to the early Greek the heavens were upborne by the mountains, and the sun traversed daily in fiery chariot from east to west. So things seemed to him. But the true Destiny of the Human Family was as little comprehended.

Man, in his origin and history, was surrounded with fable; nor was there any correct idea of the principles determining the succession of events. Revolutions of states were referred sometimes to chance, sometimes to certain innate elements of decay.

.   .   .

. . . As modern civilization gradually unfolded itself amidst the multiplying generations of men, they witnessed the successive manifestations of power,—but perceived no Law. They looked upon the imposing procession of events, but did not discern the rule which guided the mighty series. Ascending from triumph to triumph, they saw dominion extended by the discoveries of intrepid navigators,—saw learning strengthened by the studies of accomplished scholars,—saw universities opening their portals to ingenuous youth in all corners of the land, from Aberdeen and Copenhagen to Toledo and Ferrara,— saw Art put forth new graces in the painting of Raffaelle, new grandeur in the painting, the sculpture, and the architecture of Michel Angelo,—caught the strain of poets, no longer cramped by ancient idioms, but flowing sweetly in the language learned at a mother's knee,— received the manifold revelations of science in geometry, mathematics, astronomy,—beheld the barbarism of the barbarous Art of War changed and refined, though barbarous still, by the invention of gunpowder,— witnessed knowledge of all kinds springing to unwonted power through the marvellous agency of the printing-press,—admired the character of *the Good Man of Peace,* as described in that work of unexampled circulation, translated into all modern languages, the "Imitation of Christ," by Thomas à Kempis,—listened to the apostolic preaching of Wyckliffe in England, Huss in Bohemia, Savonarola in Florence, Luther at Worms; and yet all these things, the harmonious expression of *progressive* energies belonging to Man, token of an untiring advance, earnest of a mightier Future, seemed to teach no certain lesson.

The key to this advance had not been found. It was not seen that the constant desire for improvement implanted in man, with the constant effort consequent thereon in a life susceptible of indefinite Progress, caused, naturally, under the laws of a beneficent God, an indefinite advance,—that the evil passions of individuals, or of masses, while retarding, could not permanently restrain this divine impulse,—and that each generation, by irresistible necessity, added to the accumulations of the Past, and in this way prepared a higher Future.

.   .   .

To the eighteenth century belongs the honor—signal honor I venture to call it—of first distinctly acknowledging and enunciating that Law of Human Progress, which, though preached in Judea eighteen hundred years ago, failed to be received by men,—nay, still fails to be received by men. Writers in our own age, of much ability and unexampled hardihood, while adopting this fundamental law, proceed to arraign existing institutions of society. My present purpose does not require me to consider these, whether for censure or praise,—abounding as they do in evil, abounding as they do in good. It is my single aim to trace the gradual development and final establishment of that great law which teaches that "there is a good time coming,"—a Future even on earth, to arouse the hopes, the aspirations, and the energies of Man.

The way is now prepared to consider the character, conditions, and limitations of this law, the duties it enjoins, and the encouragements it affords.

Let me state the law as I understand it. Man, as an individual, is capable of indefinite improvement. Societies and nations, which are but aggregations of men, and, finally, the Human Family, or collective Humanity, are capable of indefinite improvement. And this is the destiny of man, of societies, of nations, and of the Human Family.

.   .   .

Without knowledge there can be no sure Progress. Vice and barbarism are the inseparable companions of ignorance. Nor is it too much to say, that, except in rare instances, the highest virtue is attained only through intelligence. This is natural; for to do right, we must first understand what is right. But the people of Greece and Rome, even in the brilliant days of Pericles and Augustus, could not arrive at this knowledge. The sublime teachings of Plato and Socrates—calculated in many respects to promote the best interests of the race—were limited in influence to a small company of listeners, or to the few who could obtain a copy of the costly manuscripts in which they were preserved. Thus the knowledge and virtue acquired by individuals were not diffused in their own age or secured to posterity.

Now, at last, through an agency all unknown to Antiquity, knowledge of every kind has become general and permanent. It can no longer be confined to a select circle. It cannot be crushed by tyranny, or lost by neglect. It is immortal as the soul from which it proceeds. This alone renders all relapse into barbarism impossible, while it affords an unquestionable distinction between ancient and modern times. The Press, watchful with more than the hundred eyes of Argus, strong with more than the hundred arms of Briareus, not only guards all the conquests of civilization, but leads the way to future triumphs. . . .

In receiving this law, two conditions of Humanity are recognized: first, its unity or solidarity; and, secondly, its indefinite duration upon earth. And now of these in their order.

1. It is true, doubtless, that there are various races of men; but there is but one great Human Family, in which Caucasian, Ethiopian, Chinese, and Indian are all brothers, children of *one* Father, and heirs to *one* happiness. Though variously endowed, they are all tending in the same direction; nor can the light obtained by one be withheld from any. . . . In the light of science and of religion, Humanity is an organism, complex, but still one,—throbbing with one life, animated by one soul, every part sympathizing with every other part, and the whole advancing in one indefinite career of Progress.

2. And what is the measure of this career? It is common to speak of the long life already passed by man on earth; but how brief and trivial is this, compared with the countless ages before him! According to received chronology, six thousand years have not yet elapsed since his creation. But the science of Geology, that unimpeached interpreter of the Past, now demonstrates (and here the geology of New York furnishes important evidence), that, anterior to the commencement of human history, this globe had endured for ages upon ages, baffling human calculation and imagination.

.   .   .

Admitting the Unity of Mankind, and an Indefinite Future on earth, it becomes easy to anticipate triumphs which else were impossible. Few will question that Man, as an individual, is capable of indefinite improvement, so long as he lives. This capacity is inborn. None so poor as not to possess it. Even the idiot, so abject in condition, is found at last to be within the sphere of education. Circumstances alone are required to call this capacity into action; and in proportion as knowledge, virtue, and religion prevail in a community will that sacred atmosphere be diffused under whose genial influence the most forlorn may grow into forms of unimagined strength and beauty. This capacity for indefinite improvement, which belongs to the individual, must belong also to society; for society does not die, and through the improvement of its individuals has the assurance of its own advance. It is immortal on earth, and will gather constantly new and richer fruits from the teeming generations, as they stretch through unknown time. To Chinese vision the period of the present may seem barren, but it is sure to yield its contribution to the indefinite accumulations which are the token of an indefinite Progress.

Tables speak sometimes as words cannot. From statistics of life, as recorded by Science, we learn the capacity for progress in the Human Family; the testimony is authentic, as it is interesting. A little more than two centuries have passed since Descartes predicted that improvement in human health which these figures exhibit. Could this seer of Science revisit the scene of his comprehensive labors and divine aspirations, he might well be astonished to learn how, in the lapse of so short a period in the life of Humanity, his glowing anticipations have been fulfilled. . . . [Even] the conqueror Death has been slowly driven back, and his inevitable triumph postponed. . . .

The tokens of improvement may appear at a special period, in a limited circle only, among the people, favored of God, enjoying peculiar benefits of commerce and Christianity; but the happy influence cannot be narrowed to any time, place, or people. Every victory over evil redounds to the benefit of all. Every discovery, every humane thought, every truth, when declared, is a conquest of which the whole Human Family are partakers, extending by so much their dominion, while it lessens by so much the sphere of future struggle and trial. Thus, while Nature is always the same, the power of Man is ever increasing. Each day gives him some new advantage. The mountains have not diminished in size; but Man has overcome the barriers they interpose. The winds and waves are not less capricious now than when they first beat upon the ancient Silurian rocks; but the steamboat,

> "Against the wind, against the tide,
> Now steadies on with upright keel."

The distance between two points on the surface of the globe is the same to-day as when the continents were upheaved from their ocean-bed; but the art of man triumphs over such separation, and distant people commune together. Much remains to be done; but the Creator did not speak in vain, when he blessed his earliest children, and bade them "multiply, and replenish the earth, and *subdue it.*"

There will be triumphs nobler than any over inanimate Nature. Man himself will be subdued,—subdued to abhorrence of vice, injustice, violence,—subdued to the sweet charities of life,—subdued to all the requirements of duty,—subdued, according to the Law of Human Progress, to the recognition of that Gospel Law of Human Brotherhood, by the side of which the first is only as the scaffolding upon the sacred temple. To labor for this end was man sent forth into the world,—not in the listlessness of idle perfections, but endowed with infinite capacities, inspired by infinite desires, and commanded to strive perpetually after excellence, amidst the encouragements of hope, the promises of final success, and the inexpressible delights from its pursuit. Thus does the Law of Human Progress

> "assert eternal Providence,
> And justify the ways of God to men,"

by showing Evil no longer a gloomy mystery, binding the world in everlasting thrall, but an accident, under benign Power destined to be surely subdued, as the Human Family press on to the promised goal of happiness.

While recognizing Humanity as progressive, it is important to consider a condition or limitation which may justly temper the ardors of the reformer. Nothing is accomplished except by time and exertion. Nature abhors violence and suddenness. Nature does everything slowly and by degrees. It takes time for the seed to grow into "the bright consummate flower." It is many years before the slender shoot grows into the tree. It is slowly that we pass from infancy and imbecility to manhood and strength. Arrived at this stage, we are still subject to the same condition of Nature. A new temperature or a sudden stroke of light may shock us. Our frames are not made for extremes; so that death may come, according to the poet's conceit, "in aromatic pain."

Gradual change is a necessary condition of the Law of Progress. It is only, according to the poetical phrase of Tacitus, *per intervalla ac spiramenta temporum*, "by intervals and breathings of time," that we can hope to make a sure advance. Men grow and are trained in knowledge and virtue; but they cannot be compelled into this path. This consideration teaches candor and charity towards all who do not yet see the truth as we do. It admonishes us also, while keeping the eye steadfast on the good we seek, to moderate our expectations, and be content when the day of triumph is postponed, for it cannot be always.

.   .   .

Let us, then, be of good cheer. From the great Law of Progress we derive at once our duties and our encouragements. Humanity has ever advanced, urged by instincts and necessities implanted by God,—

thwarted sometimes by obstacles, causing it for a time, a moment only in the immensity of ages, to deviate from its true line, or seem to retreat, but still ever onward. At last we know the law of this movement; we fasten our eyes upon that star, unobserved in the earlier ages, which lights the way to the Future, opening into vistas of infinite variety and extension. Amidst the disappointments which attend individual exertions, amidst the universal agitations which now surround us, let us recognize this law, let us follow this star, confident that whatever is just, whatever is humane, whatever is good, whatever is true, according to an immutable ordinance of Providence, in the sure light of the Future, must prevail. With this faith, we place our hands, as those of little children, in the great hand of God. He will guide and sustain us—through pains and perils it may be—in the path of Progress.

.　　.　　.

Technology and the Poets

To a Locomotive in Winter

WALT WHITMAN (1819–1892), following the public failure of **Leaves of Grass** (1855), continued to do necessary newspaper work while writing new poems. Deeply affected by the suffering he saw while nursing soldiers during the Civil War, he recorded his impressions in a series of poems collected in **Drum Taps** (1865). In the postwar years he earned a living in a series of government jobs, but in 1873 suffered a stroke that forced him to retire to Camden, New Jersey, where he first lived with a brother, and finally alone in a small house. "To A Locomotive in Winter" (1876), one of the many poems he continued to add to successive editions of **Leaves of Grass,** was perhaps written in the attic of his brother's house from which Whitman often watched trains go by. Like **Democratic Vistas** (1871), and "A Backward Glance O'er Travel'd Roads" (1888), two prose works, the poem reveals his continuing interest in the forces that were transforming late nineteenth-century America.

TO A LOCOMOTIVE IN WINTER. From Walt Whitman, *Leaves of Grass,* 9th ed. (1891–92).

Thee for my recitative,
Thee in the driving storm even as now, the snow, the winter-day
    declining,
Thee in thy panoply, thy measur'd dual throbbing and thy beat con-
    vulsive,
Thy black cylindric body, golden brass and silvery steel,
Thy ponderous side-bars, parallel and connecting rods, gyrating, shut-
    tling at thy sides,
Thy metrical, now swelling pant and roar, now tapering in the dis-
    tance,
Thy great protruding head-light fix'd in front,
Thy long, pale, floating vapor-pennants, tinged with delicate purple,
The dense and murky clouds out-belching from thy smoke-stack,
Thy knitted frame, thy springs and valves, the tremulous twinkle of
    thy wheels,
Thy train of cars behind, obedient, merrily following,
Through gale or calm, now swift, now slack, yet steadily careering;
Type of the modern—emblem of motion and power—pulse of the
    continent,
For once come serve the Muse and merge in verse, even as here I see
    thee,
With storm and buffeting gusts of wind and falling snow,
By day thy warning ringing bell to sound its notes,
By night thy silent signal lamps to swing.

Fierce-throated beauty!
Roll through my chant with all thy lawless music, thy swinging lamps
    at night,
Thy madly-whistled laughter, echoing, rumbling like an earthquake,
    rousing all,
Law of thyself complete, thine own track firmly holding,
(No sweetness debonair of tearful harp or glib piano thine,)
Thy trills of shrieks by rocks and hills return'd,
Launch'd o'er the prairies wide, across the lakes,
To the free skies unpent and glad and strong.

I Like to See It Lap the Miles

EMILY DICKINSON (1830–1886) surveyed her neighbors' enthusiasm
for the "progress of the age" with characteristic wit and detachment.
A leading symbol of this progress, the railroad between Belcher-
town and her home town, Amherst, Massachusetts, was a favorite
project of her father. When in 1853 it made its first run, Squire
Dickinson, his daughter reported, "went marching around the town
. . . like some old Roman general, upon a Triumph Day." A
decade later the poetess celebrated the coming of the "iron horse"
in her own way, in the selection that follows.

I like to see it lap the Miles—
And lick the Valleys up—
And stop to feed itself at Tanks—
And then—prodigious step

Around a Pile of Mountains—
And supercilious peer
In Shanties—by the sides of Roads—
And then a Quarry pare

To fit it's sides
And crawl between
Complaining all the while
In horrid—hooting stanza—
Then chase itself down Hill—

And neigh like Boanerges—
Then—prompter than a Star
Stop—docile and omnipotent
At it's own stable door—

I LIKE TO SEE IT LAP THE MILES. From Emily Dickinson, *Poems* (1891).
Reprinted by permission of the publishers and the Trustees of Amherst College from Thomas H. Johnson, Editor, *The Poems of Emily Dickinson*, Cambridge, Mass.: The Belknap Press of Harvard University Press, Copyright,
1951, 1955, by The President and Fellows of Harvard College.

Prayers of Steel

CARL SANDBURG (1878–1967) was born in Galesburg, Illinois, the son of impoverished and illiterate Swedish immigrants. After enlisting in the Spanish-American war, he attended Lombard College between 1898 and 1902 but never graduated. Joining the Socialist Party, he became a leading figure in the literary renaissance that flowered after 1912. In his use of colloquialisms, his free forms, and his devotion to democracy, he recalled Whitman, although the subtle imagery of such poems as "Fog" placed him also in the tradition of Emily Dickinson. Gaining fame for **Cornhuskers** (1918) and other volumes of poetry, he also wrote a six-volume biography of Abraham Lincoln, for which he received the Pulitzer prize in 1939.

Lay me on an anvil, O God.
Beat me and hammer me into a crowbar.
Let me pry loose old walls.
Let me lift and loosen old foundations.

Lay me on an anvil, O God.
Beat me and hammer me into a steel spike.
Drive me into the girders that hold a skyscraper together.

Take red-hot rivets and fasten me into the central girders.
Let me be the great nail holding a skyscraper through blue nights into
    white stars.

Science

ROBINSON JEFFERS (1887–1962), born in Pittsburgh, spent much of his youth abroad. A graduate of Occidental College, he studied medicine at U.S.C. and forestry at the University of Washington, in search of a genial occupation with which to support his writing. In 1912 he published **Flagons and Apples,** his first book of poems. Using an inheritance to build a house above Big Sur, he there composed **Californians** (1916). Profoundly disillusioned by the war, he preached "Inhumanism," a thoroughgoing materialism that bordered on nihilism. He appeared to say that humanity was ingrown and dying, and deserved the wars and other catastrophes that would bring its demise. Although a distortion of his position, this interpretation won Jeffers wide praise during the 1920s, and a smaller following in the 1930s among Marxists who found thus confirmed their own vision of the decadence of Western culture. More recently, critics have reassessed his work and his place in the American literary tradition. The materialism and pessimism of his poetry, fundamentally religious in purpose, obscures a basic similarity between Jeffers and the Transcendentalists. Jeffers' work, writes one leading critic, constituted "the first major poetic attempt to bring the split of the modern world together in a primarily materialistic vision." (R. Squires, **The Loyalties of Robinson Jeffers** [1956], 190.)

Man, introverted man, having crossed
In passage and but a little with the nature of things this latter century
Has begot giants; but being taken up
Like a maniac with self-love and inward conflicts cannot manage his
  hybrids.
Being used to deal with edgeless dreams,
Now he's bred knives on nature turns them also inward: they have
  thirsty points though.
His mind forebodes his own destruction;

Actæon who saw the goddess naked among leaves and his hounds tore
him.
A little knowledge, a pebble from the shingle,
A drop from the oceans: who would have dreamed this infinitely little
too much?

pity this busy monster, manunkind

E. E. CUMMINGS (1894–1962), born in Cambridge, Massachusetts,
graduated from Harvard in 1915, and served as an ambulance driver
in France during the war. **The Enormous Room** (1922), ostensibly a
war novel, affirmed the aspirations of young men caught in the
dehumanizing processes of an impersonal system. His many poems,
a terror to typesetters because of their lack of capitalization and
punctuation, are distinguished by an alternating tough and sentimental tone, and also by perhaps the most creative and strikingly
original use of the English language by any American poet. In both
his poems and essays Cummings repeatedly sounded a warning
against the danger of men becoming automatons.

pity this busy monster, manunkind,

not. Progress is a comfortable disease:
your victim(death and life safely beyond)

plays with the bigness of his littleness
—electrons deify one razorblade
into a mountainrange;lenses extend

unwish through curving wherewhen till unwish
returns on its unself.

A world of made
is not a world of born—pity poor flesh

and trees,poor stars and stones,but never this
fine specimen of hypermagical

ultraomnipotence. We doctors know

a hopeless case if—listen:there's a hell
of a good universe next door;let's go

Works and Days

RALPH WALDO EMERSON (1803–1882), born in Boston and educated at Harvard, is America's most celebrated essayist and philosopher. His career, however, was not without controversy. He
entered the ministry but resigned his parish in 1832 after deciding
he could not administer communion since the Lord's Supper was
not a sacrament. Although he accepted invitations to preach for
more than a decade, Emerson devoted full time to the public lectures and essays that gained him fame and a comfortable living.
In his "American Scholar" (1837), a speech delivered before the
Phi Beta Kappa Society at Harvard, he won warm praise for his
impassioned plea for Americans to declare intellectual independence from Europe. But his address before the Harvard Divinity
School the following year, an attack on historical Christianity that
outraged even the liberal Unitarians, made him **persona non grata**
at his alma mater most of his life. In "Nature" (1836) and the
other essays that won him fame, he expressed dissatisfaction with
much of the crudeness and commercialism of Jacksonian America.
In **Society and Solitude,** one of his last works, he surveyed the rapid
changes taking place in post–Civil War America.

Our nineteenth century is the age of tools. They grew out of our
structure. "Man is the meter of all things," said Aristotle; "the hand
is the instrument of instruments, and the mind is the form of forms."
The human body is the magazine of inventions, the patent office,
where are the models from which every hint was taken. All the tools

WORKS AND DAYS. From Ralph Waldo Emerson, *Society and Solitude*
(1870).

and engines on earth are only extensions of its limbs and senses. One definition of man is "an intelligence served by organs." Machines can only second, not supply, his unaided senses. The body is a meter. The eye appreciates finer differences than art can expose. The apprentice clings to his foot-rule; a practised mechanic will measure by his thumb and his arm with equal precision; and a good surveyor will pace sixteen rods more accurately than another man can measure them by tape. The sympathy of eye and hand by which an Indian or a practised slinger hits his mark with a stone, or a wood-chopper or a carpenter swings his axe to a hair-line on his log, are examples; and there is no sense or organ which is not capable of exquisite performance.

Men love to wonder, and that is the seed of our science; and such is the mechanical determination of our age, and so recent are our best contrivances, that use has not dulled our joy and pride in them; and we pity our fathers for dying before steam and galvanism, sulphuric ether and ocean telegraphs, photograph and spectroscope arrived, as cheated out of half their human estate. These arts open great gates of a future, promising to make the world plastic and to lift human life out of its beggary to a godlike ease and power.

Our century to be sure had inherited a tolerable apparatus. We had the compass, the printing-press, watches, the spiral spring, the barometer, the telescope. Yet so many inventions have been added that life seems almost made over new; and as Leibnitz said of Newton, that "if he reckoned all that had been done by mathematicians from the beginning of the world down to Newton, and what had been done by him, his would be the better half," so one might say that the inventions of the last fifty years counterpoise those of the fifty centuries before them. For the vast production and manifold application of iron is new; and our common and indispensable utensils of house and farm are new; the sewing-machine, the power-loom, the Mc-Cormick reaper, the mowing-machines, gaslight, lucifer matches, and the immense productions of the laboratory, are new in this century, and one franc's worth of coal does the work of a laborer for twenty days.

Why need I speak of steam, the enemy of space and time, with its enormous strength and delicate applicability, which is made in hospitals to bring a bowl of gruel to a sick man's bed, and can twist beams of iron like candy-braids, and vies with the forces which upheaved and doubled over the geologic strata? Steam is an apt scholar and a strong-shouldered fellow, but it has not yet done all its work. It already walks about the field like a man, and will do anything required of it. It irrigates crops, and drags away a mountain. It must sew our shirts, it must drive our gigs; taught by Mr. Babbage, it must calculate interest and logarithms. Lord Chancellor Thurlow thought it might be made to draw bills and answers in chancery. If that were satire, it is yet coming to render many higher services of a mechanico-intellectual kind, and will leave the satire short of the fact.

How excellent are the mechanical aids we have applied to the human body, as in dentistry, in vaccination, in the rhinoplastic treatment; in the beautiful aid of ether, like a finer sleep; and in the boldest promiser of all,—the transfusion of the blood,—which, in Paris, it was claimed, enables a man to change his blood as often as his linen!

What of this dapper caoutchouc and gutta-percha, which make water-pipes and stomach-pumps, belting for mill-wheels, and diving-bells, and rain-proof coats for all climates, which teach us to defy the wet, and put every man on a footing with the beaver and the crocodile? What of the grand tools with which we engineer, like kobolds and enchanters, tunnelling Alps, canalling the American Isthmus, piercing the Arabian desert? In Massachusetts we fight the sea successfully with beach-grass and broom, and the blowing sand-barrens with pine plantations. The soil of Holland, once the most populous in Europe, is below the level of the sea. Egypt, where no rain fell for three thousand years, now, it is said, thanks Mehemet Ali's irrigations and planted forests for late-returning showers. The old Hebrew king said, "He makes the wrath of man to praise him." And there is no argument of theism better than the grandeur of ends brought about by paltry means. The chain of Western railroads from Chicago to the Pacific has planted cities and civilization in less time than it costs to bring an orchard into bearing.

What shall we say of the ocean telegraph, that extension of the eye and ear, whose sudden performance astonished mankind as if the intellect were taking the brute earth itself into training, and shooting the first thrills of life and thought through the unwilling brain?

There does not seem any limit to these new informations of the same Spirit that made the elements at first, and now, through man, works them. Art and power will go on as they have done,—will make day out of night, time out of space, and space out of time.

Invention breeds invention. No sooner is the electric telegraph devised than gutta-percha, the very material it requires, is found. The aëronaut is provided with gun-cotton, the very fuel he wants for his balloon. When commerce is vastly enlarged, California and Australia expose the gold it needs. When Europe is over-populated, America and Australia crave to be peopled; and so throughout, every chance is timed, as if Nature, who made the lock, knew where to find the key.

Another result of our arts is the new intercourse which is surprising us with new solutions of the embarrassing political problems. The intercourse is not new, but the scale is new. Our selfishness would have held slaves, or would have excluded from a quarter of the planet all that are not born on the soil of that quarter. Our politics are disgusting; but what can they help or hinder when from time to time the primal instincts are impressed on masses of mankind, when the nations are in exodus and flux? Nature loves to cross her stocks,—and German, Chinese, Turk, Russ and Kanaka were putting out to sea, and intermarrying race with race; and commerce took the hint, and ships were built capacious enough to carry the people of a county.

This thousand-handed art has introduced a new element into the state. The science of power is forced to remember the power of science. Civilization mounts and climbs. Malthus, when he stated that the mouths went on multiplying geometrically and the food only arithmetically, forgot to say that the human mind was also a factor in political economy, and that the augmenting wants of society would be met by an augmenting power of invention.

Yes, we have a pretty artillery of tools now in our social arrangements: we ride four times as fast as our fathers did; travel, grind, weave, forge, plant, till and excavate better. We have new shoes, gloves, glasses and gimlets; we have the calculus; we have the newspaper, which does its best to make every square acre of land and sea give an account of itself at your breakfast-table; we have money, and paper money; we have language,—the finest tool of all, and nearest to the mind. Much will have more. Man flatters himself that his command over Nature must increase. Things begin to obey him. We are to have the balloon yet, and the next war will be fought in the air. We may yet find a rose-water that will wash the negro white. He sees the skull of the English race changing from its Saxon type under the exigencies of American life.

Tantalus, who in old times was seen vainly trying to quench his thirst with a flowing stream which ebbed whenever he approached it, has been seen again lately. He is in Paris, in New York, in Boston. He is now in great spirits; thinks he shall reach it yet; thinks he shall bottle the wave. It is however getting a little doubtful. Things have an ugly look still. No matter how many centuries of culture have preceded, the new man always finds himself standing on the brink of chaos, always in a crisis. Can anybody remember when the times were not hard, and money not scarce? Can anybody remember when sensible men, and the right sort of men, and the right sort of women, were plentiful? Tantalus begins to think steam a delusion, and galvanism no better than it should be.

Many facts concur to show that we must look deeper for our salvation than to steam, photographs, balloons or astronomy. These tools have some questionable properties. They are reagents. Machinery is aggressive. The weaver becomes a web, the machinist a machine. If you do not use the tools, they use you. All tools are in one sense edge-tools, and dangerous. A man builds a fine house; and now he has a master, and a task for life: he is to furnish, watch, show it, and keep it in repair, the rest of his days. A man has a reputation, and is no longer free, but must respect that. A man makes a picture or a book, and, if it succeeds, 't is often the worse for him. I saw a brave man the other day, hitherto as free as the hawk or the fox of the wilderness, constructing his cabinet of drawers for shells, eggs, minerals and mounted birds. It was easy to see that he was amusing himself with making pretty links for his own limbs.

Then the political economist thinks " 't is doubtful if all the mechanical inventions that ever existed have lightened the day's toil of one human being." The machine unmakes the man. Now that the machine is so perfect, the engineer is nobody. Every new step in improving the engine restricts one more act of the engineer,—unteaches him. Once it took Archimedes; now it only needs a fireman, and a boy to know the coppers, to pull up the handles or mind the water-tank. But when the engine breaks, they can do nothing.

What sickening details in the daily journals! I believe they have ceased to publish the Newgate Calendar and the Pirate's Own Book since the family newspapers, namely the New York Tribune and the London Times, have quite superseded them in the freshness as well as the horror of their records of crime. Politics were never more corrupt and brutal; and Trade, that pride and darling of our ocean, that educator of nations, that benefactor in spite of itself, ends in shameful defaulting, bubble and bankruptcy, all over the world.

Of course we resort to the enumeration of his arts and inventions as a measure of the worth of man. But if, with all his arts, he is a felon, we cannot assume the mechanical skill or chemical resources as the measure of worth. Let us try another gauge.

What have these arts done for the character, for the worth of mankind? Are men better? 'T is sometimes questioned whether morals have not declined as the arts have ascended. Here are great arts and little men. Here is greatness begotten of paltriness. We cannot trace the triumphs of civilization to such benefactors as we wish. The greatest meliorator of the world is selfish, huckstering Trade. Every victory over matter ought to recommend to man the worth of his nature. But now one wonders who did all this good. Look up the inventors. Each has his own knack; his genius is in veins and spots. But the great, equal, symmetrical brain, fed from a great heart, you shall not find. Every one has more to hide than he has to show, or is lamed by his excellence. 'T is too plain that with the material power the moral progress has not kept pace. It appears that we have not made a judicious investment. Works and days were offered us, and we took works. . . .

The Problem

HENRY GEORGE (1839–1897), born in Philadelphia, quit school at age fourteen, went to sea for three years, and in 1858 arrived in California where he worked as a journalist. Traveling in the east in 1869, he had the "vision," as he termed it, that shaped his entire life: under modern industrial conditions progress and poverty go hand in hand. In **Progress and Poverty** (1879), a work that sold many millions of copies in several languages, he attributed this problem to private ownership of land. After moving to New York City permanently in 1880 he crusaded actively for a Single Tax to appropriate the unearned profit accruing to owners of unimproved land. He ran unsuccessfully for mayor of the city in 1886, and died in the midst of a second campaign for this office in 1897.

The present century has been marked by a prodigious increase in wealth-producing power. The utilization of steam and electricity, the introduction of improved processes and labor-saving machinery, the greater subdivision and grander scale of production, the wonderful facilitation of exchanges, have multiplied enormously the effectiveness of labor.

At the beginning of this marvelous era it was natural to expect, and it was expected, that labor-saving inventions would lighten the toil and improve the condition of the laborer; that the enormous increase in the power of producing wealth would make real poverty a thing of the past. Could a man of the last century—a Franklin or a Priestley—have seen, in a vision of the future, the steamship taking the place of the sailing vessel, the railroad train of the wagon, the reaping machine of the scythe, the threshing machine of the flail; could he have heard the throb of the engines that in obedience to human will, and for the satisfaction of human desire, exert a power greater than that of all the men and all the beasts of burden of the

THE PROBLEM.   From Henry George, *Progress and Poverty* (1879).

earth combined; could he have seen the forest tree transformed into finished lumber—into doors, sashes, blinds, boxes or barrels, with hardly the touch of a human hand; the great workshops where boots and shoes are turned out by the case with less labor than the old-fashioned cobbler could have put on a sole; the factories where, under the eye of a girl, cotton becomes cloth faster than hundreds of stalwart weavers could have turned it out with their handlooms; could he have seen steam hammers shaping mammoth shafts and mighty anchors, and delicate machinery making tiny watches; the diamond drill cutting through the heart of the rocks, and coal oil sparing the whale; could he have realized the enormous saving of labor resulting from improved facilities of exchange and communication—sheep killed in Australia eaten fresh in England, and the order given by the London banker in the afternoon executed in San Francisco in the morning of the same day; could he have conceived of the hundred thousand improvements which these only suggest, what would he have inferred as to the social condition of mankind?

It would not have seemed like an inference; further than the vision went it would have seemed as though he saw; and his heart would have leaped and his nerves would have thrilled, as one who from a height beholds just ahead of the thirst-striken caravan the living gleam of rustling woods and the glint of laughing waters. Plainly, in the sight of the imagination, he would have beheld these new forces elevating society from its very foundations, lifting the very poorest above the possibility of want, exempting the very lowest from anxiety for the material needs of life; he would have seen these slaves of the lamp of knowledge taking on themselves the traditional curse, these muscles of iron and sinews of steel making the poorest laborer's life a holiday, in which every high quality and noble impulse could have scope to grow.

And out of these bounteous material conditions he would have seen arising, as necessary sequences, moral conditions realizing the golden age of which mankind have always dreamed. Youth no longer stunted and starved; age no longer harried by avarice; the child at play with the tiger; the man with the muck-rake drinking in the glory of the stars. Foul things fled, fierce things tame; discord turned to harmony! For how could there be greed where all had enough? How could the vice, the crime, the ignorance, the brutality, that spring from poverty and the fear of poverty, exist where poverty had vanished? Who should crouch where all were freemen; who oppress where all were peers?

More or less vague or clear, these have been the hopes, these the dreams born of the improvements which give this wonderful century its preëminence. They have sunk so deeply into the popular mind as radically to change the currents of thought, to recast creeds and displace the most fundamental conceptions. The haunting visions of higher possibilities have not merely gathered splendor and vividness, but their direction has changed—instead of seeing behind the faint tinges of an expiring sunset, all the glory of the daybreak has decked the skies before.

It is true that disappointment has followed disappointment, and that discovery upon discovery, and invention after invention, have neither lessened the toil of those who most need respite, nor brought plenty to the poor. But there have been so many things to which it seemed this failure could be laid, that up to our time the new faith has hardly weakened. We have better appreciated the difficulties to be overcome; but not the less trusted that the tendency of the times was to overcome them.

Now, however, we are coming into collision with facts which there can be no mistaking. From all parts of the civilized world come complaints of industrial depression; of labor condemned to involuntary idleness; of capital massed and wasting; of pecuniary distress among business men; of want and suffering and anxiety among the working classes. All the dull, deadening pain, all the keen, maddening anguish, that to great masses of men are involved in the words "hard times," afflict the world to-day. This state of things, common to communities differing so widely in situation, in political institutions, in fiscal and financial systems, in density of population and in social organization, can hardly be accounted for by local causes. There is distress where large standing armies are maintained, but there is also distress where the standing armies are nominal; there is distress where protective tariffs stupidly and wastefully hamper trade, but there is also distress where trade is nearly free; there is distress where autocratic government yet prevails, but there is also distress where political power is wholly in the hands of the people; in countries where paper is money, and in countries where gold and silver are the only currency. Evidently, beneath all such things as these, we must infer a common cause.

That there is a common cause, and that it is either what we call material progress or something closely connected with material progress, becomes more than an inference when it is noted that the phenomena we class together and speak of as industrial depression are but intensifications of phenomena which always accompany material progress, and which show themselves more clearly and strongly as material progress goes on. Where the conditions to which material progress everywhere tends are most fully realized—that is to say, where population is densest, wealth greatest, and the machinery of production and exchange most highly developed—we find the deepest poverty, the sharpest struggle for existence, and the most of enforced idleness.

It is to the newer countries—that is, to the countries where material progress is yet in its earlier stages—that laborers emigrate in search of higher wages, and capital flows in search of higher interest. It is in the older countries—that is to say, the countries where material progress has reached later stages—that widespread destitution is found in the midst of the greatest abundance. Go into one of the new communities where Anglo-Saxon vigor is just beginning the race of progress; where the machinery of production and exchange is yet rude and inefficient; where the increment of wealth is not yet great enough to enable any class to live in ease and luxury; where the best house is but a cabin of logs or a cloth and paper shanty, and the richest man is forced to daily work—and though you will find an absence of wealth and all its concomitants, you will find no beggars. There is no luxury, but there is no destitution. No one makes an easy living, nor a very good living; but every one *can* make a living, and no one able and willing to work is oppressed by the fear of want.

But just as such a community realizes the conditions which all civilized communities are striving for, and advances in the scale of material progress—just as closer settlement and a more intimate connection with the rest of the world, and greater utilization of labor-saving machinery, make possible greater economies in production and exchange, and wealth in consequence increases, not merely in the aggregate, but in proportion to population—so does poverty take a darker aspect. Some get an infinitely better and easier living, but others find it hard to get a living at all. The "tramp" comes with the locomotive, and almshouses and prisons are as surely the marks of "material progress" as are costly dwellings, rich warehouses, and magnificent churches. Upon streets lighted with gas and patrolled by uniformed policemen, beggars wait for the passer-by, and in the shadow of college, and library, and museum, are gathering the more hideous Huns and fiercer Vandals of whom Macaulay prophesied.

This fact—the great fact that poverty and all its concomitants show themselves in communities just as they develop into the conditions toward which material progress tends—proves that the social difficulties existing wherever a certain stage of progress has been reached, do not arise from local circumstances, but are, in some way or another, engendered by progress itself.

And, unpleasant as it may be to admit it, it is at last becoming evident that the enormous increase in productive power which has marked the present century and is still going on with accelerating ratio, has no tendency to extirpate poverty or to lighten the burdens of those compelled to toil. It simply widens the gulf between Dives and Lazarus, and makes the struggle for existence more intense. The march of invention has clothed mankind with powers of which a century ago the boldest imagination could not have dreamed. But in factories where labor-saving machinery has reached its most wonderful development, little children are at work; wherever the new forces are anything like fully utilized, large classes are maintained by charity or live on the verge of recourse to it; amid the greatest accumulations of wealth, men die of starvation, and puny infants suckle dry breasts; while everywhere the greed of gain, the worship of wealth, shows the force of the fear of want. The promised land flies before us like the mirage. The fruits of the tree of knowledge turn as we grasp them to apples of Sodom that crumble at the touch.

It is true that wealth has been greatly increased, and that the average of comfort, leisure, and refinement has been raised; but these gains are not general. In them the lowest class do not share.[1] I do not mean that the condition of the lowest class has nowhere nor in anything been improved; but that there is nowhere any improvement which can be credited to increased productive power. I mean that the tendency of what we call material progress is in nowise to improve the condition of the lowest class in the essentials of healthy, happy human life. Nay, more, that it is still further to depress the condition of the lowest class. The new forces, elevating in their nature though they be, do not act upon the social fabric from underneath, as was for a long time hoped and believed, but strike it at a point intermediate between top and bottom. It is as though an immense wedge were being forced, not underneath society, but through society. Those who are above the point of separation are elevated, but those who are below are crushed down.

This depressing effect is not generally realized, for it is not apparent where there has long existed a class just able to live. Where the lowest class barely lives, as has been the case for a long time in many parts of Europe, it is impossible for it to get any lower, for the next lowest step is out of existence, and no tendency to further depression can readily show itself. But in the progress of new settlements to the conditions of older communities it may clearly be seen that material progress does not merely fail to relieve poverty—it actually produces it. In the United States it is clear that squalor and misery, and the vices and crimes that spring from them, everywhere increase as the village grows to the city, and the march of development brings the advantages of the improved methods of production and exchange. It is in the older and richer sections of the Union that pauperism and distress among the working classes are becoming most painfully apparent. If there is less deep

[1] It is true that the poorest may now in certain ways enjoy what the richest a century ago could not have commanded, but this does not show improvement of condition so long as the ability to obtain the necessaries of life is not increased. The beggar in a great city may enjoy many things from which the backwoods farmer is debarred, but that does not prove the condition of the city beggar better than that of the independent farmer.

poverty in San Francisco than in New York, is it not because San Francisco is yet behind New York in all that both cities are striving for? When San Francisco reaches the point where New York now is, who can doubt that there will also be ragged and barefooted children on her streets?

This association of poverty with progress is the great enigma of our times. It is the central fact from which spring industrial, social, and political difficulties that perplex the world, and with which statesmanship and philanthropy and education grapple in vain. From it come the clouds that overhang the future of the most progressive and self-reliant nations. It is the riddle which the Sphinx of Fate puts to our civilization, and which not to answer is to be destroyed. So long as all the increased wealth which modern progress brings goes but to build up great fortunes, to increase luxury and make sharper the contrast between the House of Have and the House of Want, progress is not real and cannot be permanent. The reaction must come. The tower leans from its foundations, and every new story but hastens the final catastrophe. To educate men who must be condemned to poverty, is but to make them restive; to base on a state of most glaring social inequality political institutions under which men are theoretically equal, is to stand a pyramid on its apex. . . .

Letter to J. H. Twichell

MARK TWAIN (1835–1910) was the pen name of Samuel Langhorne Clemens, who grew up in the Mississippi River town of Hannibal, Missouri. Leaving school at age twelve, he worked as printer, riverboat pilot, and journalist. He gained national attention for his **Innocents Abroad** (1869), and world-wide fame for **The Adventures of Huckleberry Finn** (1885). In **A Connecticut Yankee in King Arthur's Court** (1889) he first expressed doubts concerning progress and democracy under a commercial-industrial regime. A deepening pessimism, fed by personal misfortunes during the 1890s, surfaced in **The Man that Corrupted Hadleyburg** (1900), **What Is Man?** (1906), and in his personal correspondence.

LETTER TO J. H. TWICHELL. From *Mark Twain's Letters*, Vol. II (Stormfield Edition). Copyright 1917 by Mark Twain Company; renewed 1945 by Clara Clemens Samoussoud. By permission of Harper & Row, Publishers, Inc.

To Rev. J. H. Twichell, in Hartford:

March 14, '05.

Dear Joe,—I have a Puddn'head maxim:

"When a man is a pessimist before 48 he knows too much; if he is an optimist after it, he knows too little."

It is with contentment, therefore, that I reflect that I am better and wiser than you. Joe, you seem to be dealing in "bulks," now; the "bulk" of the farmers and U. S. Senators are "honest." As regards purchase and sale with *money?* Who doubts it? Is that the only measure of honesty? Aren't there a dozen kinds of honesty which can't be measured by the money-standard? Treason is treason—and there's more than one form of it; the money-form is but one of them. When a person is disloyal to any confessed duty, he is plainly and simply dishonest, and knows it; knows it, and is privately troubled about it and not proud of himself. Judged by this standard—and who will challenge the validity of it?—there isn't an honest man in Connecticut, nor in the Senate, nor anywhere else. I do not even except myself, this time.

Am I finding fault with you and the rest of the populace? *No*—I assure you I am not. For I know the human race's limitations, and this makes it my duty—my pleasant duty—to be fair to it. Each person in it is honest in one or several ways, but no member of it is honest in all the ways required by—by what? *By his own standard.* Outside of that, as I look at it, there is no obligation upon him.

Am I honest? I give you my word of honor (private) I am not. For seven years I have suppressed a book which my conscience tells me I ought to publish. I hold it a duty to publish it. There are other difficult duties which I am equal to, but I am not equal to that one. Yes, even I am dishonest. Not in many ways, but in some. Forty-one, I think it is. We are certainly *all* honest in one or several ways—every man in the world—though I have reason to think I am the only one whose black-list runs so light. Sometimes I feel lonely enough in this lofty solitude.

Yes, oh, yes, I am not overlooking the "steady progress from age to age of the coming of the kingdom of God and righteousness." "From age to age"—yes, it describes that giddy gait. I (and the rocks) will not live to see it arrive, but that is all right—it will arrive, it surely will. But you ought not to be always ironically apologizing for the Deity. If that thing is going to arrive, it is inferable that He wants it to arrive; and so it is not quite kind of you, and it hurts me, to see you flinging sarcasms at the gait of it. And yet it would not be fair in me not to admit that the sarcasms are deserved. When the Deity wants a thing, and after working at it for "ages and ages" can't show even a shade of progress toward its accomplishment, we—well, we don't laugh, but it is only because we dasn't. The source of "righteousness"—is in the heart? Yes. And engineered and directed by the brain? Yes. Well, history and tradition testify that the heart is just about what it was in the beginning; it has undergone no shade of change. Its good and evil impulses and their consequences are the same to-day that they were in Old Bible times, in Egyptian times, in Greek times, in Middle Age times, in Twentieth Century times. There has been no change.

Meantime, the brain has undergone no change. It is what it always was. There are a few good brains and a multitude of poor ones. It was so in Old Bible times and in all other times—Greek, Roman, Middle Ages and Twentieth Century. Among the savages—all the savages —the average brain is as competent as the average brain here or elsewhere. I will prove it to you, some time, if you like. And there are great brains among them, too. I will prove that also, if you like.

Well, the 19th century made progress—the first progress after "ages and ages"—colossal progress. In what? Materialities. Prodigious acquisitions were made in things which add to the comfort of many and make life harder for as many more. But the addition to righteousness? Is that discoverable? I think not. The materialities were not invented in the interest of righteousness; that there is more righteousness in the world because of them than there was before, is hardly demonstrable, I think. In Europe and America there is a vast change (due to them) in ideals—do you admire it? All Europe and all America are feverishly scrambling for money. Money is the supreme ideal—all others take tenth place with the great bulk of the nations named. Money-lust has always existed, but not in the history of the world was it ever a craze, a madness, until your time and mine. This lust has rotted these nations; it has made them hard, sordid, ungentle, dishonest, oppressive.

Did England rise against the infamy of the Boer war? No—rose in favor of it. Did America rise against the infamy of the Philippine war? No—rose in favor of it. Did Russia rise against the infamy of the present war? No—sat still and said nothing. Has the Kingdom of God advanced in Russia since the beginning of time?

Or in Europe and America, considering the vast backward step of the money-lust? Or anywhere else? If there has been any progress toward righteousness since the early days of Creation—which, in my ineradicable honesty, I am obliged to doubt—I think we must confine it to ten per cent of the populations of Christendom, (but leaving Russia, Spain and South America entirely out.) This gives us 320,000,000 to draw the ten per cent from. That is to say, 32,000,000 have advanced toward righteousness and the Kingdom of God since the "ages and ages" have been flying along, the Deity sitting up there admiring. Well, you see it leaves 1,200,000,000 out of the race. They stand just where they have always stood; there has been no change.

N. B. No charge for these informations. Do come down soon, Joe.

With love,

MARK.

Introduction:
A Statement of Principles

The twelve contributors to **I'll Take My Stand** are native born southerners, most of whom were educated at Vanderbilt University, and include literary critics, a journalist, a historian, a political scientist, and a psychologist. The work was organized by Donald Davidson (1893–1968), John Crowe Ransom (1888–   ), and Allen Tate (1899–   ), who had earlier collaborated with Robert Penn Warren (1905–   ) in publishing the **Fugitive,** one of the more important of the literary magazines of the 1920s. Although by fortuitous circumstance their protest against the industrial regime appeared as Depression threatened the entire system, their attack on technology and commercialism had deeper roots—in revulsion at the crassness of the "New Era" of the 1920s, and rejection of the creed of the "New South," a slogan coined in the 1880s by a southern journalist, Henry Grady, who trumpeted the benefits that would accrue to an industrialized South. **I'll Take My Stand** sparked considerable debate. The editor of the **Sewanee Review** termed it "the most challenging book since Henry George's **Progress and Poverty."** Critics labeled the contributors "unreconstructed rebels" and "a socially reactionary band." The "Introduction," drafted by Ransom, announces the main themes in the essays.

Nobody now proposes for the South, or for any other community in this country, an independent political destiny. That idea is thought

INTRODUCTION: A STATEMENT OF PRINCIPLES. From *I'll Take My Stand,* by 12 Southerners. Copyright © 1930 by Harper & Row, Publishers, Inc., renewed 1958 by Donald Davidson. Reprinted by permission of Harper & Row, Publishers, Inc.

to have been finished in 1865. But how far shall the South surrender its moral, social, and economic autonomy to the victorious principle of Union? That question remains open. The South is a minority section that has hitherto been jealous of its minority right to live its own kind of life. The South scarcely hopes to determine the other sections, but it does propose to determine itself, within the utmost limits of legal action. Of late, however, there is the melancholy fact that the South itself has wavered a little and shown signs of wanting to join up behind the common or American industrial ideal. It is against that tendency that this book is written. The younger Southerners, who are being converted frequently to the industrial gospel, must come back to the support of the Southern tradition. They must be persuaded to look very critically at the advantages of becoming a "new South" which will be only an undistinguished replica of the usual industrial community.

But there are many other minority communities opposed to industrialism, and wanting a much simpler economy to live by. The communities and private persons sharing the agrarian tastes are to be found widely within the Union. Proper living is a matter of the intelligence and the will, does not depend on the local climate or geography, and is capable of a definition which is general and not Southern at all. Southerners have a filial duty to discharge to their own section. But their cause is precarious and they must seek alliances with sympathetic communities everywhere. The members of the present group would be happy to be counted as members of a national agrarian movement.

Industrialism is the economic organization of the collective American society. It means the decision of society to invest its economic resources in the applied sciences. But the word science has acquired a certain sanctitude. It is out of order to quarrel with science in the abstract, or even with the applied sciences when their applications are made subject to criticism and intelligence. The capitalization of the applied sciences has now become extravagant and uncritical; it has enslaved our human energies to a degree now clearly felt to be burdensome. The apologists of industrialism do not like to meet this charge directly; so they often take refuge in saying that they are devoted simply to science! They are really devoted to the applied sciences and to practical production. Therefore it is necessary to employ a certain skepticism even at the expense of the Cult of Science, and to say, It is an Americanism, which looks innocent and disinterested, but really is not either.

The contribution that science can make to a labor is to render it easier by the help of a tool or a process, and to assure the laborer of his perfect economic security while he is engaged upon it. Then it can be performed with leisure and enjoyment. But the modern laborer has not exactly received this benefit under the industrial regime. His labor is hard, its tempo is fierce, and his employment is insecure. The first principle of a good labor is that it must be effective, but the second principle is that it must be enjoyed. Labor is one of the largest items in the human career; it is a modest demand to ask that it may partake of happiness.

The regular act of applied science is to introduce into labor a labor-saving device or a machine. Whether this is a benefit depends on how far it is advisable to save the labor. The philosophy of applied science is generally quite sure that the saving of labor is a pure gain, and that the more of it the better. This is to assume that labor is an evil, that only the end of labor or the material product is good. On this assumption labor becomes mercenary and servile, and it is no wonder if many forms of modern labor are accepted without resentment though they are evidently brutalizing. The act of labor as one of the happy functions of human life has been in effect abandoned, and is practiced solely for its rewards.

Even the apologists of industrialism have been obliged to admit that some economic evils follow in the wake of the machines. These are such as overproduction, unemployment, and a growing inequality in the distribution of wealth. But the remedies proposed by the apologists are always homeopathic. They expect the evils to disappear when we have bigger and better machines, and more of them. Their remedial programs, therefore, look forward to more industrialism. Sometimes they see the system righting itself spontaneously and without direction: they are Optimists. Sometimes they rely on the benevolence of capital, or the militancy of labor, to bring about a fairer division of the spoils: they are Coöperationists or Socialists. And sometimes they expect to find super-engineers, in the shape of Boards of Control, who will adapt production to consumption and regulate prices and guarantee business against fluctuations: they are Sovietists. With respect to these last it must be insisted that the true Sovietists or Communists—if the term may be used here in the European sense—are the Industrialists themselves. They would have the government set up an economic super-organization, which in turn would become the government. We therefore look upon the Communist menace as a menace indeed, but not as a Red one; because it is simply according to the blind drift of our industrial development to expect in America at last much the same economic system as that imposed by violence upon Russia in 1917.

Turning to consumption, as the grand end which justifies the evil of modern labor, we find that we have been deceived. We have more time in which to consume, and many more products to be consumed. But the tempo of our labors communicates itself to our satisfactions, and these also become brutal and hurried. The constitution of the natural man probably does not permit him to shorten his labor-time and enlarge his consuming-time indefinitely. He has to pay the penalty in satiety and aimlessness. The modern man has lost his sense of vocation.

Religion can hardly expect to flourish in an industrial society. Religion is our submission to the general intention of a nature that is fairly inscrutable; it is the sense of our rôle as creatures within it. But nature industrialized, transformed into cities and artificial habitations, manufactured into commodities, is no longer nature but a highly simplified picture of nature. We receive the illusion of having power over nature, and lose the sense of nature as something mysterious and contingent. The God of nature under these conditions is merely an amiable expression, a superfluity, and the philosophical understanding ordinarily carried in the religious experience is not there for us to have.

Nor do the arts have a proper life under industrialism, with the general decay of sensibility which attends it. Art depends, in general, like religion, on a right attitude to nature; and in particular on a free and disinterested observation of nature that occurs only in leisure. Neither the creation nor the understanding of works of art is possible in an industrial age except by some local and unlikely suspension of the industrial drive.

The amenities of life also suffer under the curse of a strictly-business or industrial civilization. They consist in such practices as manners, conversation, hospitality, sympathy, family life, romantic love— in the social exchanges which reveal and develop sensibility in human affairs. If religion and the arts are founded on right relations of man-to-nature, these are founded on right relations of man-to-man.

Apologists of industrialism are even inclined to admit that its actual processes may have upon its victims the spiritual effects just described. But they think that all can be made right by extraordinary educational efforts, by all sorts of cultural institutions and endowments. They would cure the poverty of the contemporary spirit by hiring experts to instruct it in spite of itself in the historic culture. But salvation is hardly to be encountered on that road. The trouble with the life-pattern is to be located at its economic base, and we cannot rebuild it by pouring in soft materials from the top. The young men and women in colleges, for example, if they are already placed in a false way of life, cannot make more than an inconsequential acquaintance with the arts and humanities transmitted to them. Or else the understanding of these arts and humanities will but make them the more wretched in their own destitution.

.   .   .

The tempo of the industrial life is fast, but that is not the worst of it; it is accelerating. The ideal is not merely some set form of industrialism, with so many stable industries, but industrial progress, or an incessant extension of industrialization. It never proposes a specific goal; it initiates the infinite series. We have not merely capitalized certain industries; we have capitalized the laboratories and inventors, and undertaken to employ all the labor-saving devices that come out of them. But a fresh labor-saving device introduced into an industry does not emancipate the laborers in that industry so much as it evicts them. Applied at the expense of agriculture, for example, the new processes have reduced the part of the population supporting itself upon the soil to a smaller and smaller fraction. Of course no single labor-saving process is fatal; it brings on a period of unemployed labor and unemployed capital, but soon a new industry is devised which will put them both to work again, and a new commodity is thrown upon the market. The laborers were sufficiently embarrassed in the meantime, but, according to the theory, they will eventually be taken care of. It is now the public which is embarrassed; it feels obligated to purchase a commodity for which it had expressed no desire, but it is invited to make its budget equal to the strain. All might yet be well, and stability and comfort might again obtain, but for this: partly because of industrial ambitions and partly because the repressed creative impulse must break out somewhere, there will be a stream of further labor-saving devices in all industries, and the cycle will have to be repeated over and over. The result is an increasing disadjustment and instability.

It is an inevitable consequence of industrial progress that production greatly outruns the rate of natural consumption. To overcome the disparity, the producers, disguised as the pure idealists of progress, must coerce and wheedle the public into being loyal and steady consumers, in order to keep the machines running. So the rise of modern advertising—along with its twin, personal salesmanship—is the most significant development of our industrialism. Advertising means to persuade the consumers to want exactly what the applied sciences are able to furnish them. It consults the happiness of the consumer no more than it consulted the happiness of the laborer. It is the great effort of a false economy of life to approve itself. But its task grows more difficult every day.

It is strange, of course, that a majority of men anywhere could ever as with one mind become enamored of industrialism: a system that has so little regard for individual wants. There is evidently a kind of thinking that rejoices in setting up a social objective which has no relation to the individual. Men are prepared to sacrifice their private dignity and happiness to an abstract social ideal, and without asking whether the social ideal produces the welfare of any individual man whatsoever. But this is absurd. The responsibility of men is for their own welfare and that of their neighbors; not for the hypothetical welfare of some fabulous creature called society.

Opposed to the industrial society is the agrarian, which does not stand in particular need of definition. An agrarian society is hardly one that has no use at all for industries, for professional vocations, for scholars and artists, and for the life of cities. Technically, perhaps, an agrarian society is one in which agriculture is the leading vocation, whether for wealth, for pleasure, or for prestige—a form of labor that is pursued with intelligence and leisure, and that becomes the model to which the other forms approach as well as they may. But an agrarian regime will be secured readily enough where the superfluous industries are not allowed to rise against it. The theory of agrarianism is that the culture of the soil is the best and most sensitive of vocations, and that therefore it should have the economic preference and enlist the maximum number of workers.

These principles do not intend to be very specific in proposing any practical measures. How may the little agrarian community resist the Chamber of Commerce of its county seat, which is always trying to import some foreign industry that cannot be assimilated to the life-pattern of the community? Just what must the Southern leaders do to defend the traditional Southern life? How may the Southern and the Western agrarians unite for effective action? Should the agrarian forces try to capture the Democratic party, which historically is so closely affiliated with the defense of individualism, the small community, the state, the South? Or must the agrarians—even the Southern ones—abandon the Democratic party to its fate and try a new one? What legislation could most profitably be championed by the powerful agrarians in the Senate of the United States? What anti-industrial measures might promise to stop the advances of industrialism, or even undo some of them, with the least harm to those concerned? What policy should be pursued by the educators who have a tradition at heart? These and many other questions are of the greatest importance, but they cannot be answered here.

For, in conclusion, this much is clear: If a community, or a section, or a race, or an age, is groaning under industrialism, and well aware that it is an evil dispensation, it must find the way to throw it off. To think that this cannot be done is pusillanimous. And if the whole community, section, race, or age thinks it cannot be done, then it has simply lost its political genius and doomed itself to impotence.

America the Raped

GENE MARINE (1926–   ), born in San Francisco, briefly attended San Francisco State College before becoming a radio news analyst during the 1950s. West coast correspondent for the **Nation** until 1964, he served as senior editor of **Ramparts** between 1966 and 1969. An expanded version of **America the Raped** (1969) appeared in book form. His other publications include **The Black Panthers** (1969).

The old rapists—the lumbermen and miners and utilities companies —are still with us, though today they substitute seduction for rape wherever possible. The Georgia-Pacific Company still strips virgin Douglas fir from California's northern coast, but today it also contributes a few thousand dollars to a study of the habits and habitats of the American eagle.

Fortunately for the rest of us, a dozen groups have arisen to keep the old rapists in check. But while they try, the new rapists are loose upon the land; theirs, still, are the vicious, violent techniques of the *laissez-faire* turn of the century. They are not, for the most part, employed by lumber companies or mining companies—but by you and me. They work for the Port Authority of New York and New Jersey, or for the state highway commissions; the U.S. Forest Service or the National Park Service; the Army's Corps of Engineers, the Bureau of Reclamation or the Bureau of Public Roads.

They are called Engineers.

They build bridges and dams and highways and causeways and flood control projects. They *manage* things. They commit rape with bulldozers.

They are hard to fight off, because they must be fought with words, and the weapons are inadequate. In New Jersey, there is a fantastic

AMERICA THE RAPED. From *Ramparts*, 5 (April–May 1967). Copyright Ramparts Magazine, Inc. 1967. By permission of the Editors.

land of wonders, still substantially as it was when the glaciers retreated thousands of years ago. It is called the Great Swamp. The Engineers want to put a jetport on it—an absurd and irreversible crime. But— who needs a "swamp"?

The salt marshes of the Georgia coast have become an outstanding laboratory for the study of the interactions of life; there, the University of Georgia has learned much of how shrimp and other seafood depend on the unusual estuarine conditions for their life. Yet Dr. Eugene Odum, the leading researcher in the field, reports that "we are often asked, 'Of what value is the salt marsh?' or 'What can be done with all that wasted land?' "

The Engineers know: build a dam, build a levee, build a wall, dredge, fill, *change*. The marsh grass will die, the phytoplankton will die, the algae will die—and thus the shrimp and the bass will die, but the Engineers don't care. What good is a salt marsh? Who needs a swamp?

The "conservationists" can lose an isolated battle over a grove of trees or a factory on a river. We will survive, and so will trees and rivers. But the Engineers are not only straining to dam the Grand Canyon and the last wild stretch of the Missouri, to wall off the rich estuaries of Long Island and fill in the Great Swamp. They are in every section of every state, ripping, tearing, building, changing.

Theirs is a rapine from which America can never, never recover.

.   .   .

Ecology

Ecology is the study of how things fit together, or, if you prefer, the study of the interactions between life forms and their environment. We know very damned little about it, but Engineers know—or act as if they know—absolutely nothing.

Most of us have had to learn a little ecology in the past few years, in order to deal with the political problems of radioactive fallout and air and water pollution. Some of us learned about the concentration of strontium-90. Others of us learned that a harmless scattering of DDT (0.02 parts per million) in the water of Clear Lake, California, was concentrated by plankton (to 5 parts per million), concentrated again by fish (to several hundred parts per million), and ultimately killed the grebes that ate the fish. In the tissues of the birds, DDT concentration was 1600 parts per million.

The government builds dams and highways, levees and reactors, and every one rips into an ecological system far more complex than anyone yet understands. "No one," says Dr. Odum, who is one of the world's leading ecologists, "has yet identified and catalogued all the species of plants, animals and microbes to be found in any large area, as for example, a square mile of forest." But science in government is dominated by the Engineers, and the government is doing almost no work in ecology, giving almost no grants, encouraging almost no one. Instead, as could be expected of Engineers, they spend millions studying things that somebody wants to manage.

When most people think of ecology—if they've ever heard of it at all—they tend to think of food chains: minnows eat mosquitos, bream eat minnows, bass eat bream. Odum calls it the grass-rabbit-fox chain.

But there is far more to ecology than food chains and gross changes in the environment. The ignorant use of DDT and its widespread effects (it has been found in the fat of Antarctic penguins) is something most people know about; but Dr. LaMont Cole of Cornell, among others, has pointed out what we *might* have done.

Proteins—the "building blocks" of everything alive, including you and me—are nitrogen compounds. But nitrogen is a scarce element— 90 per cent of all the nitrogen there is can be found in the air, and plants can't use it directly. They depend on certain bacteria, and on blue-green algae, to convert the nitrogen to ammonia, which they can use. On top of that, there are a couple of other kinds of bacteria which change the ammonia into nitrate, which is the way most plants actually do use it. You and I get our nitrogen mostly from the plants. Even then, it would all disappear except for still other bacteria, which recover the nitrogen from dead plants and animals and turn it back into ammonia. Finally, all the nitrogen in the world would have turned into ammonia a long time ago, except for still other types of bacteria which can regenerate molecular nitrogen from nitrate.

DDT kills bacteria, and nobody has ever known exactly *what* bacteria. If DDT had proven to be toxic to any of the types of bacteria mentioned above, man—in his unthinking attempt to kill a few plant pests—would have wiped himself off the face of the earth.

This is not the kind of thinking that concerns the Engineers. They not only do not care whether they push a freeway through a wildlife refuge, nor whether they flood the Grand Canyon with a dam, they don't care whether they wipe out our only chance to understand the ecology of vast regions of the earth, and thus, perhaps, keep from killing ourselves. It is the Engineers who pollute our air and our water —and they may yet do worse than that. They may drown most of us.

.   .   .

Possibly the best and most dramatic example of the failure of the

Engineers to understand what they're doing is demonstrated by our attempt to create a completely artificial, if temporary, ecosystem: the space capsule.

The Russian manned satellite contains air—plain, simple old air, like the stuff you and I used to breathe before we moved to the city. When we Americans set out to build a capsule, however, we found out that it leaked—and in order to keep it from leaking, we would have had to make the capsule much heavier.

Leave it to us, said the Engineers. We'll make the ecosystem just that much more artificial, but we'll solve the problem. Pure oxygen can be used, at only one-fifth the pressure of air; you won't have to plug the leaks so tight, you can use rockets with less thrust; it'll all work out fine. And indeed it did—until the first astronauts for the first time confronted the fact that you can have a spark, or even light a match, in air—but not in oxygen. The Engineers improved on nature and killed three men.

Usually, of course, the dangers of ecological destruction are less dramatic. For instance, we've been extremely successful in developing and growing hybrid corn. As a result, we've almost lost hundreds of corn varieties that fell by the wayside—thereby making it impossible to experiment with new hybrids, discover possible new disease-resistant strains, or make any other use of the genetic information stored in these varieties.

This is one of the most difficult concepts of conservation to communicate—and the one least understood by conservation groups. From wanting to save the redwoods because they're pretty, some organizations have progressed to wanting to save a particular group of redwoods because of its ecological value.

But few people have yet reached the idea of the conservation of genetic information—the idea that we ought to keep every species of animal or plant alive, and in its own ecosystem, because we have no way of knowing what characteristics of what animal, plant or microbe may someday prove to be in some way valuable. The variety of corn that is not grown today, because it isn't economical in competition with today's hybrids, may be the variety which will prove, tomorrow, to be resistant to an as yet unforeseen disease. A byproduct of the whooping crane may be tomorrow's wonder drug. The ecology of the Long Island estuary may provide the clue that enables us to project a more viable ecosystem for a space station.

Everything fits together. Everything. And nobody seems to care, least of all the rampaging, rapist Engineers.

.　　.　　.

The Effluent Society

Once upon a time there was a lake.

It was a thing of magnificent beauty, left a breathtaking blue by departing glaciers. It was 30 miles wide in some places, nearly 60 in others, and more than 240 miles long. Ten thousand square miles of lake, over 200 feet deep, it lived on a still larger sister to the north, and fed a somewhat smaller sister to the east.

In 1669, a white man—Louis Joliet or Jolliet—saw the lake, and soon forts and settlements sprang up.

Today, Lake Erie is virtually dead. Detroit, Cleveland, Buffalo, Akron, Toledo and a dozen other cities pour millions of *tons* of sewage into the lake every *day*. Some of it is fairly carefully treated; much of it (especially Detroit's) is not.

The Detroit River, which feeds Lake Erie, carries every *day*, in addition to Detroit's largely untreated sewage, 19,000 gallons of oil; 100,000 pounds of iron; 200,000 pounds of various acids; and two million pounds of chemical salts. The fertilizer used on the farms of Ohio and Pennsylvania and New York drains into streams which pour into the Erie. Paper mills in the Monroe area of Michigan pour volumes of pollutant waste into the lake. Steelmakers pour in mill scale and oil and grease and pickling solution and rinse water. The Engineers of the Army dredge the harbors and channels of the area and dump the sludge into the middle of Lake Erie.

Normally, a lake receives from various sources a certain amount of nutrient material, which is consumed by plankton or algae or bottom vegetation or bacteria. The fish eat the plankton and the algae, the bacteria mess around with the nitrogen, a couple of hundred other processes simultaneously take place, and it all works out.

So you dump a bunch of sewage or fertilizer or other biologically rich material into the water, and the algae, for instance, grow faster than the fish can eat them. Algae are life forms just like you and me, but (like you and me) in large numbers they stink. They also use up whatever free oxygen might be in the water, which makes it tough for the other life forms. Beaches become covered with algae in the form of slime, and so does the surface of the lake. The lake, in ecological terms, "dies."

Lake Erie has had it.

At first glance, the solution seems easy: Stop. It may not save the lake, but at least it can be kept from getting any worse. Simply make it illegal to put anything into the lake that can remotely be construed as a pollutant.

But there's another problem. If you don't put it into the lake, what are you going to do with it?

There are a number of sophisticated techniques for dealing with a lot of water pollution. There's sand-bed filtering. There's a method called electrodialysis (one sizable California town, some of whose citizens don't know what they're drinking, gets all of its water from the electrodialysis of "waste water," mostly irrigation runoff and sewage). There's another called reverse osmosis.

The problem is that every method leaves you with *something*. After you've separated the water out, what do you do with what you separated it out of? Bury it? An urban unit of one million people produces, believe it or not, 500,000 tons of sewage a day (that's everything in the sewer, not just the most obvious component, and much of it is industrial waste). Even after you take the water out, you'll need a pretty big cemetery. Burn it? We have enough air pollution problems as it is.

Sewage aside, that same urban unit of a million people produces, every day, another 2000 tons of solid waste that has to be disposed of. On top of that, it throws into the air, every day, 1000 tons of particles, sulfur dioxide, nitrogen oxides, hydrocarbons and carbon dioxide. In 1963, American mines, every day, discarded 90,400,000 tons of waste rock and tailings. In 1965, every day, 16,000 automobiles were scrapped (joining from 25 to 40 million already on junkpiles).

Every year, America manufactures 40 billion cans, 20 billion bottles and jars, 65 billion metal and plastic caps, virtually all of which become, almost instantly, solid waste (and aluminum cans and Saran wrap don't degenerate easily like easy-rusting steel cans and paper). Of the eight billion pounds of plastics we produce, only ten per cent is reclaimed. Of the one and three quarters million *tons* of rubber products, only 15 per cent is reclaimed.

The pollution of the air is the form of pollution that most people know most about, but ecologists have some concern here, too. Nobody knows, for instance, what happens if you take one pollutant out of the witches' brew that city dwellers breathe; the chemical interactions are so complex that to take away the hydrocarbons and nitrous oxides that come out of auto exhausts may lead to difficulties with the remaining pollutants that no one can now predict.

While we search, perhaps not as frantically as we should, but at least with increasing concern, for someplace to put our solid, liquid and gaseous wastes, the Engineers gaily produce new ones. In the rush to find new sources of clean water, the technique that has most captured the popular imagination is the desalinization of sea water.

But when you've finished the desalinizing, what you have left is a bunch of hot brine. You can't dump it back into the ocean on the spot; you'll raise the temperature considerably and thus endanger all the offshore life. Besides, you'll just raise the salt concentration near your intake and have to take it all out again in your next batch.

The Engineers assure us that we can get rid of sulfur dioxide in the air and stop the ecological damage done by big dams on watersheds if we will only turn to nuclear power; but nuclear plants create radioactive wastes and "thermal pollution." Thermal pollution—the alteration of the ecosystem by changing the water temperature—is what's killing the shad near the Yankee atomic plant on the Connecticut River.

Even sewage, spewed out in large enough amounts, raises water temperature. "Sharks have appeared in waters off southern California," Congressman George P. Miller points out, "where they never previously appeared, and the studies made indicated that the slight rise in temperature through the disposal of sewage changed the ecology and caused the water to become suitable for the sharks. These are the things," the Congressman added in the understatement of his career, "that we don't know very much about."

Ultimately, it is reclamation and reuse that hold the only hope for escape from slow death by pollution. The reclamation and reuse of water is already possible, and can be done by some methods without the creation of too much solid waste. A method is being developed to make it far more economical to reclaim steel from junk automobiles. Sulfur can be reclaimed, albeit expensively, from the sulfur dioxide of stack gases. Electric automobiles, still a difficult conception for most of us, can be a reality whenever we're ready; it's a simple matter of cost.

.   .   .

La Guerre Est Finie

Consider—now that we have reached this point—the frightening depredations which the rapist Engineers are wreaking on the land.

Consider the violation of southern Florida, which, if it is not stopped, will destroy not only the beauty and the life and the economy, but the entire vital ecology of that lovely area. Consider the insistence of the Engineers who, if they are not stopped, will literally fill in the lower gorges of the Grand Canyon. Consider the rape of Storm King and the Great Swamp, the ravaging of everything natural in California for its water transfer plan. Consider the Kennecott Copper Company which intends to cut a vicious open pit into the Great Cascades to take out enough copper to supply the nation for two days.

Consider the hundreds of projects by Engineers and developers and short-range profiteers all over America, projects large and small, and the continuing rape of the environments and ecosystems on which we all depend by the forces of what they insist on calling "progress."

.   .   .

There are two simple, economy-shaking, possibly reactionary, absolutely inescapable points we have to grasp if Americans, at least, are to go on living on the earth.

The first is that we do not know what we are doing—or, rather, what we are letting the Engineers do. We *must* come to understand the incredibly complex relationships within our environment; we must come to understand our ecosystem, which means that we must come to understand as much as we can, as soon as we can, about ecosystems in general. That alone is a reason—and even when other reasons are present, it is the urgently overriding reason—for preserving the Great Swamp and the Great Smokies, the Grand Canyon and the Great Cascades.

The second is that there is nothing magical or inevitable about "progress"; we must, in fact, simply say "stop." We must recognize that we do not really need the fourth jetport or the water plan, that there is a flaw in all of our reasoning. We take it for granted that we can control the waters of the earth and the height of its mountains —and we take it equally for granted that we are slaves to the number and location of our automobiles, our factories, our populations.

It will be expensive. Kimberly-Clark's model pollution treatment plant near Mount Shasta cost $2 million.

But other "costs" are not costs at all. What New York would lose through not building its rubber jetport, some other community would gain. What Los Angeles would lose if the California Water Plan were not pursued, some other community would gain. There is enough that needs to be done—schools and hospitals are the usual examples, and they make the point—to provide work for the building trades.

Deciding simply to stop will also require changes in the law. The present federal highway law, for example, is designed to get the roads built *now*—and to hell with esthetic, much less ecological, considerations. But when it's done, the interstate highway system—leaving out all the freeways and thruways and byways built before it—will consist of enough concrete so that, as a parking lot, it could accommodate two-thirds of the automobiles in the United States (it would be 20 miles square). It will take up one and a half million acres of *new* right of way. It will use up 30 million tons of iron ore to make its steel, plus 18 million tons of coal and six and a half million tons of limestone. Its lumber requirements will take all the trees from a 400-square-mile forest.

.   .   .

Dr. Eugene Odum, in Athens, Georgia, sat back in a comfortable chair after we had finished luncheon in the state university's Center for Continuing Education, and mused about the Engineer mentality in broad, metaphoric terms. "We still think of ourselves," he said, "as waging a war against nature, conquering the land. But the war is over. We've won. We know that nature is defeated now before the advance of man—we have the weapons to fight the forest and the flood, the storm and the heat. We are even conquering space.

"But when we defeat an enemy in battle—when we defeated Germany and Japan—do we simply go on killing and slaughtering? Do we set out deliberately to massacre the population and destroy the land we've defeated? Of course not. We have defeated nature. We must do as we do with any other defeated enemy—help nature, and recognize that we must live with nature, from now on, forever. The war is over."

The war against nature is over. It is time for the war against the Engineers. It is time to learn—even if it is beyond the Engineers' ken—that we must save our ecosystems, not only because they may be pretty or because man may have a need to escape to them for recreation or meditation or the simple inhalation of fresh air, but because we may, someday, vitally need what they contain.

.   .   .

The freedom of the pike, Tawney said, is the death of the minnow. The freedom of the growth-rate planner, the builder of projects, the rapacious Engineer, is the death of man.

Report

DONALD BARTHELME (1931–   ), born in Philadelphia and raised in Houston, has been called "probably the most perversely gifted writer in the U.S." Surrealist parody in matter-of-fact prose, macabre humor masking the deepest seriousness—such are the hallmarks of his indictment of a society apparently bent on total depersonalization. His earlier stories are collected in **Come Back, Dr. Caligari**

REPORT. Reprinted with the permission of Farrar, Straus & Giroux, Inc. from *Unspeakable Practices, Unnatural Acts,* by Donald Barthelme, copyright © 1967, 1968 by Donald Barthelme.

(1964). **Snow White** (1967), his first novel, appeared originally in the **New Yorker,** as did "Report."

Our group is against the war. But the war goes on. I was sent to Cleveland to talk to the engineers. The engineers were meeting in Cleveland. I was supposed to persuade them not to do what they are going to do. I took United's 4:45 from LaGuardia arriving in Cleveland at 6:13. Cleveland is dark blue at that hour. I went directly to the motel, where the engineers were meeting. Hundreds of engineers attended the Cleveland meeting. I noticed many fractures among the engineers, bandages, traction. I noticed what appeared to be fracture of the carpal scaphoid in six examples. I noticed numerous fractures of the humeral shaft, of the os calcis, of the pelvic girdle. I noticed a high incidence of clay-shoveller's fracture. I could not account for these fractures. The engineers were making calculations, taking measurements, sketching on the blackboard, drinking beer, throwing bread, buttonholing employers, hurling glasses into the fireplace. They were friendly.

They were friendly. They were full of love and information. The chief engineer wore shades. Patella in Monk's traction, clamshell fracture by the look of it. He was standing in a slum of beer bottles and microphone cable. "Have some of this chicken à la Isambard Kingdom Brunel the Great Ingineer," he said. "And declare who you are and what we can do for you. What is your line, distinguished guest?"

"Software," I said. "In every sense. I am here representing a small group of interested parties. We are interested in your thing, which seems to be functioning. In the midst of so much dysfunction, function is interesting. Other people's things don't seem to be working. The State Department's thing doesn't seem to be working. The U.N.'s thing doesn't seem to be working. The democratic left's thing doesn't seem to be working. Buddha's thing—"

"Ask us anything about our thing, which seems to be working," the chief engineer said. "We will open our hearts and heads to you, Software Man, because we want to be understood and loved by the great lay public, and have our marvels appreciated by that public, for which we daily unsung produce tons of new marvels each more life-enhancing than the last. Ask us anything. Do you want to know about evaporated thin-film metallurgy? Monolithic and hybrid integrated-circuit processes? The algebra of inequalities? Optimization theory? Complex high-speed micro-miniature closed and open loop systems? Fixed variable mathematical cost searches? Epitaxial deposition of semi-conductor materials? Gross interfaced space gropes? We also have specialists in the cuckooflower, the doctorfish, and the dumdum bullet as these relate to aspects of today's expanding technology, and they do in the damnedest ways."

I spoke to him then about the war. I said the same things people always say when they speak against the war. I said that the war was wrong. I said that large countries should not burn down small countries. I said that the government had made a series of errors. I said that these errors once small and forgivable were now immense and unforgivable. I said that the government was attempting to conceal its original errors under layers of new errors. I said that the government was sick with error, giddy with it. I said that ten thousand of our soldiers had already been killed in pursuit of the government's errors. I said that tens of thousands of the enemy's soldiers and civilians had been killed because of various errors, ours and theirs. I said that we are responsible for errors made in our name. I said that the government should not be allowed to make additional errors.

"Yes, yes," the chief engineer said, "there is doubtless much truth in what you say, but we can't possibly *lose* the war, can we? And stopping is losing, isn't it? The war regarded as a process, stopping regarded as an abort? We don't know *how* to lose a war. That skill is not among our skills. Our array smashes their array, that is what we know. That is the process. That is what is.

"But let's not have any more of this dispiriting downbeat counterproductive talk. I have a few new marvels here I'd like to discuss with you just briefly. A few new marvels that are just about ready to be gaped at by the admiring layman. Consider for instance the area of realtime online computer-controlled wish evaporation. Wish evaporation is going to be crucial in meeting the rising expectations of the world's peoples, which are as you know rising entirely too fast."

I noticed then distributed about the room a great many transverse fractures of the ulna. "The development of the pseudo-ruminant stomach for underdeveloped peoples," he went on, "is one of our interesting things you should be interested in. With the pseudo-ruminant stomach they can chew cuds, that is to say, eat grass. Blue is the most popular color worldwide and for that reason we are working with certain strains of your native Kentucky *Poa pratensis*, or bluegrass, as the staple input for the p/r stomach cycle, which would also give a shot in the arm to our balance-of-payments thing don't you know. . . ."

I noticed about me then a great number of metatarsal fractures in banjo splints. "The kangaroo initiative . . . eight hundred thousand harvested last year . . . highest percentage of edible protein of any herbivore yet studied . . ."

"Have new kangaroos been planted?"

The engineer looked at me.

"I intuit your hatred and jealousy of our thing," he said. "The ineffectual always hate our thing and speak of it as anti-human, which is not at all a meaningful way to speak of our thing. Nothing mechanical is alien to me," he said (amber spots making bursts of light in his shades), "because I am human, in a sense, and if I think it up, then 'it' is human too, whatever 'it' may be. Let me tell you, Software Man, we have been damned forbearing in the matter of this little war you declare yourself to be interested in. Function is the cry, and our thing is functioning like crazy. There are things we could do that we have not done. Steps we could take that we have not taken. These steps are, regarded in a certain light, the light of our enlightened self-interest, quite justifiable steps. We could, of course, get irritated. We could, of course, *lose patience*.

"We could, of course, release thousands upon thousands of self-powered crawling-along-the-ground lengths of titanium wire eighteen inches long with a diameter of .0005 centimetres (that is to say, invisible) which, scenting an enemy, climb up his trouser leg and wrap themselves around his neck. We have developed those. They are within our capabilities. We could, of course, release in the arena of the upper air our new improved pufferfish toxin which precipitates an identity crisis. No special technical problems there. That is almost laughably easy. We could, of course, place up to two million maggots in their rice within twenty-four hours. The maggots are ready, massed in secret staging areas in Alabama. We have hypodermic darts capable of piebalding the enemy's pigmentation. We have rots, blights, and rusts capable of attacking his alphabet. Those are dandies. We have a hut-shrinking chemical which penetrates the fibres of the bamboo, causing it, the hut, to strangle its occupants. This operates only after 10 P.M., when people are sleeping. Their mathematics are at the mercy of a suppurating surd we have invented. We have a family of fishes trained to attack their fishes. We have the deadly testicle-destroying telegram. The cable companies are coöperating. We have a green substance that, well, I'd rather not talk about. We have a secret word that, if pronounced, produces multiple fractures in all living things in an area the size of four football fields."

"That's why—"

"Yes. Some damned fool couldn't keep his mouth shut. The point is that the whole structure of enemy life is within our power to *rend*, *vitiate*, *devour*, and *crush*. But that's not the interesting thing."

"You recount these possibilities with uncommon relish."

"Yes I realize that there is too much relish here. But *you* must realize that these capabilities represent in and of themselves highly technical and complex and interesting problems and hurdles on which our boys have expended many thousands of hours of hard work and brilliance. And that the effects are often grossly exaggerated by irresponsible victims. And that the whole thing represents a fantastic series of triumphs for the multi-disciplined problem-solving team concept."

"I appreciate that."

"We *could* unleash all this technology at once. You can imagine what would happen then. But that's not the interesting thing."

"What is the interesting thing?"

"The interesting thing is that we have *a moral sense*. It is on punched cards, perhaps the most advanced and sensitive moral sense the world has ever known."

"Because it is on punched cards?"

"It considers all considerations in endless and subtle detail," he said. "It even quibbles. With this great new moral tool, how can we go wrong? I confidently predict that, although we *could* employ all this splendid new weaponry I've been telling you about, *we're not going to do it.*"

"We're not going to do it?"

I took United's 5:44 from Cleveland arriving at Newark at 7:19. New Jersey is bright pink at that hour. Living things move about the surface of New Jersey at that hour molesting each other only in traditional ways. I made my report to the group. I stressed the friendliness of the engineers. I said, It's all right. I said, We have a moral sense. I said, *We're not going to do it.* They didn't believe me.

Questions for Discussion and Writing

1. Would an objective assessment of the history of Western civilization support Sumner's belief that man and society are "capable of indefinite improvement"? What specific developments between 1830 and 1860 convinced him and his contemporaries that this was so?

2. Compare and contrast the image of the locomotive in Whitman and Dickinson.

3. Compare Sandburg's view of technology—"Let me lift and loosen old foundations"—with that implied in the poems of Jeffers and Cummings.

4. Compare what Emerson, Sumner, and George have to say about the social and political consequences of technological advance.

5. Twain asks, "But the addition to righteousness? Is that discover-

able?" Compare his answer to his own question with that of the
other authors represented in this section.

6. Did the southern agrarians conceive of their movement as a nar-
rowly regional or broadly national one? Where did they look for
support of their program? Were their hopes realistic?

7. Has the "war against nature" abated since Marine wrote in 1967?
Who or what in addition to engineers and the engineering mentality bears responsibility for inaction?

8. Analyze the ways in which Barthelme uses the language of science
and technology so as to satirize its creators.

9. What arguments against technology have writers since 1920 added
to those of earlier critics?

Essay Topics

1. Does advancing technology increase or decrease individual freedom?
2. Material and moral progress; are they the same?
3. Is technological change a basic factor underlying the transformation of all values?

Suggestions for Further Reading

PRIMARY

EDWARD BELLAMY, *Looking Backward* (1889). A description of a fictional utopia set in the year 2000, which inspired the Nationalist
movement of the 1890s and anticipated later plans for an American
technocracy.

JOHN DEWEY, "Progress," *Characters and Events*, 2 (1929), 826. A
restatement of the doctrine of progress during the First World War
by a leading pragmatist.

JOB DURFEE, "The Influence of Scientific Discovery and Invention
on Social and Political Progress," *Complete Works* (1849); also in
American Philosophic Addresses, ed. J. Blau (1946). An adaptation
of the Enlightenment faith in science and technology toward anti-

democratic ends, anticipating later conservative uses of scientific determinism.

HENRY FORD, *My Philosophy of Industry* (1929). A celebration of the benefits of technology by one of the leading industrialists of the 1920s.

THORSTEIN VEBLEN, *Engineers and the Price System* (1921). A formulation of the technocratic ideal, with a proposal for an American "Soviet of Technicians."

SECONDARY

CLARKE A. CHAMBERS, "The Belief in Progress in 20th Century America," *Journal of the History of Ideas*, 19 (1958), 197–224. An analysis of changes in the idea of progress, and its future prospects.

ARTHUR A. EKIRCH, *The Idea of Progress in America 1815–1860* (1944). A history of the idea of progress in antebellum America, viewed against a background of European contributions.

LEO MARX, *The Machine in the Garden* (1964). A discussion of the dichotomy between technology and the pastoral ideal as revealed in American literature of the nineteenth and early twentieth centuries.

HUGO A. MEIER, "Technology and Democracy 1800–1860," *Journal of American History*, 43 (1957), 618–40. An examination of the union of the democratic ideal and a faith in technology.

HYATT WAGGONER, *The Heel of Elohim: Science and Values in Modern American Poetry* (1950). An analysis of the concern of various American poets with the place of values in a world of scientism.

THOMAS R. WEST, *Flesh of Steel: Literature and the Machine in American Culture* (1967). A study of the impact of the machine on American life in the works of eight twentieth-century authors (Anderson, Frank, Dos Passos, Lewis, Sandburg, Mumford, Veblen, and Stearns).

Working Within the System

The Office of the People in Art, Government, and Religion

GEORGE BANCROFT (1800–1891), historian and statesman, was born in Worcester, Massachusetts. A graduate of Harvard (1817) and the University of Gottingen in Germany (1820) he deserted the Federalist politics of his family to champion the Democratic party of Andrew Jackson. Serving in various public offices, he gave the order as Secretary of War pro tem that led directly to the Mexican War. In 1834 he published the first volume of his ten-volume **History of the United States** (1834–74), in which his faith in democracy sings on every page. "The Office of the People" was an oration delivered before the Adelphi Society of Williamstown College, in August 1835, the middle of Andrew Jackson's second term as President.

The material world does not change in its masses or in its powers. The stars shine with no more lustre than when they first sang together in the glory of their birth. The flowers that gemmed the fields and the forests, before America was discovered, now bloom around us in their season. The sun that shone on Homer shines on us in unchanging lustre. The bow that beamed on the patriarch still glitters in the clouds. Nature is the same. For her no new forces are generated; no new capacities are discovered. The earth turns on its axis, and perfects its revolutions, and renews its seasons, without increase or advancement.

But a like passive destiny does not attach to the inhabitants of the earth. For them the expectations of social improvement are no delusion; the hopes of philanthropy are more than a dream. The five senses do not constitute the whole inventory of our sources of knowledge. They are the organs by which thought connects itself with the external universe; but the power of thought is not merged in the exercise of its instruments. We have functions which connect us with heaven, as

THE OFFICE OF THE PEOPLE IN ART, GOVERNMENT, AND RELIGION. From George Bancroft, *Literary and Historical Miscellanies* (1855).

well as organs which set us in relation with earth. We have not merely
the senses opening to us the external world, but an internal sense, which
places us in connexion with the world of intelligence and the decrees
of God.

There is a *spirit in man:* not in the privileged few; not in those of
us only who by the favor of Providence have been nursed in public
schools: IT IS IN MAN: it is the attribute of the race. The spirit, which
is the guide to truth, is the gracious gift to each member of the human family.

. . .

If it be true, that the gifts of mind and heart are universally diffused, if the sentiment of truth, justice, love, and beauty exists in
every one, then it follows [that] . . . the best government rests on
the people and not on the few, on persons and not on property, on
the free development of public opinion and not on authority; because
the munificent Author of our being has conferred the gifts of mind
upon every member of the human race without distinction of outward
circumstances. Whatever of other possessions may be engrossed, mind
asserts its own independence. Lands, estates, the produce of mines,
the prolific abundance of the seas, may be usurped by a privileged class.
Avarice, assuming the form of ambitious power, may grasp realm after
realm, subdue continents, compass the earth in its schemes of aggrandizement, and sigh after other worlds; but mind eludes the power of
appropriation; it exists only in its own individuality; it is a property
which cannot be confiscated and cannot be torn away; it laughs at
chains; it bursts from imprisonment; it defies monopoly. A government of equal rights must, therefore, rest upon mind; not wealth, not
brute force, the sum of the moral intelligence of the community
should rule the State. Prescription can no more assume to be a valid
plea for political injustice; society studies to eradicate established
abuses, and to bring social institutions and laws into harmony with
moral right; not dismayed by the natural and necessary imperfections
of all human effort, and not giving way to despair, because every hope
does not at once ripen into fruit.

The public happiness is the true object of legislation, and can be
secured only by the masses of mankind themselves awakening to the
knowledge and the care of their own interests. Our free institutions
have reversed the false and ignoble distinctions between men; and
refusing to gratify the pride of caste, have acknowledged the common
mind to be the true material for a commonwealth. Every thing has
hitherto been done for the happy few. It is not possible to endow an
aristocracy with greater benefits than they have already enjoyed;
there is no room to hope that individuals will be more highly gifted
or more fully developed than the greatest sages of past times. The

world can advance only through the culture of the moral and intellectual powers of the people. To accomplish this end by means of the people themselves, is the highest purpose of government. If it be the duty of the individual to strive after a perfection like the perfection of God, how much more ought a nation to be the image of Deity. The common mind is the true Parian marble, fit to be wrought into likeness to a God. The duty of America is to secure the culture and the happiness of the masses by their reliance on themselves.

The absence of the prejudices of the old world leaves us here the opportunity of consulting independent truth; and man is left to apply the instinct of freedom to every social relation and public interest. We have approached so near to nature, that we can hear her gentlest whispers; we have made Humanity our lawgiver and our oracle; and, therefore, the nation receives, vivifies and applies principles, which in Europe the wisest accept with distrust. Freedom of mind and of conscience, freedom of the seas, freedom of industry, equality of franchises, each great truth is firmly grasped, comprehended and enforced; for the multitude is neither rash nor fickle. In truth, it is less fickle than those who profess to be its guides. Its natural dialectics surpass the logic of the schools. Political action has never been so consistent and so unwavering, as when it results from a feeling or a principle, diffused through society. The people is firm and tranquil in its movements, and necessarily acts with moderation, because it becomes but slowly impregnated with new ideas; and effects no changes, except in harmony with the knowledge which it has acquired. Besides, where it is permanently possessed of power, there exists neither the occasion nor the desire for frequent change. It is not the parent of tumult; sedition is bred in the lap of luxury, and its chosen emissaries are the beggared spendthrift and the impoverished libertine. The government by the people is in very truth the strongest government in the world. Discarding the implements of terror, it dares to rule by moral force, and has its citadel in the heart.

Such is the political system which rests on reason, reflection, and the free expression of deliberate choice. There may be those who scoff at the suggestion, that the decision of the whole is to be preferred to the judgment of the enlightened few. They say in their hearts that the masses are ignorant; that farmers know nothing of legislation; that mechanics should not quit their workshops to join in forming public opinion. But true political science does indeed venerate the masses. It maintains, not as has been perversely asserted, that "the people can make right," but that the people can DISCERN right. Individuals are but shadows, too often engrossed by the pursuit of shadows; the race is immortal: individuals are of limited sagacity; the common mind is infinite in its experience: individuals are languid and blind; the many are ever wakeful: individuals are corrupt; the race has been redeemed: individuals are time-serving; the masses are fearless: individuals may be false; the masses are ingenuous and sincere: individuals claim the divine sanction of truth for the deceitful conceptions of their own fancies; the Spirit of God breathes through the combined intelligence of the people. Truth is not to be ascertained by the impulses of an individual; it emerges from the contradictions of personal opinions; it raises itself in majestic serenity above the strifes of parties and the conflict of sects; it acknowledges neither the solitary mind, nor the separate faction as its oracle; but owns as its only faithful interpreter the dictates of pure reason itself, proclaimed by the general voice of mankind. The decrees of the universal conscience are the nearest approach to the presence of God in the soul of man.

Thus the opinion which we respect is, indeed, not the opinion of one or of a few, but the sagacity of the many. It is hard for the pride of cultivated philosophy to put its ear to the ground, and listen reverently to the voice of lowly humanity; yet the people collectively are wiser than the most gifted individual, for all his wisdom constitutes but a part of theirs. When the great sculptor of Greece was endeavoring to fashion the perfect model of beauty, he did not passively imitate the form of the loveliest woman of his age; but he gleaned the several lineaments of his faultless work from the many. And so it is, that a perfect judgment is the result of comparison, when error eliminates error, and truth is established by concurring witnesses. The organ of truth is the invisible decision of the unbiased world; she pleads before no tribunal but public opinion; she owns no safe interpreter but the common mind; she knows no court of appeals but the soul of humanity. It is when the multitude give counsel, that right purposes find safety; theirs is the fixedness that cannot be shaken; theirs is the understanding which exceeds in wisdom; theirs is the heart, of which the largeness is as the sand on the sea-shore.

It is not by vast armies, by immense natural resources, by accumulations of treasure, that the greatest results in modern civilization have been accomplished. The traces of the career of conquest pass away, hardly leaving a scar on the national intelligence. The famous battle grounds of victory are, most of them, comparatively indifferent to the human race; barren fields of blood, the scourges of their times, but affecting the social condition as little as the raging of a pestilence. Not one benevolent institution, not one ameliorating principle in the Roman state, was a voluntary concession of the aristocracy; each useful element was borrowed from the Democracies of Greece, or was a reluctant concession to the demands of the people. The same is true in modern political life. It is the confession of an enemy to Democracy, that "ALL THE GREAT AND NOBLE INSTITUTIONS OF THE WORLD HAVE COME FROM POPULAR EFFORTS."

It is the uniform tendency of the popular element to elevate and bless Humanity. The exact measure of the progress of civilization is the degree in which the intelligence of the common mind has prevailed over wealth and brute force; in other words, the measure of the progress of civilization is the progress of the people.

.   .   .

It is alone by infusing great principles into the common mind, that revolutions in human society are brought about. They never have been, they never can be, effected by superior individual excellence.

.   .   .

Yes, reforms in society are only effected through the masses of the people, and through them have continually taken place. New truths have been successively developed, and, becoming the common property of the human family, have improved its condition. This progress is advanced by every sect, precisely because each sect, to obtain vitality, does of necessity embody a truth; by every political party, for the conflicts of party are the war of ideas; by every nationality, for a nation cannot exist as such, till humanity makes it a special trustee of some part of its wealth for the ultimate benefit of all. The irresistible tendency of the human race is therefore to advancement, for absolute power has never succeeded, and can never succeed, in suppressing a single truth. An idea once revealed may find its admission into every living breast and live there. Like God it becomes immortal and omnipresent. The movement of the species is upward, irresistibly upward. The individual is often lost; Providence never disowns the race. No principle once promulgated, has ever been forgotten. No "timely tramp" of a despot's foot ever trod out one idea. The world cannot retrograde; the dark ages cannot return. Dynasties perish; cities are buried; nations have been victims to error, or martyrs for right; Humanity has always been on the advance; gaining maturity, universality, and power.

Yes, truth is immortal; it cannot be destroyed; it is invincible, it cannot long be resisted. Not every great principle has yet been generated; but when once proclaimed and diffused, it lives without end, in the safe custody of the race. States may pass away; every just principle of legislation which has been once established will endure. Philosophy has sometimes forgotten God; a great people never did. The skepticism of the last century could not uproot Christianity, because it lived in the hearts of the millions. Do you think that infidelity is spreading? Christianity never lived in the hearts of so many millions as at this moment. The forms under which it is professed may decay, for they, like all that is the work of man's hands, are subject to the changes and chances of mortal being; but the spirit of truth is incorruptible; it may be developed, illustrated, and applied; it never can die; it never can decline.

No truth can perish; no truth can pass away. The flame is undying, though generations disappear. Wherever moral truth has started into being, Humanity claims and guards the bequest. Each generation gathers together the imperishable children of the past, and increases them by new sons of light, alike radiant with immortality.

Civil Disobedience

HENRY DAVID THOREAU (1817–1862), opposed to slavery and the Mexican War, was arrested in the summer of 1845 for refusal to pay a poll tax. A night in the Concord jail provided the inspiration for his "Civil Disobedience," an essay that fired the imagination of later leaders from Emma Goldman, the anarchist, to Gandhi, the great Indian exponent of nonviolence, and Martin Luther King, Jr.

I heartily accept the motto,—"That government is best which governs least;" and I should like to see it acted up to more rapidly and systematically. Carried out, it finally amounts to this, which also I believe,—"That government is best which governs not at all;" and when men are prepared for it, that will be the kind of government which they will have. Government is at best but an expedient; but most governments are usually, and all governments are sometimes, inexpedient. The objections which have been brought against a standing army, and they are many and weighty, and deserve to prevail, may also at last be brought against a standing government. The standing army is only an arm of the standing government. The government itself, which is only the mode which the people have chosen to execute their will, is equally liable to be abused and perverted before the people can act through it. Witness the present Mexican war, the work of comparatively a few individuals using the standing government as their tool; for, in the outset, the people would not have consented to this measure.

This American government,—what is it but a tradition, though a

CIVIL DISOBEDIENCE. From Henry David Thoreau, *Miscellanies* (1893).

recent one, endeavoring to transmit itself unimpaired to posterity, but each instant losing some of its integrity? It has not the vitality and force of a single living man; for a single man can bend it to his will. It is a sort of wooden gun to the people themselves. But it is not the less necessary for this; for the people must have some complicated machinery or other, and hear its din, to satisfy that idea of government which they have. Governments show thus how successfully men can be imposed on, even impose on themselves, for their own advantage. It is excellent, we must all allow. Yet this government never of itself furthered any enterprise, but by the alacrity with which it got out of its way. *It* does not keep the country free. *It* does not settle the West. *It* does not educate. The character inherent in the American people has done all that has been accomplished; and it would have done somewhat more, if the government had not sometimes got in its way. For government is an expedient by which men would fain succeed in letting one another alone; and, as has been said, when it is most expedient, the governed are most let alone by it. Trade and commerce, if they were not made of India-rubber, would never manage to bounce over the obstacles which legislators are continually putting in their way; and, if one were to judge these men wholly by the effects of their actions and not partly by their intentions, they would deserve to be classed and punished with those mischievous persons who put obstructions on the railroads.

But, to speak practically and as a citizen, unlike those who call themselves no-government men, I ask for, not at once no government, but *at once* a better government. Let every man make known what kind of government would command his respect, and that will be one step toward obtaining it.

After all, the practical reason why, when the power is once in the hands of the people, a majority are permitted, and for a long period continue, to rule is not because they are most likely to be in the right, nor because this seems fairest to the minority, but because they are physically the strongest. But a government in which the majority rule in all cases cannot be based on justice, even as far as men understand it. Can there not be a government in which majorities do not virtually decide right and wrong, but conscience?—in which majorities decide only those questions to which the rule of expediency is applicable? Must the citizen ever for a moment, or in the least degree, resign his conscience to the legislator? Why has every man a conscience, then? I think that we should be men first, and subjects afterward. It is not desirable to cultivate a respect for the law, so much as for the right. The only obligation which I have a right to assume is to do at any time what I think right.

.　　.　　.

All voting is a sort of gaming, like checkers or backgammon, with a slight moral tinge to it, a playing with right and wrong, with moral questions; and betting naturally accompanies it. The character of the voters is not staked. I cast my vote, perchance, as I think right; but I am not vitally concerned that that right should prevail. I am willing to leave it to the majority. Its obligation, therefore, never exceeds that of expediency. Even voting *for the right* is *doing* nothing for it. It is only expressing to men feebly your desire that it should prevail. A wise man will not leave the right to the mercy of chance, nor wish it to prevail through the power of the majority. There is but little virtue in the action of masses of men.

.   .   .

How can a man be satisfied to entertain an opinion merely, and enjoy *it*? Is there any enjoyment in it, if his opinion is that he is aggrieved? If you are cheated out of a single dollar by your neighbor, you do not rest satisfied with knowing that you are cheated, or with saying that you are cheated, or even with petitioning him to pay you your due; but you take effectual steps at once to obtain the full amount, and see that you are never cheated again. Action from principle, the perception and the performance of right, changes things and relations; it is essentially revolutionary, and does not consist wholly with anything which was. It not only divides states and churches, it divides families; ay, it divides the *individual*, separating the diabolical in him from the divine.

Unjust laws exist: shall we be content to obey them, or shall we endeavor to amend them, and obey them until we have succeeded, or shall we transgress them at once? Men generally, under such a government as this, think that they ought to wait until they have persuaded the majority to alter them. They think that, if they should resist, the remedy would be worse than the evil. But it is the fault of the government itself that the remedy *is* worse than the evil. *It* makes it worse. Why is it not more apt to anticipate and provide for reform? Why does it not cherish its wise minority? Why does it cry and resist before it is hurt? Why does it not encourage its citizens to be on the alert to point out its faults, and *do* better than it would have them? Why does it always crucify Christ, and excommunicate Copernicus and Luther, and pronounce Washington and Franklin rebels?

One would think, that a deliberate and practical denial of its authority was the only offense never contemplated by government; else, why has it not assigned its definite, its suitable and proportionate penalty? If a man who has no property refuses but once to earn nine shillings for the state, he is put in prison for a period unlimited by any law that I know, and determined only by the discretion of those who placed him there; but if he should steal ninety times nine shillings from the state, he is soon permitted to go at large again.

If the injustice is part of the necessary friction of the machine of government, let it go, let it go: perchance it will wear smooth,—certainly the machine will wear out. If the injustice has a spring, or a pulley, or a rope, or a crank, exclusively for itself, then perhaps you may consider whether the remedy will not be worse than the evil; but if it is of such a nature that it requires you to be the agent of injustice to another, then, I say, break the law. Let your life be a counter friction to stop the machine. What I have to do is to see, at any rate, that I do not lend myself to the wrong which I condemn.

As for adopting the ways which the state has provided for remedying the evil, I know not of such ways. They take too much time, and a man's life will be gone. I have other affairs to attend to. I came into this world, not chiefly to make this a good place to live in, but to live in it, be it good or bad. A man has not everything to do, but something; and because he cannot do *everything*, it is not necessary that he should do *something* wrong. It is not my business to be petitioning the Governor or the Legislature any more than it is theirs to petition me; and if they should not hear my petition, what should I do then? But in this case the state has provided no way: its very Constitution is the evil. This may seem to be harsh and stubborn and unconciliatory; but it is to treat with the utmost kindness and consideration the only spirit that can appreciate or deserves it. So is all change for the better, like birth and death, which convulse the body.

.   .   .

Under a government which imprisons any unjustly, the true place for a just man is also a prison. The proper place to-day, the only place which Massachusetts has provided for her freer and less desponding spirits, is in her prisons, to be put out and locked out of the State by her own act, as they have already put themselves out by their principles. It is there that the fugitive slave, and the Mexican prisoner on parole, and the Indian come to plead the wrongs of his race should find them; on that separate, but more free and honorable ground, where the State places those who are not *with* her, but *against* her,—the only house in a slave State in which a free man can abide with honor. If any think that their influence would be lost there, and their voices no longer afflict the ear of the State, that they would not be as an enemy within its walls, they do not know by how much truth is stronger than error, nor how much more eloquently and effectively he can combat injustice who has experienced a little in his own person. Cast your whole vote, not a strip of paper merely, but your whole influence.

A minority is powerless while it conforms to the majority; it is not even a minority then; but it is irresistible when it clogs by its whole weight. If the alternative is to keep all just men in prison, or give up war and slavery, the State will not hesitate which to choose. If a thousand men were not to pay their tax-bills this year, that would not be a violent and bloody measure, as it would be to pay them, and enable the State to commit violence and shed innocent blood. This is, in fact, the definition of a peaceable revolution, if any such is possible. If the tax-gatherer, or any other public officer, asks me, as one has done, "But what shall I do?" my answer is, "If you really wish to do anything, resign your office." When the subject has refused allegiance, and the officer has resigned his office, then the revolution is accomplished. But even suppose blood should flow. Is there not a sort of blood shed when the conscience is wounded? Through this wound a man's real manhood and immortality flow out, and he bleeds to an everlasting death. I see this blood flowing now.

.   .   .

I know that most men think differently from myself; but those whose lives are by profession devoted to the study of these or kindred subjects content me as little as any. Statesmen and legislators, standing so completely within the institution, never distinctly and nakedly behold it. They speak of moving society, but have no resting-place without it. They may be men of a certain experience and discrimination, and have no doubt invented ingenious and even useful systems, for which we sincerely thank them; but all their wit and usefulness lie within certain not very wide limits. They are wont to forget that the world is not governed by policy and expediency.

.   .   .

They who know of no purer sources of truth, who have traced up its stream no higher, stand, and wisely stand, by the Bible and the Constitution, and drink at it there with reverence and humility; but they who behold where it comes trickling into this lake or that pool, gird up their loins once more, and continue their pilgrimage toward its fountain-head.

No man with a genius for legislation has appeared in America. They are rare in the history of the world. There are orators, politicians, and eloquent men, by the thousand; but the speaker has not yet opened his mouth to speak who is capable of settling the much-vexed questions of the day. We love eloquence for its own sake, and not for any truth which it may utter, or any heroism it may inspire. Our legislators have not yet learned the comparative value of free-trade and of freedom, of union, and of rectitude, to a nation. They have no genius or talent for comparatively humble questions of taxation and finance, commerce and manufactures and agriculture. If we were left solely to the wordy wit of legislators in Congress for our guidance, uncorrected by the seasonable experience and the effectual complaints of the people, America would not long retain her rank among the nations. For eighteen hundred years, though perchance I have no right to say it, the New Testament has been written; yet where is the legislator who has wisdom and practical talent enough to avail himself of the light which it sheds on the science of legislation?

The authority of government, even such as I am willing to submit to,—for I will cheerfully obey those who know and can do better than I, and in many things even those who neither know nor can do so well,—is still an impure one: to be strictly just, it must have the sanction and consent of the governed. It can have no pure right over my person and property but what I concede to it. The progress from an absolute to a limited monarchy, from a limited monarchy to a democracy, is a progress toward a true respect for the individual. Even the Chinese philosopher was wise enough to regard the individual as the basis of the empire. Is a democracy, such as we know it, the last improvement possible in government? Is it not possible to take a step further towards recognizing and organizing the rights of man? There will never be a really free and enlightened State until the State comes to recognize the individual as a higher and independent power, from which all its own power and authority are derived, and treats him accordingly. I please myself with imagining a State at last which can afford to be just to all men, and to treat the individual with respect as a neighbor; which even would not think it inconsistent with its own repose if a few were to live aloof from it, not meddling with it, nor embraced by it, who fulfilled all the duties of neighbors and fellowmen. A State which bore this kind of fruit, and suffered it to drop off as fast as it ripened, would prepare the way for a still more perfect and glorious State, which also I have imagined, but not yet anywhere seen.

The College Graduate and Public Life

THEODORE ROOSEVELT (1858–1919), President of the United States from 1901 to 1909, was born in New York City, the son of a

THE COLLEGE GRADUATE AND PUBLIC LIFE. From Theodore Roosevelt, *American Ideals* (1897).

well-to-do merchant. Graduating from Harvard in 1880, he might have scorned politics, like many "young gentlemen," or at least party organizations as did the independent "mugwumps." Swallowing his distaste for individual candidates, however, he repudiated his independent friends, observing later that a "mugwump" was distinguished by "small hands, small feet, a receding chin, and a culture much above his intellect." A politician to the core, he wrote "The College Graduate and Public Life" while serving on the United States Civil Service Commission in 1894.

There are always, in our national life, certain tendencies that give us ground for alarm, and certain others that give us ground for hope. Among the latter we must put the fact that there has undoubtedly been a growing feeling among educated men that they are in honor bound to do their full share of the work of American public life.

We have in this country an equality of rights. It is the plain duty of every man to see that his rights are respected. That weak good-nature which acquiesces in wrong-doing, whether from laziness, timidity, or indifference, is a very unwholesome quality. It should be second nature with every man to insist that he be given full justice. But if there is an equality of rights, there is an inequality of duties. It is proper to demand more from the man with exceptional advantages than from the man without them. A heavy moral obligation rests upon the man of means and upon the man of education to do their full duty by their country. On no class does this obligation rest more heavily than upon the men with a collegiate education, the men who are graduates of our universities. Their education gives them no right to feel the least superiority over any of their fellow-citizens; but it certainly ought to make them feel that they should stand foremost in the honorable effort to serve the whole public by doing their duty as Americans in the body politic. This obligation very possibly rests even more heavily upon the men of means; but of this it is not necessary now to speak. The men of mere wealth never can have and never should have the capacity for doing good work that is possessed by the men of exceptional mental training; but that they may become both a laughing-stock and a menace to the community is made unpleasantly apparent by that portion of the New York business and social world which is most in evidence in the newspapers.

To the great body of men who have had exceptional advantages in the way of educational facilities we have a right, then, to look for good service to the state. The service may be rendered in many different ways. In a reasonable number of cases, the man may himself rise to high political position. That men actually do so rise is shown by the number of graduates of Harvard, Yale, and our other universities who are now taking a prominent part in public life. These cases must necessarily, however, form but a small part of the whole. The enormous majority of our educated men have to make their own living, and are obliged to take up careers in which they must work heart and soul to succeed. Nevertheless, the man of business and the man of science, the doctor of divinity and the doctor of law, the architect, the engineer, and the writer, all alike owe a positive duty to the community, the neglect of which they cannot excuse on any plea of their private affairs. They are bound to follow understandingly the course of public events; they are bound to try to estimate and form judgment upon public men; and they are bound to act intelligently and effectively in support of the principles which they deem to be right and for the best interests of the country.

The most important thing for this class of educated men to realize is that they do not really form a class at all. I have used the word in default of another, but I have merely used it roughly to group together people who have had unusual opportunities of a certain kind. A large number of the people to whom these opportunities are offered fail to take advantage of them, and a very much larger number of those to whom they have not been offered succeed none the less in making them for themselves. An educated man must not go into politics as such; he must go in simply as an American; and when he is once in, he will speedily realize that he must work very hard indeed, or he will be upset by some other American, with no education at all, but with much natural capacity. His education ought to make him feel particularly ashamed of himself if he acts meanly or dishonorably, or in any way falls short of the ideal of good citizenship, and it ought to make him feel that he must show that he has profited by it; but it should certainly give him no feeling of superiority until by actual work he has shown that superiority. In other words, the educated man must realize that he is living in a democracy and under democratic conditions, and that he is entitled to no more respect and consideration than he can win by actual performance.

This must be steadily kept in mind not only by educated men themselves, but particularly by the men who give the tone to our great educational institutions. These educational institutions, if they are to do their best work, must strain every effort to keep their life in touch with the life of the nation at the present day. This is necessary for the country, but it is very much more necessary for the educated men themselves. It is a misfortune for any land if its people of cultivation take little part in shaping its destiny; but the misfortune is far greater for the people of cultivation. The country has a right to demand the honest and efficient service of every man in it, but especially of every man who has had the advantage of rigid mental and moral training; the country is so much the poorer when any class of honest men fail to do their duty by it; but the loss to the class itself is immeasurable. If our educated men as a whole become incapable of playing their full part in our life, if they cease doing their share of the rough, hard work which must be done, and grow to take a position of mere dilettanteism in our public affairs, they will speedily sink in relation to their fellows who really do the work of governing, until they stand toward them as a cultivated, ineffective man with a taste for bric-a-brac stands toward a great artist. When once a body of citizens becomes thoroughly out of touch and out of temper with the national life, its usefulness is gone, and its power of leaving its mark on the times is gone also.

The first great lesson which the college graduate should learn is the lesson of work rather than of criticism. Criticism is necessary and useful; it is often indispensable; but it can never take the place of action, or be even a poor substitute for it. The function of the mere critic is of very subordinate usefulness. It is the doer of deeds who actually counts in the battle for life, and not the man who looks on and says how the fight ought to be fought, without himself sharing the stress and the danger.

There is, however, a need for proper critical work. Wrongs should be strenuously and fearlessly denounced; evil principles and evil men should be condemned. The politician who cheats or swindles, or the newspaper man who lies in any form, should be made to feel that he is an object of scorn for all honest men. We need fearless criticism; but we need that it should also be intelligent. At present, the man who is most apt to regard himself as an intelligent critic of our political affairs is often the man who knows nothing whatever about them. Criticism which is ignorant or prejudiced is a source of great harm to the nation; and where ignorant or prejudiced critics are themselves educated men, their attitude does real harm also to the class to which they belong.

The tone of a portion of the press of the country toward public men, and especially toward political opponents, is degrading, all forms of coarse and noisy slander being apparently considered legitimate weapons to employ against men of the opposite party or faction. Unfortunately, not a few of the journals that pride themselves upon being independent in politics, and the organs of cultivated men, betray the same characteristics in a less coarse but quite as noxious form. All these journals do great harm by accustoming good citizens to see their public men, good and bad, assailed indiscriminately as scoundrels. The effect is twofold: the citizen learning, on the one hand, to disbelieve any statement he sees in any newspaper, so that the attacks on evil lose their edge; and on the other, gradually acquiring a deep-rooted belief that all public men are more or less bad. In consequence, his political instinct becomes hopelessly blurred, and he grows unable to tell the good representative from the bad. The worst offence that can be committed against the Republic is the offence of the public man who betrays his trust; but second only to it comes the offence of the man who tries to persuade others that an honest and efficient public man is dishonest or unworthy. This is a wrong that can be committed in a great many different ways. Downright foul abuse may be, after all, less dangerous than incessant misstatements, sneers, and those half-truths that are the meanest lies.

For educated men of weak fibre, there lies a real danger in that species of literary work which appeals to their cultivated senses because of its scholarly and pleasant tone, but which enjoins as the proper attitude to assume in public life one of mere criticism and negation; which teaches the adoption toward public men and public affairs of that sneering tone which so surely denotes a mean and small mind. If a man does not have belief and enthusiasm, the chances are small indeed that he will ever do a man's work in the world; and the paper or the college which, by its general course, tends to eradicate this power of belief and enthusiasm, this desire for work, has rendered to the young men under its influence the worst service it could possibly render. Good can often be done by criticising sharply and severely the wrong; but excessive indulgence in criticism is never anything but bad, and no amount of criticism can in any way take the place of active and zealous warfare for the right.

Again, there is a certain tendency in college life, a tendency encouraged by some of the very papers referred to, to make educated men shrink from contact with the rough people who do the world's work, and associate only with one another and with those who think as they do. This is a most dangerous tendency. It is very agreeable to deceive one's self into the belief that one is performing the whole duty of man by sitting at home in ease, doing nothing wrong, and confining one's participation in politics to conversations and meetings with men who have had the same training and look at things in the same way. It is always a temptation to do this, because those who do nothing else often speak as if in some way they deserved credit for their attitude, and as if they stood above their brethren who plough the rough fields. Moreover, many people whose political work is done more or less after this fashion are very noble and very sincere in their aims and aspirations, and are striving for what is best and most decent in public life.

Nevertheless, this is a snare round which it behooves every young man to walk carefully. Let him beware of associating only with the people of his own caste and of his own little ways of political thought. Let him learn that he must deal with the mass of men; that he must go out and stand shoulder to shoulder with his friends of every rank, and face to face with his foes of every rank, and must bear himself well in the hurly-burly. He must not be frightened by the many unpleasant features of the contest, and he must not expect to have it all his own way, or to accomplish too much. He will meet with checks and will make many mistakes; but if he perseveres, he will achieve a measure of success and will do a measure of good such as is never possible to the refined, cultivated, intellectual men who shrink aside from the actual fray.

Yet again, college men must learn to be as practical in politics as they would be in business or in law. It is surely unnecessary to say that by "practical" I do not mean anything that savors in the least of dishonesty. On the contrary, a college man is peculiarly bound to keep a high ideal and to be true to it; but he must work in practical ways to try to realize this ideal, and must not refuse to do anything because he cannot get everything. One especially necessary thing is to know the facts by actual experience, and not to take refuge in mere theorizing. There are always a number of excellent and well-meaning men whom we grow to regard with amused impatience because they waste all their energies on some visionary scheme which, even if it were not visionary, would be useless. When they come to deal with political questions, these men are apt to err from sheer lack of familiarity with the workings of our government. No man ever really learned from books how to manage a governmental system. Books are admirable adjuncts, and the statesman who has carefully studied them is far more apt to do good work than if he had not; but if he has never done anything but study books he will not be a statesman at all.

                     .   .   .

It is a misfortune for any people when the paths of the practical and the theoretical politicians diverge so widely that they have no common standing-ground. When the Greek thinkers began to devote their attention to purely visionary politics of the kind found in Plato's Republic, while the Greek practical politicians simply exploited the quarrelsome little commonwealths in their own interests, then the end of Greek liberty was at hand. No government that cannot command the respectful support of the best thinkers is in an entirely sound condition; but it is well to keep in mind the remark of Frederick the Great, that if he wished to punish a province, he would allow it to be governed by the philosophers. It is a great misfortune for the country when the practical politician and the doctrinaire have no point in common, but the misfortune is, if anything, greatest for the doctrinaire. The ideal to be set before the student of politics and the practical politician alike is the ideal of the *Federalist*. Each man should realize that he cannot do his best, either in the study of politics or in applied politics unless he has a working knowledge of both branches. A limited number of people can do good work by the careful study of governmental institutions, but they can do it only if they have themselves a practical knowledge of the workings of these institutions. A very large number of people, on the other hand, may do excellent work in politics without much theoretic knowledge of the subject; but without this knowledge they cannot rise to the highest rank, while in any rank their capacity to do good work will be immensely increased if they have such knowledge.

There are certain other qualities, about which it is hardly necessary to speak. If an educated man is not heartily American in instinct and feeling and taste and sympathy, he will amount to nothing in our public life. Patriotism, love of country, and pride in the flag which symbolizes country may be feelings which the race will at some period outgrow, but at present they are very real and strong, and the man who lacks them is a useless creature, a mere incumbrance to the land.

A man of sound political instincts can no more subscribe to the doctrine of absolute independence of party on the one hand than to that of unquestioning party allegiance on the other. No man can accomplish much unless he works in an organization with others, and this organization, no matter how temporary, is a party for the time being. But that man is a dangerous citizen who so far mistakes means for ends as to become servile in his devotion to his party, and afraid to leave it when the party goes wrong. To deify either independence or party allegiance merely as such is a little absurd. It depends entirely upon the motive, the purpose, the result. For the last two years, the Senator who, beyond all his colleagues in the United States Senate, has shown himself independent of party ties is the very man to whom the leading champions of independence in politics most strenuously object. The truth is, simply, that there are times when it may be the duty of a man to break with his party, and there are other times when it may be his duty to stand by his party, even though, on some points, he thinks that party wrong; he must be prepared to leave it when necessary, and he must not sacrifice his influence by leaving it unless it is necessary. If we had no party allegiance, our politics would become mere windy anarchy, and, under present conditions, our government could hardly continue at all. If we had no independence, we should always be running the risk of the most degraded kind of despotism,—the despotism of the party boss and the party machine.

It is just the same way about compromises. Occasionally one hears some well-meaning person say of another, apparently in praise, that he is "never willing to compromise." It is a mere truism to say that, in politics, there has to be one continual compromise. Of course now and then questions arise upon which a compromise is inadmissible. There could be no compromise with secession, and there was none. There should be no avoidable compromise about any great moral question. But only a very few great reforms or great measures of any kind can be carried through without concession. No student of American history needs to be reminded that the Constitution itself is a bundle of compromises, and was adopted only because of this fact, and that the same thing is true of the Emancipation Proclamation.

In conclusion, then, the man with a university education is in honor bound to take an active part in our political life, and to do his full duty as a citizen by helping his fellow-citizens to the extent of his power in the exercise of the rights of self-government. He is bound to rank action far above criticism, and to understand that the man deserving of credit is the man who actually does the things, even though imperfectly, and not the man who confines himself to talking about how they ought to be done. He is bound to have a high ideal and to strive to realize it, and yet he must make up his mind that he will never be able to get the highest good, and that he must devote himself with all his energy to getting the best that he can. Finally, his work must be disinterested and honest, and it must be given without regard to his own success or failure, and without regard to the effect it has upon his own fortunes; and while he must show the virtues of uprightness and tolerance and gentleness, he must also show the sterner virtues of courage, resolution, and hardihood, and the desire to war with merciless effectiveness against the existence of wrong.

Anarchism

EMMA GOLDMAN (1869–1940), born in Russia, emigrated to Rochester, New York, in 1886 where she worked in a factory. Befriending Alexander Berkman, a fellow anarchist, she was involved in an attempt in 1892 to assassinate Henry Clay Frick, a Carnegie lieutenant at the Homestead Steel works. She was imprisoned for inciting a riot in 1893, and deported in 1919 for interfering with the war effort. Disillusioned with the Russian Revolution she traveled to England and Canada, where she died.

The history of human growth and development is at the same time the history of the terrible struggle of every new idea heralding the

ANARCHISM. From Emma Goldman, *Anarchism and Other Essays* (1910).

approach of a brighter dawn. In its tenacious hold on tradition, the Old has never hesitated to make use of the foulest and cruelest means to stay the advent of the New, in whatever form or period the latter may have asserted itself. Nor need we retrace our steps into the distant past to realize the enormity of opposition, difficulties, and hardships placed in the path of every progressive idea. The rack, the thumbscrew, and the knout are still with us; so are the convict's garb and the social wrath, all conspiring against the spirit that is serenely marching on.

Anarchism could not hope to escape the fate of all other ideas of innovation. Indeed, as the most revolutionary and uncompromising innovator, Anarchism must needs meet with the combined ignorance and venom of the world it aims to reconstruct.

. . .

What, then, are the objections? First, Anarchism is impractical, though a beautiful ideal. Second, Anarchism stands for violence and destruction, hence it must be repudiated as vile and dangerous. Both the intelligent man and the ignorant mass judge not from a thorough knowledge of the subject, but either from hearsay or false interpretation.

A practical scheme, says Oscar Wilde, is either one already in existence, or a scheme that could be carried out under the existing conditions; but it is exactly the existing conditions that one objects to, and any scheme that could accept these conditions is wrong and foolish. The true criterion of the practical, therefore, is not whether the latter can keep intact the wrong or foolish; rather is it whether the scheme has vitality enough to leave the stagnant waters of the old, and build, as well as sustain, new life. In the light of this conception, Anarchism is indeed practical. More than any other idea, it is helping to do away with the wrong and foolish; more than any other idea, it is building and sustaining new life.

The emotions of the ignorant man are continuously kept at a pitch by the most blood-curdling stories about Anarchism. Not a thing too outrageous to be employed against this philosophy and its exponents. Therefore Anarchism represents to the unthinking what the proverbial bad man does to the child,—a black monster bent on swallowing everything; in short, destruction and violence.

Destruction and violence! How is the ordinary man to know that the most violent element in society is ignorance; that its power of destruction is the very thing Anarchism is combating? Nor is he aware that Anarchism, whose roots, as it were, are part of nature's forces, destroys, not healthful tissue, but parasitic growths that feed on the life's essence of society. It is merely clearing the soil from weeds and sagebrush, that it may eventually bear healthy fruit.

Someone has said that it requires less mental effort to condemn than to think. The widespread mental indolence, so prevalent in society, proves this to be only too true. Rather than to go to the bottom of any given idea, to examine into its origin and meaning, most people will either condemn it altogether, or rely on some superficial or prejudicial definition of non-essentials.

Anarchism urges man to think, to investigate, to analyze every proposition; but that the brain capacity of the average reader be not taxed too much, I also shall begin with a definition, and then elaborate on the latter.

ANARCHISM:—The philosophy of a new social order based on liberty unrestricted by manmade law; the theory that all forms of government rest on violence, and are therefore wrong and harmful, as well as unnecessary.

The new social order rests, of course, on the materialistic basis of life; but while all Anarchists agree that the main evil today is an economic one, they maintain that the solution of that evil can be brought about only through the consideration of *every phase* of life, —individual, as well as the collective; the internal, as well as the external phases.

A thorough perusal of the history of human development will disclose two elements in bitter conflict with each other; elements that are only now beginning to be understood, not as foreign to each other, but as closely related and truly harmonious, if only placed in proper environment: the individual and social instincts. The individual and society have waged a relentless and bloody battle for ages, each striving for supremacy, because each was blind to the value and importance of the other. The individual and social instincts,—the one a most potent factor for individual endeavor, for growth, aspiration, self-realization; the other an equally potent factor for mutual helpfulness and social well-being.

The explanation of the storm raging within the individual, and between him and his surroundings, is not far to seek. The primitive man, unable to understand his being, much less the unity of all life, felt himself absolutely dependent on blind, hidden forces ever ready to mock and taunt him. Out of that attitude grew the religious concepts of man as a mere speck of dust dependent on superior powers on high, who can only be appeased by complete surrender. All the early sagas rest on that idea, which continues to be the *leit-motif* of the biblical tales dealing with the relation of man to God, to the State, to society. Again and again the same motif, *man is nothing, the powers are everything*. Thus Jehovah would only endure man on condition of complete surrender. Man can have all the glories of the earth, but he must not become conscious of himself. The State, society, and moral laws all sing the same refrain: Man can have all the glories of the earth, but he must not become conscious of himself.

Anarchism is the only philosophy which brings to man the consciousness of himself; which maintains that God, the State, and society are non-existent, that their promises are null and void, since they can be fulfilled only through man's subordination. Anarchism is therefore the teacher of the unity of life; not merely in nature, but in man. There is no conflict between the individual and the social instincts, any more than there is between the heart and the lungs: the one the receptacle of a precious life essence, the other the repository of the element that keeps the essence pure and strong. The individual is the heart of society, conserving the essence of social life; society is the lungs which are distributing the element to keep the life essence—that is, the individual—pure and strong.

"The one thing of value in the world," says Emerson, "is the active soul; this every man contains within him. The soul active sees absolute truth and utters truth and creates." In other words, the individual instinct is the thing of value in the world. It is the true soul that sees and creates the truth alive, out of which is to come a still greater truth, the re-born social soul.

Anarchism is the great liberator of man from the phantoms that have held him captive; it is the arbiter and pacifier of the two forces for individual and social harmony. To accomplish that unity, Anarchism has declared war on the pernicious influences which have so far prevented the harmonious blending of individual and social instincts, the individual and society.

Religion, the dominion of the human mind; Property, the dominion of human needs; and Government, the dominion of human conduct, represent the stronghold of man's enslavement and all the horrors it entails. Religion! How it dominates man's mind, how it humiliates and degrades his soul. God is everything, man is nothing, says religion. But out of that nothing God has created a kingdom so despotic, so tyrannical, so cruel, so terribly exacting that naught but gloom and tears and blood have ruled the world since gods began. Anarchism rouses man to rebellion against this black monster. Break your mental fetters, says Anarchism to man, for not until you think and judge for yourself will you get rid of the dominion of darkness, the greatest obstacle to all progress.

Property, the dominion of man's needs, the denial of the right to satisfy his needs. Time was when property claimed a divine right, when it came to man with the same refrain, even as religion, "Sacrifice! Abnegate! Submit!" The spirit of Anarchism has lifted man from his prostrate position. He now stands erect, with his face toward the light. He has learned to see the insatiable, devouring, devastating nature of property, and he is preparing to strike the monster dead.

"Property is robbery," said the great French Anarchist, Proudhon. Yes, but without risk and danger to the robber. Monopolizing the accumulated efforts of man, property has robbed him of his birthright, and has turned him loose a pauper and an outcast. Property has not even the time-worn excuse that man does not create enough to satisfy all needs. The A B C student of economics knows that the productivity of labor within the last few decades far exceeds normal demand a hundredfold. But what are normal demands to an abnormal institution? The only demand that property recognizes is its own gluttonous appetite for greater wealth, because wealth means power: the power to subdue, to crush, to exploit, the power to enslave, to outrage, to degrade. America is particularly boastful of her great power, her enormous national wealth. Poor America, of what avail is all her wealth, if the individuals comprising the nation are wretchedly poor? If they live in squalor, in filth, in crime, with hope and joy gone, a homeless, soilless army of human prey.

.   .   .

Real wealth consists in things of utility and beauty, in things that help to create strong, beautiful bodies and surroundings inspiring to live in. But if man is doomed to wind cotton around a spool, or dig coal, or build roads for thirty years of his life, there can be no talk of wealth. What he gives to the world is only gray and hideous things, reflecting a dull and hideous existence,—too weak to live, too cowardly to die. Strange to say, there are people who extol this deadening method of centralized production as the proudest achievement of our age. They fail utterly to realize that if we are to continue in machine subserviency, our slavery is more complete than was our bondage to the King. They do not want to know that centralization is not only the death knell of liberty, but also of health and beauty, of art and science, all these being impossible in a clocklike, mechanical atmosphere.

Anarchism cannot but repudiate such a method of production: its goal is the freest possible expression of all the latent powers of the individual. Oscar Wilde defines a perfect personality as "one who develops under perfect conditions, who is not wounded, maimed, or in danger." A perfect personality, then, is only possible in a state of society where man is free to choose the mode of work, the conditions of work, and the freedom to work. One to whom the making of a table, the building of a house, or the tilling of the soil, is what the painting is to the artist and the discovery to the scientist,—the result of inspiration, of intense longing, and deep interest in work as a creative force. That being the ideal of Anarchism, its economic arrangements must consist of voluntary productive and distributive associations, gradually developing into free communism, as the best means of producing with the least waste of human energy. Anarchism, however, also recognizes the right of the individual, or numbers of individuals, to arrange at all times for other forms of work, in harmony with their tastes and desires.

Such free display of human energy being possible only under complete individual and social freedom, Anarchism directs its forces against the third and greatest foe of all social equality; namely, the State, organized authority, or statutory law,—the dominion of human conduct.

Just as religion has fettered the human mind, and as property, or the monopoly of things, has subdued and stifled man's needs, so has the State enslaved his spirit, dictating every phase of conduct. "All government in essence," says Emerson, "is tyranny." It matters not whether it is government by divine right or majority rule. In every instance its aim is the absolute subordination of the individual.

Referring to the American government, the greatest American Anarchist, David Thoreau, said: "Government, what is it but a tradition, though a recent one, endeavoring to transmit itself unimpaired to posterity, but each instance losing its integrity; it has not the vitality and force of a single living man. Law never made man a whit more just; and by means of their respect for it, even the well disposed are daily made agents of injustice."

.   .   .

Unfortunately there are still a number of people who continue in the fatal belief that government rests on natural laws, that it maintains social order and harmony, that it diminishes crime, and that it prevents the lazy man from fleecing his fellows. I shall therefore examine these contentions.

A natural law is that factor in man which asserts itself freely and spontaneously without any external force, in harmony with the requirements of nature. For instance, the demand for nutrition, for sex gratification, for light, air, and exercise, is a natural law. But its expression needs not the machinery of government, needs not the club, the gun, the handcuff, or the prison. To obey such laws, if we may call it obedience, requires only spontaneity and free opportunity. That governments do not maintain themselves through such harmonious factors is proven by the terrible array of violence, force, and coercion all governments use in order to live. Thus Blackstone is right when he says, "Human laws are invalid, because they are contrary to the laws of nature."

.   .   .

The most absurd apology for authority and law is that they serve to diminish crime. Aside from the fact that the State is itself the greatest criminal, breaking every written and natural law, stealing in the form of taxes, killing in the form of war and capital punishment, it has come to an absolute standstill in coping with crime. It has failed utterly to destroy or even minimize the horrible scourge of its own creation.

Crime is naught but misdirected energy. So long as every institution of today, economic, political, social, and moral, conspires to misdirect human energy into wrong channels; so long as most people are out of place doing the things they hate to do, living a life they loathe to live, crime will be inevitable, and all the laws on the statutes can only increase, but never do away with, crime. What does society, as it exists today, know of the process of despair, the poverty, the horrors, the fearful struggle the human soul must pass on its way to crime and degradation? . . .

The deterrent influence of law on the lazy man is too absurd to merit consideration. If society were only relieved of the waste and expense of keeping a lazy class, and the equally great expense of the paraphernalia of protection this lazy class requires, the social tables would contain an abundance for all, including even the occasional lazy individual. Besides, it is well to consider that laziness results either from special privileges, or physical and mental abnormalities. Our present insane system of production fosters both, and the most astounding phenomenon is that people should want to work at all now. Anarchism aims to strip labor of its deadening, dulling aspect, of its gloom and compulsion. It aims to make work an instrument of joy, of strength, of color, of real harmony, so that the poorest sort of a man should find in work both recreation and hope.

To achieve such an arrangement of life, government, with its unjust, arbitrary, repressive measures, must be done away with. At best it has but imposed one single mode of life upon all, without regard to individual and social variations and needs. In destroying government and statutory laws, Anarchism proposes to rescue the self-respect and independence of the individual from all restraint and invasion by authority. Only in freedom can man grow to his full stature. Only in freedom will he learn to think and move, and give the very best in him. Only in freedom will he realize the true force of the social bonds which knit men together, and which are the true foundation of a normal social life.

But what about human nature? Can it be changed? And if not, will it endure under Anarchism?

Poor human nature, what horrible crimes have been committed in thy name! Every fool, from king to policeman, from the flatheaded parson to the visionless dabbler in science, presumes to speak authoritatively of human nature. The greater the mental charlatan, the more definite his insistence on the wickedness and weaknesses of human nature. Yet, how can any one speak of it today, with every soul in a prison, with every heart fettered, wounded, and maimed? . . .

Freedom, expansion, opportunity, and, above all, peace and repose, alone can teach us the real dominant factors of human nature and all its wonderful possibilities. . . .

As to methods. Anarchism is not, as some may suppose, a theory of the future to be realized through divine inspiration. It is a living force in the affairs of our life, constantly creating new conditions. The methods of Anarchism therefore do not comprise an iron-clad program to be carried out under all circumstances. Methods must grow out of the economic needs of each place and clime, and of the intellectual and temperamental requirements of the individual. The serene, calm character of a Tolstoy will wish different methods for social reconstruction than the intense, overflowing personality of a Michael Bakunin or a Peter Kropotkin. Equally so it must be apparent that the economic and political needs of Russia will dictate more drastic measures than would England or America. Anarchism does not stand for military drill and uniformity; it does, however, stand for the spirit of revolt, in whatever form, against everything that hinders human growth. All Anarchists agree in that, as they also agree in their opposition to the political machinery as a means of bringing about the great social change.

"All voting," says Thoreau, "is a sort of gaming, like checkers, or backgammon, a playing with right and wrong; its obligation never exceeds that of expediency. Even voting for the right thing is doing nothing for it. A wise man will not leave the right to the mercy of chance, nor wish it to prevail through the power of the majority." A close examination of the machinery of politics and its achievements will bear out the logic of Thoreau.

What does the history of parliamentarism show? Nothing but failure and defeat, not even a single reform to ameliorate the economic and social stress of the people. Laws have been passed and enactments made for the improvement and protection of labor. Thus it was proven only last year that Illinois, with the most rigid laws for mine protection, had the greatest mine disasters. In States where child labor laws prevail, child exploitation is at its highest, and though with us the workers enjoy full political opportunities, capitalism has reached the most brazen zenith.

Even were the workers able to have their own representatives, for which our good Socialist politicians are clamoring, what chances are there for their honesty and good faith? One has but to bear in mind the process of politics to realize that its path of good intentions is full of pitfalls: wire-pulling, intriguing, flattering, lying, cheating; in fact, chicanery of every description, whereby the political aspirant can achieve success. Added to that is a complete demoralization of character and conviction, until nothing is left that would make one hope for anything from such a human derelict. Time and time again the people were foolish enough to trust, believe, and support with their last farthing aspiring politicians, only to find themselves betrayed and cheated.

It may be claimed that men of integrity would not become corrupt in the political grinding mill. Perhaps not; but such men would be absolutely helpless to exert the slightest influence in behalf of labor, as indeed has been shown in numerous instances. The State is the economic master of its servants. Good men, if such there be, would either remain true to their political faith and lose their economic support, or they would cling to their economic master and be utterly unable to do the slightest good. The political arena leaves one no alternative, one must either be a dunce or a rogue.

The political superstition is still holding sway over the hearts and minds of the masses, but the true lovers of liberty will have no more to do with it. Instead, they believe with Stirner that man has as much liberty as he is willing to take. Anarchism therefore stands for direct action, the open defiance of, and resistance to, all laws and restrictions, economic, social, and moral. But defiance and resistance are illegal. Therein lies the salvation of man. Everything illegal necessitates integrity, self-reliance, and courage. In short, it calls for free, independent spirits, for "men who are men, and who have a bone in their backs which you cannot pass your hand through."

Universal suffrage itself owes its existence to direct action. If not for the spirit of rebellion, of the defiance on the part of the American revolutionary fathers, their posterity would still wear the King's coat. If not for the direct action of a John Brown and his comrades, America would still trade in the flesh of the black man. True, the trade in white flesh is still going on; but that, too, will have to be abolished by direct action. Trade unionism, the economic arena of the modern gladiator, owes its existence to direct action. It is but recently that law and government have attempted to crush the trade union movement, and condemned the exponents of man's right to organize to prison as conspirators. Had they sought to assert their cause through begging, pleading, and compromise, trade unionism would today be a negligible quantity. In France, in Spain, in Italy, in Russia, nay even in England (witness the growing rebellion of English labor unions) direct, revolutionary, economic action has become so strong a force in the battle for industrial liberty as to make the world realize the tremendous importance of labor's power. The General Strike, the supreme expression of the economic consciousness of the workers, was ridiculed in America but a short time ago. Today every great strike, in order to win, must realize the importance of the solidaric general protest.

Direct action, having proved effective along economic lines, is equally potent in the environment of the individual. There a hundred forces encroach upon his being, and only persistent resistance to them will finally set him free. Direct action against the authority in the shop, direct action against the authority of the law, direct action against the invasive, meddlesome authority of our moral code, is the logical, consistent method of Anarchism.

Will it not lead to a revolution? Indeed, it will. No real social change has ever come about without a revolution. People are either not familiar with their history, or they have not yet learned that revolution is but thought carried into action.

Anarchism, the great leaven of thought, is today permeating every phase of human endeavor. Science, art, literature, the drama, the effort for economic betterment, in fact every individual and social opposition to the existing disorder of things, is illumined by the spiritual light of Anarchism. It is the philosophy of the sovereignty of the individual. It is the theory of social harmony. It is the great, surging, living truth that is reconstructing the world, and that will usher in the Dawn.

The Ballot or the Bullet

MALCOLM X (1925–1965), born Malcolm Little in Omaha, Nebraska, was the son of a Baptist minister who supported the teachings of the Black separatist, Marcus Garvey. Embittered by America's racism, young Malcolm also knew personal sorrow when his father was killed by a streetcar, and his mother committed to an insane asylum. He left school in the eighth grade and waited tables in Harlem, where he moved quickly into the underworld of prostitution and gambling and drew a ten-year prison sentence for burglary. Converted in prison to the Black Muslim faith of Elijah Muhammad, he was paroled in 1952. After a decade of proselytizing his new faith, he broke with Elijah Muhammad in 1963 to form his Organization for Afro-American Unity. In his autobiography (1964), certainly one of the most important books of the 1960s, he described

THE BALLOT OR THE BULLET. From *Malcolm X Speaks,* copyright © 1965 by Merit Publishers and Betty Shabazz.

his spiritual and political pilgrimage. Growing in influence, still developing his ideas, he was assassinated in 1965, allegedly by a rival faction within the Black Muslim movement.

Mr. Moderator, . . . brothers and sisters, friends and enemies: I just can't believe everyone in here is a friend and I don't want to leave anybody out. The question tonight, as I understand it, is "The Negro Revolt, and Where Do We Go From Here?" or "What Next?" In my little humble way of understanding it, it points toward either the ballot or the bullet.

.   .   .

. . . It isn't that time is running out—time has run out! 1964 threatens to be the most explosive year America has ever witnessed. The most explosive year. Why? It's also a political year. It's the year when all of the white politicians will be back in the so-called Negro community jiving you and me for some votes. The year when all of the white political crooks will be right back in your and my community with their false promises, building up our hopes for a letdown, with their trickery and their treachery, with their false promises which they don't intend to keep. As they nourish these dissatisfactions, it can only lead to one thing, an explosion; and now we have the type of black man on the scene in America today . . . who just doesn't intend to turn the other cheek any longer.

.   .   .

These 22 million victims are waking up. Their eyes are coming open. They're beginning to see what they used to only look at. They're becoming politically mature. They are realizing that there are new political trends from coast to coast. As they see these new political trends, it's possible for them to see that every time there's an election the races are so close that they have to have a recount. They had to recount in Massachusetts to see who was going to be governor, it was so close. It was the same way in Rhode Island, in Minnesota, and in many other parts of the country. And the same with Kennedy and Nixon when they ran for president. It was so close they had to count all over again. Well, what does this mean? It means that when white people are evenly divided, and black people have a bloc of votes of their own, it is left up to them to determine who's going to sit in the White House and who's going to be in the dog house.

It was the black man's vote that put the present administration in Washington, D.C. Your vote, your dumb vote, your ignorant vote, your wasted vote put in an administration in Washington, D.C., that has seen fit to pass every kind of legislation imaginable, saving you until last, then filibustering on top of that. And your and my leaders have the audacity to run around clapping their hands and talk about how much progress we're making. And what a good president we have. If he wasn't good in Texas, he sure can't be good in Washington, D.C. Because Texas is a lynch state. It is in the same breath as Mississippi, no different; only they lynch you in Texas with a Texas accent and lynch you in Mississippi with a Mississippi accent. And these Negro leaders have the audacity to go and have some coffee in the White House with a Texan, a Southern cracker—that's all he is—and then come out and tell you and me that he's going to be better for us because, since he's from the South, he knows how to deal with the Southerners. What kind of logic is that? Let Eastland be president, he's from the South too. He should be better able to deal with them than Johnson.

.   .   .

So it's time in 1964 to wake up. And when you see them coming up with that kind of conspiracy. let them know your eyes are open. And let them know you got something else that's wide open too. It's got to be the ballot or the bullet. The ballot or the bullet. If you're afraid to use an expression like that, you should get on out of the country, you should get back in the cotton patch, you should get back in the alley. They get all the Negro vote, and after they get it, the Negro gets nothing in return. All they did when they got to Washington was give a few big Negroes big jobs. Those big Negroes didn't need big jobs, they already had jobs. That's camouflage, that's trickery, that's treachery, window-dressing. I'm not trying to knock out the Democrats for the Republicans, we'll get to them in a minute. But it is true—you put the Democrats first and the Democrats put you last.

Look at it the way it is. What alibis do they use, since they control Congress and the Senate? What alibi do they use when you and I ask, "Well, when are you going to keep your promise?" They blame the Dixiecrats. What is a Dixiecrat? A Democrat. A Dixiecrat is nothing but a Democrat in disguise. The titular head of the Democrats is also the head of the Dixiecrats, because the Dixiecrats are a part of the Democratic Party. The Democrats have never kicked the Dixiecrats out of the party. The Dixiecrats bolted themselves once, but the Democrats didn't put them out. Imagine, these lowdown Southern segregationists put the Northern Democrats down. But the Northern Democrats have never put the Dixiecrats down. No, look at that thing the way it is. They have got a con game going on, a political con game, and you and I are in the middle. It's time for you and me to wake up and start looking at it like it is, and trying to understand it like it is; and then we can deal with it like it is.

The Dixiecrats in Washington, D.C., control the key committees that run the government. The only reason the Dixiecrats control these committees is because they have seniority. The only reason they have seniority is because they come from states where Negroes can't vote. This is not even a government that's based on democracy. It is not a government that is made up of representatives of the people. Half of the people in the South can't even vote. Eastland is not even supposed to be in Washington. Half of the senators and congressmen who occupy these key positions in Washington, D.C., are there illegally, are there unconstitutionally.

In the North, they do it a different way. They have a system that's known as gerrymandering, whatever that means. It means when Negroes become too heavily concentrated in a certain area, and begin to gain too much political power, the white man come along and changes the district lines. You may say, "Why do you keep saying white man?" Because it's the white man who does it. I haven't ever seen any Negro changing any lines. They don't let him get near the line. It's the white man who does this. And usually, it's the white man who grins at you the most, and pats you on the back, and is supposed to be your friend. He may be friendly, but he's not your friend.

So, what I'm trying to impress upon you, in essence, is this: You and I in America are faced not with a segregationist conspiracy, we're faced with a government conspiracy. Everyone who's filibustering is a senator—that's the government. Everyone who's finagling in Washington, D.C., is a congressman—that's the government. You don't have anybody putting blocks in your path but people who are a part of the government. The same government that you go abroad to fight for and die for is the government that is in a conspiracy to deprive you of your voting rights, deprive you of your economic opportunities, deprive you of decent housing, deprive you of decent education. You don't need to go to the employer alone, it is the government itself, the government of America, that is responsible for the oppression and exploitation and degradation of black people in this country. And you should drop it in their lap. This government has failed the Negro. This so-called democracy has failed the Negro. And all these white liberals have definitely failed the Negro.

So, where do we go from here? First, we need some friends. We need some new allies. The entire civil-rights struggle needs a new interpretation, a broader interpretation. We need to look at this civil-rights thing from another angle—from the inside as well as from the outside. To those of us whose philosophy is black nationalism, the only way you can get involved in the civil-rights struggle is give it a new interpretation. That old interpretation excluded us. It kept us out. So, we're giving a new interpretation to the civil-rights struggle, an interpretation that will enable us to come into it, take part in it. And these handkerchief-heads who have been dillydallying and pussyfooting and compromising—we don't intend to let them pussyfoot and dillydally and compromise any longer.

.   .   .

When we begin to get in this area, we need new friends, we need new allies. We need to expand the civil-rights struggle to a higher level—to the level of human rights. Whenever you are in a civil-rights struggle, whether you know it or not, you are confining yourself to the jurisdiction of Uncle Sam. No one from the outside world can speak out in your behalf as long as your struggle is a civil-rights struggle. Civil rights comes within the domestic affairs of this country. All of our African brothers and our Asian brothers and our Latin-American brothers cannot open their mouths and interfere in the domestic affairs of the United States. And as long as it's civil rights, this comes under the jurisdiction of Uncle Sam.

But the United Nations has what's known as the charter of human rights, it has a committee that deals in human rights. You may wonder why all of the atrocities that have been committed in Africa and in Hungary and in Asia and in Latin America are brought before the UN, and the Negro problem is never brought before the UN. This is part of the conspiracy. This old, tricky, blue-eyed liberal who is supposed to be your and my friend, supposed to be in our corner, supposed to be subsidizing our struggle, and supposed to be acting in the capacity of an adviser, never tells you anything about human rights. They keep you wrapped up in civil rights. And you spend so much time barking up the civil-rights tree, you don't even know there's a human-rights tree on the same floor.

When you expand the civil-rights struggle to the level of human rights, you can then take the case of the black man in this country before the nations in the UN. You can take it before the General Assembly. You can take Uncle Sam before a world court. But the only level you can do it on is the level of human rights. Civil rights keeps you under his restrictions, under his jurisdiction. Civil rights keeps you in his pocket. Civil rights means you're asking Uncle Sam to treat you right. Human rights are something you were born with. Human rights are your God-given rights. Human rights are the rights that are recognized by all nations of this earth. And any time any one violates your human rights, you can take them to the world court. Uncle Sam's hands are dripping with blood, dripping with the blood of the black man in this country. He's the earth's number-one hypocrite. He has the audacity—yes, he has—imagine him posing as the leader of the free world. The free world!—and you over here singing "We Shall Overcome." Expand the civil-rights struggle to the level of human rights, take it into the United Nations, where our African brothers can throw their weight on our side, where our Asian brothers can throw their weight on our side, where our Latin-American brothers can throw their weight on our side, and where 800 million Chinamen are sitting there waiting to throw their weight on our side.

Let the world know how bloody his hands are. Let the world know the hypocrisy that's practiced over here. Let it be the ballot or the bullet. Let him know that it must be the ballot or the bullet.

. . .

By ballot I only mean freedom. Don't you know . . . that the ballot is more important than the dollar? Can I prove it? Yes. Look in the UN. There are poor nations in the UN; yet those poor nations can get together with their voting power and keep the rich nations from making a move. They have one nation—one vote, everyone has an equal vote. And when those brothers from Asia, and Africa and the darker parts of this earth get together, their voting power is sufficient to hold Sam in check. Or Russia in check. Or some other section of the earth in check. So, the ballot is most important.

Right now, in this country, if you and I, 22 million African-Americans—that's what we are—Africans who are in America. You're nothing but Africans. Nothing but Africans. In fact, you'd get farther calling yourself African instead of Negro. Africans don't catch hell. You're the only one catching hell. They don't have to pass civil-rights bills for Africans. An African can go anywhere he wants right now. All you've got to do is tie your head up. That's right, go anywhere you want. Just stop being a Negro. Change your name to Hoogagagooba. That'll show you how silly the white man is. You're dealing with a silly man. A friend of mine who's very dark put a turban on his head and went into a restaurant in Atlanta before they called themselves desegregated. He went into a white restaurant, he sat down, they served him, and he said, "What would happen if a Negro came in here?" And there he's sitting, black as night, but because he had his head wrapped up the waitress looked back at him and says, "Why, there wouldn't no nigger dare come in here."

So, you're dealing with a man whose bias and prejudice are making him lose his mind, his intelligence, every day. He's frightened. He looks around and sees what's taking place on this earth, and he sees that the pendulum of time is swinging in your direction. The dark people are waking up. They're losing their fear of the white man. No place where he's fighting right now is he winning. Everywhere he's fighting, he's fighting someone your and my complexion. And they're beating him. He can't win any more. He's won his last battle. He failed to win the Korean War. He couldn't win it. He had to sign a truce. That's a loss. Any time Uncle Sam, with all his machinery for warfare, is held to a draw by some rice-eaters, he's lost the battle. He had to sign a truce. America's not supposed to sign a truce. She's supposed to be bad. But she's not bad any more. She's bad as long as she can use her hydrogen bomb, but she can't use hers for fear Russia might use hers. Russia can't use hers, for fear that Sam might use his. So, both of them are weaponless. They can't use the weapon because each's weapon nullifies the other's. So the only place where action can take place is on the ground. And the white man can't win another war fighting on the ground. Those days are over. The black man knows it, the brown man knows it, the red man knows it, and the yellow man knows it. So they engage him in guerrilla warfare. That's not his style. You've got to have heart to be a guerrilla warrior, and he hasn't got any heart. I'm telling you now.

I just want to give you a little briefing on guerrilla warfare because, before you know it, before you know it—It takes heart to be a guerrilla warrior because you're on your own. In conventional warfare you have tanks and a whole lot of other people with you to back you up, planes over your head and all that kind of stuff. But a guerrilla is on his own. All you have is a rifle, some sneakers and a bowl of rice, and that's all you need—and a lot of heart. The Japanese on some of those islands in the Pacific, when the American soldiers landed, one Japanese sometimes could hold the whole army off. He'd just wait until the sun went down, and when the sun went down they were all equal. He would take his little blade and slip from bush to bush, and from American to American. The white soldiers couldn't cope with that. Whenever you see a white soldier that fought in the Pacific, he has the shakes, he has a nervous condition, because they scared him to death.

The same thing happened to the French up in French Indochina. People who just a few years previously were rice farmers got together and ran the heavily-mechanized French army out of Indochina. You don't need it—modern warfare today won't work. This is the day of the guerrilla. They did the same thing in Algeria. Algerians, who were nothing but Bedouins, took a rifle and sneaked off to the hills, and de Gaulle and all of his highfalutin' war machinery couldn't defeat those guerrillas. Nowhere on this earth does the white man win in a guerrilla warfare. It's not his speed. Just as guerrilla warfare is prevailing in Asia and in parts of Africa and in parts of Latin America, you've got to be mighty naive, or you've got to play the black man cheap, if you don't think some day he's going to wake up and find that it's got to be the ballot or the bullet.

.   .   .

Our gospel is black nationalism. We're not trying to threaten the existence of any organization, but we're spreading the gospel of black nationalism. Anywhere there's a church that is also preaching and practicing the gospel of black nationalism, join that church. If the

NAACP is preaching and practicing the gospel of black nationalism, join the NAACP. If CORE is spreading and practicing the gospel of black nationalism, join CORE. Join any organization that has a gospel that's for the uplift of the black man. And when you get into it and see them pussyfooting or compromising, pull out of it because that's not black nationalism. We'll find another one.

And in this manner, the organizations will increase in number and in quantity and in quality, and by August, it is then our intention to have a black nationalist convention which will consist of delegates from all over the country who are interested in the political, economic and social philosophy of black nationalism. After these delegates convene, we will hold a seminar, we will hold discussions, we will listen to everyone. We want to hear new ideas and new solutions and new answers. And at that time, if we see fit then to form a black nationalist party, we'll form a black nationalist party. If it's necessary to form a black nationalist army, we'll form a black nationalist army. It'll be the ballot or the bullet. It'll be liberty or it'll be death.

It's time for you and me to stop sitting in this country, letting some cracker senators, Northern crackers and Southern crackers, sit there in Washington, D.C., and come to a conclusion in their mind that you and I are supposed to have civil rights. There's no white man going to tell me anything about *my* rights. Brother and sisters, always remember, if it doesn't take senators and congressmen and presidential proclamations to give freedom to the white man, it is not necessary for legislation or proclamation or Supreme Court decisions to give freedom to the black man. You let that white man know, if this is a country of freedom, let it be a country of freedom; and if it's not a country of freedom, change it.

We will work with anybody, anywhere, at any time, who is genuinely interested in tackling the problem head-on, nonviolently as long as the enemy is nonviolent, but violent when the enemy gets violent.

.   .   .

Last but not least, I must say this concerning the great controversy over rifles and shotguns. The only thing that I've ever said is that in areas where the government has proven itself either unwilling or unable to defend the lives and the property of Negroes, it's time for Negroes to defend themselves. Article number two of the constitutional amendments provides you and me the right to own a rifle or a shotgun. It is constitutionally legal to own a shotgun or a rifle. This doesn't mean you're going to get a rifle and form battalions and go out looking for white folks, although you'd be within your rights—I mean, you'd be justified; but that would be illegal and we don't do anything illegal. If the white man doesn't want the black man buying rifles and shotguns, then let the government do its job. That's all. And don't let the white man come to you and ask you what you think about what Malcolm says—why, you old Uncle Tom. He would never ask you if he thought you were going to say, "Oh, man!" No, he is making a Tom out of you.

So, this doesn't mean forming rifle clubs and going out looking for people, but it is time, in 1964, if you are a man, to let that man know. If he's not going to do his job in running the government and providing you and me with the protection that our taxes are supposed to be for, since he spends all those billions for his defense budget, he certainly can't begrudge you and me spending $12 or $15 for a single-shot, or double-action. I hope you understand. Don't go out shooting people, but any time, brothers and sisters, and especially the men in this audience—some of you wearing Congressional Medals of Honor, with shoulders this wide, chests this big, muscles that big—any time you and I sit around and read where they bomb a church and murder in cold blood, not some grownups, but four little girls while they were praying . . .

Why, this man—he can find Eichmann hiding down in Argentina somewhere. Let two or three American soldiers, who are minding somebody else's business way over in South Vietnam, get killed, and he'll send battleships, sticking his nose in their business. He wanted to send troops down to Cuba and make them have what he calls free elections —this old cracker who doesn't have free elections in his own country. No, if you never see me another time in your life, if I die in the morning, I'll die saying one thing: the ballot or the bullet, the ballot or the bullet.

If a Negro in 1964 has to sit around and wait for some cracker senator to filibuster when it comes to the rights of black people, why, you and I should hang our heads in shame. You talk about a march on Washington in 1963, you haven't seen anything. There's some more going down in '64. And this time they're not going like they went last year. They're not going singing "We Shall Overcome." They're not going with white friends. They're not going with placards already painted for them. They're not going with round-trip tickets. They're going with one-way tickets.

And if they don't want that non-nonviolent army going down there, tell them to bring the filibuster to a halt. The black nationalists aren't going to wait. Lyndon B. Johnson is the head of the Democratic Party. If he's for civil rights, let him go into the Senate next week and declare himself. Let him go in there right now and declare himself. Let him go in there and denounce the Southern branch of his party. Let him go in there right now and take a moral stand—right now, not later. Tell him, don't wait until election time. If he waits too long, brothers and sisters, he will be responsible for letting a condition develop in this country which will create a climate that will bring seeds up out of the ground with vegetation on the end of them looking like something these people never dreamed of. In 1964, it's the ballot or the bullet. Thank you.

The Third Man Emerges

Common Sense, in which the following article by Fred Farrel appeared, is a "Christian" journal dedicated to fighting "Communist Internationalism." Founded in 1946, it has condemned the United Nations, the Civil Rights Movements, and America's entry into the Second World War, a move that "put Stalin in the saddle." Defending the Third Reich, recent issues advertise Swastika armbands and such pamphlets as "The Myth of the Six Million," a refutation of the charge that Hitler's Germany massacred millions of Jews. A self-proclaimed champion of the "common man," the journal attacks both liberalism and conservatism, as these terms are ordinarily used.

It Happened in Germany—It Will Happen in the U.S.A.

The third man will taste fruits of victory because he'll refuse to take position assigned him by International Jews

We really ought to give up reading the NEW YORK TIMES Book Review Section. It raises our blood pressure to a dangerous level; not because it always tells lies, although it sometimes does. Our blood pressure rises to the most dangerous peaks when they tell the truth. In the June 21, 1970 issue, in a review of John Updike's novel BECH: A BOOK, the reviewer Thomas E. Edwards tossed off this gem: "For Gentile Middle America, now that it has so thoroughly given up its own traditions and manners, Jewishness seems more and more the

THE THIRD MAN EMERGES. By Fred Farrel. From *Common Sense* (August 1970).

repository of the experienced, skeptical wisdom it needs to understand itself."

Unhappily, this is true. Middle America has indeed thrown its own traditions to the four winds. Middle America gallops in sheeplike herds after so-called leaders like Robert Welch, Barry Goldwater, Richard M. Nixon and Spiro T. Agnew. The Jews manipulate Middle America with the greatest of ease. The Jews have thoroughly subjugated and completely destroyed the Old America. It no longer exists. It is even beyond mourning. There are, however, still a certain number of us Old Americans who yearn madly at least to punish the culprits who brought about our National downfall.

WHO ARE THE CULPRITS?

The culprits are mainly the American "Conservatives." People are constantly telling us that this or that great, bloated, phoney gasbag is a "GREAT CONSERVATIVE GENTLEMAN" or a "TRUE PATRIOT" or a "SINCERE ANTI-COMMUNIST." We are called upon to adore these gasbags and bores who lost our country to the Jews, who failed to provide really dynamic and effective political leadership, who allowed our culture to sink under Jewish control, who brayed like jackasses while America fell. They are like Nero, who played his fiddle while Rome burned.

The primary problem of contemporary history is not to seek a victory for the "Right Wing" or the "Left Wing" but to DESTROY the entire Right-Left System. The Right-Left system is the Rothschild Bank intellectual invention by means of which the Jews control much of the world. This system WILL BE DESTROYED in one way or another. If it is not destroyed by voluntary penitence and intellectual reconstruction, it will be destroyed in the violence of World War III, for War is the necessary outcome of it. The entire Right-Left orientation of political thought has become intolerable and must go.

We are now seeing the emergence into the world of THE THIRD MAN, the man who will refuse to do business either with the Right or Left Wing, but will insist absolutely upon the DESTRUCTION of these two obsolete political forms. The THIRD MAN has already had his preview in history; he was the man who emerged to power in the Third Reich; but he is not necessarily a German. He refuses to be entrapped in the asinine Right-Left orbit of thought. He has reached intellectual escape velocity and goes out to establish a new orbit of his own. Naturally, this alarms the pseudo-leaders of both the Right Wing and the Left Wing. It annoys the silly rabble of Liberal professors at Harvard. It annoys all of the politically impotent dotards of the American Establishment. Above all else, it drives the Jews to a fine frenzy. They have built a better mousetrap in which to catch the whole human race; now they see the whole thing being undone. The Jews do not remotely begin to understand what is going on. They see the THIRD MAN in action; instinctively, they try to shove him into either the Right Wing or the Left Wing. The Jews do not care whether you are on the Left or the Right, since they run both sides anyway. They see all the nice, vapid, politically obsolete and impotent chappies like Billy Buckley and Robert Welch revolving obediently in the Right Wing orbits which have been assigned to them by the Jews, while others obediently revolve in the Left Wing orbit. The Jewish intellectual planetary system seems to be functioning well. Then suddenly something goes wrong.

The THIRD MAN has made the scene.

When the Jews contemptuously tell THE THIRD MAN to get into orbit on the Right or the Left, he spits into the Jew's face. He flings down the gauntlet. He says, "Come, Little Jew! You and I are going to FIGHT." When THE THIRD MAN says "Fight" he means "FIGHT" and he does not mean something else. He means fight with BLOOD AND IRON. He means to wage total and ruthless warfare against the Right-Left system which is the backbone of Jewish power. In the future YOU are not going to be on either the Right or the Left; trying to occupy either of these political positions will be like trying to live in a house which has burned to ashes, it just isn't there anymore and you can't live in it, no matter how much you may have admired it in former times. Just so, there will be no Right and Left wings in politics. There will be only the cold intellectual ashes where these positions used to be.

THE THIRD MAN who is neither Right nor Left is the political creature of the future. He will not wear Swastica armbands, because he is not a copycat; he is quite capable of inventing his own insignia; but he is a Nazi at heart nevertheless. The Nazi is Twentieth Century political man fully developed. The Jew is an obsolete Nineteenth Century creature who simply needs to be removed from the world scene. Nobody knows this better than the Jews themselves. Suicidalism is the collective outlook of the American Jewish community today. THE THIRD MAN will be glad to help the Jews commit suicide. He thinks that the world would be a better and cleaner place without them. Since they have become insanely self-destructive, why not let them go ahead and hang themselves? As they are now firmly in control of the destinies of our Republic, it may be that they will also carry the United States to destruction with them. They quite certainly will if they remain in power. Under Jewish rule, this Republic will not possibly last more than another twenty-five years, and perhaps not that long.

Do you want to survive? Then stop chasing futile pseudo-leaders like Welch, Buckley and Hargis. If you are going to survive, you must reach ESCAPE VELOCITY and get out of the Jewish Right-Left orbit completely. The Right Wing will never save you. The Right Wing leaders will never do anything except bray like jackasses, whirl like dervishes, and scream like banshees, and in the end sell themselves like street corner whores to the Jews, as most of them have already done. They say that they are "Fighting Communism" or that they are "Upholding God and Country." When we subject them to a critical analysis, we see that they are doing absolutely nothing to implement any kind of effective political program whatsoever. They merely SAY that they are doing something, when in fact they are doing nothing. The Right Wing is firmly in the grip of a DEATH WISH. Time and again, I have seen idealistic young Americans get into these phoney Right Wing movements, hoping to accomplish something solid and real. They learn quickly that the Lord High Nabobs of the Right quickly extinguish any spark of real intelligence or effectiveness which flares in their ranks. They see that the Right, far from actually fighting Communism, secretly collaborates with Communism.

.   .   .

Thus the NEW YORK TIMES Book Review Section can boast, "The novelists who have been Updike's major competition have effectively made interior Jews of a generation of Goy leaders." The Conservative publishers sat on their hands while stupid and corrupt Jewish hack writers Judaized the nation. When they published any books at all, they published trash about how nice it would be to return to the good old Nineteenth Century. Conservative publishing of the last twenty-five years is merely the tombstone of the old American culture; it contributes nothing to any aspect of life. We have looked to the American Right for bold, decisive leadership and have heard nothing but the braying of jackasses. The Right Wing sat on its hands while the Jews took over our literature, our culture, our economy, our government. Then they demand that we approach them worshipfully and praise the great battle which they claim to be fighting. They are fighting no battle. They could not fight their way out of a paper bag. We are told that they are "Fine Christian Gentlemen." Immediately we wonder how these "Fine Christian Gentlemen" will look as they go sailing through the stratosphere atop the great mushroom clouds of World War III, along with their Jewish friends. We hope indeed that St. Peter will open the gates of heaven for them, because they are clearly finished on earth.

THE THIRD MAN is the legitimate heir, the man of tomorrow. He has no use for the old Right-Left Age. He belongs to the age which is coming, not to the age which is passing away. He will refuse to be shoved into the Right-Left orbit. He has his own position, and, like smokers of Tareyton cigarettes, would rather fight than switch. If these quaint old Nineteenth Century relics of the Jewish Right and Left are looking for a fight, THE THIRD MAN is the man who will fight them, and lick them too. You aren't going to be on either the Right or the Left in the future, because the THIRD MAN will demolish these two positions in order to make room for his own new creation; this is the only thing the THIRD MAN cares about. The Right and the Left are obsolete relics of a dead age; the only problem is to demolish them and remove them from the historical scene. There can be no question of investing any sane hopes in them.

The issue is clearly defined in the last paragraph of Oswald Spengler's THE HOUR OF DECISION: "Here possibly in our own century, the ultimate decisions are waiting for their man. In presence of these the little aims and notions of our current politics sink to nothing. He whose sword compels victory here will be lord of the world. The dice are there ready for this stupendous game. Who dares throw them?"

Yes, indeed, who dares to pick up the dice and throw them? Certainly not the Right Wing, and not the Left Wing, either. THE THIRD MAN is the man who will ACT, the man who will pick up the dice and throw them. Naturally he seems an utterly obscene creature to the sorry pack of dotards of the Right and the Left. He is going to ACT, he really is going to DO something! How utterly vulgar! Everyone who is a proper Rightist or Leftist knows that the first rule of the Right-Left game is never actually to DO anything, but always to stick to good, safe gasbaggery. THE THIRD MAN will destroy and displace this shiftless and futile rabble completely. The sooner the better.

You Don't Need a Weatherman to Know Which Way the Wind Blows

MARK RUDD (1947–   ), chairman of the Columbia University chapter of the Students for a Democratic Society, played a key role in the crisis that disrupted that university in April 1968. Collaborating with other leaders in that organization he later penned the

YOU DON'T NEED A WEATHERMAN TO KNOW WHICH WAY THE WIND BLOWS. By Mark Rudd et al. Originally published in *New Left Notes*, June 18, 1969.

following manifesto, the initial declaration of the "Weathermen," a splinter group of SDS that gained national attention for its violent tactics during the Democratic political convention in the fall of 1968. In July 1970, Rudd, already a fugitive from federal authorities, was indicted with twelve others (including several co-authors of this manifesto), for conspiracy to bomb and kill.

International Revolution

People ask, what is the nature of the revolution that we talk about? Who will it be made by, and for, and what are its goals and strategy?

The overriding consideration in answering these questions is that the main struggle going on in the world today is between US imperialism and the national liberation struggles against it. This is essential in defining political matters in the whole world: because it is by far the most powerful, every other empire and petty dictator is in the long run dependent on US imperialism, which has unified, allied with, and defended all of the reactionary forces of the whole world. Thus, in considering every other force or phenomenon, from Soviet imperialism or Israeli imperialism to "workers struggle" in France or Czechoslovakia, we determine who are our friends and who are our enemies according to whether they help US imperialism or fight to defeat it.

So the very first question people in this country must ask in considering the question of revolution is where they stand in relation to the United States as an oppressor nation, and where they stand in relation to the masses of people throughout the world whom US imperialism is oppressing.

The primary task of revolutionary struggle is to solve this principal contradiction on the side of the people of the world. It is the oppressed peoples of the world who have created the wealth of this empire and it is to them that it belongs; the goal of the revolutionary struggle must be the control and use of this wealth in the interests of the oppressed peoples of the world.

It is in this context that we must examine the revolutionary struggles in the United States. We are within the heartland of a worldwide monster, a country so rich from its world-wide plunder that even the crumbs doled out to the enslaved masses within its borders provide for material existence very much above the conditions of the masses of people of the world. The US empire, as a world-wide system, channels wealth, based upon the labor and resources of the rest of the world, into the United States. The relative affluence existing in the United States is directly dependent upon the labor and natural resources of the

Vietnamese, the Angolans, the Bolivians and the rest of the peoples of the Third World. All of the United Airlines Astrojets, all of the Holiday Inns, all of Hertz's automobiles, your television set, car and wardrobe already belong, to a large degree, to the people of the rest of the world.

Therefore, any conception of "socialist revolution" simply in terms of the working people of the United States, failing to recognize the full scope of interests of the most oppressed peoples of the world, is a conception of a fight for a particular privileged interest, and is a very dangerous ideology. While the control and use of the wealth of the Empire for the people of the whole world is also in the interests of the vast majority of the people in this country, if the goal is not clear from the start we will further the preservation of class society, oppression, war, genocide, and the complete emiseration of everyone, including the people of the US.

The goal is the destruction of US imperialism and the achievement of a classless world: world communism. Winning state power in the US will occur as a result of the military forces of the US overextending themselves around the world and being defeated piecemeal; struggle within the US will be a vital part of this process, but when the revolution triumphs in the US it will have been made by the people of the whole world. For socialism to be defined in national terms within so extreme and historical an oppressor nation as this is only imperialist national chauvinism on the part of the "movement."

.   .   .

International Strategy and the Black Vanguard

What is the strategy of this international revolutionary movement? What are the strategic weaknesses of the imperialists which make it possible for us to win? . . . The strategy . . . is what Che called "creating two, three, many Vietnams"—to mobilize the struggle so sharply in so many places that the imperialists cannot possibly deal with it all. Since it is essential to their interests, they will try to deal with it all, and will be defeated and destroyed in the process.

In defining and implementing this strategy, it is clear that the vanguard (that is, the section of the people who are in the forefront of the struggle and whose class interests and needs define the terms and tasks of the revolution) of the "American Revolution" is the workers and oppressed peoples of the colonies of Asia, Africa and Latin America. Because of the level of special oppression of black people as a colony they reflect the interests of the oppressed people of the world from within the borders of the United States; they are part of the Third World and part of the international revolutionary vanguard.

The vanguard role of the Vietnamese and other Third World countries in defeating US imperialism has been clear to our movement for some time. What has not been so clear is the vanguard role black people have played, and continue to play, in the development of revolutionary consciousness and struggle within the United States. Criticisms of the black liberation struggle as being "reactionary" or of black organizations on campus as being conservative or "racist" very often express this lack of understanding. These ideas are incorrect and must be defeated if a revolutionary movement is going to be built among whites.

The black colony, due to its particular nature as a slave colony, never adopted a chauvinist identification with America as an imperialist power, either politically or culturally. Moreover, the history of black people in America has consistently been one of the greatest overall repudiation of and struggle against the state. . . . Therefore it is no surprise that time and again, in both political content and level of consciousness and militancy, it has been the black liberation movement which has upped the ante and defined the terms of the struggle.

What is the relationship of this "black vanguard" to the "many Vietnams" around the world? Obviously this is an example of our strategy that different fronts reinforce each other. The fact that the Vietnamese are winning weakens the enemy, advancing the possibilities for the black struggle, etc. But it is important for us to understand that the interrelationship is more than this. Black people do not simply "choose" to intensify their struggle because they want to help the Vietnamese, or because they see that Vietnam heightens the possibilities for struggle here. The existence of any one Vietnam, especially a winning one, spurs on others not only through consciousness and choice, but through need, because it is a political and economic, as well as military, weakening of capitalism, and this means that to compensate, the imperialists are forced to intensify their oppression of other people.

. . .

Why a Revolutionary Youth Movement?

. . . most young people in the US are part of the working class. Although not yet employed, young people whose parents sell their labor power for wages, and more important who themselves expect to do the same in the future—or go into the army or be unemployed—are undeniably members of the working class. Most kids are well aware of what class they are in, even though they may not be very scientific about it. So our analysis assumes from the beginning that youth struggles are, by and large, working class struggles. But why the focus now on the struggles of working class youth rather than on the working class as a whole?

The potential for revolutionary consciousness does not always correspond to ultimate class interest, particularly when imperialism is relatively prosperous and the movement is in an early stage. At this stage we see working class youth as those most open to a revolutionary movement which sides with the struggles of Third World people: the following is an attempt to explain a strategic focus on youth for SDS.

In general, young people have less stake in a society (no family, fewer debts, etc.), are more open to new ideas (they have not been brainwashed for so long or so well), and are therefore more able and willing to move in a revolutionary direction. Specifically in America, young people have grown up experiencing the crises in imperialism. They have grown up along with a developing black liberation movement, with the liberation of Cuba, the fights for independence in Africa, and the war in Vietnam. Older people grew up during the fight against Fascism, during the cold war, the smashing of the trade unions, McCarthy, and a period during which real wages consistently rose—since 1965 disposable real income has decreased slightly, particularly in urban areas where inflation and increased taxation have bitten heavily into wages. This crisis in imperialism affects all parts of the society. America has had to militarize to protect and expand its Empire; hence the high draft calls and the creation of a standing army of three and a half million, an army which still has been unable to win in Vietnam. Further, the huge defense expenditures—required for the defense of the empire and at the same time a way of making increasing profits for the defense industries—have gone hand in hand with the urban crisis around welfare, the hospitals, the schools, housing, air, and water pollution. The State cannot provide the services it has been forced to assume responsibility for, and needs to increase taxes and to pay its growing debts while it cuts services and uses the pigs to repress protest. The private sector of the economy can't provide jobs, particularly unskilled jobs. The expansion of the defense and education industries by the State since World War II is in part an attempt to pick up the slack, though the inability to provide decent wages and working conditions for "public" jobs is more and more a problem.

As imperialism struggles to hold together this decaying social fabric, it inevitably resorts to brute force and authoritarian ideology. People, especially young people, more and more find themselves in the iron grip of authoritarian institutions. Reaction against the pigs or teachers in the schools, welfare pigs or the army is generalizable and extends beyond the particular repressive institution to the society and the State as a whole. The legitimacy of the State is called into question for the first time in at least 30 years, and the anti-authoritarianism which characterizes the youth rebellion turns into rejection of the State, a refusal to be socialized into American society. Kids used to try to beat the system from inside the army or from inside the schools; now they desert from the army and burn down the schools.

The crisis in imperialism has brought about a breakdown in bourgeois social forms, culture and ideology. The family falls apart, kids leave home, women begin to break out of traditional "female" and "mother" roles. There develops a "generation gap" and a "youth problem." Our heroes are no longer struggling businessmen, and we also begin to reject the ideal career of the professional and look to Mao, Che, the Panthers, the Third World, for our models, for motion. We reject the elitist, technocratic bullshit that tells us only experts can rule, and look instead to leadership from the people's war of the Vietnamese. Chuck Berry, Elvis, the Temptations brought us closer to the "people's culture" of Black America. The racist response to the civil rights movement revealed the depth of racism in America, as well as the impossibility of real change through American institutions. And the war against Vietnam is not "the heroic war against the Nazis"; it's the big lie, with napalm burning through everything we had heard this country stood for. Kids begin to ask questions: Where is the Free World? And who do the pigs protect at home?

. . .

The RYM and the Pigs

A major focus in our neighborhood and city-wide work is the pigs, because they tie together the various struggles around the state as the enemy, and thus point to the need for a movement oriented toward power to defeat it.

The pigs are the capitalist state, and as such define the limits of all political struggles; to the extent that a revolutionary struggle shows signs of success, they come in and mark the point it can't go beyond. In the early stages of struggle, the ruling class lets parents come down on high school kids, or jocks attack college chapters. When the struggle escalates the pigs come in; at Columbia, the left was afraid its struggle would be co-opted to anti-police brutality, cops off campus, and said pigs weren't the issue. But pigs really are the issue and people will understand this, one way or another. They can have a liberal understanding that pigs are sweaty working-class barbarians who over-react and commit "police brutality" and so shouldn't be on campus. Or they can understand pigs as the repressive imperialist state doing its job. Our job is not to avoid the issue of the pigs as "diverting" from anti-imperialist struggle, but to emphasize that they are our real enemy if we fight that struggle to win.

Even when there is no organized political struggle, the pigs come down on people in everyday life in enforcing capitalist property relations, bourgeois laws, and bourgeois morality; they guard stores and factories and the rich and enforce credit and rent against the poor. The overwhelming majority of arrests in America are for crimes against property. The pigs will be coming down on the kids we're working with in the schools, on the streets, around dope; we should focus on them; point them out all the time, like the Panthers do. We should relate the daily oppression by the pig to their role in political repression, and develop a class understanding of political power and armed force among the kids we're with.

As we develop a base these two aspects of the pig role increasingly come together. In the schools, pig is part of daily oppression—keeping order in halls and lunch rooms, controlling smoking—while at the same time pigs prevent kids from handing out leaflets, and bust "outside agitators." The presence of youth, or youth with long hair, becomes defined as organized political struggle and the pigs react to it as such. More and more every-day activity is politically threatening, so pigs are suddenly more in evidence; this in turn generates political organization and opposition, and so on. Our task will be to catalyze this development, pushing out the conflict with the pig so as to define every struggle—schools (pigs out, pig institutes out), welfare (invading pig-protected office), the streets (curfew and turf fights)—as a struggle against the needs of capitalism and the force of the state.

Pigs don't represent state power as an abstract principle; they are a power that we will have to overcome in the course of struggle or become irrelevant, revisionist, or dead. We must prepare concretely to meet their power because our job is to defeat the pigs and the army, and organize on that basis. Our beginnings should stress self-defense—building defense groups around karate classes, learning how to move on the street and around the neighborhood, medical training, popularizing and moving toward (according to necessity) armed self-defense, all the time honoring and putting forth the principle that "political power comes out of the barrel of a gun." These self-defense groups would initiate pig surveillance patrols, visits to the pig station and courts when someone is busted, etc.

Obviously the issues around the pig will not come down by neighborhood alone; it will take at least city-wide groups able to coordinate activities against a unified enemy—in the early stages, for legal and bail resources and turning people out for demonstrations, adding the power of the city-wide movement to what may be initially only a tenuous base in a neighborhood. Struggles in one part of the city will not only provide lessons for but materially aid similar motion in the rest of it.

Thus the pigs are ultimately the glue—the necessity—that holds the neighborhood-based and city-wide movement together; all of our concrete needs lead to pushing the pigs to the fore as a political focus:

(1) making institutionally oriented reform struggles deal with state power, by pushing out struggle till either winning or getting pigged.

(2) using the city-wide inter-relation of fights to raise the level of struggle and further large-scale anti-pig movement-power consciousness.

(3) developing spontaneous anti-pig consciousness in our neighborhoods to an understanding of imperialism, class struggle and the state.

(4) and using the city-wide movement as a platform for reinforcing and extending this politicization work, like by talking about getting together a city-wide neighborhood-based mutual aid anti-pig self-defense network.

All of this can be done through city-wide agitation and propaganda and picking certain issues—to have as the central regional focus for the whole movement.

Repression and Revolution

As institutional fights and anti-pig self-defense off of them intensify, so will the ruling class's repression. Their escalation of repression will inevitably continue according to how threatening the movement is to their power. Our task is not to avoid or end repression; that can always be done by pulling back, so we're not dangerous enough to require crushing. Sometimes it is correct to do that as a tactical retreat, to survive to fight again.

To defeat repression, however, is not to stop it but to go on building the movement to be more dangerous to them; in which case, defeated at one level, repression will escalate even more. To succeed in defending the movement, and not just ourselves at its expense, we will have to successively meet and overcome these greater and greater levels of repression.

.   .   .

The Need for a Revolutionary Party

The RYM must also lead to the effective organization needed to survive and to create another battlefield of the revolution. A revolution is a war; when the movement in this country can defend itself militarily against total repression it will be part of the revolutionary war.

This will require a cadre organization, effective secrecy, self-reliance among the cadres, and an integrated relationship with the active mass-based movement. To win a war with an enemy as highly organized and centralized as the imperialists will require a (clandestine) organization of revolutionaries, having also a unified "general staff"; that is, combined at some point with discipline under one centralized leadership. Because war is political, political tasks—the international communist revolution—must guide it. Therefore the centralized organization of revolutionaries must be a political organization as well as military, what is generally called a "Marxist-Leninist" party.

How will we accomplish the building of this kind of organization? It is clear that we couldn't somehow form such a party at this time, because the conditions for it do not exist in this country outside the black nation. What are these conditions?

One is that to have a unified centralized organization it is necessary to have a common revolutionary theory which explains, at least generally, the nature of our revolutionary tasks and how to accomplish them. It must be a set of ideas which have been tested and developed in the practice of resolving the important contradictions in our work.

A second condition is the existence of revolutionary leadership tested in practice. To have a centralized party under illegal and repressive conditions requires a centralized leadership, specific individuals with the understanding and the ability to unify and guide the movement in the face of new problems and be right most of the time.

Thirdly, and most important, there must be the same revolutionary mass base mentioned earlier, or (better) revolutionary mass movement. It is clear that without this there can't be the practical experience to know whether or not a theory, or a leader, is any good at all. Without practical revolutionary activity on a mass scale the party could not test and develop new ideas and draw conclusions with enough surety behind them to consistently base its survival on them. Especially, no revolutionary party could possibly survive without relying on the active support and participation of masses of people.

These conditions for the development of a revolutionary party in this country are the main "conditions" for winning. There are two kinds of tasks for us.

One is the organization of revolutionary collectives within the movement. Our theory must come from practice, but it can't be developed in isolation. Only a collective pooling of our experiences can develop a thorough understanding of the complex conditions in this country. In the same way, only our collective efforts toward a common plan can adequately test the ideas we develop. The development of revolutionary Marxist-Leninist-Maoist collective formations which undertake this concrete evaluation and application of the lessons of our work is not just the task of specialists or leaders, but the responsibility of every revolutionary. Just as a collective is necessary to sum up experiences and apply them locally, equally the collective inter-relationship of groups all over the country is necessary to get an accurate view of the whole movement and to apply that in the whole country. Over time, those collectives which prove themselves in practice to have the correct understanding (by the results they get) will contribute toward the creation of a unified revolutionary party.

The most important task for us toward making the revolution, and the work our collectives should engage in, is the creation of a mass revolutionary movement, without which a clandestine revolutionary party will be impossible. A revolutionary mass movement is different from the traditional revisionist mass base of "sympathizers." Rather it is akin to the Red Guard in China, based on the full participation and involvement of masses of people in the practice of making revolution; a movement with a full willingness to participate in the violent and illegal struggle. It is a movement diametrically opposed to the elitist idea that only leaders are smart enough or interested enough to accept full revolutionary conclusions. It is a movement built on the basis of faith in the masses of people.

The task of collectives is to create this kind of movement. (The party is not a substitute for it, and in fact is totally dependent on it.) This will be done at this stage principally among youth, through implementing the Revolutionary Youth Movement strategy discussed in this paper. It is practice at this, and not political "teachings" in the abstract, which will determine the relevance of the political collectives which are formed.

The strategy of the RYM for developing an active mass base, tying the city-wide fights to community and city-wide anti-pig movement, and for building a party eventually out of this motion, fits with the world strategy for winning the revolution, builds a movement oriented toward power, and will become one division of the International Liberation Army, while its battlefields are added to the many Vietnams which will dismember and dispose of US imperialism. Long Live the Victory of People's War!

Rebels Without a Program

GEORGE F. KENNAN (1904–   ), like George Bancroft a distinguished diplomatist and historian, was born in Milwaukee, Wiscon-

REBELS WITHOUT A PROGRAM. From *Democracy and the Student Left* by George F. Kennan, by permission of Atlantic—Little, Brown and Co. Copyright © 1968 by George F. Kennan.

sin. Graduating from Princeton in 1925, he served with the State
Department in a variety of posts from 1926 to the 1960s. Author of a
popular study of **American Diplomacy** (1951), he has written several
volumes on the relations of the West with Russia, where he served
as ambassador. "Rebels Without a Program," delivered to an undergraduate audience at Swarthmore College, is printed with the many
replies and rebuttals it attracted in **Democracy and the Student
Left** (1968).

. . . The world seems to be full, today, of embattled students. The
public prints are seldom devoid of the record of their activities. Photographs of them may be seen daily: screaming, throwing stones,
breaking windows, overturning cars, being beaten or dragged about
by police and, in the case of those on other continents, burning libraries. That these people are embattled is unquestionable. That they
are really students, I must be permitted to doubt. I have heard it freely
confessed by members of the revolutionary student generation of
Tsarist Russia that, proud as they were of the revolutionary exploits
of their youth, they never really learned anything in their university
years; they were too busy with politics. The fact of the matter is that
the state of being *enragé* is simply incompatible with fruitful study.
It implies a degree of existing emotional and intellectual commitment
which leaves little room for open-minded curiosity.

I am not saying that students should not be concerned, should not
have views, should not question what goes on in the field of national
policy and should not voice their questions about it. Some of us, who
are older, share many of their misgivings, many of their impulses. Some
of us have no less lively a sense of the dangers of the time, and are no
happier than they are about a great many things that are now going
on. But it lies within the power as well as the duty of all of us to
recognize not only the possibility that we might be wrong but the
virtual certainty that on some occasions we are bound to be. The fact
that this is so does not absolve us from the duty of having views and
putting them forward. But it does make it incumbent upon us to
recognize the element of doubt that still surrounds the correctness of
these views. And if we do that, we will not be able to lose ourselves in
transports of moral indignation against those who are of opposite opinion and follow a different line; we will put our views forward only
with a prayer for forgiveness for the event that we prove to be mistaken.

I am aware that inhibitions and restraints of this sort on the part of
us older people would be attributed by many members of the student
left to a sweeping corruption of our moral integrity. Life, they would

hold, has impelled us to the making of compromises; and these compromises have destroyed the usefulness of our contribution. Crippled by our own cowardice, prisoners of the seamy adjustments we have made in order to be successfully a part of the American establishment, we are regarded as no longer capable of looking steadily into the strong clear light of truth.

In this, as in most of the reproaches with which our children shower us, there is of course an element of justification. There is a point somewhere along the way in most of our adult lives, admittedly, when enthusiasms flag, when idealism becomes tempered, when responsibility to others, and even affection for others, compels greater attention to the mundane demands of private life. There is a point when we are even impelled to place the needs of children ahead of the dictates of a defiant idealism, and to devote ourselves, pusillanimously, if you will, to the support and rearing of these same children—precisely in order that at some future date they may have the privilege of turning upon us and despising us for the materialistic faintheartedness that made their maturity possible. This, no doubt, is the nature of the compromise that millions of us make with the imperfections of government and society in our time. Many of us could wish that it might have been otherwise—that the idealistic pursuit of public causes might have remained our exclusive dedication down into later life.

But for the fact that this is not so I cannot shower myself or others with reproaches. I have seen more harm done in this world by those who tried to storm the bastions of society in the name of utopian beliefs, who were determined to achieve the elimination of all evil and the realization of the millennium within their own time, than by all the humble efforts of those who have tried to create a little order and civility and affection within their own intimate entourage, even at the cost of tolerating a great deal of evil in the public domain. Behind this modesty, after all, there has been the recognition of a vitally important truth—a truth that the Marxists, among others, have never brought themselves to recognize—namely, that the decisive seat of evil in this world is not in social and political institutions, and not even, as a rule, in the will or iniquities of statesmen, but simply in the weakness and imperfection of the human soul itself, and by that I mean literally every soul, including my own and that of the student militant at the gates. For this reason, as Tocqueville so clearly perceived when he visited this country a hundred and thirty years ago, the success of a society may be said, like charity, to begin at home.

.   .   .

. . . If you accept a democratic system, this means that you are prepared to put up with those of its workings, legislative or administrative, with which you do not agree as well as with those that meet with your concurrence. This willingness to accept, in principle, the workings of a system based on the will of the majority, even when you yourself are in the minority, is simply the essence of democracy. Without it there could be no system of representative self-government at all. When you attempt to alter the workings of the system by means of violence or civil disobedience, this, it seems to me, can have only one of two implications: either you do not believe in democracy at all and consider that society ought to be governed by enlightened minorities such as the one to which you, of course, belong; or you consider that the present system is so imperfect that it is not truly representative, that it no longer serves adequately as a vehicle for the will of the majority, and that this leaves to the unsatisfied no adequate means of self-expression other than the primitive one of calling attention to themselves and their emotions by mass demonstrations and mass defiance of established authority. It is surely the latter of these two implications which we must read from the overwhelming majority of the demonstrations that have recently taken place.

I would submit that if you find a system inadequate, it is not enough simply to demonstrate indignation and anger over individual workings of it, such as the persistence of the Vietnam war, or individual situations it tolerates or fails to correct, such as the condition of the Negroes in our great cities. If one finds these conditions intolerable, and if one considers that they reflect no adequate expression either of the will of the majority or of that respect for the rights of minorities which is no less essential to the success of any democratic system, then one places upon one's self, it seems to me, the obligation of saying in what way this political system should be modified, or what should be established in the place of it, to assure that its workings would bear a better relationship to people's needs and people's feelings.

If the student left had a program of constitutional amendment or political reform—if it had proposals for the constructive adaptation of this political system to the needs of our age—if it was *this* that it was agitating for, and if its agitation took the form of reasoned argument and discussion, or even peaceful demonstration accompanied by reasoned argument and discussion—then many of us, I am sure, could view its protests with respect, and we would not shirk the obligation either to speak up in defense of institutions and national practices which we have tolerated all our lives, or to join these young people in the quest for better ones.

But when we are confronted only with violence for violence's sake, and with attempts to frighten or intimidate an administration into doing things for which it can itself see neither the rationale nor the electoral mandate; when we are offered, as the only argument for change, the fact that a number of people are themselves very angry and excited; and when we are presented with a violent objection to what exists, unaccompanied by any constructive concept of what, ideally, ought to exist in its place—then we of my generation can only recognize that such behavior bears a disconcerting resemblance to phenomena we have witnessed within our own time in the origins of totalitarianism in other countries, and then we have no choice but to rally to the defense of a public authority with which we may not be in agreement but which is the only one we've got and with which, in some form or another, we cannot conceivably dispense. People should bear in mind that if this—namely noise, violence and lawlessness—is the way they are going to put their case, then many of us who are no happier than they are about some of the policies that arouse their indignation will have no choice but to place ourselves on the other side of the barricades.

These observations reflect a serious doubt whether civil disobedience has any place in a democratic society. But there is one objection I know will be offered to this view. Some people, who accept our political system, believe that they have a right to disregard it and to violate the laws that have flowed from it so long as they are prepared, as a matter of conscience, to accept the penalties established for such behavior.

I am sorry; I cannot agree. The violation of law is not, in the moral and philosophic sense, a privilege that lies offered for sale with a given price tag, like an object in a supermarket, available to anyone who has the price and is willing to pay for it. It is not like the privilege of breaking crockery in a tent at the county fair for a quarter a shot. Respect for the law is not an obligation which is exhausted or obliterated by willingness to accept the penalty for breaking it.

To hold otherwise would be to place the privilege of lawbreaking preferentially in the hands of the affluent, to make respect for law a commercial proposition rather than a civic duty and to deny any authority of law independent of the sanctions established against its violation. It would then be all right for a man to create false fire alarms or frivolously to pull the emergency cord on the train, or to do any number of other things that endangered or inconvenienced other people, provided only he was prepared to accept the penalties of so doing. Surely, lawlessness and civil disobedience cannot be condoned or tolerated on this ground; and those of us who care for the good order of society have no choice but to resist attempts at its violation, when this is their only justification.

Now, being myself a father, I am only too well aware that people of my generation cannot absolve ourselves of a heavy responsibility for the state of mind in which these young people find themselves. We are obliged to recognize here, in the myopia and the crudities of *their* extremism, the reflection of our own failings: our faintheartedness and in some instances our weariness, our apathy in the face of great and obvious evils.

I am also aware that, while their methods may not be the right ones, and while their discontent may suffer in its effectiveness from the concentration on negative goals, the degree of their concern over the present state of our country and the dangers implicit in certain of its involvements is by no means exaggerated. This is a time in our national life more serious, more menacing, more crucial, than any I have ever experienced or ever hoped to experience. Not since the civil conflict of a century ago has this country, as I see it, been in such great danger; and the most excruciating aspect of this tragic state of affairs is that so much of this danger comes so largely from within, where we are giving it relatively little official attention, and so little of it comes, relatively speaking, from the swamps and jungles of Southeast Asia into which we are pouring our treasure of young blood and physical resources.

For these reasons, I do not mean to make light of the intensity of feeling by which this student left is seized. Nor do I mean to imply that people like myself can view this discontent from some sort of smug Olympian detachment, as though it were not our responsibility, as though it were not in part our own ugly and decadent face that we see in this distorted mirror. None of us could have any justification for attempting to enter into communication with these people if we did not recognize, along with the justification for their unhappiness, our own responsibility in the creation of it, and if we did not accompany our appeal to them with a profession of readiness to join them, where they want us to, in the attempt to find better answers to many of these problems.

I am well aware that in approaching them in this way and in taking issue as I have with elements of their outlook and their behavior, it is primarily myself that I have committed, not them. I know that behind all the extremisms—all the philosophical errors, all the egocentricities and all the oddities of dress and deportment—we have to do here with troubled and often pathetically appealing people, acting, however wisely or unwisely, out of sincerity and idealism, out of the unwillingness to accept a meaningless life and a purposeless society.

Well, this is not the life, and not the sort of society, that many of us would like to leave behind us in this country when our work is done. How wonderful it would be, I sometimes think to myself, if we and they—experience on the one hand, strength and enthusiasm on the other—could join forces.

Questions for Discussion and Writing

1. Bancroft notes that "the best government rests on the people and not on the few, on persons and not on property, on the free development of public opinion and not on authority." Has the American democratic system followed these precepts in its development?

2. Bancroft says that "individuals claim the divine sanction of truth for the deceitful conceptions of their own fancies," while Thoreau believes "the only obligation which I have a right to assume is to do at any time what I think is right." Discuss the role of conscience in public affairs in relation to these two statements.

3. When Thoreau says, "I came into this world, not chiefly to make this a good place to live in, but to live in it, be it good or bad," does he thus abjure the role of political reformer?

4. Does Thoreau's theory of civil disobedience differ from that put into practice by leaders inspired by his example, such as Gandhi and Martin Luther King, Jr.? Would Thoreau approve of contemporary mass demonstrations for civil rights and peace?

5. Discuss Theodore Roosevelt's views concerning the role of "elites" in a democracy. Would he approve of the contemporary student activist?

6. May Goldman correctly claim Thoreau as a founder of anarchism?

7. When, according to Malcolm X, is violence justified in the pursuit of freedom? Do modern conditions justify the use of violence by the black man?

8. Evaluate Malcolm X's rhetorical use of the refrain. How is this kind of repetition useful in oral argument?

9. Would it be correct to say that the failure of the melting pot leads directly to political extremism? Discuss.

10. Discuss Farrel's use of scapegoats in his article on "the third man." Does he support his argument with evidence and logic?

11. Why have blacks and young people contributed so much to the international revolution described by Mark Rudd?

12. Evaluate Rudd's contention that students are part of America's working class.

13. How does Kennan's view of human nature influence his conception of the role of civil disobedience in a democratic society? Compare his view of human nature in its relation to politics, with that of other writers represented in this section.

14. Define and discuss, with reference to the selections in this section: the people, *civil* disobedience, the system.

Essay Topics

1. Is compromise the *sine qua non* of democracy? Discuss.
2. Discuss James Reston's statement that "the principle of 'majority *decision*' is unarguable and unavoidable if the nation's business is to go on, but this is quite different from the notion that 'majority opinion' is the right opinion."
3. What political tactics, if any, do you consider "un-American"? Explain.

Suggestions for Further Reading

PRIMARY

FISHER AMES, "No Revolutionist," *Works* (1809). An attack on all revolution by an American Federalist.

NOAM CHOMSKY et al., "On Civil Disobedience," *New York Times Magazine* (November 26, 1967). A discussion by a leading theoretician of the New Left.

"FREE" (ABBIE HOFFMAN), *Revolution for the Hell of It* (1968). A statement of the Yippie creed by one of the founders of the movement.

PAUL GOODMAN, "Reflections on Civil Disobedience," *Liberation*, 13 (July–August 1968), 11–15. A penetrating discussion by the author of *Growing Up Absurd*.

JACK LONDON, *The Iron Heel* (1907). A fictional account of a bloody revolution in Chicago, ruthlessly suppressed by plutocracy's "iron heel."

LINCOLN STEFFENS, *Autobiography* (1931). The life of a leading muckraker who later praised the Russian Revolution.

WOODROW WILSON, "Democracy and Efficiency," *Public Papers*, eds. Baker and Dodd, I. A reassessment of democracy by the future President, an example of the New Liberalism of the progressive era.

SECONDARY

DANIEL AARON, *Writers on the Left* (1961). A literary history of American communism in the 1930s.

RALPH H. GABRIEL, *The Course of American Democratic Thought* (rev. ed., 1956). An intellectual history of the symbols and myths that constitute America's democratic faith.

KENNETH KENISTON, *Young Radicals* (1968). A study of fourteen young activists who worked for Vietnam Summer, examining the roots of their radicalism.

STAUGHTON LYND, *Intellectual Origins of American Radicalism* (1968). A provocative assessment of the radical tradition by a New Left historian.

JOSEPH MARTIN, *Men Against the State: Individualist Anarchism in America 1827–1908* (1953). A history of a minor but significant movement in American political history, forerunner of much present-day radicalism.

WALTER B. RIDEOUT, *The Radical Novel in the United States 1900–1954* (1956). A literary history of the response to socialism in the pre–First World War period, and to communism in the 1930s and later.

Epilogue

Without Marx or Jesus: The New American Revolution Has Begun

JEAN-FRANÇOIS REVEL, born in Marseilles in 1924, was educated at the Sorbonne. Active in the French Resistance, he later taught literature and philosophy in Mexico, Florence, and Lille, before becoming an editor in Paris. In addition to contributing a weekly column to the French news magazine **L'Express,** he has published a novel and several volumes of essays, including **The French** (English translation, 1966).

The revolution of the twentieth century will take place in the United States. It is only there that it can happen. And it has already begun. Whether or not that revolution spreads to the rest of the world depends on whether or not it succeeds first in America.

I am not unaware of the shock and incredulity such statements may cause at every level of the European Left and among the nations of the Third World. I know it is difficult to believe that America—the fatherland of imperialism, the power responsible for the war in Vietnam, the nation of Joe McCarthy's witch hunts, the exploiter of the world's natural resources—is, or could become, the cradle of revolution. We are accustomed to thinking of the United States as the logical target of revolution, and of computing revolutionary progress by the rate of American withdrawal. Now, we are being asked to admit that our revolutionary slide rule was inaccurate and to face the future without that comfortable tool.

If we draw up a list of all the things that ail mankind today, we will have formulated a program for the revolution that mankind needs: the abolition of war and of imperialist relations by abolishing states

WITHOUT MARX OR JESUS: THE NEW AMERICAN REVOLUTION HAS BEGUN. By Jean-François Revel, translated by Jack Bernard. Translation copyright © 1971 by Doubleday & Company, Inc. Used by permission of the publisher. Originally appeared in *Saturday Review* in somewhat different form.

and also the notion of national sovereignty; the elimination of the possibility of internal dictatorship (a concomitant condition of the abolition of war); worldwide economic and educational equality; birth control on a planetary scale; complete ideological, cultural, and moral freedom, in order to ensure both individual happiness through independence and a plurality of choice, and in order to make use of the totality of human creative resources.

Obviously, this is a utopic program, and it has nothing in its favor, except that it is absolutely necessary if mankind is to survive. The exchange of one political civilization for another, which that program implies, seems to me to be going on right now in the United States. And, as in all the great revolutions of the past, this exchange can become worldwide only if it spreads, by a sort of political osmosis, from the prototype-nation to all the others.

The United States is the country most eligible for the role of prototype-nation for the following reasons: It enjoys continuing economic prosperity and rate of growth, without which no revolutionary project can succeed; it has technological competence and a high level of basic research; culturally it is oriented toward the future rather than toward the past, and it is undergoing a revolution in behavioral standards and in the affirmation of individual freedom and equality; it rejects authoritarian control and multiplies creative initiative in all domains —especially in art, life-style, and sense experience—and allows the coexistence of a diversity of mutually complementary alternative subcultures.

It is evident from the above that the various aspects of a revolution are interrelated—so much so that, if one aspect is missing, the others are incomplete. There are five revolutions that must take place either simultaneously or not at all: a political revolution; a social revolution; a technological and scientific revolution; a revolution in culture, values, and standards; and a revolution in international and interracial relations. The United States is the only country, so far as I can see, where these five revolutions are simultaneously in progress and are organically linked in such a way as to constitute a single revolution. In all other countries, either all five revolutions are missing, which settles the problem, or one or two or three of them are lacking, which relegates revolution to the level of wishful thinking.

The most common error concerning the United States is to try to interpret that nation in terms of the revolutionary guidelines with which we are familiar, and which are usually purely theoretical. Then, when we see that those guidelines are not applicable to the American situation, we conclude that America is a reactionary country.

The revolutionary plans that we know, and that we usually try to apply, are all based on the existence of opposition, of antagonism: the peasants against the proprietors of the land; workers against factory owners; colonials against colonizers. The present American revolution, however, resembles more a centrifugal gyration than a clash between opposing camps. It has certain characteristics in common with old-style revolution. There are the oppressed and the oppressors; the exploited and the exploiters; the poor and the rich. There are people who are morally dissatisfied with the present state of affairs—an essential condition of revolution—and there is a serious rift within the governing elite.

There are also traits that are entirely new and peculiar to America. The "poor" are an unusual kind of poor; they earn between $1,500 and $3,000 a year, and, if their income falls below the former figure, they are eligible for government aid. In Europe, such an income would place a family considerably above the poverty level—although, common opinion to the contrary, the cost of living in European urban centers is not much less than in America. In America, however, the phenomenon of prosperity makes everything relative, and, in consequence, some of the moral and psychological factors that are important in Europe do not play nearly so large a part in establishing revolutionary goals in America. The American revolution is, without doubt, the first revolution in history in which disagreement on values and goals is more pronounced than disagreement on the means of existence. American revolutionaries do not want merely to cut the cake into equal pieces; they want a whole new cake. This spirit of criticism of values, which is still more emotional than intellectual, is made possible by a freedom of information such as no civilization has ever tolerated before—not even within and for the benefit of the governing class, let alone at the level of the mass media. This accessibility of information has resulted in a widespread and strong feeling of guilt, and a passion for self-accusation that, on occasion, tends to go to extremes. And that result, in turn, has produced a phenomenon unprecedented in history: a domestic revolt against the imperialistic orientation of American foreign policy.

This revolt, however, is not the only indication of a new revolutionary direction. There has never been another society that faced a situation like that of the United States with respect to the blacks. In the face of this contagious domestic problem and of the demands of the Afro-American community, American society is being divided into factions and is entering upon the path of cultural polycentrism. And this process, of course, is playing havoc with our prejudices concerning the "conformity" and "uniformity" of American society. The truth of the matter is that American society is torn by too many tensions not to become more and more diversified.

Another unprecedented characteristic of the American revolution is the revolt of the young—the contagion of which, at both the national and international levels, was so virulent in the years between 1965 and 1970. This is, moreover, a new development within the context of upper-class divisions during revolutionary periods, since these young revolutionaries are mostly students; that is, members of the privileged class. It should be pointed out that this "privileged class" is less and less exceptional; it is a case, so to speak, of mass privilege. The current upheavals are due not only to the great number of young people in proportion to the rest of the population, but also to the great number of students in proportion of young people. Out of a population of two hundred million, there are presently seven million students; and it is estimated that by 1977 there will be eleven million.

It has been said that there are three nations in the United States: a black nation; a Woodstock nation; and a Wallace nation. The first one is self-explanatory. The second takes its name from the great political and musical convention held at Woodstock, New York, in 1969, which has been documented by the film *Woodstock*. It includes the hippies and the radicals. The third nation is embodied in Governor George Wallace of Alabama, and is composed of lower-middle-class whites, whose symbol is the hard hat worn by construction workers. Each of these nations has its own language, its own art forms, and its own customs. And each has a combat arm: the Black Panthers for the blacks; the Weathermen for Woodstock; and the Ku Klux Klan and various citizen organizations for Wallace. We could add other "nations"; e.g., members of the Women's Liberation movement, who have declared war on sexism and who take their methods from those of the black power and student power movements.

There is also a large group of citizens who are neither black nor particularly young nor especially intellectual. Far from being reactionary, they are sometimes militantly progressive and are vaguely categorized as liberals. This group includes citizens with a wide range of opinion; from what, in Europe, we call the democrats, to the progressives. The liberals often have been able to contribute the appearance of a mass movement to demonstrations that, without them, would have attracted only the extremists. They demonstrated alongside the blacks throughout the great Southern revolt that began in 1952 and against the Vietnam War in the various moratoriums. They are on the side of the students, the Indians, and the Third World. On May 21, 1970, for instance, thousands of New York lawyers—what we might call the governors of the governing class—descended on Washington to protest American intervention in Cambodia. On the same day, the hardhats demonstrated in New York in favor of this intervention, and, still on the same day, prices dropped sharply on the New York Stock Exchange, indicating, according to some American commentators, that the financiers, like the lawyers, were not in agreement with the administration over the conduct of the war. No nineteenth-century class distinctions are sufficient to convey the nature of these new political classes—which are also sexual, racial, and esthetic; that is, they are based on the rejection of an unsatisfactory life-style. Each of these categories has specific economic, racial, esthetic, moral, and religious or spiritual characteristics; each has its own customs, its own way of dressing and eating—even though, as a whole, they are referred to as a "community." In this instance, the image of a series of superimposed circles rather than of stratified social levels describes the nature of this community.

The "hot" issues in America's insurrection against itself, numerous as they are, form a cohesive and coherent whole within which no one of them can be separated from the others. These issues are as follows: a radically new approach to moral values; the black revolt; the feminist attack on masculine domination; the rejection by young people of exclusively economic and technical social goals; the general adoption of non-coercive methods in education; the acceptance of the guilt for poverty; the growing demand for equality; the rejection of an authoritarian culture in favor of a critical and diversified culture that is basically new, rather than adopted from the old cultural stockpile; the rejection both of the spread of American power abroad and of foreign policy; and a determination that the natural environment is more important than commercial profit. None of the groups concerned with any one of these points, and none of the points themselves, would have been able to gain as much strength and attention as they have if they had been isolated from other groups and other points.

The moral, cultural, and political revolutions are but a single revolution. In San Francisco, a group composed of women and homosexuals (members of the Women's Liberation Front and the Gay Liberation Front), shouting "Cambodia is obscene! Sex is not obscene!" burst into a psychiatrists' convention that was discussing the "treatment" of homosexuality. The criticism of paternalistic and moralistic psychiatry, in this instance, not only takes on a political form but also produces new courage in the affirmation of self.

The interconnection between counter-cultural themes appeared again on June 10, 1970, at the Venice Biennale when a group of American artists promoting an "artists' strike against racism, sexism, and war" withdrew their works from the exposition as a protest against the policies of their government. This group comprised thirty-three of the forty-four persons selected to represent the United States at the festival and included the cream of contemporary American artists, such as Josef Albers, Leonard Baskin, John Cage, Sam Francis, Jasper Johns, Roy Lichtenstein, Robert Morris, Claes Oldenburg,

Robert Rauschenberg, and Andy Warhol. So far as I know, there was never a similar large-scale protest of first-rate French artists during the Indochina war or the Algerian war—I mean a protest involving a real sacrifice in terms of one's career. The same sort of phenomenon is taking place in all the visual arts: in the modern American theater, where drama has been recast and joined to an instinctual explosion; in such films as Andy Warhol's *Lonesome Cowboys,* which is a homosexual parody of cowboy Westerns and which I saw in a commercial movie theater one afternoon in Chicago; in stage plays in which the sex act is performed on the stage; or in *Macbird,* a take-off on *Macbeth,* in which the President of the United States and his wife are openly accused of having had John Kennedy assassinated. Examples could be multiplied indefinitely to demonstrate the thesis that liberation must be complete, or it will not exist at all.

There have been political revolutions that failed because, among other reasons, they were limited to a single area, to politics or economics, and therefore were not able to generate the "new man" who could have given meaning to new political or economic institutions. In *Prolégomènes à un troisième manifeste du surréalisme,* André Breton writes: "We must not only stop the exploitation of man by man, but we must also re-examine—from top to bottom, without hypocrisy and without dodging the issues—the problems involved in the relationship between men and women." And Charles Fourier pointed out that the revolutionaries of 1789 had failed because "they bowed before the concept of the sanctity of marriage." If women had been allowed to become their own rulers, he says, "it would have been a scandal, and a weapon capable of undermining the foundations of society." It should be noted, however, that even the divorce law passed by the revolutionaries, and subsequently adopted by the Napoleonic Code, was so far ahead of its time that it was abolished during the Restoration. It was revived only at the time of the Third Republic, but in such a limited form as to be more restrictive than it had been at the beginning of the nineteenth century.

.   .   .

I certainly do not mean to imply that the battle against sexual repression is the whole of the revolutionary struggle; but it is undoubtedly one of the surest signs of an *authentic* revolutionary struggle.

In practice, sexual repression indicates the existence of authoritarianism in a diversity of areas: in family life and religion; in relations between the sexes, between age groups, and between races and social classes. Conversely, the appearance of sexual liberty is symptomatic of freedom from authoritarianism in those areas. When culture is "directed," we may be certain that it is involved in a relationship of authority; that is, it is subjected to force. One of the most striking characteristics of the revolutionary movement in America is that it is the first such movement in which all demands are part of a single front, and are advanced simultaneously on the same program. Demands belonging to the individualist-anarchist tradition, and those referring to the organized political struggle of the oppressed (or of the less non-oppressed, as the case may be), are, for once, all included in one demand.

There is, therefore, a basis common to all manifestations of the American revolt, and to its European extensions. That basis consists in the rejection of a society motivated by profit, dominated exclusively by economic considerations, ruled by the spirit of competition, and subjected to the mutual aggressiveness of its members. Indeed, beneath every revolutionary ideal we find a conviction that man has become the tool of his tools, and that he must once more become an end and a value in himself. The hippies are characterized by a particularly vivid awareness of that loss of self-identity and of the perversion of the meaning of life. A competitive society, for instance, or a spirit of rivalry, is a source of suffering to them. But they do not self-righteously condemn such societies nor attempt to refute them theoretically; they simply refuse to have any part in them. A hippie, therefore, is above all someone who has "dropped out"; a boy or girl who decided, one day, to stop being a cog in the social machine. Baudelaire suggested adding two additional rights to the Declaration of the Rights of Man: the right to contradict oneself and the right to walk away. Hippies make use of both those rights. This use, when it is so widespread as to be no longer marginal is much more revolutionary than one is willing to admit if one insists on viewing everything dogmatically, in terms of classic political activity. When societies decline seriously, it is because of this internal absenteeism, because its people have discovered new forms of commitment.

Certainly, one can make a good case against the hippies for their political indifference and for their naïveté in rejecting every form of violence—for these are the attitudes that distinguish the hippies. One can even fault them for forgetting that the hippie way of life is possible only in an affluent society and because of a surplus in production (even though the hippie personally may be willing to live in comparative poverty). One can make fun of their nebulous ideology, which is a mixture of confused Orientalism and adulterated primitivism (although they are likely to retort that they prefer pop music to ideology). One can jeer at their simplistic confidence in the strength of universal love as the key to all problems. And one can be astonished at their belief that it is possible for an individual to have absolute freedom without infringing the rights of others. All these things are, no doubt, open to criticism from many standpoints; and they are all no doubt very limited concepts. The fact remains, however, that the hippies' refusal to accept regimentation in any form gives them a mysterious strength and a means of exerting pressure; the same sort of strength and pressure that is exerted by, say, a hunger strike. To those who try to persuade them to give their revolt a political or religious structure, the hippies offer a patient, but absolutely inflexible, resistance. The May uprisings in Paris and the demonstrations at the Renault plant in France all seem to the hippies to be too much the product of the harsh society that they are trying to escape. Plossu says of those who were involved in these events that "their ideas of revolt were, in the long run, chains" and their "attempt at liberation, only a form of slavery."

Such words as Plossu's are guaranteed to strike a sour note among lovers of the revolutionary praxis. Nonetheless, this rejection of solutions that are too immediate and too concrete originates in a basic intuition that one of the foundations of revolution that we most need today is the elimination of pathological aggression. Unless that elimination is achieved, no revolution can do anything but lead to a new form of oppression. We do not need a political revolution so much as an antipolitical revolution; otherwise the only result will be the creation of new police states. Human aggression is a determining factor in human behavior; and it is accepted even more gratuitously, and is even more murderous, than all of the sacred causes by which it justifies itself and on which it bases itself. Unless this root evil is extirpated, the hippies believe, then everything else will be corrupted. By reflecting that belief in their attitudes and behavior, the hippies at very least perform a useful function; they remind us constantly that a revolution is not simply a transfer of power, but also a change in the goals for the sake of which power is exercised and a new choice in the objects of love, hate, and respect. Also, the hippies have the advantage of being able to point out, to those who still talk about "freedom at gunpoint" in a world dripping with blood that has been shed in vain, that this slogan is nothing more than an outdated jingoism.

It is not impossible that intimations of a new and even more thoroughgoing technological advance, and a radical extension of the applications of biological science, may have already decided the question of a "return to nature." The same sort of intimations, or presentiments, acted as a warning signal to man in the 1760s, before the first great technological revolution. And today, as in the time of Rousseau, the struggle for the preservation of the beauty and benefits of nature reveals our need to believe in the goodness of man, or of oneself, and the need to prove that goodness to ourselves. It is making us turn away from a single culture to several cultures. For that reason, it is absurd to regard the ecological battle as a mere skirmish or a spin-off from the main war. The ecological battle is one of the pieces of the revolutionary puzzle, and it is necessary to complete the picture. It gives us the emotional energy necessary, for example, to challenge the omnipotence of the great industrial empires; and such energy is not engendered by a political program, no matter how clear it may be. Not a week passes that we do not hear talk of a law forbidding the use of internal combustion engines by 1975, or of legal actions by New York State or other states to force the airlines to filter their jet-exhaust fumes.

We should have no illusions about the immediate efficacy of these steps, for it seems that the graver the problem, the less money the nation-state can devote to its solution. The protection of the environment, in effect, presents problems the solutions to which it is difficult to envision; indeed, some experts see the situation as desperate. In any case, the alarm has been sounded more energetically and more passionately in the United States than anywhere else. And, characteristically, it has taken two forms: that of scientific and technical research, and that of a collective emotion that is incomparably more intense and widespread in the United States than anywhere else. "Earth Day" in America was one huge pantheistic feast. Some say it is because "America is more polluted than any other country." Europeans always believe that nature is non-existent in the United States. They think of the whole country as one vast Chicago. They forget that the populations of the United States and the nations of the Common Market are approximately equal—but that the area of the latter could fit comfortably into one-eighth the area of the United States. It comes as a surprise to a European, when he flies over America, to see that the country has more open space than it does cities. And we see many American cities surrounded by open countryside, and practically hidden by greenery because of the practice (even in cities of a million people) of building houses on wooded lots.

The young men and women who, on a Saturday in California, walk naked through the forests, singing and playing their guitars and flutes, those who lie down in front of bulldozers to prevent trees from being uprooted, those who go to live in hippie communes—these people rarely come from places as suffocated by bad air and garbage as New York, or Paris, or London. There is a good deal more to the ecological movement than the effect of a practical determinism. After all, for thousands of years mankind has lived (and, for the most part, still lives) by drinking contaminated water, and he has survived the resulting dysentery and typhoid epidemics. Suffering apparently is not enough to move one to fight for a better environment. Malaria has never caused a revolution. In order to fight, one must be able to see a clear relationship among nature, technology, economic power, and political power.

One must also be able to rise to the belief that nature belongs to every man, and to the realization that an oil slick on the ocean affects one's own good or, better, one's own happiness. The development of such a belief therefore implies the existence of a political awareness that calls for the reshaping of intrasocial relations, for co-proprietorship, for co-dependence, for co-responsibility. Those who still believe that the ecological movement is part of a plan to distract people, a sort of political smoke screen, may not have seen a *New Yorker* cartoon in which one elderly and obviously wealthy golfer expresses his belief to another that the whole "ecology business" is "just another Commie trick." Hardly. The Communists, in fact, are as backward about ecology as they are about women and contraception. But, just as Europeans still believe that Americans are puritanical, they still picture Americans as slaves to "gadgets" and pollution-creating machines. The truth is that there is no country in the world where automobiles, for example, are treated more like ordinary tools—or where people drive less like maniacs. Moreover, it is in America that the moral revolution, and the ecological revolution that is part of it, have initiated an era of caution, if not of outright mistrust, with respect to machines and "the techno-electronic society."

We can therefore conclude that a counter-culture, a counter-society, has already sprung up in the United States. And it is, as it must necessarily be, a counter-society that has nothing marginal about it. It is a revolutionary universe, characterized by the demand for equality of sexes, races, and age groups; by the rejection of the authoritarian relationship on which rest all societies that have been stratified by force and despotism; by the transformation of directed culture into productive culture; by the rejection of nationalism in foreign policy; by the realization of the outdated character of the "authority of the state," constituted without sufficient participation by the people, and exercised under conditions that allow an abuse of power to a degree that has become intolerable; by an insistence on economic and educational equality; by a radical reappraisal of the goals of technology and its consequences; by a demand for absolute individual and cultural freedom, without moral censorship—which is a variant in the rejection of an authoritarian relationship. When all these demands have been met, it is highly probable that we will have a *homo novus,* a new man very different from other men.

These incentives for revolution, by their cohesiveness, by the great number of Americans who support them, and by the changes in depth that they have already achieved in the sensitivity, conduct, habits, thoughts and acts of Americans, can be described as the first stage of a revolution. What usually happens is that a political revolution occurs at the top, and that no social revolution follows to make the political revolution durable. In the United States, however, the social revolution has been largely achieved. What remains to be seen is the possible political application of the reservoir of energy constituted by this mass counter-society.

A revolutionary force therefore exists. The results of its activity also exist: There are two societies, two humanities now confronting each other whose views on the future can hardly be reconciled. We can therefore say that a point of crisis has been reached. Not a halfway point. Not a crisis over this or that particular thing. But a crisis over society itself. What will be the outcome? The true revolutionary solution is to place oneself at the point at which the lines being drawn will converge, and to refrain from adopting any solution from the past.

The American "movement" has been compared to primitive Christianity, sometimes favorably in order to hail the dawning of a new era; and sometimes unfavorably, in order to analyze the narcissistic elements of dissent. The Black Panthers, on the other hand, call themselves "Marxist-Leninists"; and the students of the Free Speech Movement, who play a dominant role in the New Left, call upon Marx, Lenin, Guevara, and Mao. (In one scene from *The Strawberry Statement*, a female student asks, "Did you know that Lenin liked large breasts?"—as she uncovers her own enormous pair.) The pro-Chinese Progressive Labor Party, whose student branch (WSA, or Workers-Students Alliance) set off the occupation of the Harvard campus in the spring of 1969, still clings to the dogma of the working class as the only revolutionary avant-garde—a position which, given the American situation, is rather quaint. The Weathermen, on the other hand, following in the footsteps of Trotsky, Guevara, and Marcuse, believe that a world revolution can only come from the Third World and from the blacks.

The religious element of the American movement is undeniable. The *need for sacredness* is being satisfied by the confused adoption and the hit-or-miss practice of Oriental religions, and by a return to the Indian cult of natural foods, to astrology (according to which we have now entered the Age of Aquarius, and the astral implications of that fact are being studied diligently), and to a rediscovery of Christianity. Above all, however, this need is being satisfied by the application of a traditional principle that has always been successful in America: The best religions are those that you find for yourself.

America has never had a state religion, either officially or otherwise. European wits who make fun of the endemic religiosity of America, as exemplified by the presence of Bibles in hotel rooms and the inscription "In God We Trust" on money, would do better to reflect on the consequences of a very important cultural fact: that no church of any kind has ever dominated, either by law or de facto, the moral, intellec-

tual, artistic, or political life of that immense country. It is true that
the President of the United States swears his oath of office on the Bible,
and that the President of France does not. The President of France,
however, is not the one who is more free of confessional influence. And
the same can be said if we compare the two countries (not to speak of
Italy or Spain) from the standpoint of freedom from religious influence in the classroom, in the newspaper office, and in the publishing
house. *The Yearbook of American Churches* (1969 edition) lists
seventy-nine established religions in the United States—and by "established" it means those which have no fewer than 50,000 members. If
we go below the 50,000 mark, the various churches may be numbered
in the thousands. Just in Los Angeles, one could change one's religion
every day of the year, if one wished to do so; for some of these religions
last only a few months, or until their founders tire of the whole thing.

Standing in front of the Berkeley campus at noontime, one can see
a group of "Buddhist monks" go dancing by in long yellow robes,
their feet bare, their heads shaved—all natives of Oregon or Arizona.
Meanwhile, a group of Christian hippies tries to drown out the Buddhists' drums by shouting the name of Jesus, and a "naturist pantheist"
sells fruits and vegetables grown without fertilizer. Jesus has always
been an honored figure in hippie mythology, and there is a group that
calls itself "Street Christians" or "Jesus Freaks." The name Jesus
Freaks was at first a term of derision, but the adherents of the cult
took it over for themselves. They had no difficulty in finding rich, and
generous, benefactors. One of them brought up the aspect of "primitive Christianity," of which some of the Woodstock people were
already conscious. "I think you are being *very first century*," he told
his friends. The Jesus Freaks have founded several hundred communes,
both rural and urban, and they have their own underground newspaper,
called *Right On,* in which they inveigh against sexual promiscuity,
homosexuality, and drugs. They admit, however, that the drug culture
possesses a spirituality that is lacking in the alcohol culture. (The
religious connotation of drugs is important; as is the opposition between the two cultures: that of pot and that of the dry martini.)

Even though the Jesus Freaks are in favor of restrictions on personal
liberty and call for a renunciation of "permissiveness" (a reversal
which would be difficult to bring about), their movement may con-
solidate itself solely under its religious aspect and lead to a gigantic
dropping-out. Or millions of people may drop out and invent religious
cults of their own. I once read this graffito on a wall of the Santa Cruz
campus: "When peace is outlawed, only outlaws can have peace." Thus,
a massive counter-society continues to develop, one which lives on the
fringes of technological society. For the moment, the latter is wealthy
enough to afford a counter-society; but if the counter-society begins

to grow excessively, it is obvious that the rate of economic growth in America will immediately begin to slow.

This effect upon economic growth is a possibility. It will not, however, resolve the crisis. One can conceive of a sort of suicide of technological society, an asphyxiation of American power from within, an immense boycott that would weaken and disorganize production. Then America, inhabited by vagrant mystics and ruined bankers, would crumble and sink into the Third World. At that point, international justice would be established, and, with imperialism dead at its source, the world would once again move toward democratic socialism. But there is one catch: Without scientific and technical progress backed by economic power—progress and power of which America is the main source—the world's problems are insoluble. Moreover, this fictive withdrawal of America into itself would aggravate the country's domestic problems, since it would destroy the very means of satisfying the demands of the blacks, the poor, women, students, and the cities. These groups would then rise up once more, and the result would be a process of decomposition without the possibility of a solution, instead of a revolution—which is a process of disintegration *with* a solution and a new integration of conflicting forces. America's economic and social downfall would make almost certain a drift to the right among the middle classes, and an authoritarian political regime. It is nonetheless possible that a new religion of the future is being born in the world of the American underground. I do not know for certain. If that is the case, however, I doubt very much that it will be productive, from a revolutionary standpoint, in the immediate future.

These perspectives—or rather, this lack of perspectives—serve to show the limitations of dissent. These limitations have often been discussed—by psychiatrists particularly, and with great perception—as childish efforts to skirt the "principle of reality." Regarding the ability of dissent to transform reality, Bruno Bettelheim, in the United States, has much the same reservations as those expressed in Europe by André Stéphane in *L'Univers contestationnaire*. According to Stéphane, no revolution can be based on a rejection of reality. The middle-class youth (i.e., today's student and dissenter) is not so much in revolt against his father as he is unwilling to recognize his father's presence as it exists. Youth, Stéphane says, is dominated by narcissism, self-admiration, and intolerance—all of which are characteristic of the phases of sexual development anterior to the Oedipus complex. A true revolutionary spirit, however, leads one, not to run away from his father, but to take his father's place; not merely to do away with his father, but to *become* his own father. This doing away with the father (only in the youth's imagination, of course) brings us to the Oedipal universe; that is, a universe dominated by the mother, who is simultaneously good and evil, indulgent and frustrating—that is, the prototypical consumer society—from whom youth demands everything and whom he wishes to destroy.

What characterizes the narcissistic stage is the child's desire to have everything at once. If he is not satisfied, then he takes refuge in the hallucinatory fulfillment of his desires. The need for omnipotence makes progressive action impossible, for narcissism ignores the principle of reality and refuses to admit the incompatibility of contradictory solutions. To the narcissistic child, the idea of making choices is unbearable.

We know how difficult it is for dissenters to describe the kind of society they long for. This lack of precise ideas, it is sometimes said, is justifiable; after all, it is up to adults to supply solutions. The role of the young is merely to express dissatisfaction, *modo grosso*. This explanation, however, ignores two facts. First, that the spirit of dissent is far from being the exclusive property of the young; and second, that the spirit of dissent excludes all concrete solutions, for solutions are always partial and always subject to expiration, either short-term or long-term.

Any technical discussion, any reservation concerning details—even on the part of those who approve of the dissenters' demands, but who emphasize the difficulties inherent in their practical realization—is regarded by the dissenter as an overall rejection and as an act of hostility. To begin a technical discussion is to call the dissenter back to reality, and that is something intolerable to someone for whom only total and instantaneous gratification exists, and who therefore cannot accept either the *quid pro quo* or the step-by-step progress of revolutionary action—let alone of reformism. Everything that contradicts the magical power of words is experienced as a repetition of the original narcissistic wound that was inflicted upon the infant when he first discovered his lack of independence with respect to his environment.

In this universe of all or nothing, of black and white, there is no question of action, but only of redemption. It is not by chance that dissent has been absorbed into some major branches of Christianity and then refurbished and translated into religious terms. The redeemer may be the workman, the black, or the poor. All the dissenter needs is someone who is suffering, a victim that he can help. Since the Six-Day War, he has found it difficult to forgive the Jews for no longer being downtrodden. Victorious Jews do not make good subjects for crucifixion. The rapidity with which some of Israel's friends have dropped that country, without bothering to analyze in detail the causes of the 1967 conflict, indicates that being pro-Israeli has lost its power to absolve from guilt. By the same token, we can easily see why it is necessary for workers to be miserable. "Are you hungry?" students asked the striking workers at the Renault plant—to the astonishment, and amusement, of the workers. If the workers are happy, they can no longer be the dissenter's means of redemption. This is the source of the Marcusian critique of the consumer society, which has as its purpose to reinstate the proletariat in its role as victim—this time by means of the subterfuge of "alienation." Therefore, we are not allowed to admit that the situation of the blacks in America has improved in the past twenty years. Thus to equate the well-being of the proletariat with a sort of counter-revolutionary terrorism presupposes serious distortion of the revolutionary ideal, and the existence of major conflicts within oneself.

No revolution can result from a pretension that one embodies absolute good and opposes absolute evil. For that reason, the ease with which purveyors of the irrational have taken over the movement of dissent is disturbing—as disturbing as the spirit of intolerance that has resulted. I am not the first one to notice the similarities between certain themes of dissent and certain themes of prewar fascism. We find the most rabid diatribes against the flabbiness of the French people as exemplified by illustrated magazines, paid vacations, retirement benefits, before-dinner drinks, and the national lottery, in the works of Brasillach, Rebatet, and Céline—all celebrated fascists. And Mussolini himself pronounced high-sounding words against those who longed for the "easy life"—words that would have easily evoked applause in 1968 from certain student audiences so long as one did not mention Mussolini's name. (In fact, some practical jokers did exactly this in Berlin, with great success.)

Must we then conclude that dissent leads to counter-revolution? I do not think we can go that far, but it seems certain that dissent, in itself, does not constitute a revolution. In today's societies, dissent is a necessary condition of revolution, but it is not a sufficient condition; it must be completed by something else.

By what? This brings us to a second hypothesis (the religious hypothesis being the first). For the most enterprising among the adherents of the Free Speech Movement, the necessary "something else" is the classic Marxist revolution; that is, the overthrow of capitalism and its political system by the oppressed classes. And this is also the view of all the partisans of the various "power" movements: black power, brown power (the Mexican-Americans), red power (the Indians), sex power (women), student power—all of which are united under the motto "Power to the People." Marxist groups and Christian groups easily find common ground in "Zen Marxism" and "Pop Marxism"; and young people for whom "Jesus is the best trip" and the Mao-Guevara group arrive at an easy understanding with each other. The only problem is that such understandings are more likely to lead them to the comforts of religion than to the joys of power.

Revolution has been defined, quite accurately, as "a movement of dissent that succeeds in attaining power." Within that context, we may add that the crucial question of our time is this: How does one go from dissent to revolution? The answer, I think, depends on the meaning that we attach to the words "attaining power" in the above definition. In societies where government has a rudimentary and centralized form, the process of attaining power is relatively simple and quick. In a nation as complex as the United States, however, power does not fall into the hands of anyone who succeeds in mounting an attack on the Capitol. And that is why the urban guerrilla warfare that we hear so much about is not actually a war of revolution, nor a transition from dissent to revolution, but only a form of armed dissent. It is merely the intensification of a form of action, and not the adoption of a new form. The anarchists who, at the end of the nineteenth century, made a practice of killing customers in Parisian cafés with bombs were belligerent dissenters, but they were not revolutionaries. Their chances of gaining power were zero. And the *sine qua non* of revolution is that power must change hands. Sometimes this transfer takes time, even though it is a revolutionary process; that is, it is brought about by means that go beyond, and violate, the normal rules of the political game. These means, however, must be relevant to the composition of a society and proportionate to the forces involved.

In the case of the United States, one can hardly pretend that there really exists a Silent Majority and that, at the same time, the only possible course of action is civil war. For absolute insurrection to succeed, the Army and the police must stand side by side with the insurgents, and that seems hardly likely in a country where the notion of a Constitutional consensus is so deeply ingrained. The only thing that could bring about civil war would be a military disaster, accompanied by a state of acute physical want, such as occurred in Russia in 1917, or a war of national liberation, like that in China. And both those hypotheses are hopelessly unrealistic. Moreover, civil war presupposes the existence of certain sociological conditions that are not found in the United States. In America class warfare is not a battle of "class against class." This psychological Manichaeism exists only in the minds of those who have fallen victim to it. America is not composed of a monolithic Silent Majority on one side (first of all, because it is not a majority at all; and second, because it is never silent) and, on the other side, a bloc of "victims of capitalism."

When Michael Harrington's book on poverty in America (*The Other America*) was published in March 1962, the news that poverty existed in the midst of abundance came as a great shock to certain optimistic economists. At that time, $3,000 was regarded as the minimum income necessary for an urban family of four; an income below that level represented poverty. In 1968, this minimum income was raised to $3,553. By the end of 1970, it reached $3,700. Below that level, a family of four is eligible for public assistance, in the form of additional income. The average annual income in the United States— not by family, but per capita (in 1968)—was $3,412. In Portugal, it was $412. In Spain, $719. In Italy, $1,300. In France $1,436. And in West Germany, $1,753. In these circumstances, poverty (which is defined in terms other than that of income—by housing, for example, and educational opportunity) affects between one-sixth and one-fifth of the American people. This percentage allowed Michael Harrington to speak of "the first poverty minority known to history"—meaning not that the number of poor was small, but that, for the first time, the usual breakdown of society into a few wealthy families and a vast majority of poor families had been reversed. Politically speaking, this fact necessitates a revision of one's tactics. We can no longer say that the oppressed at least have numbers on their side, and that, at the first weakening of the repressive system, it will be enough for them to rise and the whole apparatus of government will crumble.

.   .   .

American Marxism-Leninism and Maoism, in fact, proceed on the basis of an error in analysis, since the white working class is, on the whole, conservative; since the business world favors reform; since the federal government, for the past twenty years, has been on the side of the blacks and against local racism; and since in 1969 and 1970 the Senate (with strong Republican backing) inflicted a humiliating defeat on the White House by refusing to confirm two Nixon nominees to the Supreme Court, both Southerners, one of whom, many years before, had made a racist speech.

Paradoxically, the United States is one of the least racist countries in the world today. A large black minority has lived alongside the whites for many years, and the fight against racism, its extirpation and the analysis of its symptoms, a preoccupation with its rejection in others and with its domination in oneself—all these things are a reality with which America lives. Many other countries, however, are experiencing an upsurge in popular racism: the French, the Swiss, and the English, who, for the first time in their history, now find large North African, Portuguese, Jamaican, or Senegalese minorities in their midst. The problem is particularly serious because the social traditions of these countries contain no antibody against the disease of racism. . . .

The demands of black Americans are, after all, more *cultural* demands than *class* demands. The blacks are divided into several social classes among themselves. Their two chief preoccupations are poverty in the ghettos and cultural alienation. The latter is expressed uncompromisingly by the 400,000 to 500,000 black university students (out of a total student population of some seven million) who do not want merely to enter the universities in large numbers—as they are actually doing, thanks to the lavish distribution of scholarships—but who also, within the universities, want to receive an education that has no connection with that given to the whites. They do not wish to know about white literature, white science, white history, or white theater; and they do not want white teachers—an attitude that will contribute greatly to an explosion in America in the years to come.

Black Marxism-Leninism does not seem able to become either politically operative or intellectually illuminating in American society. But then, neither does white Marxism-Leninism. It comes as no surprise that the "theoretical" works of the Yippie leaders—Jerry Rubin's *Do It!* and Abbie Hoffman's *Revolution for the Hell of It*—are as puerile as they are incoherent. Nor should anyone be astonished by the fact that American "Marxists" are particularly fascinated by Mao, whose vague slogans save one the trouble of serious analysis. The tone of Maoism is that of a summary of Marxism-Leninism, embellished with folksy moral advice such as "We make progress when we are modest" and "The hardest thing is to act properly throughout one's whole life." Then there are truisms: "An army without culture is an ignorant army" and "Unilateral examination consists in not knowing how to see a question under all its aspects." Mao is not a theoretician, or at least he is not an original theoretician. His few theoretical works, such as *On Practice* and *On Contradiction,* are limited to popularizing and simplifying Lenin's *Materialism and Empirio-Criticism.* These writings, like all his texts, are products of circumstance and of battle, intended to bring political pressure to bear on a particular tendency either within or outside of the Chinese Communist party. The Leninist-Stalinist ideology, once adopted by Mao, was never rethought by him. When he appears to be creating an ideology, he is really pursuing a tactic.

The idea of a "cultural army" goes far back in Mao's works. There again, however, he is not innovating: Culture is always the reflection of political and social reality. Once the economic revolution has been accomplished, therefore, one must look to the cultural revolution. This view is entirely in conformity with that of militant Leninism, without the slightest personal variation. I should make it clear that it is not my intention to formulate a political judgment with respect to China. I wish only to say that a study of Mao's texts leads me to conclude that, philosophically, the little Red writer does not exist; there is no "Chinese version" of Marxism; and there is no "thought of Mao."

The worst that could happen to the Free Speech Movement in

America would be for it to become involved with a nineteenth-century ideology and to see its creativity emasculated by a desire to make it conform to concepts forged in the prehistoric period of modern revolutions. The strength of the American movement is that, up to now, it has been able to discover modes of action that are suited to its circumstances and that work effectively at all levels of the society it is fighting. If this revolutionary inspiration is allowed to be trapped in the theoretical dustbins of Europe, where one spends more time asking whether it is possible to make a non-Marxist revolution than in making revolutions, it will weaken and waste away. Let me repeat: Revolution is not imitation. Revolution is not a settling of accounts with the past, but with the future. American revolutionaries sense this; and that is the reason for American originality in comparison to Europe—as unpleasant as that fact may be for European students, who consider themselves to be more Left than Americans, and especially more intelligently Left. It is also the reason why American youth is actually *creating* a revolution in place of, and prior to, visualizing a revolution.

.   .   .

Of course, one can never exclude the possibility, in any country, of a trend toward authoritarianism. We can say, however, that the past decade gives no indication of a shift in that direction, even though unrest, riots, great changes in the style and principles of life, and a hardening of demands of all kinds are naturally resulting in fear, surprise, misapprehension, and anger in those who are becoming the captives of a new America of which they have not had the imagination to become the creators.

Never, in any country or at any time, has public opinion, however well informed it may have been (which was hardly ever the case), reflected an element of dissent sufficiently strong to make known its condemnation of its government's abuses in foreign policy, and thereby to create a real political problem. Public opinion can, on occasion, turn against domestic injustices, but it has never before been known to rebel against external crimes. The American student uprisings are directly associated with the students' rejection of the war in Vietnam. And this rejection is not merely the position of minorities—as proved by the state of semi-insurrection that greeted the announcement of the Cambodian intervention, and by the Senate vote on a document recalling the Constitutional obligation of a President to consult with the Congress before any commitment of American troops abroad.

.   .   .

It is significant that protests against . . . imperialism originate among the American people, for this represents an important change in historical patterns—just as it would be an extraordinary sign of human evolution if there were even an abortive mass demonstration in Russia against the invasion of Czechoslovakia, anti-Semitism, and intervention in Egypt. Just as we seem able to ignore the fact that we Europeans exterminated the Indians; that we Europeans sold the blacks into slavery; that we Europeans started the process, and developed the methods, of subjecting the whole planet to the white race; so now, we want to forget the fact that the very existence of white America is a result of our invasion of the whole earth and, as it were, an extension and a continuation by proxy of Europe's onslaught against the rest of the world.

Today in America—the child of European imperialism—a new revolution is rising. It is *the* revolution of our time. It is the only revolution that involves radical, moral, and practical opposition to the spirit of nationalism. It is the only revolution that, to that opposition, joins culture, economic and technological power, and a total affirmation of liberty for all in place of archaic prohibitions. It, therefore, offers the only possible escape for mankind today: the acceptance of technological civilization as a means and not as an end, and—since we cannot be saved either by the destruction of the civilization or by its continuation—the development of the ability to reshape that civilization without annihilating it.

Questions

1. Compare and contrast Revel's view of the coming American revolution with that of Reich, Malcolm X, and the Weathermen.
2. Is Revel's judgment, "This spirit of criticism of values . . . is still more emotional than intellectual," a fair characterization of the critics represented in this reader?
3. Elsewhere Revel has insisted that the "profound changes that transform American society can take place without wrecking its institutions." Do you agree?
4. Comparing readings from any two sections of this book, what evidence do you find that the current criticism of values forms "a cohesive and coherent whole"?
5. Has not disagreement on values and goals been a perennial feature of American thought? If not, when did the "new American revolution" begin?

Suggestions for Further Reading
on American Values

CORA DUBOIS, "The Dominant Value Profile of American Culture," *American Anthropologist*, 57 (155), 1232–39. An anthropologist, taking a monist view of American values, discusses three "focal" values—material well-being, conformity, and "effort-optimism."

JOHN GILLIN, "National and Regional Cultural Values in the United States," *Social Forces*, 34 (1955), 107–13. An examination by a sociologist of regional variations from the national value system representing the pluralist approach to values.

OSCAR HANDLIN, ed., *American Principles and Issues: The National Purpose* (1961). A symposium on national purpose that appeared in *Life* in 1960 with selections illustrating the historical development of the values discussed.

MICHAEL MCGIFFERT, ed., *The Character of Americans* (1964). An excellent selection of readings on national character and values that contains a rich bibliography.

MARGARET MEAD, *And Keep Your Powder Dry* (1942). A seminal study of American character by an anthropologist concerned with the future of America in the post–Second World War period.

GUNNAR MYRDAL, *An American Dilemma* (1944), Chapter 1. A perceptive survey of American values prefacing a ground-breaking study of American race relations by a Swedish sociologist.

DAVID POTTER, *People of Plenty* (1954). An analysis by a leading historian of the role of abundance in shaping American values.